# Fire and Snow

# Fire and Snow

## Climate Fiction from the Inklings to *Game of Thrones*

## Marc DiPaolo

Cover image "Ice on Fire" photographed by John Perry.

Published by State University of New York Press, Albany

For information, contact State University of New York Press, Albany, NY
www.sunypress.edu

**Library of Congress Cataloging-in-Publication Data**

Names: Di Paolo, Marc author.
Title: Fire and snow : climate fiction from The inklings to Game of thrones / Marc DiPaolo.
Description: Albany : State University of New York Press, 2018. | Includes bibliographical references and index.
Identifiers: LCCN 2017038441 | ISBN 9781438470450 (hardcover : alk. paper) | ISBN 9781438470467 (pbk. : alk. paper) | ISBN 9781438470474 (ebook)
Subjects: LCSH: Fantasy fiction, English—History and criticism. | Science fiction, English—History and criticism. | Fantasy fiction, American—History and criticism. | Science fiction, American—History and criticism. | Climatic changes in literature. | Environmentalism in literature.
Classification: LCC PR830.F3 D45 2018 | DDC 823/.0876609—dc23
LC record available at https://lccn.loc.gov/2017038441

10 9 8 7 6 5 4 3 2 1

No human being should ever have to fear for his own life because of political or religious beliefs. We are all in this together, my friends: the rich, the poor, the red, white, black, brown and yellow. We share responsibility for Mother Earth and those who live and breathe upon her . . . never forget that.

—Leonard Peltier


If we don't put aside our enmities, we will die.
Then it doesn't matter whose skeleton sits on the Iron Throne.

—Ser Davos Seaworth (Liam Cunningham), *Game of Thrones*


If we burn, you burn with us!

—Katniss Everdeen, "The Girl Who Was on Fire,"
to President Corialanus Snow in *The Hunger Games: Mockingjay*

*For Bill Murphy, Brian Stevens, and Mitchell Sherry*

# Contents

# Acknowledgments

[C]lassics are the books that come down to us bearing the traces of readings previous to ours, and bringing in their wake the traces they themselves have left on culture or cultures they passed through (or, more simply, on language and customs).

—Italo Calvino, "Why Read the Classics?"

Faced with information overload, we have no alternative but pattern-recognition.

—Marshall McLuhan, *Counterblast*

Authors need a lot of emotional, intellectual, and financial support to find the time, energy, and inspiration to craft a monograph. I owe a great debt to everyone who helped me see this project to its conclusion. I would like to begin by thanking the Southwest Commission on Religious Studies for funding my research for this book with a 2015 Junior Scholar Grant. I am especially grateful to the close friends I have made through SWCRS while serving on the presidential line of the American Academy of Religion-SW, including Katherine Downey, Allen Redmon, Darren Middleton, Rachel Toombs, Joerg Rieger, and B. J. Parker. I would also like to thank theologian Robin Meyers for lending me the use of his cabin in Colorado to get away from it all and write, and Laura Schmidt, archivist at the Marion E. Wade Center of Wheaton College, for locating research materials regarding Treebeard and Lewis's alleged plagiarism of Tolkien's Númenor.

My friends and former colleagues Karen Schiler, Brooke Hessler, and Marc Lucht deserve my heartfelt gratitude for introducing me to *A Song of Ice and Fire* and for reassuring me that my somewhat unusual vision of C. S. Lewis was spot on. They helped me learn to love the fantasy genre more than I ever had, completing a transformation in my thinking begun by my old college roommate Bill Murphy, now a visiting assistant professor of history at SUNY Oswego. He introduced me to Lewis through urging me to read *The Great Divorce*, and assured me time and again over the years that I would love *The Silmarillion* thanks to my research into medieval cosmology and *The Cosmographia* at SUNY Geneseo. Bill was one of the manuscript reviewers for this book, as was Arrash E. Allahyar, Nicholas Birns, Catherine DiPaolo, David C. Downing, Robert Colin Earle, Salwa Khoddam, Kenneth Kimbrough, and Janine Surmick. (And Tory Doherty did some mean typesetting for me.) Meanwhile, the following people recommended some truly excellent sources that I may not have found otherwise: Sofia Ahlberg, Kate Henley Averett, Amit Rahul Baishya, Ashley Bellet, Nancy Blankenship, Jim Buss, Bryan Cardinale-Powell, Rosanne Carlo, Susan M. Comfort, Matthew T. Dickerson, Daniel Farris, Tracy Floreani, Christopher Gonzalez, Erik Heine, Joe Jenen, Abigail Keegan, Marsha Keller, Joseph E. Kraus, Diana Maltz, Erin McCoy, Joe Meinhart, Frederic Murray, Rebecca Wisor Muszynski, Benjamin Myers, John Nelka, Santiago Piñón, Jo Pressimone, Stephen Prilliman, Rob Roensch, Nathan Ross, Amrita Sen, and Jerry Vigna.

My participation in two National Endowment for the Humanities Summer Seminars for College Teachers helped lay the groundwork for this book by exposing me to key concepts and sources that I employed in this monograph. They included "The Decadent 1890s: English Literary Culture and the Fin de Siècle," directed by Joseph Bristow at the William Andrews Clark Memorial Library (June 22–July 24, 2009) and "Adaptation and Revision: The Example of Great Expectations" directed by Hilary Schor and Paul Saint-Amour at the University of California, Santa Cruz (July 1–27, 2007).

As I developed the idea for this book, I taught two sections of an honors junior/ senior seminar at Oklahoma City University called *Apocalyptic and Dystopian Literature* in which I assigned many of the texts I examine in these pages. The students who enrolled were among the finest—the smartest, most engaged, and biggest-hearted—I've met during my nearly two decades teaching college classes. I would like to thank the director of the OCU Honors Program, Karen Youmans, for asking me to teach the course (and for just being her fantastic self). I also owe thanks to the many honors students whose fascinating insights helped stoke my enthusiasm to commit to this book: Megan Adkins, Kristine Bachicha, Ronald Bercaw, Madeline Boehlke, Noelle Bradley, R. E. Darby-McClure, Tiesha N. Davis, Audrey C. Harris, Sylvia Hayes, Kathryn Hirsch, Erin N. Langer, Kaitlin Moews, Eleanor Nason, Dana Nicole, Felicity Owens, Blakeley Pearson, Katie R. Schneider, Dylan Smith-Sutton, Rayne Sofley, Victoria Trujillo, Kyle E. Wardwell, Ken O. Williams, Kathryn Wonderly, and Damaila L. Young.

At this point, I am still getting to know my new colleagues at Southwestern Oklahoma State University, but I would like to express my heartfelt thanks to those who have made me feel welcome already, including James South, vice president of Academic Affairs; Peter Grant, dean of the College of Arts and Sciences; Kelley Logan, chair of the Department of Language and Literatures; and English faculty members Fred Alsberg, John Bradshaw, Kevin Collins, Christi Cook, Victoria Gaydosik, Tee Kesnan, Denise Landrum-Geyer, Amanda Smith-Chesley, Taylor Verkler, and Camilo Peralta.

I would also like to thank my journalism mentors at *The Staten Island Advance,* Tom Wrobleski, Paul McPolin, Rob Wolf, Eileen AJ Connelly, and Robin Eisner; my spiritual gurus, Tom Bierowski, Christian Matuschek, and James J. Mayzik, and my teachers, Frank Battaglia, Bill Cook, Daniel Fuchs, Jim Hala, Ronald Herzman, Janice Katz, Wes Kennison, Wendy Kolmar, Dennis Lord, Nadine Ollman, Blandford Parker, Anne-Marie Reynolds, Michael Shugrue, Gary Towsley, and Jim Wakeham.

Also, the world must be made aware: Dr. Preethi Krishnan is the best physician on the planet! She was the first doctor to ever get my *ridiculous* body to function somewhat properly.

Finally, I want to express my love and appreciation for my wonderful family: my wife Stacey, my children Keira and Quentin, my brother Brian, and my parents Ted and Cathy.

# Introduction

## Reclaiming Enemy-Occupied Territory: Saving Middle-earth, Narnia, Westeros, Panem, Endor, and Gallifrey

I used to think the top environmental problems were biodiversity loss, ecosystem collapse, and climate change. I thought that with thirty years of good science we could address those problems. But I was wrong. The top environmental problems are selfishness, greed, and apathy, and to deal with those we need a spiritual and cultural transformation. And we scientists don't know how to do that.

—Gus Speth, founder, Natural Resources Defense Council

The struggle of justice against oppression, hope against despair, is hard. But it has long been the work of humanists, and of literature in particular, to put before the world both terms in each of these dyads—justice as well as oppression, hope as well as despair—to help people commit to the first in each case. . . . It is out of fashion to say this, but it is nonetheless true: liberal activist texts have transformative power. They play a profound role in the fight for human justice and planetary healing that so many of us recognize as the urgent struggle of our time. Words on the page more than reach our minds. They call up our feelings. They call out our spirits. They move us to act.

—Elizabeth Ammons, *Brave New Words: How Literature Will Save the Planet*

### Margaret Atwood and the Newfound Importance of Climate Fiction

In "Climate Fiction: Can Books Save the Planet?" (August 14, 2015), *Atlantic* columnist J. K. Ullrich described the unexpected rise of popularity of "cli-fi," a subgenre of speculative fiction created by Jules Verne in the nineteenth century, further developed by J. G. Ballard in the 1960s, and recently named and popularized by environmentalist

1

Dan Bloom and novelist Margaret Atwood via the power of social media. Thanks to growing awareness of the environmental, social, and economic consequences of climate change, the subgenre has grown in popularity in recent years. Evidence of its omnipresence may be found in hashtags, Facebook groups, Goodreads lists, and the fact that, as Ullrich observed, "searching for the term 'climate fiction' on Amazon today returns over 1,300 results." According to Ullrich, "Unlike traditional sci-fi, its stories seldom focus on imaginary technologies or faraway planets. Instead the pivotal themes are all about Earth, examining the impact of pollution, rising sea levels, and global warming on human civilization. And the genre's growing presence in college curriculums, as well as its ability to bridge science with the humanities and activism, is making environmental issues more accessible to young readers—proving literature to be a surprisingly valuable tool in collective efforts to address global warming."[1]

Ullrich cites as key examples of canonical cli-fi the films *The Day After Tomorrow* (2004), *Snowpiercer* (2013), and *Interstellar* (2014); Young Adult novels *Breathe* (2012) by Sarah Crossan, and both *The Drowned Cities* (2013) and *Ship Breaker* (2011) by Paolo Tadini Bacigalupi, as well as the shows *Game of Thrones* and *The Handmaid's Tale*, adapted from books by George R. R. Martin and Atwood. Other key texts in the genre not cited by Ullrich include the short story "That Bus Is Another World" (2015) by

Fig. I.1. *The Hunter* (2011) is an Australian film based on a novel by Julia Leigh. A military biotech film hires Martin David (Willem Dafoe) to get a DNA sample from the last surviving Tasmanian tiger before killing it. During his quest to find the tiger, Martin experiences a crisis of conscience, finding himself wanting no part of these plans. The book and the film both form a part of a growing canon of multimedia works of climate fiction taught in university courses. Magnolia Pictures.

Stephen King, the comic books *Dark Fang* (2017) by Miles Gunter and Kelsey Shannon, and both *The Silver Surfer: Rebirth of Thanos* (1990) and *Infinity Gauntlet* (1991) by Jim Starlin and Ron Lim, as well as the books *Walden Two* (1948) by B. F. Skinner, *A Canticle for Leibowitz* (1959) by Walter M. Miller, *The Drowned World* (1962) by Ballard, *The Wall* (1962) by Marlen Haushofer, *The Lorax* (1972) by Dr. Seuss, *Ecotopia: The Notebooks and Reports of William Weston* (1975) by Ernest Callenbach, *Woman on the Edge of Time* (1976) by Marge Piercy, *The Children of Men* (1992) by P. D. James, *The Tropic of Orange* (1997) by Karen Tei Yamashita, and *Green Earth* (2015) by Kim Stanley Robinson. Additional climate fiction narratives include the television shows *The Fire Next Time* (1993) and *Treme* (2010–2013) and the films *La Jetée* (1962), *Silent Running* (1972), *Soylent Green* (1973), *Long Weekend* (1978), *C.H.U.D.* ["Contamination Hazard Urban Disposal"] (1984), *The Stuff* (1985), *On Deadly Ground* (1994), *Safe* (1995), *Idiocracy* (2006), *Wall-E* (2008), *Promised Land* (2012), *The East* (2013), *The Only Lovers Left Alive* (2013), *Asterix: The Mansions of the Gods* (2014), *Moana* (2016), *Wonder Woman* (2017), *First Reformed* (2017), the filmography of Hayao Miyazaki, and multiple *Godzilla* and *Mothra* films, including *Godzilla* (1954) and *Shin Godzilla* (2016).

Texts such as these have appeared on English classroom reading lists around the world in recent years as the social and intellectual import of the genre has become more widely known. In addition, several notable works of scholarship have also been published that deal with climate fiction in whole or in part, including the anthology *Green Planets: Ecology and Science Fiction* (2014), edited by Gerry Canavan and Kim Stanley Robinson, and the monographs *Anthropocene Fictions: The Novel in a Time of Climate Change* (2015) by Adam Trexler, *Environmentalism in the Realm of Science Fiction and Fantasy Literature* by Chris Baratta (2012), and *Apocalyptic Transformation: Apocalypse and the Postmodern Imagination* (2008) by Elizabeth K. Rosen.[2] It is also significant that, in 2017, Amy Brady debuted the cli-fi column "Burning Worlds" for *The Chicago Review of Books*. In the first few months of the column, Brady examined texts such as *Flight Behavior* (2013) by Barbara Kingsolver, *Odds Against Tomorrow* (2014) by Nathaniel Rich, *Not Dark Yet* (2015) by Berit Ellingsen, and *California* (2015) by Edan Lepucki, as well as *The End We Start From* by Megan Hunter, *South Pole Station* by Ashley Shelby, and *Mr. Eternity* by Aaron Their, all published in 2017.

For Atwood, "climate fiction" is most effective when it is more about character and story than it is about sermonizing and assaulting the audience with sobering scientific data and doomsday prophecies. As she explained in a February 6, 2015, interview with *Slate* reporter Ed Finn: "It's rather useless to write a gripping narrative with nothing in it but climate change because novels are always about people even if they purport to be about rabbits or robots. . . . In the *MaddAddam* books, people hardly mentioned 'climate change,' but things have already changed. For instance, in the world of Jimmy, who we follow in *Oryx and Crake*, the first book, as he's growing up as an adolescent, they're already getting tornadoes on the East Coast of the United States, the upper East Coast, because I like setting things in and around Boston. It's nice and flat, and when the sea rises a bunch of it will flood. It's the background, but it's not in-your-face a sermon."[3]

On March 21, 2016, *The Chronicle of Higher Education* published "The Subfield that is Changing the Landscape of Literary Studies," an article about climate fiction by Rio Fernandes, which argues that the genre is "changing the curricula of English departments across the country" and around the world.[4] The full professors and graduate students quoted in the piece include those who have presented panels on climate fiction at conferences, run seminar classes, and included climate fiction in their courses: Ted Howell, Temple University; Richard Crownshaw, the University of London; Sina Farzin, the University of Hamburg; and Wai Chee Dimock, Yale University. Among the books that are staples of courses on climate fiction are the *MaddAddam* trilogy, *The Stand* (1978) by Stephen King, *The Road* (2006) by Cormac McCarthy, and *Solar* (2010) by Ian McEwan. Not all the above books would pass muster with the champion of the traditional Western Canon, Harold Bloom, as being of high literary quality and worthy of study, but many of these professors see value in contrasting how both high-brow and low-brow art confront similar themes. Fernandes addresses the popularity of the courses, their importance in the revitalization of freshman seminar and core course requirements, and the evolution of the English major. The article also raises the specter of complaints that these courses have received from conservative students and climate change deniers who regard the genre of cli-fi as fundamentally propagandistic and dangerous. However, the professors interviewed express that they are aware of their moral responsibility to promote the truth and continue educating their students despite such complaints.[6] Indeed, Elizabeth Ammons writes in *Brave New Words: How Literature Will Save the Planet* (2010) that teachers have a moral imperative to tell students the truth, which most students have already grasped, and discuss the ramifications of climate change with them, which they haven't come to terms with.

> Five centuries of Western colonialism, capitalism, enforced Christianity, racism, systemic sexism, and ever-more-sophisticated warfare have brought the globe to a perilous brink. Soil depletion so destroyed agriculture in Haiti even pre-2010 that street vendors in Port-au-Prince sell pies made of clay, salt, and shortening as food. Arctic ice melts and with it the habitats of bears who have lived there for millennia. Life expectancy for an indigenous person on the Wind River Reservation in the United States of America is forty-nine years. Worldwide desertification now consumes an area larger than Canada and the U.S. combined. . . . As George Monbiot explains in *Heat*, the United States needs to cut carbon emissions by 90 percent by 2030 . . . to avert irreversible global catastrophe.
>
> Many of my students know and fear these truths. Others try not to know out of feelings of despair and powerlessness. What can any one person or even group of people do to halt, much less reverse, devastation of such magnitude? Still others cling to technology. . . . Science will have the answers. Deep in our hearts, however, we know that science and technology

do not have the answer. The crisis is one of values. It can be met . . . only by a radical shift in belief, a profound realignment of thought and spirit.[7]

Interdisciplinary education, modeled by the Association for the Study of Literature and Environment (ASLE), is vital to the effort to foster this profound realignment of thought and spirit that Ammons argues for. It is in the tradition of such interdisciplinary education that this book fits.

## The Inklings and Religiously Informed Ecological Fiction

This book focuses on the works of two of the innovators of environmentalist fantasy and science fiction, J. R. R. Tolkien and C. S. Lewis, and considers how they confront the evils of pollution, deforestation, and warfare in their religiously and morally informed writings, including their heroic fiction, scholarly essays, and personal correspondences. This book then explores the works by authors, filmmakers, and writers of television serials who were inspired by Lewis and Tolkien to write environmentalist speculative fiction of their own, sometimes expressing concern for the earth in equally religious terms, sometimes employing secular arguments.

Lewis and Tolkien wrote speculative fiction imbued with forms of Christianized Norse and Greco-Roman Mythology that promoted environmental ethics and the values of sustainability within the fantasy and science fiction genres. They could not have, themselves, referred to their works as being part of the "climate fiction" or "cli-fi" subgenre, since the subgenre has been identified only recently. However, they did indeed write an early species of climate fiction, and its use of apocalyptic imagery from mythology to warn of the potential ecological collapse of the planet was as idiosyncratic and groundbreaking as it was inspiring to many authors who followed. The two academic colleagues, friends, and fellow Inklings belonged to different branches of the Christian faith, had competing visions of what Christian allegory could (and should) do in novel form, and had a falling out over personal, religious, and professional conflicts mid-career. Their differences aside, they were united in their interest in countering fascism, utilitarianism, and the excesses of industrial capitalism with a Christian environmentalist ethic that they explored in their Narnia and Middle-earth sagas. This monograph examines how different writers on both sides of the Atlantic revisited and rewrote these Inklings' apocalyptic fantasy tropes and environmentalist ethics, especially novelists Margaret Atwood, Octavia Butler, Suzanne Collins, George R. R. Martin, Philip Pullman, and a variety of writers and producers who have shaped more than five decades' worth of multimedia *Doctor Who* adventures. Notably, these authors often express starkly different religious views than the Inklings' that inspired them, and yet mirror their predecessors' ecological and genre concerns. Pullman, Collins, Martin, and the *Doctor Who* scriptwriters all revisit the Inkling fascination with the Norse conception of Ragnarök: the ice and fire cycle of apocalypse and renewal. Philip Pullman used Ragnarök imagery to call for a halting of climate change and the abolishing of authoritarian organized religion in the trilogy of novels *His Dark Materials*. Collins's *Hunger Games* trilogy used Ragnarök symbolism ("the Girl Who Was on Fire" versus "President Snow") to condemn war, racism, and the enormous wealth disparity found in contemporary America. Martin's *A Song of Ice and Fire* (a.k.a. *Game of Thrones*) calls for a balancing of oppositional social, natural, and religious forces in the world, and warns that unchecked sectarianism and totalitarianism, and an endless, unbroken cycle of intergenerational violence creates a society divided against itself that descends into chaos and summons monsters.

One recurring source of tension within scholarly, religious, and fan communities is the question of whether to embrace a work of speculative fiction as good art and ethical storytelling depending on whether the work being examined appears to promote religious or secular values. Anecdotally, cultural commentators in the mass media and on social media appear to be divided over which fantasy books and authors to favor and which to condemn as being unsuitable for young minds. Atheists sometimes seem to champion the critic of establishment Christianity Philip Pullman, while being dismissive of Christian apologist C. S. Lewis. For their part, Christians tend to be predictable in their favoring of Lewis and condemnation of Pullman.[8] For example, Lewis scholar Alister McGrath's concern about whether certain fantasy texts promote secular humanism or Christianity stems from his position as a Christian apologist; he has adopted the role of contemporary public Christian intellectual that Lewis played so well in his lifetime. Nevertheless, there are more interesting questions to ask than whether climate fiction authors somehow "harm" Christianity by promoting secular humanism. *Fire and Snow* is about *what kind of secular humanism* and *what kind of Christianity* the authors promulgate in the texts and subtexts of their environmentalist writings. There are benign and pernicious species of secular humanism just as there are benign and pernicious species of Christianity. Significantly, several of the authors already identified share deep ecological concerns with Lewis, even if they don't share his Christian worldview. The connective ecological thematic framework of Lewis's imitators and Tolkien's imitators is of far greater import than the questions of how to best pit their respective religious beliefs against one another on behalf of the contemporary American culture wars. In contrast to McGrath, fantasy aficionados concerned more with good storytelling than with ideological content tend to embrace all the finest books by Lewis and Pullman as good art. This monograph will argue that the fantasy fans who unreservedly enjoy reading all the canonical works of the fantasy genre may have stumbled upon a truth that has been lost because of the various ideological factions that have claimed one author over another as a champion: there is more commonality of ecological sentiment and ethics uniting these works thematically than any divisive ideological label should be allowed to undermine. *Fire and Snow* uses thematic criticism as a means of building rhetorical bridges between sometimes fiercely divided religious factions in the interests of finding a common ground for environmentalists of different personal belief systems. Despite their sometimes (in)significant ideological differences, these very similar and very different authors may be regarded as, essentially, working in solidarity with one another on the same ideological project: using spiritually informed genre fiction to help save the planet from annihilation. (Notably, another scholar who has argued for the importance of studying genre fiction from an ecocritical perspective is Anthony Lioi, who examines "green" multimedia science fiction, horror, and fantasy narratives in 2016's *Nerd Ecology: Defending the Earth with Unpopular Culture*.)

Scholar Farah Mendlesohn describes thematic criticism as a potentially "powerful and threatening" interpretive approach most often taken to works of fantasy by both scholars and fans alike. She notes that "Thematic criticism is a form of archaeology that excavates the layers of a text and compares that text with those found in other excavations." Elaborating, Mendlesohn notes that thematic criticism is "often deployed in comparative work, in order to create clusters of texts which can be discussed together"[9] What is accomplished when works considered part of the same genre are clustered together and examined thematically? Mendlesohn writes, "The process of thematic criticism can be understood as a deconstructionist route into a text's deeper meaning, finding it richer and more meaningful than it might otherwise be read. . . . Thematic criticism is also, however, a mode of reader response criticism and as such contributes an extra layer to the text, the role of the reader who brings to the text his own prior reading and may slot the text into a pattern of thematic reading which the author did not envisage. . . . For both author and reader, thematic criticism can feel like a challenge to the 'ownership' of a text."[10]

Mendlesohn observes that, even though many authors are hostile to thematic criticism, some are particularly worthy subjects of it, especially authors, such as Tolkien, who embed recurring themes in their work. Mendlesohn suggests Tolkien as a case study because he was opposed to allegorists reading his works as straightforward moral parables even as he himself clearly wove environmentalist messages into his fiction. Indeed, his private correspondences were filled with ecological allusions and allegories, and Tolkien referred to the pollution in Britain as a "Mordor in our midst." He also offered a pointed condemnation of some of his unquestioningly pro-war and pro-pollution fellow Catholics when discussing the moral significance of the "Scouring of the Shire" epilogue of *Lord of the Rings*, in which even Hobbits began despoiling their own land. Tolkien observed that those in the Shire who attempted to use the magic and technology of Mordor to achieve "good" aims were as morally misguided and destined to inevitably advance the cause of evil as Catholics who, with the best of intentions, research poison gases.[11]

This monograph marries thematic criticism to ecocriticism, and uses both as a means of interpreting climate fiction. In "Literary Studies in an Age of Environmental Crisis," which serves as the introduction to *The Ecocriticism Reader: Landmarks in Literary Ecology* (1996), Cheryll Glotfelty defines ecocriticism as "the study of the relationship between literature and the physical environment."[12] Glotfelty observes that it took far longer for ecological criticism to develop in the thinking of academics, especially in the humanities, than it did to become a concern to scientists and the broader populace, but—in recent decades—the different branches of the humanities have developed independent responses to the ecological crisis appropriate to their respective fields. These different, autonomous branches have come together in the blossoming field of ecocriticism, especially thanks to the work of scholarly organizations such as Association for the Study of Literature and Environment and the work of ecologically minded and interdisciplinary scholars. The branches of the humanities of most interest to this book include literary studies, philosophy, and religious studies. As Glotfelty argues, "Literary scholars specialize in questions of value, meaning, tradition, point of view, and language, and it is in these areas that they are making a substantial contribution to environmental thinking."[13] Philosophy's subfield of ecofeminism has, in part, informed the thinking of the author of this text because, as Glotfelty explains, ecofeminism understands and critiques "the root causes of environmental degradation and [formulates] an alternative view of existence that will provide the ethical and conceptual foundation for right relations with the earth. Theologians, too, are recognizing that. . . . While some Judeo-Christian theologians attempt to elucidate biblical precedents for good stewardship of the earth, others re-envision God as immanent in creation and view the earth itself as sacred. Still other theologians turn to ancient Earth Goddess worship, Eastern religious traditions, and Native American teachings, belief systems that contain much wisdom about nature and spirituality."[14]

Glotfelty's discussion of the overlap in approach to ecocriticism between the disciplines of philosophy and theology suggests a kinship between the perspective of ecofeminism and of Stewardship of the earth—a kinship that *Fire and Snow* explores as it suggests that the Christian Stewardship of the earth advocated by Lewis, Tolkien, Pope Francis, and St. Francis of Assisi has enormous spiritual and thematic resonance with the writings of ecofeminist philosophers, artists, theologians, writers, journalists, and activists, ranging from Rosemary Radford Ruether, Sallie McFague, and Naomi Klein to Margaret Atwood, Ursula K. Le Guin, and Octavia Estelle Butler.

Climate fiction reaches into several different genres and is identifiable in its dramatizing of issues such as deforestation, pollution, climate change, sustainability, animal welfare, extinction-level events, the evils of industrialization, the ecological ravages caused by large-scale and extended military conflicts, the preservation of nature, the rights of indigenous peoples, the sins of capitalism, the equitable care and allocation of natural resources, and the oppression of women and ethnic minorities to create a self-contained "ecosystem" of oppression. Some of these issues might seem far afield from the question of the ethical stewardship of the Earth. However, these concepts radiate outward from a central concern of maintaining a well-balanced ecosystem without polluting it, squandering it, destroying it, or keeping all its bounty for the privileged few. In a sense, for a climate fiction narrative to be centrally concerned with the environment is for climate fiction to be centrally concerned with life itself. As Atwood observes, therein lies the problem of the somewhat limiting umbrella term of "climate change" when discussing these issues: "I would rather call it the 'everything change,' because when people think climate change, they think maybe it's going to rain more or something like that. It's much more extensive a change than that because when you change patterns of where it rains and how much and where it doesn't rain, you're also affecting just about everything. You're affecting what you can grow in those places. You're affecting whether you can live there. You're affecting all of the species that are currently there because we are very water dependent. . . . The other thing that we really have to be worried about is killing the oceans, because should we do that there goes our major oxygen supply, and we will wheeze to death."[15]

Since climate fiction—or everything fiction—straddles multiple genres, genre criticism terminology is important to clarify as well. When the real-world issues of the wages of pollution are depicted as taking place in a reality much like our own, but the story itself is a narrative conceit, the work is climate fiction but not speculative fiction. When these issues that touch us in our reality are dramatized as taking place in Westeros, Panem, Middle-earth, or other such invented worlds, the climate fiction is taking place within the realm of a speculative fiction narrative, but we have the right to draw several notable parallels between the events taking place in these fictional worlds and the ones unfolding in our own. It is also possible to find works of climate fiction by climate change deniers—with the late Michael Crichton's *State of Fear* (2004) being the most notable work by the world's most famous climate change denier. However, most works in this vein accept the truth of climate change and consider its ramifications in a series of "what if" scenarios. This does not always mean that a well-meaning environmentalist cli-fi writer will always get the climate science right—*The Day After Tomorrow* has often been ridiculed for its bad science and good intentions—or offer a solution that climate change activists would approve of—for example, the defeatist and improbable plan to abandon the Earth in *Interstellar*.

Returning to the issue of terminology: several of Lewis's fantasy novels set in the land of Narnia may be considered speculative fiction because they featured worlds that he designed, but they are also climate fiction because of their apocalyptic ecological concerns. Notably, the Narnia novels are not science fiction. However, Lewis also wrote *The Space Trilogy* (aka *The Ransom Trilogy*), a series of Christian science fiction novels. These books are also treated as works of climate fiction in this study, with book three, *That Hideous Strength*, a frequent touchstone.

Whether the climate fiction narrative in question is "secular" or "religious," or whether the original book or the filmed adaptation is the focus of analysis, the multimedia cli-fi text provides rich fodder for discussion in these environmentally troubled times. The goal of this book is to show how these popular franchises are recognized (or not recognized) by the broader public as climate fiction narratives offering critical moral instruction on the urgency of conservation. The moral urgency of these stories may be underpinned by overt or covert Christian ethics, a Native American spirituality, or by a species of secular humanism, but the shared interest in saving our forests and saving our planet transcends ideological differences and bridges gaps between science fiction and fantasy texts. Each of these narratives offers up—almost like a musical refrain—images of trees being destroyed: cut down, burned to the ground, or devoured by monsters. None of the authors of these works support the mass destruction of trees. The Christians, atheists, and agnostics who penned these works all agree that we need to put aside our cultural differences and transcend our personal, socioeconomic circumstances to work together to save our environment. These stories show us how.

## (Un)Intentional Cli-Fi Authors: Philip Pullman, Octavia Butler, and George R. R. Martin

Whether their works lean more toward the fantasy genre or science fiction, or more toward dystopian or postapocalyptic, several of the authors of speculative fiction set out to craft narratives that are a conscious climate change allegory and intentionally written to be part of the climate fiction subgenre. Other authors have different concerns when they begin their projects, and the climate change commentary seems to manifest itself in the narratives more subconsciously, or even wholly unintentionally. In still other instances, readers identify a given narrative's relevance to a world with a changing climate when the authors themselves are resistant to seeing their works branded "cli-fi." Octavia E. Butler, Philip Pullman, and George R. R. Martin represent this spectrum of climate fiction writers: Butler wrote her climate change commentary intentionally, Pullman partly subconsciously, and Martin unintentionally.

One of the most respected authors of climate fiction and the winner of a 1995 MacArthur Fellowship, Butler wrote two volumes of a planned trilogy, *Parable of the Sower* (1993) and *Parable of the Talents* (1998), before her death in 2006. *Parable of the Sower* is a dystopian novel about Lauren Olamina, a teenage empath who leads a multiethnic assemblage of suburban refugees north along the highways of California to find a new sanctuary after drug-addicted pyromaniacs destroy their walled-off community, Robledo. In an interview, Butler explained that her books project a speculative future extrapolated from the social and political trends of her present, "I looked at the growing rich/poor gap, at throwaway labor, at our willingness to build and fill prisons, our reluctance to build and repair schools and libraries, and at our assault on the environment. . . . There's food-price driven inflation that's likely because, as the climate changes, some of the foods we're used to won't grow as well in the places we're used to growing them. . . . I considered spreading hunger as a reason for increased vulnerability to disease. And there would be less money for inoculations or treatment. . . . I imagined the United States becoming, slowly, through the combined effects of lack of foresight and short-term unenlightened self-interest, a third world country. And the only way of cleaning up, adapting, and compensating for all this in *Parable of the Sower* and *Parable of the Talents* is to use our brains and our hands—the same tools we used to get ourselves into so much trouble."[16]

Philip Pullman's *His Dark Materials* trilogy is also informed by his passionately held personal and ideological beliefs. It includes the books *Northern Lights* (aka *The Golden Compass*, 1995), *The Subtle Knife* (1997), and *The Amber Spyglass* (2000), and is about a multiracial insurrection led against an imposter "God" who has supplanted the Creator God and ruled all species across the multiverse with a merciless, totalitarian hand. The series includes a subplot in which the melting of arctic lands robs the heroic King Iorek Byrnison of his kingdom, and leaves his people—an armored, articulate race of polar bears—without food or shelter. In the process, a once proud and resilient race is reduced in stature to splintered, nomadic refugees. Pullman claims that the polar bear diaspora storyline was a partly conscious commentary on the melting of arctic lands in the real world, noting that the ecological catastrophe in his fantasy multiverse "wasn't an entirely unconscious echo."[17] Pullman is also interested in the role that religion plays in confronting the challenges of a changing climate: "[T]he stories that the global warming prophets tell us (let's call them that, to distinguish them from the sceptics), take their place right slap-bang in the middle of the prophetical tradition, along with the prophets of the Old Testament. But the prophets of the Old Testament were not very successful because they were generally hounded out of the city and cast adrift on the waves. People don't like hearing what prophets tell them: it's generally uncomfortable. It's full of doom; it's full of warnings; it's full of denunciations and threats to mend their ways or suffer for it. So it's not a popular message. And the struggle that the climate-change prophets have had to undertake to get their message heard, I suppose, is similar."[18]

Like *His Dark Materials*, the book series *A Song of Ice and Fire* works well as a climate change allegory, though Martin has said that he did not intend the books to

Fig. I.2. In Philip Pullman's *His Dark Materials* trilogy, the melting of arctic lands robs the polar bear Iorek Byrnison of his kingdom and reduces his people to starving refugees. Pictured are Lyra Belacqua (Dakota Blue Richards) and Iorek (voiced by Ian McKellen) from the adaptation of Book One, *The Golden Compass* (2007). New Line Cinema.

be regarded, first and foremost, as climate fiction. In Martin's books, magical forces threaten to engulf the fictional realm of Westeros in an eternal winter, setting the stage for an invasion of ice zombies that will transform all humanity into the frozen undead. As Martin has explained in interviews, he was most concerned with crafting an original universe inspired by the real-world history of the Wars of the Roses and the genre fiction he read in his formative years. While Martin may have been prepared for his readers to make note of his deliberate tributes to the Inklings, he seemed surprised when he first learned that viewers of the HBO television series *Game of Thrones* have grown inclined to see the Westeros narrative writ large as a climate change metaphor. Uncommon when Martin began the decades-long journey towards completion of his Westeros series in the early 1990s, mighty superstorms, lengthy droughts, record hot summers, blistering cold winters with record snowfalls, and devastating brushfires have become common in recent years. Martin's readership and viewers of the HBO adaptation of his books have noticed these weather patterns and seen echoes of them in his grand narrative. Initially, Martin seemed reluctant to grant the climate change interpretation of his books credence or own that climate change concerns were a primary motivating force in his writing the Westeros books. Consequently, during a question-and-answer session for fans at Dymock's Literary Luncheon in Sydney, Australia, in 2013, he said, "Like Tolkien I do not write allegory, at least not intentionally. . . . [I]f I really wanted to write about climate change in the 21st century, I'd write a novel about climate change in the 21st century."[19] More recently, the liberal Democrat and frequent critic of the Trump administration has embraced the interpretation. In a 2014 interview with *Al-Jazeera America*, he said that his work has tremendous contemporary relevance because climate change is "ultimately a threat to the entire world. But people are using it as a political football instead of . . . [getting] together."[20]

As the thoughts of Butler, Pullman, and Martin illustrate, science fiction and fantasy narratives have enormous potential to educate the public, inspire them, and galvanize them into action. This is true whether the writer of that book series *intended* to craft a climate allegory, *somewhat* intended to, or wrote one *almost entirely by accident*. In "Cli-Fi; Climate Change Fiction as Literature's New Frontier?" (July 23, 2015), *Huffington Post* columnist Bethan Forrest argues that entertaining speculative fiction narratives have the potential to educate the public about environmental issues in a way that juried journal articles and PowerPoint presentations have failed to do: "In our glib, 24-hour-news-cycle world, the unrestrained drip of an iceberg in the Arctic or the slow encroachment of water onto the land of southern hemisphere islands, debated in lengthy terms by austere scientists at dry conferences, doesn't strike us with the immediacy and urgency that it deserves. Perhaps that's where the responsibility of true challenge to an uninformed and inactive audience has fallen, as it always has, to the arts."[21]

However imperfect the science may be or how subtle the social message, these cli-fi stories still have the potential to educate the public on environmental issues—and the potential to inspire activism. The one-third-complete film adaptation of Pullman's *His Dark Materials*, *The Golden Compass* (2007), was a financially unsuccessful film that has yet to achieve the success of other fantasy multimedia franchises. The DVD release of the movie was a fixture of bargain basement outlet stores in the years following the film's failure, but even this failed adaptation may have played a part in educating the few that saw it. For example, the home video version begins with a public service announcement on behalf of the World Wildlife Fund narrated by actress Dakota Blue Richards, who addressed the young fans of the series in character as series heroine Lyra Belacqua. "Lyra" talked of her armored polar bear friend Iorek, exhorting the children of our reality to protect the polar bears of our world—to "be their armor"—and join the WWF in defending them from global climate change, which "is reducing the size of their home and shortening the season in which they are able to find food. World Wildlife Fund works every day to study how global warming impacts the earth and what we can do to stop it. . . . You can help save it and our entire planet. For bears, for yourself, and for future generations."[22] The World Wildlife Fund blurred the line between fiction and reality when it asked a child actress to voice a fictional character, Lyra Belacqua, to make a plea on behalf of real polar bears in the name of the fictional Iorek. Ecological organizations are forever looking for charismatic champions to enter the public discourse to bring a sense of urgency to the causes they are fighting for, and to make their messages more marketable. Appropriately, several actors associated with film and television adaptations of climate fiction brought the issue of pollution greater attention by participating in a high-profile advertising campaign in Great Britain. Sixty celebrities took part in activist and fashion designer Dame Vivienne Westwood's *Save the Arctic* initiative with Greenpeace. These celebrities included actors famous for playing characters from the lands of Westeros, Middle-earth, and Gallifrey on film and television. Among the participants were those who played the Doctor on *Doctor Who* (Peter Capaldi, David Tennant, and John Hurt), Gandalf in *Lord of the Rings* (Ian McKellen), Loki in *The Avengers* (Tom Hiddleston), and Arya Stark and Brienne of Tarth in *Game of Thrones* (Maisie Williams and Gwendoline Christie). The actors were photographed wearing *Save the Arctic* T-shirts and their likenesses were displayed near the corporate offices of Shell as part of a campaign to discourage the oil company from drilling in the Arctic. Shell representatives decried the initiative as a public relations stunt, but the intent of the campaign is clear. It is one thing for celebrities to protest environmental devastation. It is another to imagine that the beloved fictional characters that they play on television and in films are the ones denouncing Shell.[23] In an interview, Williams explained her motivation in participating in the campaign: "The Arctic is a unique and beautiful ecosystem, providing a home to both Indigenous Peoples and endangered species. Now it's under threat and we must act."[24] In speaking these words, Williams is not the only one issuing a climate change warning; Arya Stark of Westeros is as well.

This blending of fiction and reality cuts both ways, of course. *Atlantic* columnist J. K. Ullrich notes that the potential problem with using speculative fiction to comment upon real world problems is that it is too easy for the fans to think it is all just an entertaining story and not a parable with real world applications. Still more troubling, the fantasy elements of multimedia cli-fi narratives sometimes make the vast problem of climate change seem as fictional and grotesque as the menace posed by the ice zombies in *Game of Thrones*. For example, George Marshall, founder of the Climate Outreach Information Network, has expressed concern that cli-fi adds more fuel to the fire of climate skepticism than it does educate the uniformed.[25] In a related critique, Amitav Ghosh calls upon global literary fiction—not just popular fiction or speculative fiction—to present the world with *realistic* models of collective action to help us rethink our relationships to one another and to the world. In *The Great Derangement: Climate Change and the Unthinkable* (2016), Gosh is concerned with distinctions between high and low art, and the creation of new literary representations that conform to a particular, respectable artistic tradition of realism. His concern is, arguably, overstated, especially since critics such as Jesse Oak Taylor have attested that the "pure" realist novel becomes almost impossible to achieve after the first major manifestations (and literary representations) of the Anthropocene in Victorian England. However, Gosh's argument that individual action on climate change is laudable but likely insufficient—and that all of us must work together toward more sweeping societal change—is an important one made from a global perspective.

Cli-fi stories have another significant problem: they tend to be operatically depressing. As Ursula K. Le Guin wrote in her 1969 introduction to her novel *The Left Hand of Darkness*, "Science fiction is often described, and even defined, as extrapolative. The science fiction writer is supposed to take a trend, or phenomenon of the here-and-now, purify and intensify it for dramatic effect, and extend it into the future. 'If this goes on, this is what will happen.' A prediction is made . . . [that generally arrives] somewhere between the gradual extinction of human liberty and the total extinction of terrestrial life. This may explain why many people who do not read science fiction describe it as 'escapist,' but when questioned further, admit they don't read it because 'it's so depressing.' "[26] There is, indeed, the problem of the bleakness of the narratives causing the readers to shut down emotionally, overwhelmed by the scope of the problem. Ullrich observes, "Cli-fi, like the science behind it, often presents bleak visions of the future, but within such frightening prophecies lies the real possibility that it's not too late to steer in a different direction."[27]

Apocalyptic as these stories are, fans of Young Adult fiction gravitate to them, and postapocalyptic, dystopian narratives from *The Hunger Games* trilogy to the *Divergent* series to *The Maze Runner* books and films are voraciously consumed by young readers who at least enjoy the thrilling adventures—and charismatic heroes such as Katniss Everdeen—even if they might not always embrace the notes of fatalism and the specter of death hanging over the main story. Of course, some young readers like the books precisely because of the apocalyptic content, and are not averse to meditating on the ramifications of climate change through these adventures. Some readers even hope to write apocalyptic fiction of their own. The genre of cli-fi has now become so popular that there is a handbook for prospective writers of the genre, *Saving the World One Word at a Time: Writing Cli-Fi* (2015) by Ellen Szabo. Szabo's book shows emerging writers how to use "knowledge of science and climate to imagine and create apocalyptic

Fig I.3. A scene from the original *Godzilla* (1954), directed by Ishirō Honda, in which the invincible prehistoric beast sets Tokyo aflame with its radioactive breath in an allegorical reenactment of the atomic bombings of Hiroshima and Nagasaki. The climate fiction film spawned several environmentalist sequels, including *Godzilla versus Hedorah* (1971), *Godzilla vs. Biollante* (1989), *Shin Godzilla* (2016), and Gareth Edwards's American *Godzilla* (2014). Toho.

or dystopian worlds with the goal of changing how humans think about, inhabit and interact with our planet," thereby "taking the issue out of politics and into the realm of the personal."[28]

This monograph is designed to complement existing scholarship on green topics, some of which theorize ecology, others focus on taking the political temperature of international relations in an era of climate change and globalization, while still others examine how ecological concerns are treated in the arts and popular culture. Some notable works of extant ecocriticism include *The Future of Environmental Criticism: Environmental Crisis and Literary Imagination* (2005) by Lawrence Buell, *Ecology Without Nature* (2007) by Timothy Morton, *Living in the End Times* (2010) by Slavoj Žižek, and *Slow Violence and the Environmentalism of the Poor* (2011) by Rob Nixon. There are several notable collected editions of ecological writings. One of the enduring examples of this library edition–style publication is *The Ecocriticism Reader: Landmarks in Literary Ecology* (1996), edited by Glotfelty and Harold Fromm. More works in this vein come out each year. Morton's work is more theoretical than mine and Nixon's is more a work of political science, but traces of their influence can be found in these pages. *Fire and Snow* is written in the style of extant works of literary and film criticism, such as *The Child to Come: Life After the Human Catastrophe* (2016) by Rebekah Sheldon and the two monographs on the ecological sensibilities of the Inklings co-written by Matthew Dickerson and published for the University of Kentucky Press: Dickerson co-wrote *Ents, Elves, and Eriador: The Environmental Vision of J. R. R. Tolkien* (2006) with Jonathan Evans and *Narnia and the Fields of Arbol: The Environmental Vision of C. S. Lewis* (2009) with David O'Hara. This book is indebted to the work already done on the Inklings and literary environmentalism, and seeks to build upon extant scholarship by showing how the precedent set by the Inklings was followed by the later writers of speculative fiction, who took the environmental concerns of the Lost Generation and placed them in the context of the twenty-first-century climate crisis.

The environmentalist and scientific writers and thinkers who are addressed in these pages include Carol J. Adams, Elizabeth Ammons, Wendell Berry, William R. Cook, John Elder, Bill Gates, Joy Harjo, Michio Kaku, Naomi Klein, Ursula K. Le Guin, Sallie McFague, Bill McKibben, Timothy Morton, Rob Nixon, Pope Francis, Rosemary Radford Ruether, Mark Ruffalo, Neil deGrasse Tyson, and Karen Warren. Some of these thinkers contribute activist-styled ecological commentary to middlebrow venues such as PBS, NPR, or periodicals such as *The Atlantic* and *Rolling Stone*, while others have published more scholarly works in journal articles and monographs released by academic presses.

The book is organized into eleven chapters and an epilogue. Chapter 1, "*Star Wars*, Hollywood Blockbusters, and the Cultural Appropriation of J. R. R. Tolkien," is an assessment of how the film adaptations of Tolkien's Middle-earth saga downplay the author's ecological sensibilities while lengthening the percentage of narrative time spent on depicting armed combat and romanticizing war. Consequently, in the wake of the "war on terror"–era Peter Jackson film adaptations of *The Hobbit* and *The Lord of the Rings*, Tolkien's original work has been perceived as an imperialist text by cultural critics on the left and right political wings of the spectrum. Fortunately, literary critics and environmental activists such as John Elder and Matthew Dickerson are aiding in the effort to return readers' attention to the ecological core of Tolkien's work. Indeed, despite Tolkien's opposition to writing transparent, pedagogical allegory, his Middle-earth stories work well as environmentalist fables that explore how industrialization destroys nature in both the real world and Middle-earth. This chapter also considers how big-budget genre films now tend to be "action movies" modeled after both *Star Wars* and a transparently limited understanding of Joseph Campbell's monomyth theories. This ubiquitous storytelling model, dictated by Hollywood marketing gurus, is another reason the Jackson film adaptations of Tolkien's works were repurposed as action movies. This marketing mandate is also part of the reason why it is so difficult to make a thoughtful climate fiction movie in this cultural moment.[29]

Chapter 2 is "Of Treebeard, C. S. Lewis, and the Aesthetics of Christian Environmentalism." It offers contrasting biographical interpretations of the nature of the friendship between Tolkien and Lewis and ponders the extent to which their personal relationship shaped their religious beliefs and genre fiction writing. Two central figures in this chapter are Professor Ransom, the Christian hero of Lewis's *Space Trilogy* (whom Lewis modeled partly after Tolkien), and Treebeard, the supernatural champion of trees that Tolkien based somewhat on Lewis. The chapter also concerns Lewis's efforts to encourage Tolkien to publish faster, and to build textual links between the Middle-earth, Arthurian Romance, and *Space Trilogy* adventures, thereby designing one ecological narrative in the same "shared universe."

Chapter 3, "The Time Lord, the Daleks, and the Wardrobe," is about the apocalyptic, centuries-long conflict between the Doctor and the space fascists known as the Daleks. The alien time-traveler protagonist of the British science fiction television series *Doctor Who* has seen planet Earth consumed by fire and has been responsible for the destruction of both his own home world, Gallifrey, and the Daleks' home planet of Skaro. He considers himself an enemy of fascist and totalitarian regimes, but fears that he has more than enough blood on his hands to be considered a genocidal Nazi himself. To atone for his past mistakes, he endeavors to save as many lives as he can. In one adventure that is relevant to this book, "The Green Death" (1973), he stops an evil corporation from continuing to pollute the community of Llanfairfach in South Wales. In another, "The Doctor, the Widow, and the Wardrobe" (2012), he transports the souls of trees to the stars shortly before their forest is destroyed. This "Christmas special" was the *Doctor Who* adventure most overtly inspired by the writings of Lewis. This chapter also explores what *Doctor Who* owes to the morality of Tolkien, especially in its *Silmarillion*-like representations of apocalyptic-level warfare throughout the Time War storyline.

Chapters 4 and 5 work together as a unified whole. They include "Noah's Ark Revisited: *2012* and Magic Lifeboats for the Wealthy," and the direct follow-up, "Race and Disaster Capitalism in *Parable of the Sower*, *The Strain*, and *Elysium*." These chapters explore how comics writer and filmmaker Mark Millar crafted two narratives in which the wealthy elite (popularly referred to as the 1 percent) conspire to create a Noah's Ark haven for themselves to survive climate catastrophe. In the process, they sacrifice most of the planet's common people (the 99 percent). These stories, which satirize Ayn Rand's *Atlas Shrugged*, include *Kingsman: The Secret Service* and *The Fantastic Four: The Death of the Invisible Woman*. To demonstrate where Millar's anger with the ruling classes comes from, this chapter will examine both Republican politicians who have refused to confront the climate crisis and the sweeping, well-funded propaganda campaigns funded by members of the fossil fuel industry designed to debunk scientific research that calls for environmental protections. Books, films, and television shows examined in these paired chapters include Michio Kaku's *Physics of the Future*, Octavia Butler's *Parable of the Sower*, Dan Brown's *Inferno*, Michael Crichton's *State of Fear*, and the films and television shows *Elysium*, *2012*, *Noah*, *Daybreakers*, and *The Strain*.

The sixth chapter examines environmentalist and feminist theology by Catholic writers, as well as writers from different faith traditions who advocate a similar rapprochement between humanity and nature, including Jewish, Protestant, and Muslim environmentalists. In total, "Eden Revisited: Ursula K. Le Guin, St. Francis, and the Ecofeminist Storytelling Model" explores the ideological overlap between ecofeminist theorists and science fiction writers who have written political and literary tracts about the moral imperative to reorient the world away from imperial patriarchy, pollution profiteering, colonialism, and institutional racism and sexism. These writers argue that the dominant profit-over-people mindset fostered by global corporate capitalism will soon destroy the planet, and that a new, populist, feminist, environmentalist mindset is needed to save humanity. The argument is gendered and appears to promote a pagan or earth goddess form of religious worship, but the worldview is compatible with the Christianity of female theologian Sallie McFague and male mystic St. Francis of Assisi. Indeed, McFague and Assisi express a view of ecological stewardship compatible with Lewis and Tolkien.

The somewhat self-explanatory title of the seventh chapter is "*MaddAddam* and *The Handmaid's Tale*: Margaret Atwood and Dystopian Science Fiction as Current Events." This chapter explores Atwood's four dystopian novels, placing them in a contemporary sociopolitical context, examining Atwood's commitment as an author and public scholar to challenging totalitarianism and the systemic persecution of women. The chapter also considers the possibility that Atwood is an agnostic equivalent of a Hebrew prophet— even if she herself rejects the label. This chapter hearkens back to the previous chapter, demonstrating how Atwood's writing fits the ecofeminist writer's manifesto of Ursula K. Le Guin and acts as a sequel to the "wolf of Gubbio" story from *The Little Flowers of St. Francis*, also covered in chapter 6.

Chapter 8 is titled "Ur-Fascism and Populist Rebellions in *Snowpiercer* and *Mad Max: Fury Road*." The works considered in this chapter explore societies that have survived a catastrophic event that ended civilization as we currently understand it, in most cases leaving only a small band of survivors living under an oppressive regime in which power is divided starkly based on class, race, and gender. Eventually, the oppressed masses rebel against their Ur-fascist overlords, and the above narratives depict different potential outcomes for rebellions. Umberto Eco provides the methodological framework for this chapter.

Chapter 9 is "Tolkien's Kind of Catholic: Suzanne Collins, Empathy, and *The Hunger Games*." This chapter places Roman Catholic climate fiction author Suzanne Collins squarely in the Catholic social justice tradition occupied by Tolkien, St. Francis of Assisi, Oscar Wilde, Dorothy Day, Pope Francis, and Stephen Colbert. It offers a close reading of the *Hunger Games* series as a subversive text arguing for a bottom-up revolution of empathy within our own reality as well as the world of Panem. This chapter also considers how some conservative Catholic critics have failed to see the book as a liberal Catholic text, or recognized it as such and condemned it for not advocating a right-wing form of Catholicism.

The tenth chapter of this book is called "The Cowboy and Indian Alliance: Collective Action against Climate Change in *A Song of Ice and Fire* and *Star Trek*." As this chapter demonstrates, *A Song of Ice and Fire* is an incisive commentary on climate change that resonates with the message of political solidarity found in Naomi Klein's real-world assessment of the political dimension of combatting climate change in *This Changes Everything* (2014) and in the final *Star Trek* story with the original cast, *Star Trek VI: The Undiscovered Country* (1991).

Chapter 11 is "What Next? Robert Crumb's 'A Short History of America' and Ending the Game of Thrones." Right now, readers of Martin's books do not know if his heroes will save Westeros from the coming of the most devastating winter in its history. Similarly, people in the real world do not know if they can halt and/or reverse the already devastating and alarming effects of climate change. Martin offers us suspense. Naomi Klein, in her provocative and controversial book *This Changes Everything*, offers one possible plan for collective action in the real world to confront our own equivalent of ice zombies on the march. Considering both together is an eye-opening process.

Finally, the epilogue asks the question: Who today can legitimately stake a claim to being an inheritor of Tolkien's legacy, as both an author and an environmentalist?

Overall, this book examines the various prophetic scenarios presented by climate fiction and considers the role these works play in offering us all critical food for thought as we face the challenges of the twenty-first century.

# 1

# *Star Wars*, Hollywood Blockbusters, and the Cultural Appropriation of J. R. R. Tolkien

Every tree has its enemy, few have an advocate. (Too often the hate is irrational, a fear of anything large and alive, and not easily tamed or destroyed, though it may clothe itself in pseudo-rational terms). . . . In all my works I take the part of trees as against all their enemies.

—J. R. R. Tolkien

"Primroses and landscapes," [the Director of Hatcheries and Conditioning] pointed out, "have one grave defect: they are gratuitous. A love of nature keeps no factories busy. It was decided to abolish the love of nature, at any rate among the lower classes."

—Aldous Huxley, *Brave New World*

## Joseph Campbell's Monomyth and the Cinematic Ecological War Narrative

Over the course of six *Star Wars* films, George Lucas told the story of Anakin Skywalker, the tragically flawed Jedi Knight who fell from grace, transformed into the evil Sith Lord known as Darth Vader, and was redeemed through his son Luke's belief in his enduring potential for goodness. The story unfolded in two trilogies: the original trilogy that recounted the coming of Luke Skywalker, a new hope for the future of the Republic, and the redemption of Vader—comprising *Star Wars* (1977), *The Empire Strikes Back* (1980), and *Return of the Jedi* (1983)—and the prequel trilogy that recounts the fall of Anakin Skywalker and the rise of the Empire—*The Phantom Menace* (1999), *Attack of the Clones* (2002), and *Revenge of the Sith* (2005). The main arc of this story is supplemented by

21

several comic books, novels, television shows, and video games, as well as new live-action films produced by Disney Studios that take place during, between, before, and after these films. Some series aficionados are vocal in their loathing of Lucas's prequel trilogy—and his many alterations to the original trilogy—but the *Star Wars* saga is beloved worldwide nevertheless. Its appealing science fantasy appropriation of Buddhism as an awareness of the "Force" that binds all the Cosmos, and its melodramatic depictions of the Force's chief disciples known as the Jedi, have inspired millions. Indeed, a surprising number of fans identified themselves as Jedi in religious affiliation questions on global census surveys in 2001, causing Jediism to be recognized as a religion by some governments. Though the first film was released at the beginning of the Carter administration, the blossoming popularity of the series coincided with the rise of the Reagan Revolution in the late seventies and early eighties; consequently, its predominantly male cast, emphasis on action over characterization, and depiction of messianic heroism has caused some cultural commentators to deem the series politically reactionary. However, critic Doug Williams championed the Lucas films as representing progressive values and depicting environmentalist, anti-imperial ideals.[1] Also, journalist Kate Aronoff praised 2016's *Rogue One: A* Star Wars *Tale* as a timely and subversive antifacist narrative.[2] As many scholars and fans are aware, the series offers up a positive role model for the young through Luke's popularization of narratologist Joseph Campbell's conception of the hero.[3] In some respects, the series is a hybrid of these value systems—reactionary and patriarchal as well as Buddhist and ecological.

The story of Darth Vader—told by Lucas in collaboration with co-writers Lawrence Kasdan and Leigh Brackett and fellow directors Irvin Kershner and Richard Marquand—concerns a misguided man who thought that he was taking positive, heroic action to combat institutionalized injustice and slavery, but instead transformed into everything that he himself hated. In the six Lucas *Star Wars* films, Anakin Skywalker/Darth Vader is depicted as a man who surrendered himself to the system of a totalitarian military industrial complex and became "more machine than man"—the physical embodiment of mechanized warfare and fascistic impulses. Vader serves Emperor Palpatine, who lives on Coruscant, a planet that is, essentially, one vast city devoid of vegetation. Vader himself lives atop a skyscraper when on Coruscant and has a primary home in a black castle located on the volcanic, Mordor-like planet Mustafar. Vader's goal is to lure his son onto the same path he treads in life so that they can overthrow the Emperor and rule the galaxy together. However, for Luke to join his father, he would have to embrace authoritarianism so completely that he, too, would become more machine than man. The more tempted he is to be like his father, the darker his clothes become and the more machine parts begin to be grafted onto his body. However, Luke has chosen to reject what his father stands for. Luke has chosen the side of nature. He grew up on a farm, embracing the natural order, and has been tutored by the Jedi master Yoda, who lives on Dagobah, a planet covered in wetlands. In *Star Wars*, the moral side is represented by pacifists, inept left-wing politicians, and the radical liberal terrorists of the Rebel Alliance who are associated with nature imagery and who base themselves on forest and desert planets. In contrast, the Imperial side is replete with humans who cover themselves in so much armor that they are indistinguishable from androids, and barely alive enough to be considered murdered when they are shot by rebels. When the heroes suffer their most grievous losses, it is on planets such as Coruscant, or on ice- or snowfall-covered planets, when the seasonal cycle is symbolically linked with death. Significantly, the final battle between the Rebels and the Empire on the forest planet Endor sees the imperial Stormtroopers routed by the moral authority of the diminutive indigenous peoples called the Ewoks. From a strategic perspective, the Ewoks should not have been able to defeat the Stormtroopers, but the power of Nature and the subtle guidance of the Force helped ensure the victory of life over death and nature over mechanization.

As Campbell has observed, Vader is an intellectually dishonest figure who lies to himself about his own value system. Like Thanos, the tragic Malthusian ecoterrorist who erotically enjoys the act of killing (*Infinity Gauntlet/Infinity War*), the mass-murdering Vader has convinced himself he is a champion of Life. He has extended his own life unnaturally with cybernetics. He is—like his successor Voldemort in the

Fig. 1.1. In the six George Lucas *Star Wars* films, Anakin Skywalker is depicted as a man who surrendered himself to the system of a totalitarian military industrial complex and became "more machine than man." He is transformed into Darth Vader, the physical embodiment of mechanized warfare and fascistic impulses. The iconic villain returned to the screen in 2016's *Rogue One: A Star Wars Story* (pictured here). Lucasfilm.

*Harry Potter* saga—a perpetrator of genocide who started down a dark path only because of an intense dread of death and anger over the impermanence of life. If Vader would embrace Yoda's Buddhist-like philosophy of the Force, he would not be so angry and misguided—but Vader is no Buddhist. The tension between the good intentions of his heart and the false logic of his ideologically shaped intellect has driven him mad. As Campbell said, "If a person insists on a certain program, and doesn't listen to the demands of his own heart, he's going to risk a schizophrenic crackup. Such a person has put himself off-center. He has aligned himself with a program for life, and it's not the one the body is interested in at all. The world is full of people who have stopped listening to themselves or have only listened to their neighbors to learn what they ought to do, how they ought to behave, and what the values are they should be living for."[4]

The Hero's Journey model of storytelling is as famous as it is problematic. It is widely associated with geek culture and adolescent male power fantasies. In scholarly circles, Campbell, the mythologist who popularized the model, is considered too much of a public scholar, self-help guru, and promoter of cultural sameness to be taken seriously. In contemporary anthropology, his name is anathema, and Alan Dundes famously condemned Campbell's work in a 2004 Presidential Plenary Address to the American Folklore Society. And yet, despite such strong opposition from respected anthropologists, Campbell is, essentially, the patron saint of screenwriting courses. In each case, Campbell's writings are vastly under- and overestimated. Contrary to popular assumptions, Campbell is not promoting an establishment narrative in which St. George kills a dragon in a triumphal, fascistic manner that is pro-war, pro-patriarchy, antifeminine, and antiegalitarian. In fact, Campbell's dragon is a metaphor for the internal temptation that heroes face. They are tempted to surrender their wills to the dictates of an oppressive society rather than to heed the urgings of their own hearts. The dragon represents the hero's temptation to "sell out"—to justify acquiescing to the demands of establishment forces through sophistry, and to do just what parents, religious leaders, and community leaders say needs to be done for success to be achieved in contemporary society. Campbell explains that the dragon represents the dominant ideological system of the day, which can be gleaned from whatever building is tallest in the community—the Gothic church in medieval times, the government building in the Renaissance, and the skyscraper headquarters of conglomerates in modern times. Those who fail to slay the dragon within become the dragon themselves and sacrifice themselves to a corrupt system.[5] For Campbell, meditating upon the hero's journey teaches us all to follow our bliss, and Jhumpa Lahiri dramatized the transformative power of this philosophy for good and ill in her novel *The Namesake* (2003).

Significantly, Campbell's book *The Hero with a Thousand Faces* (1949) was one of the sources of inspiration for Lucas when he was writing *Star Wars*.

For Campbell, the power of the Hero's Journey cycle is that it models resistance to indoctrination and encourages those who immerse themselves in such stories to resist adopting a programmatic life. In popular culture, the hero's journey is most famously exemplified in Luke Skywalker's refusal to become his father.

Ever since the release of *Jaws* (1975), the first summer blockbuster, and *Star Wars*, a film that shaped the aesthetic and ideological sensibilities of Generation X to an astounding and incalculable degree, special effects–saturated film narratives have accounted for a growing percentage of the motion pictures released each year by Hollywood. Far from becoming weary of action movies with apocalyptic plots, global audiences have continued to patronize them, filling the lists of the highest-grossing films of all time with such blockbusters. Indeed, as special effects technologies have grown steadily more sophisticated, and the spectacle associated with these escapist narratives has grown more dazzling, audience demand for apocalyptic special effects extravaganzas seems to have increased in kind. This voracious hunger for these epic stories has encouraged studio executives to regard such films—expensive as they are to produce—as so lucrative that they have continued to produce a multitude of film franchises based on the same basic, market-tested formula. It is apparent to any film scholar, critic, fan, or even casual filmgoer that most Hollywood blockbusters follow the exact same storytelling formula: they have a generic plot informed by Campbell's Hero's Journey model filtered through the corporate scriptwriter model of Christopher Vogler. If Vogler's template isn't proscriptive enough, the script is also expected to adhere to the minute-by-minute "beat sheet" movie formula developed by Blake Snyder for his screenwriting Bible *Save the Cat*, and to be vetted by marketing consultants such as statistician Vinny Bruzzese, of Worldwide Motion Picture Group, who analyze scripts to make sure they contain no scenes, plot twists, or character personality traits that have been statistically proven to alienate audiences.[6] In the wake of the huge success of the *Terminator, Matrix, Harry Potter*, and *Spider-Man* films, studios and premium television stations now appear to be engaged, more than ever, in search of ready-made properties to adapt into their next multimedia franchises. In recent years, some of the most popular and profitable fantasy and science fiction franchises have included *Game of Thrones, The Hunger Games, Lord of the Rings*, and *Doctor Who*. These texts are all continuations of (or reboots of) serialized narratives of the past or adaptations of intellectual properties with a proven market value. For decades now, investors have banked on their tapping into the ascendant geek culture zeitgeist, and tap in they have. The multimedia adaptations based upon bestsellers gave the narratives still greater exposure than they had in print format, ensuring that the authors and the architects of the adaptations became household names (if they weren't already). Whether these adaptations are all quality productions or are truly faithful to the source material is oft-debated. Indeed, the adaptations of *Game of Thrones, Lord of the Rings*, and *The Hunger Games* have all been embraced or rejected to varying degrees by readers of the novels. There have been many insightful discussions of the artistic merit of these adaptations. There have been reasonable calls for them to be judged based upon their own merits and not merely upon their level of fidelity to their sources. Nevertheless, it is important to note that these adaptations' persistent failure to bring the climate fiction sensibilities of their source novels to the screen is deeply troubling.

Any process of adaptation that minimizes the social commentary embedded in apocalyptic, dystopian, or climate fiction narratives and maximizes the length and scope of the battle scenes for marketing reasons suppresses much of the progressive or subversive qualities of the source material. Instead, it excavates and amplifies the more retrograde, pro-war potential of that narrative. Any "action movie" version of a cli-fi book is potentially dumbed-down enough to privilege a "reading" of the source book that transforms it into a piece of pro-war escapist art with the potential to bolster the power of reactionary political movements. In this manner, a book that was written to *challenge* fascistic forces in the real world is often transformed into a movie that, in many significant ways, appears to *promote* the very fascist causes the story was written to oppose.

A successful environmentalist narrative needs to be *identifiable as environmentalist*, in both its original written form and in adapted form. Whether it is an older climate fiction narrative by one of the Inklings or a pressing contemporary parable by a living author, it needs to be compelling enough dramatically—and convincing enough morally—to move an audience to action on ecological issues. The *Game of Thrones* series brings enough of the environmental sensibilities of the novels to the television screen that viewers have noticed them despite the ratcheted-up sex and violence. The rising ocean waters and other climate change conditions that helped create the stark class divisions of Panem were excised from *The Hunger Games* film adaptations, but they were more part of the back story of the books than the action of the plot proper, so those omissions were understandable, if unfortunate. Omissions such as these might have been made from some sinister attempt to keep any discussion of climate change as anything but a hoax out of the mass media. However, it is also possible that these thematically important moments were dropped from various film adaptations of cli-fi novels because they didn't "advance the plot" like a runaway train to its inevitable climax. Thematically important moments are often deemed boring and superfluous, and are excised by screenwriters or directors even if they are centrally important to the author and the experience of reading the novel.

On a related issue, thanks in part to Vogler, studio executives often look to Campbell's hero's journey model as a template for the plot structure of their movies. However, the Hollywood reworking of Campbell frequently omits the usage of what is one of the most important of the many stages of the hero's journey—the "Return"—in which the hero comes home to a blighted society with the grail artifact. Thanks to the grail, the hero brings new life and fertility home, "where the boon may redound to the renewing of the community, the nation, the planet, or the ten thousand worlds."[7] This imagery helps add an ecologically minded coda to the heroic fiction narrative template that makes it far more progressive and enlightening than the idea that the hero's journey is solely concerned with the slaying of monsters. The easiest way to co-opt Campbell's "hero's journey" model is to deemphasize the psychological richness of Campbell's interpretations and eschew his efforts to illustrate global interconnectedness through promoting awareness of similar storytelling concerns found in different cultures. Furthermore, instead of depicting the dragon as an inner demon, reactionary forces that co-opt Campbell's storytelling model tend to be more concerned with presenting the dragon as either dangerously female or as a racially "other" figure that must be subdued and slain. In some of the most martial iterations of the hero narrative, the moment of the kill—when the hero slays the dragon—is given the greatest dramatic weight. That moment of the kill is triumphalist and presented as the end of the story. Omitting Campbell's Return stage, or including it as a brief, perfunctory epilogue without giving it the proper dramatic weight, makes murdering monsters the most important (if not the sole) function of the story. In other, still more problematic iterations of the hero's journey, the moment of the kill is repeated over and over and over again as the hero slays monster after monster after monster in a narrative that takes several hours and includes few moments of plot, characterization, or thematic richness. Sometimes the hero kills hundreds or thousands of monsters during the story, and yet his fundamental "goodness" is unquestioned. As Marina Warner observed in "Boys Will Be Boys," video games are notorious for multiplying the moment of the kill at the expense of all other stages of the hero's journey.[8] (Note: It is clear that Warner is basing her observations upon video games in the militarist, gun-and-war-festish mold of *Ikari Warriors*, *Call of Duty*, *Tomb Raider*, *Mortal Kombat*, *Panzer General*, and *Hogan's Alley*, and not talking about more narratively complex, psychological interesting, and socially aware video games such as *Unmanned*, *Tender Loving Care*, *Destroy All Humans!*, or the Sierra strategy games of the 1980s and 1990s.) As motion pictures become more like the worst of the shoot-'em-up, Walmart–fare video games, they have multiplied the numbers of enemies slain, extended the lengths of battle scenes, and given shorter shrift to plot, theme, and character.

Climate fiction made for the screen that has not been based upon long novels has also faced creative and political opposition from executives. These executives seem to dislike the tenor of the ecological message and fear that a political film will not be as lucrative as an "apolitical" film. For example, writer-director James Cameron was challenged in his intention to make *Avatar* (2009) at once an environmentalist parable and a condemnation of the legacy of American imperialism from the Indian wars to the 2003 invasion of Iraq. The film concerns the corporate-military forces of the human empire destroying the home of the peaceful, tribal alien culture, the Na'vi. The humans hope to drive the Na'vi out of lands humanity needs to exploit for natural resources necessary for the continuance of their interstellar hegemony. After the film's release, Cameron reported, "We're getting a tremendous amount of feedback from environmental groups, from people with specific causes . . . whether it's indigenous people being displaced by companies to do mining or to do oil drilling, or if it's environmental groups saying, 'let's do some curriculum around *Avatar*.' " Despite this enthusiastic response from certain quarters, Cameron revealed that executives at the studio sponsoring the film, Fox, were not pleased by the green sensibilities of the script during preproduction: "When they read it, they sort of said, 'Can we take some of this tree-hugging, *FernGully* crap out of this movie?'. . . . And I said, 'No, because that's why I'm making the film.' "[9] With corporate executives consistently privileging marketing concerns over artistic ones, it should not be surprising whenever an environmentalist sentiment is excised from a film script during production. Instead, it may be more surprising when, against all odds, an ecological message somehow finds its way into a film, and its meaning and significance is apparent to discerning audience members.

Fig. 1.2. In *Avatar* (2009), the Na'vi, the indigenous peoples of Pandora, face conquest and exploitation from the soldiers and businessmen of the Earth empire. Writer-director James Cameron revealed that executives at the studio sponsoring the film, Fox, were not pleased by the green sensibilities of the script during preproduction: "When they read it, they sort of said, 'Can we take some of this tree-hugging, FernGully crap out of this movie?'. . . . And I said, 'No, because that's why I'm making the film.'" 20th Century Fox.

Even this assessment may be optimistic, as Max Horkheimer and Theodor W. Adorno would have predicted all the above scenarios. These members of the Frankfurt School of Critical Theory would argue that, since the chief goal of mass culture is to indoctrinate the masses into submissiveness, any even remotely revolutionary material called upon to be translated from written word to film would be stripped of its liberating power before being distributed. Consequently, Horkheimer and Adorno would not be surprised, then, that Campbell's message was co-opted by the system he was attempting to criticize, or that the morals of works of climate fiction would be turned upon their head sometime during their journey from the page to the screen. Nor would they be surprised by the notion that the public would *demand* that these works be adapted and co-opted and betrayed, because they are too challenging, revolutionary, and "boring" in their original forms. After all, as Adorno observes in "The Schema of Mass Culture": "All mass culture is fundamentally adaptation," a "pre-digested" product marketed to "those who cannot digest anything not already pre-digested. It is baby-food: permanent self-reflection based upon the infantile compulsion toward the repetition of need which it creates in the first place."[10]

In their landmark works, Horkheimer and Adorno were concerned with uncovering the origins of totalitarianism within the very Enlightenment philosophies that were designed to prevent such a sociopolitical calamity from happening in the first place. In the years following the writing of their works, fascism "fell," but their observations about tyranny in European and American industrial society remained apt in a postwar world, they explain in the introduction to their perennially controversial *Dialectic of Enlightenment* (1944). As Horkheimer and Adorno observe in an essay included in that collection, "The Culture Industry: Enlightenment as Mass Deception":

> The consumers are the workers and the salaried employees, the farmers and petty bourgeoisie. Capitalist production hems them in so tightly, in body and soul, that they unresistingly succumb to whatever is proffered to them. However, just as the ruled have always taken the morality dispensed to them by the rulers more seriously than the rulers themselves, the frauded masses today cling to the myth of success still more ardently than the successful. They, too, have their aspirations. They insist, unwaveringly, on the ideology by which they are enslaved. The pernicious love of the common people for the harm done to them outstrips even the cunning of the authorities. It surpasses the rigor of the Hays Office, just as, in great epochs, it has inspired renewed zeal in greater agencies, directed against it, the terror of the tribunals. It calls for Mickey Rooney rather than the tragic Garbo, Donald Duck rather than Betty Boop. The industry bows to the vote it has itself rigged. . . . Under the ideological truce between them, the conformism of the consumers, like the shamelessness of the producers they sustain, can have a good conscience. Both content themselves with the reproduction of sameness.[11]

These thinkers are describing a species of fascism that the average American refuses to acknowledge permeates American culture. It is an assertion that has earned Horkheimer and Adorno more than their share of detractors, especially since the term *fascism* is so loaded and overused. In order to determine, in a sober state of mind, the extent to which their diagnosis of American culture as fascist is accurate, it is important to first settle upon a definition of fascism. For the purposes of clarity, fascism shall best be understood in these pages in the manner presented by Ian Adams in *Ideology and Politics in Britain Today* (1999): "The common elements of fascism—extreme nationalism, social Darwinism, the leadership principle, elitism, anti-liberalism, anti-egalitarianism, anti-democracy, intolerance, glorification of war, the supremacy of the state and anti-intellectualism—together form a rather loose doctrine. Fascism emphasises action rather than theory, and fascist theoretical writings are always weak. Hitler's Nazism had rather more theory, though its intellectual quality is appalling. This greater theoretical content is mostly concerned with race, and it was Hitler's racial theories that distinguished Nazism from Italian fascism."[12]

Upton Sinclair's epigrammatic definition of fascism, "Fascism is capitalism plus murder," first appeared in *Presidential Agent II* (1944) and has rediscovered fame recently as an internet meme. Another significant work on the subject, Bertram Gross's *Friendly Fascism* (1990), presciently argues that fascists could be voted into power in America by using an entertaining mass media campaign to tell the American people what they want to hear, thereby concealing a totalitarian agenda behind a populist veneer. It is also important to note that some of the most notable antifascist thinkers working within the traditions of Western theology include Reinhold Niebuhr, John Hick, and C. S. Lewis. Peter Watkins, meanwhile, is one of the most critically respected antifascist filmmakers and documentarians.

The looseness of the definition of fascism has posed problems over the years, and has enabled people to employ it as a derogatory term in political and online debates to mean simply, "someone I find personally repellent," thereby eroding the usefulness of the label (per Godwin's Law). Nevertheless, the fascist (or Ur-fascist) villain is such a ubiquitous presence in climate fiction, from Lewis's writings up through Margaret Atwood's and George R. R. Martin's novels—and is so consistently portrayed from narrative to narrative—that it remains an important concept to understand and examine, especially, as you will see, in its implications for ecology.

Horkheimer and Adorno have not achieved the widespread respect within the United States that their work warrants because they are so critical of America. However, their contestation that American popular culture is fascist because it is anti-intellectual, Puritanical, militarist, sexist, racist, and designed to pacify an unruly mob of an audience rings alarmingly true in a culture that immerses itself in hundreds of channels worth of corporate dross on television and in limitless propagandistic websites online all hours of the day. Since entertainment is expected to be unintelligent and uniform in tone, content, and message, it is no wonder that climate change has no secure place in popular culture. It is too serious a concept, and it is too challenging to a mindset invested in the perpetration of the cultural sameness of the status quo. In this regard, and in many others, a "fascist" or a "diet fascist" mindset is the archenemy of environmentalism and alarmingly omnipresent in contemporary America.

Would that it were possible to break free of the influence of such a pervasive, all-encompassing fascistic narrative. Would that it were possible to refuse to participate in the crafting and enforcement of this pernicious ideology that we are all complicit in crafting, to one degree or another. Would that it were possible to change the narrative somehow.

## Tolkien's Skeptical View of Film Adaptations

In 1958, John Ronald Reuel Tolkien learned of a planned animated film adaptation of his epic *Lord of the Rings* saga, a book that he had published in three volumes between 1954 and 1955. Although not against the idea of an adaptation in principle, he was disappointed when he read Morton Grady Zimmerman's synopsis of the proposed project. To Tolkien, Zimmerman's treatment violated the spirit of his narrative. In June, Tolkien wrote to the adaptation's sponsor—publisher, agent, and genre film memorabilia archivist Forrest J. Ackerman—explaining his "irritation" and "resentment" at finding his work treated "carelessly in general, in places recklessly, and with no evident signs of any appreciation of what it is all about. . . . The canons of narrative art in any medium cannot be wholly different; and the failure of poor films is often precisely in exaggeration, and in the intrusion of unwanted matter owing to not perceiving where the core of the original lies."[13]

In 2004, prominent Tolkien scholar Tom Shippey explained that the English writer and philologist had reservations about any adaptation of *Lord of the Rings* that granted dramatic weight to all the wrong elements of his stories, thereby changing the tone and meaning of the Middle-earth cycle: "What Tolkien feared in particular was the subordination of what he called the 'Prime Action,' the story of the Ring-bearers Frodo and Sam, to the 'Subsidiary Action' of the great battles at Isengard, at Helm's Deep, at Cormallen, at the Black Gate. It is very much part of the core meaning of *The Lord of the Rings* that the highly visual and traditional heroic displays from Aragorn and Théoden and the other high-status characters would be futile, as they themselves recognize, without Frodo and Sam, whose heroism is an entirely different and much less visible style. . . . Yet in some respects [Jackson's film adaptation of] *The Lord of the Rings* remains 'an action movie,' even a 'special effects movie.' " When speculating upon the reasons why Tolkien's book was transmuted into an action film, Shippey concludes that a "moviemaker . . . operating with a budget measurable in millions of dollars per day, very obviously has to consider recovering the return on his expenses, and is accordingly susceptible to 'audience pressure': he has to guess what his audience will like and won't like and adjust his production accordingly. Experimentation is much cheaper in a written medium, conformism much more of a threat in movies."[14]

Those who are inclined to defend Peter Jackson as a Tolkien fan and his films as labors of love have a compelling case to make. There is no questioning Jackson's devotion to Tolkien and the Middle-earth saga. As he himself explained, "I read the book when I was eighteen-years-old and thought, 'I can't wait 'til the movie comes out!' Twenty years later, no one had done it, so I got impatient."[15] Jackson initially made a two-picture deal with the film studio Miramax to produce *The Lord of the Rings* adaptation, but became disillusioned with the partnership when executive Bob Weinstein made creative demands that Jackson objected to. Weinstein dictated that the films be told in flashback by an elderly Frodo and that Jackson kill off at least one of the four main Hobbit characters, all of whom survive in Tolkien's original. Taking a risk, Jackson broke with Miramax and shopped the project around to other studios. Bob Shaye, head of New Line Cinema, picked up the project. Many Tolkien fans look upon Shaye kindly because he made fewer specific demands than Bob Weinstein did and was the one to willingly offer Jackson a three-picture deal, giving Jackson the freedom to make one full-length film for each book in the series.[16] Given how happily this tale of preproduction business and creative wrangling concluded, it is unfortunate that the film series born out of this stressful process was not more thematically faithful to Tolkien's vision. Ultimately, what filmgoers got were three films that were faithful to the *letter* of Tolkien's narrative but not to its *spirit*.

In general, the Jackson films devote too much screen time to the battle segments from the books and excise too much thematically central ecological material with the Hobbits and Treebeard—especially in the briefer, more commonly seen theatrical "cuts" (or "edits"). Jackson reserved much of this ecologically themed material for the extended edition home video versions of the films marketed to the hardcore Tolkien fans, suggesting that those scenes are "optional" or "extras" that only a niche audience could appreciate, instead of forming the backbone of the saga. Jackson's strategy of producing different cuts of the films for mass audiences and for hardcore fans is savvy in many ways, and probably was the only way he could think of to please *both* his corporate backers and serious Tolkien fans—by releasing a *marketable* cut and a *faithful* cut. Nevertheless, viewers of the theatrical cuts of the films are still cheated of the material closest to the heart of Tolkien's original, and even Jackson's execution of the "faithful" extended cuts are problematic. The bloated battle scenes featured in both the theatrical cuts and extended versions of Jackson's *Lord of the Rings* and *The Hobbit* often go too far in glorifying the heroism of Aragorn and Thorin Oakenshield and romanticizing the battle scenes at the expense of the Roman Catholic and environmentalist themes inherent in the Hobbit-centric segments of Tolkien's epic. Even the extended editions of Jackson's films do not adapt to film the critically important "Scouring of the Shire" segment at the end of the book *The Return of the King*. They also slice the "green" character Tom Bombadil out of the story. Horkheimer and Adorno would not be surprised to learn that even the most hardcore Tolkien fans predicted that these omissions would be made before the films were released, and preemptively approved of such omissions. The "Scouring of the Shire" segment would, arguably, have made an already overlong film epilogue still lengthier, and Bombadil was widely regarded as too whimsical a figure for Jackson's version of the story. However, both omissions add to an overall effect of a film trilogy adaptation that diminishes the dramatic and thematic significance of all the original story's environmental sensibilities and takes every opportunity to inject as much militarism as possible into the narrative. Another consequence of leaving out the "Scouring" is that much of the antiwar element of the work is lost. Tolkien believes war is sometimes necessary, but his story is in part about the cost of war on those who fight it, and how things are never the same after you go home. That sentiment is mostly lost in the Jackson films. Indeed, one might well imagine an alternative reality in which a low-budget, ninety-minute Masterpiece Theater adaptation of just the "Scouring of the Shire" chapter of *Lord of the Rings* exists, and that such an adaptation would, potentially, feel tonally and thematically closer to the spirit of Tolkien's narrative than Jackson's proudly completist adaptation, filled to bursting with action scenes and wholly lacking in the core of the thematically critical epilogue.

Given the epic battle scenes featured in the book *Lord of the Rings*, it was perhaps inevitable that a twenty-first-century film adaptation of that book would feature overlong battle segments. What is more surprising is how many extended and unnecessary battle scenes were shoehorned into the three-part Jackson film adaptation of *The Hobbit*— especially those with no analogue in the novel. Beginning with a discussion of how different adaptations of *The Hobbit* dramatize military and ecological themes will help us understand better what went wrong with the film adaptations of the more sprawling and ambitious narrative, *Lord of the Rings*.

## How to Ruin *The Hobbit*—Or— So Much Depends upon Black Emperor Butterflies

The classic children's book *The Hobbit* was published in 1937. Over the decades, it has been read by generations of children and adults and has been the subject of a range of adaptations and merchandising initiatives. Most famously, the book was adapted into a widely seen 1977 Rankin/Bass television cartoon special with an all-star voice cast and a motion picture trilogy directed by Jackson comprised of the films *An Unexpected Journey* (2012), *The Desolation of Smaug* (2013), and *The Battle of Five Armies* (2014). *The Hobbit* has also the subject of numerous stage adaptations, comic book adaptations, a 1968 BBC 4 radio series, and "The Ballad of Bilbo Baggins" (1968) sung by Leonard Nimoy, which one might listen to after hearing German power-metal band Blind Guardian's *Silmarillion* concept album *Nightfall on Middle-earth* (1998). A strategy game version of *The Hobbit* designed by Sierra was released across multiple platforms in 2003, and it strives to recreate a sense of the entire book as a playable experience. In contrast, several board game and role-playing game companies, including TSR and Games Workshop, have developed *Hobbit*-themed tabletop games, most frequently in the form of war strategy games recreating the Battle of Five Armies from the book. Additionally, the 1970s art of Greg and Tim Hildebrandt depicting scenes from the Middle-earth stories has appeared in calendars, on paperback covers, and in limited edition books and trading card sets for years.

When fantasy genre fans discuss the extent to which they like *The Hobbit*—or their willingness to forgive it or not forgive it for being written by Tolkien as a children's book, instead of one intended for older audiences like its sequel—it is hard to tell whether they are talking about the original book, Peter Jackson's films, the Rankin/Bass cartoon, or its various toy, board game, or art-book merchandise tie-ins. Each version of *The Hobbit* presents much the same story. One may find Bilbo in the art of the Hildebrandt brothers, voiced by Orson Bean in the Rankin/Bass cartoons, played onscreen by Ian Holm and Martin Freeman in the Jackson films, or sung about on the album "The Two Sides of Leonard Nimoy." However, there are subtle differences between each of these iterations of Bilbo Baggins, and of *The Hobbit* story. These differences have great potential to influence how the story is interpreted. For example, one might argue that any board game that focuses on fighting and winning the Battle of Five Armies might be missing the point of a book in which war is depicted as being a senseless waste of life. In the novel, Bilbo spends a great deal of energy trying to prevent the battle from occurring in the first place. Also, Thorin dies filled with remorse for instigating the conflict—he had greedily refused to share the wealth recovered from the slain dragon

Smaug with all those desperate humans whose homes Smaug burned to the ground. So why would a game be created to make such a battle entertaining and suggest that the glory of war and the importance of expert military strategy should be viewed as the central thematic focus of *The Hobbit*? Strategy games are admittedly fun, but a "Battle of Five Armies" game seems . . . *inappropriate.*

Tolkien's novel *The Hobbit* is an underdog tale—a small band of Dwarves enlists the aid of a callow, provincial Hobbit named Bilbo Baggins to journey with them to their ancestral seat, the Lonely Mountain (also called Sindarin Erebor). There they hope to kill the dragon Smaug, who has driven them from their home and stolen their gold. The dwarves wish to raise Thorin, pretender King of the Dwarves, to power in the Kingdom Under the Mountain. During the episodic, briskly paced quest narrative, the malcontented and dandyish Bilbo grows into a seasoned adventurer who has challenged, defeated, or escaped from giant spiders, hostile wood Elves, trolls, goblins, a cannibal river-folk Hobbit called Gollum, and Smaug himself. The Dwarves—who are motivated as much by greed, revenge, and selfishness as they are by a desire for justice and a home of their own—eventually learn from Bilbo's kindhearted example how to cultivate a healthy sense of their culture's place in the larger world. Their basic characters do not change, but Bilbo helps them curb some of their darker impulses.

Fig. 1.3. In Peter Jackson's *The Hobbit: An Unexpected Journey* (2012), the dwarves invite themselves over to Bilbo's house to recruit him to their quest. From left to right: William Kircher as Bifur, Graham McTavish as Dwalin, Martin Freeman as Bilbo, James Nesbitt as Bofur, John Callen as Oin. Warner Bros.

One of the most compelling moments in *The Hobbit* story—in all its major permutations—is the black emperor butterflies segment. Bilbo, the constant complainer, reluctantly climbs to the top of a tree in Mirkwood Forest to get a better vantage point to spy a path out of the dense forest his party is lost in. At the tree's summit, he discovers a breathtaking view of the sun and spies hundreds of glorious, midnight black butterflies in flight. However, Bilbo fails to discern a way out of the forest from his vantage point because the tree he chooses isn't tall enough. Upon his return to the ground, he breaks the bad news to the dwarves that they are still lost but tries to console them by telling them the story of his beautiful encounter with nature. Unfortunately, "they did not care tuppence about the butterflies, and were only made more angry when he told them of the beautiful breeze, which they were too heavy to climb up and feel."[17]

Since it is a moment of a small-town man making life-changing contact with the natural beauty of the wider world, the black emperor butterfly encounter is of central importance to this book. Additionally, the distinction between Bilbo's attitude toward the butterflies and the Dwarves' is of extraordinary significance. Throughout Tolkien's Middle-earth stories, the Dwarves are presented as indoor and underground industrial workers who see the natural world as raw material for the machines and weapons they produce. As Vala Yavanna, the angelic champion of nature, predicted in Tolkien's Middle-earth creation myth *The Silmarillion*, these Dwarves, like the first generation of Dwarves, "will love first the things made by their own hands, as doth their father [the angel who created them, Yavanna's mate Aulë]. They will delve in the earth, and the things that grow and live upon the earth they will not heed. Many a tree shall feel the bite of their iron without pity."[18] Like the Ferengi of *Star Trek: Deep Space 9*, the Dwarves are the comically-villainous-but-potentially-redeemable pragmatists, misers, and businessmen of Middle-earth (and both fictional species bear more than a hint of ethnic stereotyping and anti-Semitic sentiment in their design). They have little respect for the beauty of nature and little appreciation of either mysticism or aesthetics. Certain Hobbits have a similar form of tunnel vision given how little of the world they have seen beyond their small enclave of fellow Hobbits. However, Hobbits lack the industriousness of the Dwarves, and appreciate a good indolent afternoon smoking pipe-weed and eating multiple breakfasts, giving them the open, even temperament that makes spiritual growth and empathy with non-Hobbit outsiders more culturally possible for them than for Dwarves. In the butterfly segment, the Dwarves viewed the tree only as a tool—something to requisition as a crow's nest. Should the edge of the forest have been seen from the tree, and its location reported back to the Dwarves, then both Bilbo (the scout) and the tree (his lookout post) would have been deemed useful and successful. Significantly, the utilitarian aspect of this enterprise is an utter failure. Bilbo did not see the edge of the forest, so the Dwarves deemed him and his tree useless and, therefore, worthy of only dismissal, ridicule, and disgust. The questers are, indeed, close to the edge of the forest, as the narrator reveals, but they have not chosen a tree that is positioned well enough to help them see that. When Bilbo returns to the Dwarves with no good news, he is coerced by peer pressure into feeling their uniform disappointment and utter disregard for the moral and aesthetic significance of breathtaking views and moments of communion with nature. The Dwarves' anger gives an anticlimactic feel to the segment. And yet, one gets the impression that the older Bilbo, who has settled down to write the text of *The Hobbit* (aka *There and Back Again*, his memoirs contained in the Red Book of Westmarch), recalls his encounter with the butterflies fondly and feels its gravity in retrospect, removed by the passage of time from the influence of the Dwarves. The segment in the book shows how precious a moment it is when a provincial, practical-minded person has his horizons widened by contact with nature beyond the outskirts of even an admittedly beautiful home village. It also demonstrates how difficult it is for one to hold onto that truly spiritual moment when one returns to the "real world" cares and tries to share perspective-altering experiences with philistines who try to debunk an experience they neither understand nor appreciate.

What the Rankin/Bass cartoon adaptation strives to do is augment the emotion Tolkien infuses into Bilbo's moment of communion with the butterflies. In the *Hobbit* cartoon, Orson Bean's Bilbo narrates as Bilbo climbs the twisted, anthropomorphized trees. "One day, we decided that someone should climb to the top of the tallest tree and have a look about. I couldn't argue. My contract is vague on several points." When Bilbo reaches the top, there is a close-up on his animated face, which is basked in sunlight so intense that he shields his eyes. The cartoon then cuts to a shot of the sun that fills the screen. The viewer's perspective changes as the image pulls back from the sun to reveal a flutter of black butterflies hovering over the treetops. Bilbo's voice-over continues, "There are moments which can change a person for all time." His eyes well with tears. "And I suddenly wondered if I would ever see my snug Hobbit hole again." The visual of the gathering of butterflies is superimposed over Bilbo's humble hillside home. "I wondered *if I actually wanted to*." A folk song by Glenn Yarbrough, "The Road Goes Ever On," begins playing on the soundtrack to underscore the beauty of the moment. The final shot of the scene is a bird's-eye view looking down on Bilbo. The butterflies are foregrounded. The viewer sees Bilbo through the kaleidoscope of butterflies, far away, on the tree horizon line, looking up from an inferior position. He is small. The butterflies are large. They surround him. He is only a little Hobbit awed by the beauty of the larger universe. The scene then fades out. When the story fades back in, it is after a commercial break in the original television broadcast (and after a brief black screen in the home video version). The fade-in brings viewers to the next moment of tension, when Bilbo finds himself menaced by spiders in his sleep. Clearly, some time has passed. The fade-out provides a thematic and visual barrier between the butterflies and the spider attack that allows the butterflies to have their "moment in the sun" before the episodic action narrative resumes its breakneck pace. Taken in total, the butterfly segment of the Rankin/Bass cartoon is a classic moment of 1970s "Hollywood liberal" environmentalism, adapting the work of one of the most environmentalist Inklings as a suitable echo of the ecological sensibilities of the time.

The butterfly segment in the Jackson film is an entirely different audiovisual experience. Bilbo's party has wandered off the safe trail in Mirkwood, has become lost, and is traveling in circles. They have fallen under the spell of the forest, which dulls their senses, and casts them into a stupor somewhere in the no man's land between drunkenness, entrancement, and possession. Bilbo (Martin Freeman) decides that he must climb the trees to help find the way back to the path. He does so under his own initiative, not telling the others, because he has the clearest head of them all and no one else is in a fit state to perform the task. Fearlessly and uncomplaining, he climbs trees coated with mammoth spiderwebs, suggesting the presence of equally massive spiders. When he reaches the summit, breaking through the canopy of leaves, we see his face in close-up, basking in radiant sunlight. The sun gradually burns away the enchantment the forest has placed over his senses. He smiles. He is exhausted but exorcised of Mirkwood's influence. The camera pulls back to a medium shot, revealing the sea of autumn leaves he has emerged from. His hands disturbed the foliage, alarming dozens of pale blue butterflies that had been resting amid the leaves into flight. The butterflies scatter in the air about him and begin an aerial dance, almost as if they are responding to his command to perform for him alone. The camera pulls back into a long shot, spins around to position itself behind Bilbo, sharing his perspective. Howard Shore's orchestral score fills the soundtrack with strings and choral vocalizing, underlining the moment's majestic quality. From his vantage point, Bilbo sees everything he needs to help the Dwarves find their way out of the wood and resume their journey to Erebor. He shouts down to his comrades on the ground, "I can see a lake, and a river, and the Lonely Mountain. We're almost there!" They do not respond, so he becomes concerned. He peers down into the dark below and loses his footing. He falls, lands in one of the enormous spiderwebs he had avoid getting trapped in on the way up, and is instantly set upon by a gigantic spider. Viewers of the film then learn that an army of giant spiders has launched an attack on the Dwarves. The members of the stupefied party are shocked into fighting for their lives and have rallied themselves into action. The extended battle scene that follows shows Bilbo escape from his spiderweb snare and launch himself into fierce combat. He dispatches the spiders with savage brutality as Gollum's enchanted ring fuels his rage and moral corruption. Unexpectedly, the Elves Legolas (Orlando Bloom) and Tauriel (Evangeline Lilly) appear on the scene, intervening to save the Dwarves, using blades, bow and arrow, and martial arts maneuvers to slay the remaining spiders.

The segment in the Jackson film makes several notable alterations to Tolkien's text. One minor but notable change is that the butterflies are pale blue, not black, providing sharper color contrast between the view above the treetops and below, but also challenging the idea that black-colored wildlife can be good or beautiful. Bilbo does not stumble upon the butterflies already in flight and spy upon them without disturbing them. Here he scares them into flight and they seem to dance *for him*. Also, unlike in the book, Bilbo's scouting mission is a success; he sees the edge of the forest, the river, and the mountain in the distance. Traveling to the treetops breaks the spell of the forest, gives him much-needed information, and provides him with wildlife entertainment that he enjoys, but not in the same spiritual way. All this undermines what is achieved in Tolkien's text. In the Jackson film, the utilitarian purpose of the climb is achieved and the tree makes an excellent requisitioned crow's nest. So, in this version, the important element of this scene is not the communion with nature but that Bilbo has *made use of nature* to help him attain his practical goals and move his entourage farther along on their quest. Finally, in the Jackson film, there is no stark scene break between the moment of contact with the butterflies and the next major action scene. Instead, spiders barge in on the butterfly dance segment so quickly and intensely that the emotional potency of the segment is undermined almost entirely by frantic action. During the fight itself, the overemphasis on the gallant performance of the Dwarves fighting the spiders, the combat expertise of Tauriel (a character created for this film), and the sidelining of Bilbo does for this segment what most of the Jackson films do—reduces the moral and dramatic importance of the Hobbits in favor of showcasing warrior heroism, reveling in the glory of combat, and failing to communicate that the epic is a climate fiction narrative.

Comparing these three versions of the same scene—Tolkien's original, the Rankin/Bass cartoon adaptation, and the Jackson live-action dramatization—illustrates how the production teams of the two adaptations made choices in what they depicted, what they didn't, and how they shaped dramatic tone and message. The adaptations do not simply transpose the words of Tolkien's novel to the screen as plastic images. They are both, strictly speaking, faithful in their visualization of the butterfly scene, but both versions show how specific choices on the parts of the filmmakers brought different readings of the novel to the screen: one reading (Rankin/Bass) is ecological, while the other (Jackson) is concerned with depicting the courage and combat prowess demonstrated by comrades-in-arms on the battlefield, marshaling their inner resolve to stand firm against impossible odds. The message of the Jackson film is one calculated to resonate with American audiences during the age of the endless war on terrorism.

One might also make the case that Jackson's films are not only weighted down by their lengthy action segments, but cluttered up with too many special effects for the films to succeed in presenting the illusion of an authentic reality. Viggo Mortensen, who played Aragorn in the *Lord of the Rings* trilogy, explained it best when he observed that "Peter was always a geek in terms of technology but, once he had the means to do it, and the evolution of the technology really took off, he never looked back. In the first movie, yes, there's Rivendell, and Mordor, but there's sort of an organic quality to it, actors acting with each other, and real landscapes; it's grittier. The second movie already started ballooning, for my taste, and then by the third one, there were a lot of special effects. It was grandiose, and all that, but whatever was subtle, in the first movie, gradually got lost in the second and third. Now with *The Hobbit* . . . it's like that to the power of 10."[19]

One literary critic who shares Viggo Mortensen's negative assessment of the Jackson films is Loren Wilkinson, who wrote in "Tolkien and the Surrendering of Power" (2007) that "one of the more grievous liberties the filmmakers took with Tolkien's text was turning Faramir into a power-hungry kidnapper [when Faramir is a gardener at heart] . . . but it seems to me to be in keeping with a general tendency to play down the nature of the gardener, or steward role."

Wilkinson's point about Faramir deserves explication, especially since the character is, indeed, quite different between the book and the film, and people may have a muddled impression of him as a result. Tolkien uses the character Faramir specifically to decry the rising glorification of violence in the world during his lifetime, which he saw as a sign of degradation and decay. In the chapter "The Window on the West" from *The Two Towers*, Faramir explains to Frodo that the people of Gondor, his home, are the last remnant of Númenórean society—a high culture in which knowledge and art and curiosity were more valued than skill in combat. Faramir is troubled that Gondor has abandoned Númenórean ideals: "We now love war and valour as things good in themselves, both a sport and an end; and though we still hold that a warrior should have more skills and knowledge than only the craft of weapons and slaying, we esteem a warrior, nonetheless, above men of other crafts. Such is the need of our days. So even was my brother, Boromir; a man of prowess, and for that he was accounted the best man in Gondor."[20]

The contrast between the brothers is an important one. Boromir is the warrior who thinks in terms of power and advantage. Desperate to save his people and thinking that salvation can only come from warfare, he tries to take the Ring from Frodo. He pays for his betrayal with his life, even though he redeems himself before dying. "Alas for Boromir! It was too sore a trial!" [Faramir said], "Not if I found it on the highway would I take it, I said. Even if I were such a man as to desire this thing, and even though I knew not clearly what this thing was when I spoke, still I should take those words as a vow, and be held by them. But I am not such a man. Or I am wise enough to know that there are some perils from which a man must flee. Sit at peace!"[21]

Later, Faramir's father, Denethor, berates him for *not* doing as Boromir wanted to do, and bringing him the Ring. In the Jackson adaptation, Faramir is indeed tempted by the Ring and does try to take Frodo to his father, making the same mistake Boromir did. In this and other ways, the movies glorify war and violence, while Tolkien's original epic does not. One of Tolkien's central themes is that—even if there is such a thing as a "just war"—war should never be desired or glorified. And so, one of the characters Tolkien uses to illustrate this point is turned into a warrior scarcely distinguishable from Boromir on screen, completely undermining Tolkien's wishes to make Faramir espouse a thoughtful, antimilitarist philosophy. The changes also, as Wilkinson observes, downplay the role of the steward in the narrative.

Wilkinson concludes, "It is a sad fact of history—and of our own time in particular—that the Christian story has been seen as an elevation of the warrior hero. . . . For the Christian story, too, is about the surrendering of power—indeed, about gardening. . . . The unheroic gardener is the hero of Tolkien's story—and of the even greater Christian story that informs it. Perhaps necessarily, the medium of film fails when it tries to tell such a story."[22] Wilkinson contends that *The Lord of the Rings* is written in a style that predicts the character-driven, environmentalist storytelling model of Ursula K. Le Guin's "Carrier Bag Theory of Fiction" (see chapter 6), but the films stripped Tolkien's narrative of its green sensibilities and altered its "carrier bag" story structure so that it could fit into Vogler's prefabricated, plot-driven, cinematic hero's journey mold. The result is a film series that is indistinguishable from all other contemporary escapist tentpole franchises. Wilkinson's observation that the era of the blockbuster film seems particularly ill-equipped to handle a story with truly humane or authentically Christian and environmentalist sensibilities is, indeed, correct.

## Unsuitable for Adaptation: *Lord of the Rings*

It is difficult to overstate the importance of the environment to Tolkien himself and of environmental themes to his entire corpus of fantasy literature, especially his Middle-earth stories. In 1972, Paul H. Kocher was the first critic to identify Tolkien as an ecologist. Other scholars have followed suit, including Patrick Curry, Marta Garcia de la Puerta, Don Elgin, Dinah Hazell, Marcella Juhren, Christina Ljungberg Stücklin, and Verlyn Flieger. Matthew Dickerson and Jonathan Evans—the authors of the definitive, book-length study of Tolkien's ecological views, *Ents, Elves, and Eriador: The Environmental Vision of J. R. R. Tolkien* (2006)—explain that "the concluding sections of 'On Fairy-stories' make "it clear that literary concerns and environmental ideas were not merely cultural matters for Tolkien, but fundamentally theological ones. His views of the environment grew out of the belief that the world originated as the good creation of a good God, that environmental responsibility is nothing more and nothing less than good stewardship, and that failure to exercise such stewardship is a form of evil."[23]

Those already familiar with the novel know that it is a sequel to *The Hobbit*. Its central conflict involves the demonic Sauron and his allies—including the turncoat white wizard Saruman and the vast Orc armies of Mordor—seeking to conquer, industrialize, and pollute all the lands of Middle-earth. Sauron also hopes, in this effort, to find and regain control of the lost "One Ring" he had forged in an earlier age to help grant him power over the world. At the start of the story, the good wizard Gandalf has determined that the ring has fallen into the possession of his elderly friend Bilbo, who has served as its guardian for many years without understanding its true nature. Some of Gandalf's allies are briefly tempted to use the Ring as a weapon against Sauron, but he convinces them that they cannot truly defeat force with force and evil with evil. Instead, Gandalf argues that the young Hobbits Frodo and Sam should travel into Mordor on a quest to melt down the ring in the fiery pit in which it had been forged. As Frodo undergoes his arduous quest, Aragorn, heir to the throne of Gondor, strives to build alliances between the fragmented peoples of Middle-earth who find themselves under siege by rampaging Orcs. Aragorn's expectation is not to achieve a conclusive military victory; he hopes merely to keep the armies of darkness at bay until Frodo and Sam have the time to complete their quest and bring Sauron's power to an end with the annihilation of the One Ring.

Fig. 1.4. Hobbits Frodo and Sam journey into Mordor on a quest to destroy the Ring of Sauron in the fiery pit in which it was forged. Pictured are Elijah Wood (left) as Frodo and Sean Astin (right) as Sam, in the three-part film adaptation directed by Peter Jackson and released in installments between 2001 and 2003. New Line Cinema.

Critic Kristen M. Burkholder has observed that the rural Hobbit homeland, the Shire, symbolizes everything that the forces of good in *The Lord of the Rings* are fighting to preserve. The Shire also stands for everything in the natural order that the forces of good in the real world are failing to protect from being "sullied by factories, pollution, and modernization." Exploring the preindustrial scope of the Shire, she notes that

[t]here is a mill on the north bank of the Water, the river near Hobbiton, but it is operated by a waterwheel, a type of mill dating back to European antiquity. Under Bilbo's cousin Lotho Sackville-Baggin's direction, this old mill is destroyed. Its replacement is industrial in nature and produces pollutants and filth, fouling the water. Tolkien abhorred the destruction of the landscape in real life, although he lived nearly his entire life in town suburbs. Tolkien couldn't do anything about industrialization in England, but he could create a bucolic, peaceful countryside for Middle-earth in his writing. After the Battle of Bywater and the eviction of Saruman's adherents from the Shire, the new mill is torn down.[24]

"The Scouring of the Shire" epilogue of *Lord of the Rings* is Tolkien's wish-fulfillment reversal of industrialization, in which evil machines are destroyed and polluted lands reclaimed following the defeat of Sauron. The segment was intended to serve as an object lesson for what readers should be doing to challenge the foul, Mordor-like technology of the real world. The conflict also gave the Hobbits a real stake in the war they had been fighting. Had they come home to an unchanged and unsullied Shire, they would have been caught up in events that affected other realms but not their own. They would have saved others but not themselves and their own people in any tangible way. Since evil had come to the Shire, the Hobbits were fighting to save their own homes and people, too—and have been the whole time, though they may not have realized it until then. The Hobbits were also, in Gandalf's words, trained for it; their other adventures had prepared them to confront evil in their own land and defeat it.

Furthermore, the "Scouring" segment, like the saga taken in toto, represents the triumph of nature over technology, good over evil, and life over death. It depicts the epic struggle it takes to win this battle, and the high price heroes pay to fight on the side of right. When one considers what *The Lord of the Rings* is about—environmentalism—the central thematic and heroic importance of the Hobbits becomes clear. As charismatic and romantic a figure as Aragorn is, it is, indeed, the humble Hobbits who are supposed to command the most admiration from readers. Aragorn himself kneels before the Hobbits, and commands all the armies of Gondor to "praise them with great praise!" Hugh T. Keenan's description of the Hobbits, from 1968's "The Appeal of *The Lord of the Rings*: The Struggle for Life," remains apt:

> Like rabbits or country folk, the Hobbits emphasize family and fertility as manifested by their love for genealogical facts and by their well-populated, clan-sized burrows. Their love of domestic comforts is in line with their dual nature. Like children they enjoy birthday parties as frequent as those in *Alice in Wonderland*, the receiving of presents, and the eating of snacks plus full meals, while they do little work and mostly play. Yet furry and fat like rabbits (or country squires) though they may be, they prove to be the human-like creatures most interested in preserving life. The Hobbits combine the strongest traditional symbols of life: the rabbit for fertility and the child for generation. They represent the earthly as opposed to the mechanic or scientific forces. Therefore, they are eminently suitable heroes in the struggle of life against death.[25]

As a biographical aside, it is important to note that Tolkien also modeled his chief Hobbit protagonists on himself. He observed in a 1958 letter to an admirer of his work, Deborah Webster, "I am in fact a hobbit in all but size. I like gardens, trees, and unmechanized farmlands; I smoke a pipe and like good plain food (unrefrigerated), but detest French cooking. I like, and even dare to wear in these dull days, ornamental waistcoats. I am fond of mushrooms (out of a field); have a very simple sense of humour (which even my appreciative critics find tiresome); I go to bed late and get up late (when possible). I do not travel much." Tolkien makes a convincing argument here that he and his hobbits are indistinguishable.

Keenan also underscores the recurring significance of trees throughout Tolkien's saga, from the Elves that revere them, speak their language, and live in them, to the people of Gondor, whose sense of vitality is linked to the health of the White Tree in the courtyard of Minas Tirith.[26] But one of the most important characters for Keenan is Sam, the Hobbit most dedicated to the preservation of nature within the Shire, and who steadfastly aids Frodo in his quest to destroy the One Ring. When the Ring tempts Sam, it attacks him through his greatest virtue—his love of nature:

> [Primarily, the Ring] grants one the power to rule and to achieve his chief desire. For instance, when Sam puts on the Ring, he has a vision of controlling the world and making it one large garden. As gardening is the idée fixe of Sam, for him the promise the Ring gives is the world cultivated as a magnificent garden . . .[27]

The "Fascist gardener" temptation is a fascinating moment in the book, reminding environmentalists how easily their good intentions can become corrupted if they grow too angry and despairing in their efforts to take on the global problem of pollution. Conquest is not the answer, even if it is conquest in the service of the green planet. Sam does emerge as an ecological hero by the end of the book, but he goes about becoming a champion of life in the correct way—without the help of the evil ring. He ends his life as he always lived it, as a champion of life instead of as a misguided eco-tyrant. As Keenan observes, "This life strength of Sam's comes from his gardening, his relation to the soil. He is the good country person par excellence. . . . One may notice that the last volume closes with Sam happily married, a fulfilled adult, the father of his first child. It is he to whom Galadriel entrusts the magic dust which makes the seedlings sprout into saplings in one season, thus replacing the Shire trees destroyed by the Enemy's minions."[28] Sam is the true hero of *Lord of the Rings* and the character Tolkien most wants his readers to emulate.

## The Problem of the Uniformly Evil Orc Race

Tolkien did not want to write a transparent ecological allegory. Nevertheless, *Lord of the Rings* has a strong environmentalist message and may be experienced as Tolkien's requiem for the loss of life caused by two world wars. Despite some moments when Legolas and Gimli engage in witty banter during battle and overcome their culture differences fighting against a common enemy, *The Lord of the Rings* is not a celebration of the glory of combat. And yet, several cultural commentators have made strong, difficult-to-refute arguments that *The Lord of the Rings* is a white supremacist, pro-war epic. Since the story is about a hive-minded, irredeemably evil army of Orcs swarming over Middle-earth, laying waste to everything in its path, both Tolkien's books and their film adaptations are open to the charge that they endorse genocidal warfare. Critics who make this observation feel that the good versus evil sensibilities of the narrative encourage readers to embrace the idea that all Orcs must be wiped from the face of the Earth for peace to be restored to the lands. The heroes of the saga could endorse ruthless, genocidal thinking since the Orcs are *not human, after all*. . . . This attitude suggests racist thinking, a Manichean worldview, and an imperialist mindset that celebrates the virtues of endless warfare and apocalyptic-level conflicts.

C. S. Lewis, for one, challenged this interpretation of the story. In 1955, Lewis observed in "The Dethronement of Power" that Tolkien's ethics could be boiled down to this: the distinction between good and evil should always be apparent to anyone with a heart and a brain. Therefore, all good people are called upon to defend the Good, especially in times when evil forces are ascendant. "This is the basis of the whole Tolkienian world," Lewis writes. "I think some readers, seeing (and disliking) this rigid demarcation of black and white, imagine they have seen a rigid demarcation between black and white people. Looking at the [chess] squares, they assume (in defiance of the facts) that all the pieces must be making bishops' moves which confine them to one color. . . . Motives, even on the right side, are mixed. Those who are now traitors usually began with comparatively innocent intentions. Heroic Rohan and imperial Gondor are partly diseased. Even the wretched Smeagol, til quite late in the story, has good impulses and, by a tragic paradox, what finally pushes him over the brink is an unpremeditated speech by the most selfless character of all."[29]

Years later, Dickerson and Evans also challenged the notion that the evils perpetrated by the Orcs should be interpreted as a justification of any attempt to wipe out an entire people in the real world. They argue, "It should be noted that the race of Orcs (also called Goblins)—which in Tolkien's mythology are spawned from Elves who are twisted and corrupted by Morgoth—also represents some aspects of the human race, such as the potential for devious creativity and petty jealousy. However, they represent fallen and corrupted humans and illustrate little if anything of what humans in our world are *supposed* to be like."[30]

With the release of the Jackson films, many critics were horrified by the representations of Orcs as having dreadlocks and an aboriginal or African appearance, making many who had not read the books, or not read them in some time, wonder if the racism of the films was Jackson's or Tolkien's. In 2004, Anderson Rearick III published "Why is the Only Good Orc a Dead Orc? The Dark Face of Racism Examined in Tolkien." For Rearick, Humphrey Carpenter's biography of Tolkien paints a picture of a good-hearted man free of the racism he is accused of exhibiting in his writing. He also references passages of Tolkien's correspondences, in which Tolkien deconstructs the Nazi view of Aryanism as absurd and historically unsound, since the Aryans were an "Indo-Iranian group that spoke Hindustani, Persian, gypsy, or any related dialect."[31] Furthermore, Tolkien told his publisher not to certify the German editions of his Middle-earth works as being published by a non-Jew because he did not want to make any gesture that could be perceived as endorsing Nazi race hatred. He writes, "If you are enquiring whether I am of Jewish origin, I can only reply that regret that

I appear to have no ancestors of that gifted people."[32] Tolkien also wrote emotionally of Hitler's toxic influence upon the public perception of Norse mythology—and of all things of the North: "I have in this War a burning private grudge against that ruddy little ignoramus Adolf Hitler for ruining, perverting, misapplying, and making forever accursed, that noble northern spirit, a supreme contribution to Europe, which I have ever loved, and tried to present in its true light."[33]

After offering close readings of these pieces of biographical evidence, Rearick turns his attention to *Lord of the Rings*. He concludes that racism is always in the support of the acquisition of power, imperial ends, and the constant undervaluing of entire groups. Since *Lord of the Rings* is about fighting the imperial ends of Mordor, surrendering the power of the ring, and celebrating the undervalued Hobbits, who face prejudice for their diminutive height and lack of power throughout the series, Rearick sees only one conclusion: "Racism claims that one can tell the value of an individual just by looking at his or her outward appearances. But nothing could be more overtly counter to the Christian worldview that Tolkien functions in even as he creates his fantasy. 'Man [Elf, Dwarf and Ent] looketh on the outward appearance, but the LORD looketh on the heart' (1 Sam. 16:7). Nothing could be more contrary to the assumptions of racism than a Hobbit as a hero."[34]

To a large degree, how one morally assesses and emotionally responds to *The Lord of the Rings* story (either in book or film form) is determined by how one "reads" the figures of the Orcs—as locating "evil" within a real-world people and (possibly) advocating their extermination, or as locating evil within a destructive ideology, psychological tendency, social trend, or technological movement. The critic who has offered the most incisive critique of what the Orcs represent on film is Kristen Whissel, who dissected the Jackson films in her 2014 book *Spectacular Digital Effects: CGI and Contemporary Cinema*. In one extended passage, Whissel argues that "spectacular images of multitudes function as emblems of apocalypse,"[35] which is to say that the vast armies of monsters besieging outnumbered and terrified humans in films such as *Arachnophobia* (1990), *Independence Day* (1996), *Starship Troopers* (1997), *The Matrix* (1999), and *Attack of the Clones* (2002) are a common occurrence in contemporary special effects cinema and indicative of the end-of-times mood of society in the late twentieth and early twenty-first century. Whissel observes that the filmmakers design these apocalyptic images to be multivalent to evoke the cultural anxieties of a broad swath of viewers from a variety of political and ideological backgrounds without pinning an overt political meaning to this multitude. Since these images are multivalent, they do not divide the audience reaction along political lines. The result is a film that might mean all things to all viewers, which maximizes viewer anxiety and corporate profits while making little coherent or controversial sociopolitical commentary.

Turning her attention to the apocalyptic cinematic images of multitudes found in the Jackson films, Whissel examines how the director represents the Orc and Uruk-hai army on screen: "[I]n *The Two Towers*, long shots show an Uruk-hai army stream across an open landscape in Middle-earth like a massive black river that engulfs everything in its path, making it an emblem for an unstoppable force of sweeping historical change able to overcome an entire civilization."³⁶

In a shot-by-shot analysis, Whissel demonstrates how one of the most charged moments of the film, Saruman's unveiling of his Uruk-hai army to Grima Wormtongue at Isengard, creates the illusion that there are enough Uruk-hai to fill the entire horizon-line of Middle-earth, giving them the literal capacity to block out the sun and bring about the final dusk of humanity.

Defenders of the Jackson films may argue convincingly that moments such as this are so well executed that they justify the film as art. Whissel also discusses scenes in which the director is adept at using visuals to bring key themes from the book to life on screen:

> In the *Lord of the Rings* trilogy, much is made of the fact that the alliances that once existed between the various kingdoms of Middle-earth no longer stand. A key scene in *Fellowship of the Ring* foregrounds the idea that Sauron's consolidation of power depends upon the fragmentation of Middle-earth: after the representatives of each kingdom gather in Rivendell, they argue stridently over what is to be done with the Ring. A close-up of the Ring shows their images reflected on its surface as Sauron is heard on the soundtrack voicing pleasure at the bitter acrimony his Ring sows among his enemies. All of this emphasizes that the protagonist's world is vulnerable to the multitude precisely because it is divided by internal power struggles, selfish motivations, and the too-sharp individuation of those who populate

Fig. 1.5. The Orcs gather, preparing for combat in *The Hobbit: The Battle of Five Armies* (2014), directed by Peter Jackson. Critic Kristen Whissel argues in *Spectacular Digital Effects: CGI and Contemporary Cinema* (2014) that "spectacular images of multitudes [of monsters] function as emblems of apocalypse." Warner Bros.

it. Indeed, at the level of appearance, the representative members of the Fellowship—Hobbits, Elves, Dwarves, Wizards, and Men—perfectly embody the variety and differentiation that initially seem to doom Middle-earth. To resist the multitude, the protagonists must aspire to a degree of the unity, singularity of purpose, *and* selflessness that enables the multitude to pursue its destructive force with the fearsome singularity of purpose and, in the process, to serve as an emblem of apocalypse.[37]

If the Orcs are symbols of the apocalypse, what manner of apocalypse would the 2001 film be depicting? Tolkien wrote the source book between 1937 and 1949, and published it between 1954 and 1955, which is why some readers looking for real-world parallels between the forces of Sauron and Saruman in the book looked no farther than Hitler and the Nazi menace, despite Tolkien and Lewis both asserting that the book was more about World War I than World War II. The interpretation of Tolkien's epic tale that is the most evocative for this moment in our history is an ecological reading that interprets the destruction wrought by Sauron, the Orcs, and their allies as the ravages of industrial society, and as the threat that global, free-market capitalism poses to the

Fig, 1.6. In Peter Jackson's *Hobbit* film trilogy, Ian McKellen (left) plays Gandalf the Grey and Sylvester McCoy (right) plays Radagast the Brown, an analogue to Saint Francis of Assisi. The wizards are angelic Maiar charged with defeating the Sauron's plans to destroy the world. Both wizards are stewards of Nature, though Radagast prefers the company of animals to people—especially birds. Warner Bros.

environment. Of course, once a reader accepts the notion that the book is an ecological narrative and that the Orcs are the forces of pollution personified, the question remains: What does the book teach us about ecological devastation and ecological preservation?

When readers look to green readings of Tolkien, they soon discover that some environmental humanities scholars are more enthusiastic about the value of Tolkien's brand of environmentalism than others. Timothy Morton, an ecological theorist, argues in *Ecology Without Nature: Rethinking Environmental Aesthetics* (2007) that Tolkien's conservationist thinking is too bent on creating a world-bubble, a wish-fulfillment "safe place" or "snow globe" for green spaces. Morton views this thinking as of little use to ecologists in the real world.[38]

John Elder offers a contrasting view, in his foreword to *Ents, Elves, and Eriador: The Environmental Vision of J. R. R. Tolkien* (2006). He posits that

> [i]ndeed, if the landscape around Hobbiton were to be valued primarily for its thatched roofs and home-brewed beer, it might well be dismissed as no more than an appealing anachronism. But it is in fact presented as one distinctive region within a carefully graduated range of locales in Middle-earth. The rolling downs of Rohan, the deep woods of the Ents and Huorns, and the damaged but resilient gardens of Gondor offer the broader context in which to appreciate the specific importance of the Shire.

Elder also grapples with the argument that the anachronistic political structure of Middle-earth prevents the saga from modeling political action in our own times. "Just as the Shire could be dismissed as provincial or sentimental . . . so too the idea of stewardship might be considered irrelevant because of its association with lordly structures of authority that are distant from our present democratic institutions. And in a figure like Denethor, the domineering steward of Gondor, all those aristocratic and authoritarian connotations are strongly sounded. But such an example is more than counterbalanced by the stewardship of the good gardener Sam Gamgee." Elder observes that Sam, like Frodo and Gandalf, models stewardship as a "faithful and discerning action on behalf of a beloved landscape and community." Consequently, *Lord of the Rings* has the potential to model a form of ecological heroism that can be useful in the real world, at this moment of grave ecological crisis. Elder writes that "the environmental movement is now looking beyond the dichotomy of wilderness preservation and the more utilitarian definitions of conservation that have prevailed in environmental thinking throughout much of the twentieth century. In fact, maps of ecological and social health must encompass both these values, just as Tolkien's hand-drawn maps do. And stewardship, the knowledgeable and practical service of living communities, is called on to affirm and protect the full diversity of landscapes through which the members of the fellowship pass."[39]

As Gandalf says to Denethor in Minas Tirith, " '[T]he rule of no realm is mine, neither of Gondor nor any other, great or small. But all worthy things that are in peril as the world stands, those are my care. And for my part, I shall not wholly fail of my task, though Gondor should perish, if anything passes through this night that can still grow fair or bear fruit and flower again in days to come. For I too am a steward. Did you not know?' And with that he turned and strode from the hall with Pippin running at his side."[40]

Both Elder and Morton make valid points about different ways we might interpret Tolkien's environmental allegory. As a further example, Dickerson and Evans provide some practical advice for confronting climate change that can be gleaned from a book as fantastical as *Lord of the Rings*. They acknowledge that most middle- and working-class readers living in a democracy do not have the political clout of an Aragorn and are not angels such as Gandalf, but they may glean some knowledge from Treebeard, who is an authority figure that goes to great lengths to build political consensus among the Ents and urges even the stubborn ones to environmental action. Readers may also look to the humble hobbits for inspiration. The scholars write, "It is in the hobbits and in the Shire where readers see models of leadership that are more applicable to our own situation. Just as in Fangorn, the rousing of the Shire requires leaders with a plan. Once the recovery of the Shire is well under way, Farmer Cotton says, 'I said we could master them. But we needed a call. You came back in the nick o' time, Mr. Merry.' Like Treebeard, when Merry and Pippin lead, other hobbits follow and are able to bring about change."[41]

Perhaps the most valuable ecological lesson one might glean from *Lord of the Rings* comes from the One Ring. As the product of evil industrial manufacturing and an object that should never have been made in the first place, the Ring symbolizes the false promise and the destructive potential of unrestrained industrialism. The Ring is the product of and symbol of the military industrial complex and corporate capitalism run amok on a global scale. One might be tempted to try to use the forces of industrialization and unregulated capitalism for the greater good. Tolkien seemed to be more skeptical of any effort to use force to fight force, industrialization to fight industrialization, fighting wars to end wars, and using magic wand solutions to solve problems that were created by magic wands in the first place. Certainly, Gandalf believed that one cannot use evil forces to promote good causes. He would argue that those of us in the real world must turn away from the false promise of industrialization in its current form—which is about subduing the Earth instead of respecting it, nurturing it, and acting as its steward— and embrace greener technologies, more ecologically sound means of feeding ourselves, and fight tooth and nail to heal and sustain our environment on behalf of all human, plant, and animal life. We need to abandon the dead-end road of profits-above-all-else, power-for-its-own-sake, and technology-over-nature. We need to cast the One Ring of false promises back into the industrial fires that forged it. It is a grim task in and of itself. The mission that will follow, the scouring of the shire on a global scale, places an enormous burden of responsibility upon our shoulders and upon the shoulders of our descendants. The alternative is still more horrifying to contemplate—a world turned to ashes by the armies of the Saurons and Sarumans of the real world.

The original text of Tolkien's *Lord of the Rings* makes the full weight of this message clear. The film adaptations, sadly, do not. Consequently, it is to Tolkien's novels we must turn to for wisdom in this hour of crisis, and not to their bastardized film incarnations.

We are all called to act like real-world analogues of Frodo in the great ecological endeavor of our time. It is his grim resolve to do what needs to be done that we need to emulate. Frodo would prefer living a quieter life to shouldering this overwhelming burden. Many of us feel much the same way about having to face the climate crisis that he felt about becoming the Ring-bearer. It is in the heroism of Frodo that we, as readers, may see yet another of Tolkien's models for how to move forward to create a more sustainable world. At the beginning of *The Fellowship of the Ring*, Gandalf tells Frodo of the grave times they are living in and explains the necessity of the Hobbits coming out of their protected, provincial bubble to face up to the challenges that lie ahead, for the sake of all the peoples of the world. Devastated, Frodo doesn't want any part of this conflict, but he understands what he needs to do.

"I wish it need not have happened in my lifetime," says Frodo.

"So do I," said Gandalf, "and so do all who live to see such times. But that is not for them to decide. All we have to decide is what to do with the time that is given us."[42]

# 2

# Of Treebeard, C. S. Lewis, and the Aesthetics of Christian Environmentalism

[C. S.] Lewis and [J. R. R.] Tolkien mourned the loss of the Britain of their youth and generations past, a rural Britain of ancient social hierarchies, unspoiled by automobiles and factories. Theirs was a conservatism that led them to rail against a grab-bag of phenomena ranging from coed schools to real-estate development. Though neither was politically active (and Lewis boasted of never reading newspapers), some of their strongest political feelings align with what we would now call environmentalism.

—Laura Miller, *The Magician's Book*

How will the legend of the age of trees
Feel, when the last tree falls in England?
When the concrete spreads and the town conquers
The country's heart; when contraceptive
Tarmac's laid where farm has faded,
Tramline flows where slept a hamlet
And shop-fronts, blazing without stop from
Dover to Wrath, have glazed us over?

—C. S. Lewis, "The Future of Forestry"

## The Devastation of Nature in *Lord of the Rings*

Aragorn, the warrior-king hero of *The Lord of the Rings*, leads his comrades-in-arms to Isengard seeking to destroy the military-industrial stronghold of the evil wizard Saruman. He arrives to find the battle over and the enemy base destroyed. He and his men are greeted by two long-lost friends of theirs, the Hobbits Meriadoc ("Merry") Brandybuck and Peregrin ("Pippin") Took, who are drunk on wine and good food and celebrating amid the flooded ruins of the enemy stronghold. They explain to a bewildered Aragorn that, not long ago, they had encountered a sentient, fourteen-foot, ambulatory tree creature named Treebeard in Fangorn forest. The eldest of the Ents, Treebeard, had been distressed to learn from Merry and Pippin that Saruman was involved in a massive project of deforestation and pollution that had already killed countless numbers of his tree brethren and threatened to murder untold more trees throughout the whole of Middle-earth.

When they discovered just how many trees had died, the revelation shocked Treebeard, the Ents, and the far wilder tree creatures, the Huorns. They were all doubly distressed because the killings of so many trees occurred while the Ents were neglecting their duties as guardians of the forest. Consequently, the normally inactive and peaceful Ents responded by springing into action to avenge their fallen tree friends. They waged war on Isengard, broke a dam, and destroyed Saruman's foundry by flooding it. Commenting upon this powerful segment, critic Anne C. Petty explains that Tolkien "never marched in mass demonstrations against the location of oil pipelines, didn't carry signs protesting pollution of rivers, never served as whistle-blower when houses were built over chemical dumpsites, never drove spikes into trees to prevent them from being logged. But the dismantling of Isengard by Ents and Huorns is one of the most satisfying acts of [environmentalist] retribution committed to paper."[1] Petty posits that Tolkien's "role as crusader for nature in the face of mechanized progress seems to have been triggered when his mother [Mabel] moved the family from rural Sarehole to industrial Birmingham, and escalated after his return from the war—an attitude you can see developing if you read his collected letters sequentially."[2]

It is also important to note here that, while Tolkien himself never protested the placement of a pipeline, contemporary environmentalists and indigenous rights activists have often referenced Tolkien and *Lord of the Rings* in their efforts to challenge fossil fuel industry initiatives that threaten to pollute water supplies and artificially generate earthquakes. For example, in early November 2016, Native American filmmaker Sterlin Harjo traveled to the site of the anti–Dakota Access Pipeline protests to chronicle them in a documentary. He found himself seated next to the wife of a fossil fuel industry champion on an arduously long flight, and couldn't believe his terrible luck. He described the scene vividly in "Debate on a Plane" in the Nov. 8, 2016, edition of *The Tulsa Voice*: "She glanced at me. A glance that, I know now, was one of dark pleasure. I had fallen into her trap. Like Frodo and the giant spider in *The Lord of the Rings*, I was about to be wrapped in her unrelenting web. . . . How did this happen? Of all the folks that I could've sat by on a flight to Standing Rock I'm next to Republican Congressman Kevin Cramer's wife. Kevin Cramer the climate change denier, Kevin Cramer who wants Planned Parenthood abolished, Kevin Cramer who wants less regulations on drilling, Kevin Cramer who helped draft Donald Trump's energy bill. That Kevin Cramer." They soon fell into a quietly heated debate about the Standing Rock Protests. Mrs. Cramer quoted Dominionist Christian theology to justify the fossil fuel industry's God-given right to extract oil from the ground—and to remove Native peoples from their sacred grounds in the process. Harjo politely but firmly disagreed and made no dent in the moral certainty she exhibited. By the end of the article, it was clear why Harjo had felt as if he was Frodo falling into the clutches of Shelob. It was a frightening conversation, indeed. Shortly before this article was published, the "Honest Government Advert—Dakota Access Pipeline," released by thejuicemedia on Oct 21, 2016, mocked the financiers of the pipeline as being like Saruman and predicted that the lands and bodies of water that the pipeline would be built across would look like Mordor before long. In both these narratives, the environmentalists and Native Americans symbolically link themselves to Tolkien's heroes, the Hobbits, Treebeard, and the Ents, and compare their real-world enemies to Tolkien's villains.

As these examples indicate, Tolkien's ecological message endures in our contemporary political landscape. And yet, one may ask, what was it that first drew Tolkien's sympathy so strongly to nature, when so many others were—and are—indifferent to it? Perry correctly credits Mabel. Tolkien's favorite period of his life was when he lived with Mabel and his brother Hilary in Sarehole. He soon came to symbolically associate Mabel with the English countryside—a nostalgic and emotional connection that eventually haunted him, especially since her decline and death coincided with his removal to more urban locales. Thanks to this unhappy mental and emotional correlation, Tolkien relived feelings of his mother's death every time he contemplated a felled tree. As Tolkien biographer Humphrey Carpenter makes clear, Mabel was, in some respects, a Dryad in his mind.[3] Furthermore, one of the reasons that Tolkien came to develop a romanticized view of his own wife is because he began to associate Edith with trees during the early years of their marriage, and imagine her as being an elf in a mythic forest.

Carpenter described the child Tolkien as an imaginative figure who often pretended to be a Native American and regularly pestered Mabel to find him a bow and arrow to play with. He enjoyed reading the Fairy Books of Andrew Lang, which—like the American Indian fixation—mixed his romantic imagination with an appreciation of Nature. Tolkien "was good at drawing, too, particularly when the subject was a landscape or a tree. His mother taught him a great deal of botany, and he responded to this and soon became very knowledgeable. But again, he was more interested in the shape and feel of a plant than its botanical details. This was especially true of trees. And though he liked drawing trees he liked most of all to be *with* trees. He would climb them, lean against them, even talk to them. It saddened him to discover that not everyone shared his feelings toward them. One incident in particular remained in his memory: 'There was a willow hanging over the mill-pool and I learned to climb it. It belonged to a butcher on the Stratford Road, I think. One day they cut it down. They didn't do anything with it: the log just lay there. I never forgot that.' "[4]

Tolkien's love of trees inspired his creation of the Ents and Treebeard—his version of Dryads—and the Ents, in turn, inspired similar defenders of tree-kind, including the title character of *The Lorax* (1971) and the murderous trees of *The Happening* (2008). There were, reportedly, many sources of inspiration for Treebeard. One grew out of Tolkien's desire to make the battle in which "Fanghorn Forest has come to Isengard" far more surprising and dramatic than the moment in *Macbeth* when "Birnham Wood is come to castle Dunsinane." Another possible source of inspiration was a large black pine in the Oxford Botanic Garden that was a favorite of Tolkien's. In a cruelly ironic twist of fate that angered many members of the Tolkien Society, that same tree was deemed unsafe when two large limbs fell from it in the summer of 2014. The Oxford City Council and Oxford University ordered it cut down on July 26, 2014, despite protestations that it could be preserved and cordoned off.[5]

The fictional origins of Treebeard could be found in Tolkien's creation narrative for Middle-earth. In *The Silmarillion*, posthumously published in 1977, Tolkien revealed that Eru Ilúvatar (his representation of God) created the Ents to serve as Shepherds of the Forest to protect them from being felled en masse as raw materials for the industrial projects of Dwarves and Men. Vala Yavanna, Queen of the Earth, Giver of Fruits, and champion of trees, had predicted the possibility of many future crimes against the environment spearheaded by these groups. She foresaw Dwarves and Men committing countless crimes against all tree life throughout their history thanks to their inborn tendency toward indifference to the beauty of the natural order and their preference for the manufactured over the organic. Over the ages, the numbers of Ents dwindled, they lost their mates, the Entwives, and grew isolated from news of the outside world because of their reluctance to venture forth from Fangorn Forest. It was under these circumstances that Merry and Pippin discovered the Ents during *The Lord of the Rings*.

In "The Dethronement of Power," a positive 1955 review of *The Lord of the Rings*, C. S. Lewis praises Tolkien's epic for its realistic portrayal of a fantasy war that "has the very quality of the war my generation knew"—World War I. Lewis also finds inspiring its moral vision urging fortitude and goodheartedness even in the face of an apocalyptic-level conflict. Citing Tolkien's vivid, compelling characters, Lewis singles out Treebeard for approbation, noting that the Tree herder is merely one of a vast ensemble cast featured in *Lord of the Rings* but is compelling enough that he "would have served any other author (if any other could have conceived him) for a whole book." In his discussion of Treebeard, Lewis posits a possible connection between Treebeard and Tolkien, though he does not want to push the notion that "Treebeard can be regarded as a 'portrait of the artist'" too far.[6] Treebeard makes a feasible stand-in for Tolkien, especially since both Tolkien and his creation are gentle, retiring souls capable of being raised to great anger at the sight of thoughtless ecological devastation.

Despite Lewis's suspicion that Treebeard was primarily a stand-in for Tolkien, Carpenter reveals that, in fact, *Lewis* was a partial model for Treebeard. Carpenter wrote that Treebeard is "the ultimate expression of Tolkien's love and respect for trees. When eventually he came to write [the scenes with Treebeard] (so he told Nevill Coghill), he modeled Treebeard's way of speaking, 'Hrum, Hroom,' on the booming voice of C. S. Lewis."[7] It is an odd and teasingly affectionate tribute. One might argue that the character Lewis based partly upon Tolkien, the heroic philologist Dr. Elwin Ransom of *The Space Trilogy* (also known as *The Ransom Trilogy*) was a more flattering homage. (Notably, David C. Downing has contended that Ransom was modeled primarily on

Lewis himself, and morphed into Charles Williams as the trilogy progressed, but Tolkien "saw in Ransom some of his own ideas 'Lewisified.' ")[8]

Tolkien and Lewis thought of one another when contemplating Treebeard because both were environmentalists and each had much in common with the other. Indeed, it is uncanny how much the two men had in common. For most of their lives, both men were religious Christian university professors with an affinity for Norse mythology who created their own fantasy worlds and wrote speculative fiction based within those worlds that promoted environmental ethics. Tragically, their differences in temperament, career arcs, and views on aesthetics and theology were significant enough to make them forget their commonalities and grow apart as they aged.

## The Devastation of Nature in *The Last Battle*

*The Last Battle* (1956) chronicles the invasion of Lewis's fantasy world of Narnia by hostile forces that have hidden behind a false God and a phony piety to bring deforestation and slavery to the land. The true God of Narnia is the magical lion Aslan, who uses cryptic language to reveal to the young heroine Lucy Pevensie that he is, in fact, the same being as the Judeo-Christian God, only made manifest in Narnia. The implication is that, as a fictional character, Aslan is not an allegorical representation of Christ but is, per the literary conceit of the Narnia series, *Christ himself.* This revelation is particularly significant when one considers the central conflict of *The Last Battle*; it means that the villains of *The Last Battle* are false Christians fighting under the banner of an antichrist advocating slavery, industrialization, deforestation, and pollution. The villains are Lewis's warning to the British people: we didn't win the war against fascism abroad only to lose the war with fascism within Britain itself in the aftermath of the war. This thesis is the British equivalent of the sentiment issued by James Waterman Wise Jr., who wrote in *The Christian Century* in 1936 that if fascism reaches American shores, it will probably be "wrapped up in the American flag and heralded as a plea for liberty and preservation of the Constitution."[9] In the following scene from *The Last Battle*, King Tirian and his most trusted advisors learn of the swath of destruction the invaders are cutting through Narnia, and a Dryad races to meet him in the forest, pleading for him to protect the trees and animals from further attacks:

> "Woe, woe, woe!" called the voice. "Woe for my brothers and sisters! Woe for the holy trees! The woods are laid waste. The axe is loosed against us. We are being felled. Great trees are falling, falling, falling. . . . Come to our aid. Protect your people. They are felling us in Lantern Waste. Forty great trunks of my brothers and sisters are already on the ground."
>
> "What, Lady! Felling Lantern Waste? Murdering the talking trees?" cried the King, leaping to his feet and drawing his sword. "How dare they? And who dares it? . . ."

"A-a-a-h," gasped the Dryad shuddering as if in pain—shuddering time after time as if under repeated blows. Then all at once she fell sideways as suddenly as if both her feet had been cut from under her. For a second they saw her lying dead on the grass and then she vanished. They knew what had happened. Her tree, miles away, had been cut down.[10]

This segment in the final, apocalyptic book in the Narnia cycle reads much like *Lord of the Rings* in terms of its thematic content, if not in the style of its writing, characters, and plot structure. Like the villains featured in the concluding volume of Lewis's *Space Trilogy, That Hideous Strength* (1945), these totalitarian, materialist, industrialist despoilers of nature are ideological equivalents of Tolkien's villains, Sauron, Saruman, and the Orc army. As Hugh T. Keenan observed, the two authors were concerned about pollution and industrialization and the self-destructive course of humanity, but each identified a different source of that corruption: "In Tolkien's trilogy as in the science fiction trilogy of C. S. Lewis (especially the final volume *That Hideous Strength*), man is bent on destroying himself through sociological, technological, and psychological means. Man's technology is the enemy of humanity. But whereas [Lewis] . . . traces the source of man's perversity to the influence of the Devil . . . [Tolkien] traces the perversity of his creatures—in the Shire and outside it—to their own twisted natures."[11]

## The Question of Allegory: *The Space Trilogy, The Chronicles of Narnia, The Silmarillion,* and *The Lord of the Rings*

Both Lewis and Tolkien could be said to have been writing environmentalist fiction embedded in classical mythology. Tolkien saw himself as creating (or "sub-creating," to use his term) an entire fictional world, which readers could examine and contemplate in all manner of ways. In contrast, Tolkien regarded Lewis as primarily a Christian apologist who proselytized through lay sermons, religious tracts, and allegorical novels for adults and children. Tolkien's perception of Lewis is widely known in the circles of lay fantasy fandom and has colored many readers' perceptions of Lewis. Lewis himself denied that he wrote allegory, and his own assessment of his work is more apt than Tolkien's. The men are often compared, and often as a means of determining which writer is superior. Such an evaluative project is of limited value. It is far more interesting and important to reflect upon how their works have similar morals, arguing for humans to be better stewards of the earth and that all societies abandon an industrialization that will lead to the extinction of all life on earth. Part of the problem in the discussions of their virtues as writers—and debating the relative sophistication of the religious themes in their stories—is the muddying of the definition of the word *allegory*. In one sense, neither Tolkien nor Lewis used allegory, since the God and Devil figures in Middle-earth and Narnia are literally supposed to be the Christian God and the Christian devil, just as angels in both the Lewis and Tolkien universes are just that:

angels. While Gandalf does not reveal himself to be an angel in the text proper of *Lord of the Rings*, Tolkien revealed in *The Silmarillion* that Gandalf is, indeed, an angel—a Maia—outranked by the higher order of Tolkien's equivalent of Archangels, the Valar. Consequently, Gandalf cannot be called a wizard who acts *allegorically* or *symbolically* as an angel. He *is* an angel. And Tolkien's God, Eru Ilúvatar, is implicitly the creator God of the Judeo-Christian tradition, since Middle-earth *is* our earth, only from a lost period of history. The characters of Maleldil and Aslan in Lewis's works proclaim themselves to be one and the same with Yahweh and Christ at various key moments in the narrative. Again, Lewis's Eldils or Oyarsas are literally angels. The fallen angel (or Vala), who is, essentially, Lucifer, appears in Tolkien's works as Melkor (or Morgoth) and as "the bent Oyarsa" in Lewis's novels. In other words, Lewis and Tolkien identified their fictionalized versions of God, the Devil, and the Messiah with alternative names befitting their appearances at other points in recorded history, on other worlds, and in other dimensions, but they are intended to be God, the Devil, and the Messiah. In this respect, the fictional worlds of both writers are Miltonic. Milton's Satan and Christ are not representatives of Satan and Christ—they *are* Satan and Christ. Consequently, neither Tolkien nor Lewis wrote allegory. It might be venturing too far to say that Tolkien and Lewis wrote environmentalist "allegory." It is certainly fair to say that Tolkien and Lewis both wove Christian environmentalist sensibilities into their climate fiction.

Fig. 2.1. In the third book of *The Chronicles of Narnia, The Voyage of the Dawn Treader* (1952), the lion Aslan cryptically reveals to Lucy Pevensie that he is the Judeo-Christian God made manifest in Narnia. This scene, from the 2010 film adaptation directed by Michael Apted, features (left to right): Aslan (voiced by Liam Neeson), Lucy (Georgie Henley), Edmond (Skandar Keynes), and King Caspian (Ben Barnes). 20th Century Fox.

In the fictional context of the first volume of *The Space Trilogy*, *Out of the Silent Planet* (1938), Dr. Ransom exhorts the book's narrator-amanuensis to relate the true story of Ransom's trip into space—and first contact with alien races on Mars—as if it were a work of fiction. Ransom argues that it is sensible to present fact as if it were fiction in this case since the world is not ready to embrace such strange truths consciously. And yet, Ransom argues that revealing the truth disguised as fiction is better than not revealing the truth at all. The narrator agrees, and the text of *Out of the Silent Planet* is the result. Ransom's goal in publishing the truth in the guise of "speculative fiction" is to begin educating the public about a rise in imperialistic and racist sentiments across human civilization. Ransom has discovered a reprehensible conspiracy of opportunistic capitalists and xenophobic warmongers to extend the legacy of colonialism onto other planets inhabited by intelligent alien indigenous peoples. Ransom wants to expose this conspiracy by telling an entertaining story to a public that is allergic to the idea of moralizing and conspiracy theories.

Ransom has another message to spread along with this first one. He hopes to familiarize humanity with the concept that their world should be considered enemy-occupied territory in the grip of an evil force that mythological tradition identifies as Lucifer (but that he knows is called "the bent Oyarsa"). If humanity is to reclaim Earth, it must strive to reconnect with God, the ultimate force of creation and good in the universe (a force he has come to know as Maleldil). In *Out of the Silent Planet*, the villains are the warmongers and profiteers in league with the bent Oyarsa. The hero, Ransom, symbolizes the compassion, intellectualism, anti-imperialism, and environmental values that the followers of Maleldil embrace. Again, Ransom believes that readers are only likely to accept this weighty message in the trappings of an escapist science fiction tale. He fears that they would not be likely to embrace it as a religious Jeremiad by a seemingly insane preacher.[12]

This mission statement provided by Ransom and the narrator justifying their writings within the fictional context of *The Space Trilogy* reads like Lewis's own justification of presenting Christianity and ecology to the public in the guise of one of his fantasy or science fiction novels. Significantly, Lewis is doing more than merely asking his readers to embrace a Christianity informed by a faith in a Divine Jesus. He is asking his readers to fight fascism. Lewis's reputation as a Christian apologist is widely known and discussed. What is less widely known and discussed is Lewis's employment of political and social satire to challenge racist and imperialist thinking.

In his works, Lewis offers a savage critique of twentieth-century England from the perspective of the Christian social justice tradition that excoriates polluters, secularists, elitists, militarists, scholars of the historic Jesus, communists, fascists, capitalists, journalists, sociologists, and psychologists for destroying the soul of his country. Some of Lewis's targets are worthier of condemnation than others.

(For example, Lewis flays sociologists, casting them as establishment figures when history has not borne out this view of the discipline, as Harvey J. Graff makes clear in his 2015 study, *Undisciplining Knowledge*. Significantly, Lewis's disdain for the field is probably rooted in his unease about the Social Darwinism of early sociologist and biologist Herbert Spencer, whose ideas are arguably part of the intellectual lineage of the Eugenics movement and the racist philosophy of the Nazis.)

However, Lewis's thinking has a solid internal logic. For Lewis, what is the result of the combined pernicious efforts of these various groups to "reform" society and move it forward? More colonialism, more pollution, less God, less freedom, and an England that looks "almost as if we'd lost the war."[13] The last quote, from the heroic Mrs. Dimble in *That Hideous Strength*, describes how jackbooted thugs working for the bent Oyarsa come to take over a small town in England in a speculative postwar future written while World War II was still raging. It is one of many pieces of cultural commentary in the book that earmarks it as at least as prescient as President Dwight D. Eisenhower's final speech on Jan. 17, 1961, warning of the dangers of the growing power of the military industrial complex over American and world affairs.

Lewis's totalitarian villains are an odd assortment of far-right and far-left establishment figures, and count among them evil British nationals, grotesquely Orientalist foreign evil, the over- and undersexed, the overly intellectual and the appallingly simpleminded. Whatever flag they wave, racial background they come from, or ideological label they place upon themselves, these villains are all, at their core, totalitarians and Satanists. Some of these villains are self-aware enough to know they are totalitarians and Satanists. Others delude themselves into thinking they are merely worker bees or patriots. As David C. Downing observed in *Planets in Peril: A Critical Study of C. S. Lewis' Ransom Trilogy* (1992), one of N.I.C.E.'s leaders, Lord Feverstone, presents the goals of the organization as "to continue interplanetary expansion; to rid the planet of species that compete with humans for resources; and to purify the human species itself, through 'sterilization of the unfit [and] liquidation of backward races.' (The parallels between the animating ideas of N.I.C.E. and those of Nazism would certainly not be lost on the novel's original readers in 1945.) Even more radical than Feverstone are those at N.I.C.E., like Filostrato, who want to dispense with organic life altogether, retaining only Mind."[14]

The Nazi/Satanist villains of *That Hideous Strength* are working to increase their hold upon the world. In many respects, they have already won at the time the novel begins. When Lewis discusses planet Earth as "enemy-occupied territory" in both *Mere Christianity* and *The Space Trilogy*, he is describing a Christian universe that seems bleak enough to be borderline heretical, but one that is not incompatible with the theology of Dante, who depicted the sectarian, blood-soaked Italy of 1300 as a form of hell on Earth. Most importantly, the bleak view of the material world Lewis presents is certainly understandable in the historical context of the Blitz and two consecutive world wars that Lewis lived through as he conceived of the theology of *Mere Christianity*. *Mere Christianity* is a text that began life as a series of patriotic, antifascist radio lectures broadcast by Lewis meant to rally the faith and determination of the British people against the Nazi menace. The polished and edited radio talks first appeared in print as *Broadcast Talks* (1942), *Christian Behaviour* (1943), and *Beyond Personality* (1944). Lewis later revisited these published versions of the radio talks, combined and rewrote them, and they became *Mere Christianity*. American poet, essayist, and spiritualist Kathleen Norris argues that it is of central importance that contemporary readers understand the circumstances of the writing of *Mere Christianity* and not read it ahistorically as a timeless theological document. As she observes in her foreword to the 2000 edition:

> [*Mere Christianity*] begs to be seen in its historical context, as a bold act of storytelling and healing in a world gone mad. In 1942, just twenty-four years after the end of a brutal war that had destroyed an entire generation of its young men, Great Britain was at war again. Now it was ordinary citizens who suffered, as their small island nation was bombarded by four hundred planes at night, in the infamous "Blitz" that changed the face of war, turning civilians and their cities into the front lines. . . . We can only wonder about the metaphors that connected so deeply with this book's original audience; images of our world as enemy-occupied territory, invaded by powerful evils bent on destroying all that is good, still seem very relevant today. . . . Like Soren Kierkegaard before him and his contemporary Dietrich Bonhoeffer, Lewis seeks in *Mere Christianity* to help us see the religion with fresh eyes, as a radical faith whose adherents might be likened to an underground group gathering in a war zone, a place where evil seems to have the upper hand, to hear messages of hope from the other side.[15]

Lewis's antifascist form of Christianity took hold especially strongly during World War II, but he opposed far right-wing and fascist ideologies throughout his life, and was wary of fascism's potential manifestations in the postwar world. Indeed, *The Space Trilogy* was his prediction that fascism would somehow survive the fall of Germany and Italy and take root in Great Britain.

Part of Lewis's most prescient and frightening social satire in *That Hideous Strength* is his representation of the fascistic, futuristic British oligarchy and its use of N.I.C.E. (National Institute for Co-ordinated Experiments) to exert power over the British people. Lewis's villains present themselves as "nice" in their intentions, but they begin their efforts by taking control of Bracton College and the forest of Bragdon Wood and the town of Edgestow surrounding it. The new rulers install their own secret police, drive the townies out of their homes, and privatize the local prison, transforming it into a "mental hospital" from which there is no hope of release (think Randle Patrick McMurphy's open-ended sentence in *One Flew Over the Cuckoo's Nest*). They also begin rapidly despoiling all the nature in the region, gleefully engaging themselves in "the conversion of an ancient woodland into an inferno of mud and noise and steel and concrete."[16] All of these aspects of Lewis's dystopian, post–World War II Britain resonate with the contemporary experience of globalization and corporate rule in the twenty-first century, from the prison industrial complex, to the corporate university, to media consolidation's killing reliable investigative journalism and co-opting the entertainment industry. For an idea of how *That Hideous Strength* prophetically anticipated the crisis in contemporary higher education, consider Steve Mims's 2016 documentary *Starving the Beast* and Henry A. Giroux's *University in Chains: Confronting the Military-Industrial-Academic Complex* (2007). In addition, "Prioritization Anxiety," Colleen Flaherty's August 16, 2016, article in *The Chronicle of Higher Education,* unintentionally and indirectly reveals how Lewis's vision of a Satanic academic computer called "the Pragmatometer"—which rates what majors are worth studying based on profitability and "practicality" metrics—is employed in the real world, today.[17] Notably, the narrative of Satanic forces taking over a school, corrupting curriculum, and firing teachers seems to have influenced the plot of J. K. Rowling's *Harry Potter and the Order of the Phoenix* (2003).

As a body of work, Lewis's theological writings express his ideas about religion, animal rights, politics, and environmentalism in laymen's terms designed to reach a thinking-but-not-scholarly audience of adults. Lewis expressed many of these same ideas in a more coded form in books written for children. Inserting these ideas in the text and subtext of the Narnia series was Lewis's means of teaching better values to the next generation. Since he did not approve of allegory, Tolkien saw this enterprise as a sin against aesthetics. Philip Pullman sees this enterprise as a sin against education. Pullman is deeply troubled by the notion of a Christian apologist brainwashing generations of children into becoming Christians, noting that he is sometimes "tempted to dig [Lewis] up and throw stones at him."[18] Pullman and Tolkien offer assessments of the Narnia books that are defensible and understandable, but too harsh.

Fig. 2.2. Tilda Swinton plays Jadis, the White Witch, in director Andrew Adamson's 2005 film adaptation of C. S. Lewis's *The Chronicles of Narnia: The Lion, the Witch and the Wardrobe.* The 1950 source novel is about the efforts of four British schoolchildren to help overthrow Jadis's tyrannical rule over the magical land of Narnia. As reigning queen, she had brought one hundred years of winter to Narnia, and her overthrow is prophesized to bring springtime once again. Walden Media.

When Lewis wrote several Narnia books in which the animals and magical beings of Narnia—whether they are talking beavers and horses or fawns and centaurs and unicorns—are sold into slavery, whipped, killed, eaten, or frozen by villains such as the Witch or King Miraz or Shift the ape, he was teaching children to respect animal life. He was exhorting children—and readers of all ages—not to behave the way the villains of Narnia do in the real world. When Lewis depicts Narnia devastated, shows arrogant human villains launching campaigns of genocide against dwarves, and killing not only trees but also the Dryads they are linked to, he is teaching children about war crimes, deforestation, slavery, and ethnic cleansing. When Lewis depicts treasonous Narnians aiding foreign enemies in the exploitation of Narnia's peoples and natural resources, he is making a compelling case concerning the need to protect the environment from internal and external threats. Throughout his works, Lewis makes a distinction between education designed to foster love and reverence for learning and the Created order and an education that is about achieving worldly wealth and fame. His environmentalist perspectives and his critique of industrial progress and unrestrained capitalism made him an ideological enemy of Ayn Rand, who wrote a series of invectives against his worldview in the margins of her copy of *The Abolition of Man*. In her marginalia, she dubbed him "an 'abysmal bastard,' a 'monstrosity,' a 'cheap, awful, miserable, touchy, social-meta-physical mediocrity,' a 'pickpocket of concepts,' and a 'God-damn, beaten mystic.'"[19]

What Lewis lacks in subtlety—and, perhaps, originality—he makes up for in trenchant cultural criticism, especially in his depictions of how the villains manipulate the news media and pit liberal and conservative citizens against one another so that the elite can continue to rule the country, unopposed by an ideologically divided populace. In this scene, the chief of N.I.C.E.'s secret police, "Fairy" Hardcastle, explains to the group's newest member, Mark Studdock, that he is no longer his own man and should no longer see himself as an ivory tower academic. Instead, he has been drafted to become their go-to propaganda writer for the mass media. Flabbergasted and uninterested in his new responsibilities, Mark tells Hardcastle that he doesn't understand what kinds of articles he will be writing and for what kinds of newspapers.

"Is it Left or Right papers that are going to print all this rot?" [Mark asked.]

"Both, honey, both," said Miss Hardcastle. "Don't you understand anything? Isn't it absolutely essential to keep a fierce Left and a fierce Right, both on their toes and terrified of the other? That's how things get done. Any opposition to the N.I.C.E. is represented as a Left racket in the Right papers and a Right racket in the Left papers. If it's properly done, you get each side outbidding the other in support of us—to refute the enemy slanders. *Of course* we're non-political. The real power always is."

"I don't believe you can do that," said Mark. "Not with the papers that are read by educated people."

"Why you fool, it's the educated reader that can be gulled. All our difficulty comes from the others. When did you meet a workman who believes in the papers? He takes it for granted that they're all propaganda and skips the leading articles. He buys his paper for the football results and the little paragraphs about girls falling out of windows and corpses found in Mayfair Flats. He is our problem. We need to recondition him. But the educated public, the people who read the highbrow weeklies, don't need reconditioning. They are all right already. They'll believe anything."[20]

Hardcastle is one of the central villains of the piece, a grotesque lesbian dominatrix who may have helped inspire later James Bond villains Rosa Klebb, Pussy Galore, and Xenia Onatopp. While she is a villain, Lewis grants her dialogue that might well explain why he, himself, does not read the newspapers. In the epigraph that opens this chapter, Laura Miller implies that Lewis didn't read the newspapers because he was out of touch and had a fuddy-duddy streak. However, there is a long tradition in multimedia social satire narratives in which authors will occasionally use the villain as their vehicle of expressing a truth that is too unpleasant or controversial for the hero to give utterance to, but which the author agrees with. This passage of Hardcastle feels like just such a passage, suggesting that Lewis didn't read newspapers, in part, because he knew that the fourth estate had been compromised and no longer served the interest of the public against the forces of the establishment. (Lewis also lampoons yellow journalism in his poem "Iron Will Eat the Old World's Beauty Up.") In this segment, Lewis simultaneously reveals something about his own attitudes, makes a wise observation about contemporary culture, develops the characters of his villain (Hardcastle) and his deeply flawed protagonist (Mark), all the while advancing the plot and generating palpable suspense. If this multilayered approach to storytelling may be called allegorical, it is not the substandard form of rhetoric and artistic expression that Tolkien thinks it is. Lewis wrote works of climate fiction in both the fantasy and science fiction genres with demonstrable real-world applicability that offered readers a road map for how to lead a good life and be a good Christian in a war-torn twentieth-century environment. Tolkien, meanwhile, had a different view of what good art constituted. A Roman Catholic sensibility informed his work, but he believed that the religious underpinnings of his stories were handled with greater finesse, originality, and artistry.

## Tolkien's Cordial Dislike of Allegory

Unlike many of his academic peers, Tolkien felt the best way to understand the primary sources in his field of specialization was not to write secondary texts critiquing them but by writing works of his own in the same vein. His desire to "sub-create" his own pseudo-medieval literature via his Middle-earth stories was fueled, in part, by his desire to better understand Arthurian romance, fairy tales, the Icelandic sagas, and epics through composing fresh tales in these traditions. He also felt that he would best understand linguistics by creating organically evolving languages of his own. By creating this new body of literature, Tolkien hoped to write entertaining stories that might amuse others as well as himself. He also had the ambitious goal of creating a more coherent, less overtly Christian mythic origin story for Great Britain by way of the Middle-earth saga. With these complex and ambitious goals underpinning Tolkien's literary efforts, it should be little surprise that he spent years writing and rewriting and refining his works of fiction. He was forever concerned that he had not achieved his stated purpose and needed to keep revising his corpus until the stories were worthy of publication. Thanks to his perfectionism, he finished *The Hobbit* and *The Lord of the Rings* during his lifetime but died before completing *The Silmarillion*. Some theorize that the reason he didn't finish *The Silmarillion* is because it was his Magnum Opus. It was the work that interested himself the most and which he also feared would interest readers the least. He started it decades before he wrote the other Middle-earth stories and he was still working on it when he died, probably because it was both so complex and so personal.

In the years following the publication of *The Lord of the Rings*, Tolkien found himself confronted by critics—some hostile, some not—who interpreted his work as a transparent World War II allegory. Since Tolkien was not trying to write an allegory in any form, least of all a World War II retelling with Orcs instead of Nazis, he found these interpretations frustrating. In his "Foreword to the Second Edition" of *The Lord of the Rings*, Tolkien explained: "I cordially dislike allegory in all its manifestations, and always have done so since I grew old and wary enough to detect its presence. I much prefer history, true or feigned, with its varied applicability to the thought and experience of readers. I think that many confuse 'applicability' with 'allegory'; but the one resides in the freedom of the reader, and the other in the purposed domination of the author."[21] Tolkien's effort to privilege the right of the reader to make meaning over the author's right to inflict a single, correct interpretation of a text onto the mind of a reader through obvious symbolism and narrative signposting anticipates some of the reader response criticism sentiments of Roland Barthes's 1967 essay "The Death of the Author" (though Tolkien would quarrel with some of the atheistic sentiments Barthes expresses).[22]

In this foreword, Tolkien also reveals to readers that he had devised the plot of *Lord of the Rings* before the rise of the Nazi menace and well before the development of the hydrogen bomb, which is why the forces of Sauron could not be called Nazis and the heroes' refusal to use the destructive potential of the One Ring to ensure victory for the side of light could not be regarded as a negative commentary upon the destruction of Hiroshima and Nagasaki. Tolkien also appears offended by the intimation that his work should be read as a ripped-from-the-headlines narrative retelling of events of the recent past. In Tolkien's view, any intimation that *Lord of the Rings* is such a narrative cheapens and conceals his great enterprise. The World War II allegory interpretation fails to give Tolkien the proper credit for the years of work he did developing his own languages, mythology, and history of Middle-earth based on genre conventions and his knowledge of storytelling tropes, history, and linguistics only. Tolkien's statement dismissing allegory as a style of storytelling also serves to distance him from what he perceived to be the excessive proselytizing embedded in the more allegorical writing of Lewis.

However, it is important to remember that Tolkien's objections to early reviews of his book should liberate readers to make their own meanings from his texts. It should not place a chilling effect on all future scholarship or deeper readings of his work. Sometimes Tolkien devotees tend to dismiss any interpretation of the Middle-earth narrative that goes beyond a naive reading, or they insist that Dwarves are only Dwarves and symbolize nothing whatsoever. That assertion is absurd and not what Tolkien had in mind when he was composing his frustrated and defensive response to his early critics. In a letter he wrote to his publisher, Sir Stanley Unwin, on July 31, 1947, Tolkien revealed that, despite his objections to attempts to decipher the one, true way to read *The Lord of the Rings*, he does not object to readers finding a "moral" to his work—possibly even an allegorical one.[23]

## The Lewis and Tolkien Relationship

While Lewis and Tolkien disagreed about the relative merit of "allegory" as a literary genre, the two authors certainly had much in common. The striking similarities between Tolkien and Lewis no doubt helped them become friends in the first place. When the two academics met in 1926 at a Merton College English Faculty meeting, they were initially wary of one another because of their differences in disposition—Lewis was an extroverted literature scholar and Tolkien was a more introverted linguist and historian. Before long, the men realized just how much they had in common. They both had a fascination with Norse mythology, and with mythology and religion in general, which scholars such as Marjorie Burns and Salwa Khoddam have explored.[24] Also, they shared deep emotional scars from both the untimely deaths of their parents and their traumatic memories of service in World War I.[25] Most significantly, both men had a tendency to escape the pain of the real world—and, simultaneously, plunge themselves deeper into that same pain to confront it directly—by creating for themselves fantasy realms populated by characters facing emotional burdens that mirrored their own.[26] Tolkien created Middle-earth; Lewis created Narnia. Lewis's hero, Digory Kirke, is haunted by his sick and dying mother in *The Magician's Nephew* (1955), and his pain is clearly Lewis's pain at the memory of his mother's death, just as Treebeard's pain at the sight of so many downed trees is clearly Tolkien's anguish at seeing the wonders of the natural world soiled by industrialization. They grew close. Tolkien called Lewis by his preferred name: "Jack." Lewis called Tolkien "Tollers."

During the early days of their friendship, the most significant distinction to be drawn between them was that Tolkien was religious and Lewis was not initially Christian. As Lewis explained in his autobiography, *Surprised by Joy* (1955), during his formative years he had enjoyed reading tales of Thor and Loki, but his sympathies had been for the intellectual trickster figure Loki over the musclebound establishment hero Thor. Immersing himself in these tales, Lewis came to believe that the obvious falsity of Norse mythological texts pointed to the obvious falsity of the Judeo-Christian tradition. As Alister McGrath reveals in his biography of Lewis, *C. S. Lewis—A Life: Eccentric Genius, Reluctant Prophet* (2013), the death of Lewis's father in 1929 began to change his feelings about religion, as did Lewis's friendship with Tolkien.

Tolkien was a devout Roman Catholic who strove to convert Lewis to Christianity through an appeal to the objective truth of Christianity. Tolkien eventually convinced Lewis that the body of tales comprising the old Norse religions and the sacred scriptures of Christianity could both be categorized as "myth," only the Norse tales were false and the Christian narratives were "true myth." As Ethan Gilsdorf related in "J. R. R. Tolkien and C. S. Lewis: A Literary Friendship and Rivalry" (2006), Tolkien finally succeeded in breaking down Lewis's resistance to the Christian faith "on September 19, 1931, during an intense conversation that lasted until 3 a.m. . . . among the swaying trees of Magdalen Grove . . . Tolkien's logic was enough to persuade Lewis to become a Christian. But to Tolkien's dismay, Jack chose to join the Anglican Church. This didn't sit well with Tolkien, who was a Catholic. Tolkien had helped Lewis see the light, but Jack's fame and celebrity, which arrived soon after, was at odds with Tolkien's quiet and devout ways. Lewis's popularity as 'Everyman's Theologian,' as Tolkien put it, was disturbing. He had become a disappointment."[27]

McGrath confirms these sources of tension, but he takes pains to demonstrate that the men continued to nominate one another for honors, awards, and jobs during periods in their lives when the most sensationalist biographers paint them as being furious with one another. Depending on whether you are reading Gilsdorf, McGrath, Carpenter, the Zaleskis, Colin Duriez, or Diana Pavlac Glyer, different biographers place a different emphasis on the friendship between Tolkien and Lewis, the points at which it was strongest, when it was most frayed, and why. These Inklings knew one another for thirty-seven years, so it would be unreasonable to assume that such a relationship would be without incident. Remarks that the two men had made to others reflecting upon their friendship included moments of venting that critics have both overstated and underestimated in significance. There is some agreement that, around the time Lewis became a national figure, their friendship faltered slightly and that they grew farther apart in 1954 when Lewis left Oxford and became chair of Mediaeval and Renaissance Literature at Magdalene College, Cambridge. Some biographies of the authors focus upon how Lewis enjoyed Tolkien's writings more than Tolkien enjoyed Lewis's, that Tolkien sometimes was jealous of the friendship that Lewis developed with Charles Williams, and that Tolkien objected to Lewis's "strange" marriage to American divorcée Joy Davidman (a romance dramatized in the popular 1993 film *Shadowlands*). Gilsdorf concludes, "The causes of any waning friendship are hard to fathom. Sometimes, people simply outgrow the need for each other. In 1949, towards the beginning of their unspoken falling-out, Lewis wrote to Tolkien, 'I miss you very much.' Upon Lewis' death in 1963 (on the same day John F. Kennedy was killed), Tolkien was moved to write to his daughter Priscilla that Jack's passing 'feels like an axe-blow near the roots.' "[28]

However their friendship concluded, its beginning was a momentous event in the history of Christian thought, British literature, genre fiction, and the development of climate fiction. Early in their friendship, the two began showing one another drafts of their works in progress, be it scholarship, poetry, or fictional works. Tolkien showed Lewis pages of *The Hobbit* manuscript and Lewis showed Tolkien *The Pilgrim's Regress.* More than writing manuscripts alone, Tolkien was engaged in the project of creating an entire fictional universe, and Lewis was fascinated by the enterprise. "Sub-creating" (or "subcreating") was a term Tolkien used to describe the process by which he constructed his own fictional universe of Middle-earth. Each author gave the other encouragement and feedback. They prodded one another to write more and to publish. From these humble beginnings, *The Lord of the Rings* and *The Chronicles of Narnia* were born.

The cultural significance of the friendship between Tolkien and Lewis was profound. As Baylor University professor Alan Jacobs has observed, "They were convinced that they were two oddball weirdos who cared about stories that nobody else cared about, who were interested in periods of literary history that no one else was interested in. They were very convinced of their own isolation from the mainstream of intellectual culture, but through that mutual encouragement, they produced these works that ended up changing the mainstream of intellectual culture, which I'm sure they would not have believed possible."[29]

What started out as just Tolkien and Lewis sharing as-yet-unpublished works grew to a larger circle of writers and scholars and interested parties listening to works in progress read aloud and commenting upon them. Before long, the fabled discussion group known as the Inklings was born. The group met regularly throughout the 1930s and 1940s, holding gatherings in Lewis's private quarters and in The Eagle and Child pub, which has since become a site of pilgrimage for fantasy and science fiction fans and for Christians wanting to pay homage to their favorite writers. Beyond Tolkien and Lewis, Tolkien's son Christopher, and Lewis's older brother Warnie, the most regular members included Owen Barfield, Charles Williams, J. A. W. Bennett, Lord David Cecil, Nevill Coghill, Hugo Dyson, Adam Fox, Roger Lancelyn Green, and Robert Havard. As McGrath explained, "Serious literary discussion often seems to have been limited to around half a dozen people in Lewis' rooms at Magdalen College after dinner on Thursday evenings. . . . The Inklings read texts aloud to each other for comment and criticism as and when they were ready. This did cause a certain degree of gentlemanly awkwardness, as Tolkien did not read particularly well—perhaps explaining why his university lectures were poorly attended. This problem eventually resolved itself when his son Christopher began to attend, and read his father's works with a clear and attractive voice."[30]

It is difficult to ascertain the extent to which the group helped Tolkien hone his ideas and overcome his bouts of writers' block. In some ways, the Inklings seemed *unhelpful* to him, given the description of "gentlemanly awkwardness" described above and the fact that, because of it, Hugo Dyson sometimes vetoed a reading from Tolkien and moved that the group hold an intellectual conversation instead. On the other hand, there is no doubt that Lewis championed Tolkien's efforts to finish composing his own works. In *I am in Fact a Hobbit: An Introduction to the Life and Work of J. R. R. Tolkien* (2003), Perry C. Bramlett wrestles with this issue, and concludes that: "Tolkien appreciated Lewis for his 'sheer encouragement' and because Lewis saw [*The Silmarillion*] as more than Tolkien's 'private hobby' and urged him to see the book through and try to have it published."[31]

There is much mythology spun around the Inklings and many who are aware of their existence hold preconceived notions—both positive and negative—of who they were that may be based more on a stereotypical view of them than upon reality. In *The Oxford Inklings: Lewis, Tolkien, and Their Circle* (2015), Colin Duriez places the writing circle in its proper historical context and posits several alternative and complimentary ways of understanding its cultural and literary significance. Duriez observes that Tolkien can be credited for founding the group by successfully converting Lewis to Christianity (as part of a multipronged effort with Dyson, Owen Barfield, and Lewis's friend Arthur Greeves) and, consequently, creating a circle of Christian friends and writers from a variety of professions.[32] Rather than regarding this circle as a reactionary outpost of Christianity in an otherwise modern age, Duriez suggests that it is more helpful to see the Inklings as part of a broader, surprising Renaissance of Christian writing during that period, produced by figures such as Francis Berry, T. S. Eliot, Graham Greene, Rose Macaulay, Edwin Muir, Dorothy Sayers, Helen Waddell, Evelyn Waugh, and Andrew Young.[33]

Duriez also emphasizes the Inklings' own tendency to see themselves as the inheritors of the tradition of British Romanticism, with its love of nature and desire for spiritual Transcendence, carrying the flames of Coleridge, Keats, and Wordsworth into the twentieth century.[34] Lewis saw the canon of British literature beginning with Beowulf and ending with Jane Austen, one of the last British writers to produce great art before the age of machines took over the world, corrupting all religion, politics, art, and literature with its robot-like, inhuman sensibilities. Consequently, Lewis regarded his writings, and the writings of the other Inklings, as picking up where Jane Austen left off—championing real literature for real people.[35] While this perspective may seem quaint, it dovetails provocatively with Jesse Oak Taylor's *The Sky of Our Manufacture: The London Fog in British Fiction from Dickens to Woolf* (2016), which posits that Victorian and Edwardian literature (read: post–Jane Austen literature) is the dawn of the literature of the Anthropocene. Taylor examines literary and journalistic narratives that reflect the wages of fin de siècle industrialization (accelerated pollution, urbanization, and climate change), focusing primarily on depictions of the wrongfully romanticized smog-covered streets of London. Since the Inklings mourned the accelerated industrialization they witnessed in their lifetimes, they did not want to immerse themselves in fiction and nonfiction that dwelled upon the kinds of depictions of contemporary life in the Anthropocene that Taylor explores. Instead, they wanted to read works written *before* industrialization and read and write narratives calling for a concerted effort to restore the world to its more blessed, preindustrial state.

In his book-length study of the Inklings, Duriez also considers how the environmentalism of the group's core membership is linked to the culture of the "walking tour" and the rebirth of the travel-writing genre in Great Britain of the 1930s. Barfield, Tolkien, Lewis, and Warnie all enjoyed taking walking holidays and writing about them. Indeed, the simple pleasure of the long walk along a beautiful landscape is a fixture of the Middle-earth and Narnia tales. Furthermore, Frodo and Sam's long walk along a blighted landscape in *Lord of the Rings* is a mournful contrast to the joys of the long nature walks celebrated by this cultural and literary movement. Duriez explains that "[w]alking was popular with both the middle classes and the intelligentsia. With the rapid expansion of towns and cities, for many it was a part of a new appreciation of nature, which was seen as increasingly precious."[36]

Finally, Duriez suggests that, during their Golden Age of creative productivity, the Inklings operated as a moral support group and an antitotalitarian site of resistance dedicated to producing art that challenged the evil ideals of the Axis powers. During World War II, the Inklings met frequently and threw themselves into their work because they were terrified of Hitler (and of Britain's ally, Stalin). Several of them were veterans of World War I who were heartbroken that it had not been, after all, the "war to end all wars." Their ages and occupations exempted them from military service in this war, so they fought the good fight against fascism with their words.[37] In his reminiscences of his times with the Inklings, Dr. Robert Havard recalled that, the day the Inklings first heard of Hitler's invasion of Poland, those who were gathered felt "[t]heir spirits were dashed as they realized that war was inevitable. Lewis quipped, 'Well, at any rate, we now have less chance of dying of cancer,' which raised a hearty laugh." It is easy to see how moments such as these—Christian friends bonding and laughing thanks to Lewis's stress-releasing graveyard humor—held the Inklings together throughout the war.[38]

This construction of the Inklings is validated by Tolkien's satirical and mythologized account of the group in *The Notion Club Papers*, an unfinished novel manuscript he worked on in 1944 and 1945, in which Tolkien created a fictional analogue of the Inklings with a comically similar name: the Notion Club. He called his central counterpart Michael George Ramer, Hugo Dyson's alter ego Alwin Arundel Lowdham, and C. S. Lewis's "Frankley." A "Warnie" was also present, but most of the other Notion Club members are other aspects of Tolkien's personality and not analogues to other Inklings. The book is at once a dramatization of the meetings of the Inklings and an attempt to connect the Middle-earth mythology to the present day through the narrative conceit of psychic time travel. In connecting the Númenor narrative of the distant past to the present day, this manuscript revisits themes Tolkien had explored in a previous, unfinished work, *The Lost Road* (1936), and revisits/rewrites Lewis's own efforts to connect the Númenor story to the modern day via his 1945 novel *That Hideous Strength*.

The dual purpose of the narrative provocatively blends fiction and reality, giving it a Jorge Luis Borges metanarrative feel. As a dramatization of the Inklings meetings, *The Notion Club Papers* is part "history" and part "myth." Using the Notion Club as a stand-in for the Inklings, Tolkien provocatively suggests that, should any future historian try to reconstruct what the Inklings meetings were like "historically," whatever conclusions they might come to via studying nonfiction documents such as letters and meeting minutes would be more mythologically true than historically true. It is a fascinating, amusing, and humbling notion for any scholar to contemplate, although Tolkien also has the Christopher Tolkien character, Jeremy, remark that "the distinction between history and myth might be meaningless outside the Earth."[39]

In its recreation of the mundane details of the "real world" Inklings meetings, *The Notion Club Papers* depicts an amusing conversation between the Notioners about the moral and aesthetic value of contemporary slang and onomatopoeia that seems to be a tongue-in-cheek (but largely accurate) depiction of the kinds of conversations the Inklings had during their meetings. The narrative then becomes unexpectedly mystical. When the Inklings begin to workshop an in-progress story about the drowned kingdom of Númenor, they come to the shocking conclusion that at least three of their members have all had independent psychic visions of a very real, Atlantis-like land that has reached into their dreams in the present day, demanding that the Notioners chronicle its story in the present. Since several of the members independently develop this "calling" to warn the people of the present day of the hubris of the modern world, and of the potential that England might sink as Númenor did after its fall from grace, Tolkien suggests that several of the Inklings, in real life, had a calling to embed religious and ecological-minded prophecy in their fiction. While the book is incomplete, Bruce G. Charlton makes a convincing case concerning where the story was intended to go and what its moral was. Charlton observes that "Tolkien wanted his works about Middle-earth/Arda to be regarded as fictional and also containing genuine knowledge about the 'real world'—a combination made possible by the unconscious processes of literary invention as it is described in *The Notion Club Papers*." Charlton argues that the fictional action of *The Notion Club* papers would involve Inklings stand-ins encountering Middle-earth elves and learning from this supernatural contact how "to adopt an attitude of love towards nature; to become 'elvishly' capable of disinterested craft, art, science and scholarship as things to be loved for their own sakes, rather than as a means to another end." Tolkien's secondary concern would be to have his readers, in the real world, contemplate the lessons that the Notion Club members learn in their fictional reality, and try to enact an ecological transformation of the "real" world modeled in fiction.[40]

Tolkien's mythic portrayal of the Inklings in *The Notion Club Papers* is far removed from his satirical treatment of their meetings in the very same novel fragment. While the distinction between myth and history may be inconsequential in the eternal realm, that distinction is still of import to Earthly scholars. Duriez's even-handed approach to understanding the Inklings is the one that seems the most salient. In the conclusion to his history of the group, Duriez explains that "it is equally mistaken to see the literary club simply as a group of friends, or as a doctrinaire group driven by a highly defined common purpose. A set of aims does not neatly distil when we zealously tidy up the seeming randomness and chaos of what we know of the group's life."[41] Nevertheless, all the views of the Inklings that Duriez explores are accurate to a degree and valuable to consider; together, they were, indeed, an integral part of a British Christian Renaissance, standard-bearers of twentieth-century British Romanticism, 1930s "walking tour" environmentalists, and staunch antitotalitarians.

Colin Duriez paints a positive portrait of the historical and literary significance of the Inklings. Percy Bramlett concludes that the Inklings were, ultimately, of some use to Tolkien and aided him in his efforts to write and publish his works. There are other, less flattering constructions of the Inklings—and of Lewis in particular—that suggest that they were a source of frustration for Tolkien and took more from him than they gave. Indeed, some Tolkien scholars dislike Lewis principally because they see in him someone who mimicked Tolkien to the point of plagiarizing his art and his theology, casting Lewis as a "talented" Mr. Ripley figure trying to be more like Dickey Greenleaf. This portrayal of Lewis as pure mimic goes a bit too far. It is undeniable that Tolkien had enormous influence on Lewis, but it is possible to read Lewis's writings as a tribute to Tolkien's work, just as George R. R. Martin's writings pay tribute to Tolkien, *Dungeons & Dragons* pays tribute to Tolkien, and all other contemporary fantasy pays tribute to Tolkien. If Lewis "borrowed" too much from Tolkien when he wrote his fantasy stories, he's the first of a long line of writers who treated Tolkien in much the same way. Also, scholars who have condemned Lewis for plagiarism have not discerned what may have been Lewis's true motivations for making his works resemble Tolkien's: he wanted his stories to take place in the same theological and environmental universe as Tolkien's.

Tolkien inspired Lewis to write works of his own that took cues from the Middle-earth tales. Lewis acknowledged his debt to Tolkien in print and used the writing and publication of his own stories as an occasion to encourage Tolkien to finish his books and publish them simultaneously, as part of a unified, grand Christian environmentalist narrative. In fact, by the time Lewis published *Perelandra* (1943) and *That Hideous Strength* (1945), he had laid the textual groundwork in his works for future readers—especially veteran science fiction and fantasy fans—to read the entire climate fiction corpus of Lewis and Tolkien as being part of one "shared universe" that includes both Middle-earth and Narnia. This concept of a Middle-earth and Narnia "shared universe" may seem new and unlikely to most Inklings experts, since they are not accustomed to thinking of Narnia and Middle-earth occupying the same "continuity," so it bears explaining. A "shared universe" comes into being when a fictional character (or complete world) with its own autonomous history and narrative continuity is linked to another, seemingly unrelated character (or complete world) with its own autonomous history and narrative continuity. Points of connection between unrelated texts create the shared universe in the imaginations of readers; allowing them to mentally bring the two separate narratives together onto a larger, imagined canvas. The process can be initiated by an author who is paying tribute to work (s)he admires by linking new stories to extant work and "continuing" or "expanding" the admired narrative. It is a process that is also instigated by fans that see points of similarities between narratives that (interestingly) may not have been placed there intentionally by the original authors. Fans build shared universes by making note of common settings (often London or New York), bloodlines (positing potential relations between characters such as Sherlock Holmes, Nero Wolfe, Dick Grayson, and Mr. Spock), or multiverse gateways (portals into other realities accessed via the TARDIS, the forest and the many lakes in *The Magician's Nephew*, or Stephen King's Dark Tower). The final, most frequent form of shared universe is created when corporations seek to turn one narrative into a franchise, sometimes with the same team of writers, sometimes with a diverse array of storytellers charged with maintaining narrative consistency as new stories are added to the existing continuity. The most famous examples of "shared universes" of all of the above varieties occurs when movies or comic books based on Victorian Gothic heroes posit that characters created by Arthur Conan Doyle, H. Rider Haggard, Robert Lewis Stevenson, Bram Stoker, H. G. Wells, and Oscar Wilde all knew one another (see the Universal Monsters, the Wold Newton Universe, *The League of Extraordinary Gentlemen*, *Penny Dreadful*, *Anno Dracula*, Nicholas Meyer's Sherlock Holmes novels, and *Thursday Next*) or when spinoffs of television shows link multiple shows through the use of shared characters (in a Norman Lear or Tommy Westphall Universe manner), or when superheroes with their own histories join up to form a team of heroes, suggesting they occupy the same world when their solo adventures frequently provide evidence to the contrary (see the Avengers, the Justice League, and so on).[42]

Tolkien initially conceived of *The Hobbit*, *The Silmarillion*, and the tale of the fall of Númenor as distinct narratives, though he eventually brought the Númenor story into *The Silmarillion* and wrote *The Lord of the Rings*, in part, to tie the continuity of his works together into one grand narrative. This is widely known. It is also known that *The Chronicles of Narnia* had a clear continuity of its own and an internal logic identified and explicated by scholar Michael Ward in *Planet Narnia: The Seven Heavens in the Imagination of C. S. Lewis* (2010). What many readers of both authors have not noticed is that Lewis established in *That Hideous Strength* that he saw his *Space Trilogy* and Tolkien's writings as occupying the same "shared universe" when he made repeated reference to "Numinor and the True West" and used the figure of Merlin to forge a path from his *Space Trilogy* to *The Silmarillion* through the causeway of the collected works of Arthurian Romance.

Tolkien had created Númenor as an analogue of Atlantis in his history of Middle-earth. The fallen island civilization was west of Middle-earth and was once home to a race of supremely advanced Men, but their downfall came when they turned upon God (Eru Ilúvatar). As Tolkien reveals in *The Silmarillion*, the Númenóreans had been good humans blessed by the Valar with lifespans between three and five times that of other Men because of their good service in fighting against Morgoth. They were rewarded with an island kingdom on which the Elves and the Valar helped them build an idyllic, utopian society. Númenor, the greatest civilization of humans, is renowned for showing a respect for nature almost comparable to the Elves' ecological sensibilities. They also become powerful craftsmen, building great cities and tools and weapons, and become so powerful that, all on their own, they launch a war against Sauron and destroy his army. In the process, the Númenóreans save the Elves and take Sauron prisoner. Tragically, during the time Sauron spends among the Númenóreans, he corrupts them with forbidden knowledge that they use to increase their wealth and power. Still worse, he tempts them to turn against the natural order of the world by making them thirst for immortality. In his narration, Tolkien describes death as "the gift of Ilúvatar," and writes of death as God's plan for humanity. The Númenóreans cannot find it in themselves to view death as a gift, especially when they know that Elves live forever. Sauron convinces them to attack Valinor, misleading them into believing, incorrectly, that possessing the "Undying Lands" where the Valar and most of the Elves live will by itself give them immortality. Rather than resist this invasion themselves, the Valar turn over control of the world directly to Ilúvatar. He breaks the world to punish the Númenóreans, causing the sea to rise and swallow their homeland. The few Númenórean survivors of the catastrophe are the Faithful, a group that never turned evil; they had rejected Sauron's teachings and remained friendly with the Elves. These refugees survive to found Gondor and Arnor in Middle-earth.

Lewis was intrigued by Tolkien's history of Númenor and built it into the overarching narrative of the clash between the forces of the good and bent Oyarsa in *That Hideous Strength*. In the process, he established that the legendary Merlin was the last magician to keep the flame of Middle-earth magic alive in Britain. In his preface to *That Hideous Strength*, composed on Christmas Eve, 1943, Lewis explained: "Those who would like to learn further about Numinor [*sic*] and the True West must (alas!) await the publication of much that still exists only in the MSS. of my friend, Professor J. R. R. Tolkien."[43]

Lewis had heard several unpublished Middle-earth tales and the story of Númenor read aloud at meetings of the Inklings. He knew of Tolkien's plan to publish the fall of Númenor as the final story in the *Silmarillion*. He also knew that Tolkien planned to publish *The Silmarillion* and *Lord of the Rings* as a two-volume book and hoped that his reference to "Numinor" would serve as an early advertisement for the imminent publication of both. When Tolkien's publisher rejected *The Silmarillion* manuscript and said that the lengthy *Lord of the Rings* manuscript needed to be broken up into three volumes, Lewis's plan was spoiled—at least as far as publishing his shared universe works concurrently with Tolkien's books. Nevertheless, the crossover arguably works to this day when readers go through all the fictional works of both Inklings together within a short span of time and the connective tissue between the Tolkien and Lewis fantasy worlds becomes more apparent.

## The Fruits of "Shared Universe" Building: Reading Lewis's *The Space Trilogy* (1938–1945) as a Sequel to Tolkien's *Lord of the Rings* (1954)

In connecting the timelines together, Lewis certainly made gestures in the direction of suggesting that his angels and analogues of God and the Devil were also one and the same characters as Tolkien's. Lewis also made repeated gestures toward establishing what was at the least a multiverse, but which was still more likely a single "shared universe" in which *The Silmarillion*, *The Hobbit*, and *The Lord of the Rings* represent the early history of our planet, followed by the "after the Fall" events of the Judeo-Christian Bible, then by Arthurian Romance. This single timeline culminates in *The Chronicles of Narnia* and *The Space Trilogy*, with the open ending of *That Hideous Strength* suggesting that more epic clashes between the forces of good and evil lie in the future. Furthermore, toward the end of *That Hideous Strength*, Dr. Dimble and his wife discuss the evolution of the Valar without identifying the Valar by Tolkien's name.[44] They posit that the Valar, like elves, dwarves, and other faerie folk and Middle-earth figures, are more neutral and unpredictable during the early years of man—which is why some characters in Tolkien's world seem unaffiliated or neutral in a Gary Gygax, *Dungeons & Dragons*–style alignment system and yet may not be regarded as evil because of their lack of firm commitment to the forces of Good. However, according to the heroes of *That Hideous Strength*, the Valar likely evolved into the angels of pure good and pure evil found in more recent Christian iconography in a manner that suggests that, as the war between good and evil "comes to a point" in the twentieth century, neutrality becomes a luxury affiliation that no race and no individual can afford to adopt. In this discussion, neutrality is presented as a pose that can only serve the interests of the forces of evil, and a strong allegiance to God/Maleldil is the only moral option. The connections to *The Silmarillion* found in *That Hideous Strength* link the universes of *The Space Trilogy* to the whole Middle-earth saga. The conversation about the many faces of Maleldil in *Perelandra*, the song of Creation sung by Aslan in *The Magician's Nephew*, and the alternative faces of Aslan discussed in *Voyage of the Dawn Treader* and *The Last Battle* link Aslan, Maleldil, Eru Ilúvatar, and Christ into one God, thereby linking the Narnia books to *The Space Trilogy* and the Middle-earth saga.

Tolkien was not impressed by Lewis's efforts to connect their works in this fashion. On September 11, 1955, Tolkien wrote a letter to Hugh Brogan, explaining to a puzzled Brogan what an incorrectly spelled reference to Númenor was doing in a Lewis novel, "Your discovery of 'Numinor' in C.S.L.'s *That Hideous Strength* is discovery of a plagiarism: well, not that, since he used the word, taken from my legends of the First and Second Ages, in the belief that they would soon appear. They have not, but I suppose now they may. The spelling Numinor is due to his hearing it and not seeing it."[45] It is interesting that Tolkien does not seem to know how to react to Lewis's use of Númenor and that he has understandably mixed feelings about it. In *The Company They Keep: C. S. Lewis and Tolkien as Writers in Community* (2007), Diana Pavlac Glyer writes, "In including references to Tolkien's work, Lewis was not trying to be sneaky. . . . He clearly believed that Tolkien's work would soon be published and that his use of Tolkien's material would be viewed with favor, recognized as an indirect tribute or deliberate literary allusion. But whatever Lewis's perceptions or motives might have been, Tolkien clearly believed that some trespass had been committed."[46] In 1944 and 1945, when Tolkien was writing *The Notion Club Papers*, he chose to dramatize several Inklings stand-ins independently being called to tell the story of Númenor in their own way. The element of that narrative appears to offer a mythic validation to *That Hideous Strength*—and even supports the view that the Inklings corpus can be seen as occupying a shared universe—but it is one that he may have second-guessed by the time he joked darkly about "plagiarism" in the letter written to Hugh Brogan ten years later. Furthermore, as his son Christopher has revealed, Tolkien was also frustrated that Lewis gave Jane Studdock prophetic dreams in *That Hideous Strength* not long after Tolkien had shared his belief in "true dreams" with Lewis.[47] Imitation may be the sincerest form of flattery but, as the other cliché maintains, there can also be too much of a good thing.

Despite Tolkien's misgivings, anyone who reads the above works together, in the order in which they are intended to take place, is rewarded with a grand, epic narrative clash that begins with the Middle-earth saga and ends with *That Hideous Strength*. Lewis must have had some sense of what he was doing when he connected *That Hideous Strength* to *The Silmarillion*, but one wonders what he might think of the possibility of anyone using his references to Numinor as a justification for reading his *Space Trilogy* (1938–1945) as a sequel to Tolkien's *Lord of the Rings* (1954). While the *Space* and *LOTR* trilogies were by different authors and published in reverse order, *The Space Trilogy* works well as a sequel to the saga it preceded (or, if you prefer, *The Lord of the Rings* works well as a *prequel* to *The Space Trilogy*).

In *Lord of the Rings*, hope lies in the fact that many of the peoples of Middle-earth value nature and live in harmony with it instead of destroying nature to replace it with the artifacts of their own culture—most notably the elves, hobbits, and anthropomorphized Nature characters. The alliance of these like-minded peoples helped keep the forces of anti-Nature in check long enough for Frodo to complete his quest and destroy the ultimate anti-Nature artifact, the One Ring. Also, in Tolkien's works, especially *The Silmarillion*, *Lord of the Rings*, and *Unfinished Tales*, the forces of evil use pollution as a means of destroying the power of Good on Earth. Tolkien depicts the Valar as chief stewards of nature, and their powers are connected to nature. The destruction of—or corruption of—nature reduces their influence over the world. Ulmo, the Valar who is the Lord of Waters, exerts influence in Middle-earth through the waters of Middle-earth; he can communicate through the ocean, rivers, streams, and lakes. However, his power withdraws from the waters if they become polluted. Other Valar with nature-related powers have similar responsibilities as stewards of the Earth and suffer a similar loss of power when they fail to protect the cosmos from being ravaged by evil. These Valar include Manwë, the lord of the air; Varda, the maker of the Sun, Moon, and Stars; Yavanna, the giver of fruits and protector of all trees and growing things; Aulë, the smith and master of all craftsmanship, and Orome, the protector of animals. Melkor—and Sauron after him—pursues a deliberate strategy of destroying and befouling nature in part because ecological devastation weakens the Valar. The theological ramification of this concept is stunning: the act of pollution literally diminishes the power of the Earth's Guardian Angels, and a wholly polluted planet literally drives these Angels off-world and hands complete control of the planet to Lucifer. In Tolkien's theology, nothing makes less sense than for a Christian to argue then the idea that Christians have the right to pollute the Earth because God gave them the planet to soil as they see fit. In Tolkien's theology, polluting the planet is the act of a *Satanist,* not a Christian.

If we are to read *That Hideous Strength* as a sequel to Tolkien's writings, then it takes place during the period immediately following World War II, when the theological crisis described above has come to pass. So much of Nature has been befouled by twentieth-century industrialization that—to mix Tolkien and Lewis terminology in the name of understanding "shared universe" continuity—the Valar have no real influence left over the world and the Earth has become a "silent planet" governed only by the bent Oyarsa. Meanwhile, the allies of Nature despondently inform their new and unexpected ally—a reborn Merlin—that, unlike in his time, no culture on Earth in the twentieth century values Nature. The forces of "progress" have disdain for Nature and only want to see life extinguished, not preserved. They wish to see all human beings turned into immortal cyborgs and all of Earth transformed into a natureless world that is, effectively, one giant city or computer. This nature-less planet would appear in various iterations in other science fiction narratives, including the planet Trantor in Isaac Asimov's *Foundation Trilogy,* Coruscant in the *Star Wars* saga, and Cybertron in *Transformers.* The apocalyptic arc of this continuity means that the situation in *That Hideous Strength,* though presented in the more civilized setting of sitting rooms, think tank hallways, and pubs, is direr than on the battlefields of Middle-earth because there is less Nature left to protect, fewer allies of nature to speak for it, and a general global hive-mind that sees pollution as preferable to conservation. Far from being merely the stuff of science fiction conjecture, the nature-less planet is the direction our own world is heading in, and the Earth may soon look like a vast suburban strip mall version of Cybertron. According to a study in *Current Biology,* in the last twenty years, one-tenth of the remaining wilderness on our planet was lost to "large-scale land conversion, industrial activity, or infrastructure development," an area equivalent to half of the Amazon and double the size of Alaska.[48] The loss occurred primarily in South America and Africa. "'Even though 10 percent is quite a small number in some ways, it really means that if we keep this trajectory going we will lose all wilderness in the next 50 years,' said James Watson, lead author and director of science and research initiative at the Wildlife Conservation Society. . . . 'Without any policies to protect these areas, they are falling victim to widespread development. . . . We probably have one to two decades to turn this around.'"[49]

A person should not be considered an enemy of science or an enemy of "progress" to be troubled by a real-life unfolding story like the one cited above. Lewis was concerned about pollution and deforestation during his lifetime and he predicted our current, escalating deforestation crisis. That didn't make him a pure Luddite. As Downing observed, many have "assumed that Lewis, as one of the century's most well-known advocates of Christianity, felt a natural antipathy for science because of his religious convictions. But this assumption is wide of the mark."[50] Lewis himself argues that the only bona fide scientist in N.I.C.E. is murdered for having left the organization in protest when he discovered their insane agenda. Lewis "intended the trilogy as a cautionary tale against totalitarians who use 'scientific planning' as their catch-phrase to attract popular support. He says that the underlying theme of *That Hideous Strength* is not, as [J. B. S.] Haldane claims, 'That scientific planning will certainly lead to hell,' but rather that 'under modern conditions any effective invitation to hell will certainly appear in the guise of scientific planning—as Hitler's regime in fact did.'"[51]

In *That Hideous Strength*, Lewis models an alternative relationship between humans and the natural world by dramatizing a community of good people who refuse to participate in industrial society. They drop out and form their own community in St. Anne's-on-the-hill, in which they enjoy picnicking outdoors in the rain, have animals living with them indoors, break down the differences between the genders and classes in a more egalitarian household, and have healthy sex lives. Dickerson and O'Hara remark that Lewis offers as many chapters depicting the good society at St. Anne's as he does illustrating the evil one in the N.I.C.E. headquarters at Belbury. They note, "At St. Anne's, readers see a compelling model of how to live in healthy relationships with other people, with other creatures, and with the earth."[52] This community is presented as the polar opposite of the society found at Belbury, in which the predominantly male community is engaged primarily in political one-upmanship, is afraid of going outside into the elements, keeps animals in cages to experiment on them, and thinks the best destiny for the human race is for us all to become celibate, zombie-like cyborgs on a nature-free planet. When Merlin arrives toward the end of the book, and is drawn to the ecologically friendly community at St. Anne's and sides with them against Belbury, his presence seems, at first, as incongruous as if Gandalf had shown up during a climactic moment of *Rosemary's Baby* to save Mrs. Woodhouse from the witches. What prevents Merlin's sudden appearance in post–World War II Britain from being dramatically ridiculous is that the jarring anachronistic nature of his presence is precisely the point. Dickerson and O'Hara conclude their chapter on *That Hideous Strength* by quoting Ransom's observations about what modern people might learn from Merlin now that he has returned during Earth's darkest hour. The legendary figure, who is "forbidden by the rules of his order to use any edged tool on any growing thing" represents a return to reverence for nature and a return to a true feeling of interconnection between humans and nature. Merlin represents an extreme position, but one that is intended to act as a corrective, and to demonstrate just how extreme our own position is: cutting plants *is all we ever do*.

C. S. Lewis's *Space Trilogy* may be read as a sequel to J. R. R. Tolkien's *Lord of the Rings* thanks to the efforts of Lewis to tie *That Hideous Strength* to Tolkien's as-yet-unpublished work *The Silmarillion*. It is an admittedly odd mental exercise, but one justified by the way in which Lewis treats the same themes as Tolkien does in *Lord of the Rings*. The fall of Bragdon Wood and Edgestow make for a chilling contemporary follow-up to the "Scouring of the Shire" epilogue of Tolkien's epic, in which pollution and devastation once relegated to far off lands (or what Naomi Klein calls "sacrifice zones" in 2014's *This Changes Everything*) come back home to despoil a homeland. Even if Tolkien would not have approved of his works being linked to Lewis's, reading the writings of the Inklings as being part of a larger, thematic whole links *Lord of the Rings* ever closer to our own time and our own society. *That Hideous Strength* calls upon us to not treat this "shared universe" narrative as a grand fiction but as a disguised documentary. As we consider the various attitudes toward nature represented in these works, we are asked by the authors of these documentaries disguised as climate fictions to emulate the behaviors of Treebeard and St. Anne's, and to avoid as much as possible walking in the footsteps of Saruman and Belbury.

# 3

# The Time Lord, the Daleks, and the Wardrobe

C. S. Lewis meets H.G. Wells meets Father Christmas. That's the Doctor.

—Verity Lambert, co-creator of *Doctor Who*,
in *An Adventure in Space and Time*

CLARA: Why would trees want to kill us? We love trees.

THE DOCTOR: You've been chopping them down for furniture for centuries. If that's love, no wonder they're calling down fire from the heavens!

—Frank Cottrell Boyce, *Doctor Who*,
"In the Forest of the Night"

## The Doctor and the Inklings

"The Professor, the Queen, and the Bookshop," a 2011 comic strip that appeared in *Doctor Who Magazine* #429, paid tribute to C. S. Lewis by retelling two Narnia novels—*The Lion, the Witch, and the Wardrobe* (1950) and *The Magician's Nephew* (1955)—as if they were *Doctor Who* adventures. The comic, by writer Jonathan Morris and artist Rob Davis, acknowledges the enduring influence of Lewis's works upon the multimedia science fiction franchise since its television premiere on November 23, 1963—the day after the death of Lewis and the assassination of President Kennedy.

Morris's strip begins during the Blitz, when two child heroes, Amelia and Rory, delay their evacuation of London to visit Phoenix Books, a quaint shop that has a modest exterior but is a cavernous library within. The mysterious proprietor calls himself "the Professor," but he is drawn to resemble the Doctor (as played by actor

Matt Smith on television in 2011). The Professor warns the children not to open any of the books, because doing so will transport the entire store and its occupants into the book's fictional reality. As he says, "This is no ordinary bookshop. It moves! . . . It can travel into the pages of any book ever written! We can be in any story, anywhere in the imagination!" Despite the warning, Amelia opens the book *Shada* and the trio are transported to a dead landscape drawn to resemble both the Death Zone on the Doctor's home planet of Gallifrey (from 1983's "The Five Doctors") and the devastated civilization Charn discovered by Digory and Polly in *The Magician's Nephew*.

Amelia, Rory, and the Professor encounter a regal female with stone skin dressed in Time Lord robes. She is drawn to resemble both the Lewis villain Jadis and a Weeping Angel from *Doctor Who*. The Professor identifies her as the White Queen and orders the children back to the bookstore. They leave immediately, believing they have escaped from the prison world, but the White Queen had perceived where their escape route would take them, followed their trajectory, and manipulated the timelines so that she could arrive at their destination before them. When the bookstore lands in Narnia, the three travelers find that the Queen has conquered the land. She has blanketed Narnia in ice and snow, turning unruly animal and fairy tale creature subjects into trees, and making more malleable subjects into warrior-slaves. The Queen orders the Professor killed and attempts to enslave the children, but Amelia shields herself with *Shada*. She opens the book and draws the White Queen back into its pages, imprisoning her once more. Then Amelia turns to a blank leaf in the book and writes a new ending for the Professor, revealing that he was not dead after all. At the final stroke of her pen, the Professor returns to life.

The story-within-a-story ends here and the comic strip then begins a new scene in which C. S. Lewis is presenting the above narrative as an unpublished manuscript to the Inklings at a gathering in The Eagle and Child. He asks for their thoughts. Tolkien replies, "Well, I thought it was a bit juvenile . . . A jumble of unrelated mythologies . . . All rather derivative, I'm afraid . . . And I wasn't convinced by the allegorical element at all."

Lewis says, "Blunt as always, John. Your honesty is appreciated. What about our new Inklings? What did you make of it?" In the next comic panel, the Doctor and Amy Pond are revealed, lounging with the Inklings and enjoying libations.

THE DOCTOR: Me? Oh, I loved it!

AMY POND: Yeah. Ignore old misery guts. He's just upset because it didn't include half-a-dozen made-up languages!

THE DOCTOR: I do have a small, tiny suggestion, though . . .

LEWIS: Yes, Doctor? Go on?

THE DOCTOR: It might work even better with a wardrobe.

The strip is in the tradition of multiple *Doctor Who* time-travel stories with circular narratives in which the Doctor goes back in time to witness a significant historical event only to discover—through some causal loop or bootstrap paradox—that he himself was responsible for bringing about the event he had hoped to observe. In Paul Cornell's slyly blasphemous 1994 novel "Goth Opera," the Doctor explains that he traveled back in time to experience the delivering of the Ten Commandments unto the Hebrew peoples and wound up helping Moses write the Commandments themselves. In the Inklings comic strip described above, Morris creates a fictional narrative in which the Doctor tells Lewis about his Gallifreyan heritage, Lewis transforms the Doctor's biography into an allegorical fairy tale for children, and teaches the world about the "true" story of the Time Lord from Gallifrey by disguising it as fiction. The strip is intended as an affectionate tribute to the Inklings, but it reduces them to figures of fun: Tolkien is the "misery guts" whose dismissal of Lewis's tale amounts to a dismissal of *Doctor Who*, and Lewis is an unoriginal composer of childishly allegorical literary pastiche.

## *Doctor Who* as Climate Fiction

The *Doctor Who* story is a multimedia one, related in part through Virgin Publishing's original novels, Titan Press's licensed comic books, and Big Finish Productions's full-cast audio dramas. However, *Doctor Who* began life as a television series, and the broadcast stories remain the only ones that fans of the franchise agree may be considered "canonical" adventures in the life of the Doctor. A bohemian, anti-imperialist figure who combats Nazis, demons, cyborgs, and the demonic Nazi cyborgs known as the Daleks, the Doctor is a time-traveling extraterrestrial who can regenerate his mortally wounded body twelve times, thereby living thirteen lives. The series mythology concept of regeneration was created for a practical reason—to help viewers willingly suspend their disbelief that a recast lead actor is still playing the same character as his predecessor. Somewhat like the Doctor, the series itself has died twice and regenerated twice. It had a twenty-six season run from 1963 through 1989, returned in the 1996 television movie that failed to lead into a new series as was expected, and returned in 2005 as a revival series created by Russell T. Davies that is, as of the writing of this book, still broadcasting new episodes.

As *Doctor Who* adventure writer and scholar Kim Newman observed, over the years the show has mimicked themes and styles of "the blood-and-thunder Gothicism of Hammer horror, panto humor, conspiracy thriller, studio-bound fantasia, social satire . . . deliberate and unintentional camp, and even ambitious philosophizing."[1] These shifts in style and tone may be accounted for by changing times, production teams, and casts, as well as efforts on behalf of storytellers to shape the episodes to appeal to the broadest possible viewership demographics. As series star Peter Capaldi observed, the important thing to remember is that, first and foremost, the show belongs to the children in the audience. That having been said, he and the writers and directors also strive to entertain "hipsters and students, and middle-aged men who should know better.

So sometimes there is a kind of metaphysical and intellectual aspect to it, which is more to the fore than other times. But, generally, we just blow up monsters."[2]

There are, of course, the oft-cited criticisms of the classic series: that it is difficult for modern viewers to watch because it is dated by its "filmed play" production values (shared by other old, excellent British shows such as *Fawlty Towers* and *Poldark*) and that there is an odd "offness" of the pacing one experiences when watching in one sitting a six- or seven-part serial intended to be watched once a week with cliffhangers intact. Despite budgetary limitations, the production team often excelled at costume, creature, and set design, but was just as often inept at lighting the sets and monsters in a flattering or atmospheric way. Also, they tended to film futuristic guns and miniature spaceships and cities in a manner that made it clear they were not "real." More damning than the (*somewhat* unjustifiably) infamous visual effects limitations, however, is the fact that both the classic and new series of *Doctor Who* are often criticized for their treatment of women and minority characters. Series co-creator and founding producer Verity Lambert bestowed feminist and multicultural sensibilities upon *Doctor Who*. However, since her early departure from the program, it has not been as consistently liberal as she intended it to be. For example, up until 2017, the only woman to ever play the Doctor was Joanna Lumley, in the comedy sketch "The Curse of the Fatal Death" (1999), which depicted a newly regenerated female Doctor discovering with amazed glee that her sonic screwdriver had a vibrator setting. Better late than never, Jodie Whittaker inherited the title role from Capaldi in "Twice Upon a Time," becoming the first-ever female star of the series in time for its thirty-seventh season, delighting progressive fans and distressing more conservative ones in the process. Supporting roles for women in the series have also been a source of controversy. For example, the Doctor's female traveling companions often have been defined by their sex appeal and tend to exist for the Doctor to: (1) explain plot points to and (2) rescue. Series stars Tom Baker, Nicola Bryant, and Janet Fielding have made similar assessments of the treatment of women in *Doctor Who*.

These not insignificant caveats aside, there is a subversive quality to the series typical of the best aspects of "camp" narratives and an intelligence, humor, and imagination to the storytelling that rewards viewers who can see past the limitations of the show's production values and jarring mix of progressive and reactionary sentiments. Indeed, producer, writer, and gay rights activist Russell T. Davies said as much during a March 27, 2017 *Telegraph* interview when he explained why the series has such a strong following among gay men: "It takes a lot of nerve and a lot of work to love *Doctor Who*. I'm going to be really bold now and say you've got to be cleverer than the normal viewer. You've got to take more of a risk, you've got to invest in it. Because you need to fill those gaps where it's looking cheap or it's looking poor. It's a very imaginative act to watch *Doctor Who*. And I think gay people are better and cleverer and more imaginative than anyone else!"

Offering still loftier praise for the low-budget, oft-disparaged series, Davies's successor as series producer, Steven Moffat, argued in a *Metro News* interview on December 14,

2017, that *Doctor Who* is, literally, "the greatest television show ever made," surpassing *The Office, I Claudius,* and *The Wire,* not in ratings or critical acclaim, but in its generations of cultural influence worldwide. "Count the scientists, the musicians, the scholars, the writers, the directors, the actors, who became what they are because of this show," he said. "Count, as you might say, the hearts that beat a little faster because of *Doctor Who.* I do not even know what is in second place, but without doubt, and by that most important measure, *Doctor Who* is the greatest television show ever made." This is a hyperbolic statement from a highly biased source. Nevertheless, if Moffat's contention is even remotely true that "people become scientists, people change their view of the world and what they're capable of, because of a silly show about a man who travels around in time and space in a police box," then it is all the more important to consider what cultural values the series represents and what view of science—and of ethics—it promotes.

Consequently, one must ask, "What is *Doctor Who* and what kind of character is the series' main hero, 'The Doctor?'" Most importantly, for the purposes of this book, the Doctor is one of the world's most famous fictional environmentalist heroes. Whether his tactics are gentle or ruthless, the heroic protagonist known as the Doctor is presented as combating imperialism and supporting the oppressed. Significantly, the Doctor has often championed the forces of Nature over industrialization, especially in episodes such as "Inferno" (1970), "The Green Death" (1973), "The Invasion of the Dinosaurs" (1974), "The End of the World" (2005), and "In the Forest of the Night" (2014).

In "Inferno" (1970), written by Don Houghton, the Doctor tries to escape from an exile on Earth that the Time Lords have imposed upon him by experimenting with his wardrobe-like time machine, the TARDIS. He is accidentally shunted into a parallel universe five years in the future, arriving in a fascist version of England engaged in a project to drill into the Earth's crust to release Stahlman's Gas, a substance that promises to provide limitless reserves of cheap energy. Unfortunately, despite its positive press clippings, the gas escapes into the atmosphere and mutates humans into monsters. As the human populace turns zombie-like, an endless gush of lava bursts from the drill shaft, coating the surface of the planet and setting it aflame. The Doctor escapes back to his own reality and works to prevent the same catastrophe that he witnessed on an alternate Earth from happening on *his* version of Earth. After all, in his timeline, the project to drill to find Stahlman's Gas has begun in earnest and is about to reach a critical stage. Unfortunately, the project is expected to be profitable and promises energy independence, so no one in government wants to listen to the ravings of an eccentric environmentalist.

In "The Green Death" (1973), written by Robert Sloman (and an uncredited Barry Letts), a Global Chemicals oil plant in Llanfairfach in South Wales boasts the development of a new process that can "produce 25% more petrol and diesel fuel from a given quantity of crude oil" with very little waste. In reality, Global Chemicals is dumping gallons of toxic waste into nearby mines, poisoning miners to death and transforming tiny maggots into giant, man-eating creatures. The Doctor discovers that the executives at Global Chemicals are in the thrall of an insane computer called

BOSS, whose only goals are efficiency and increased profit margins for the corporation. Inhuman and insane, BOSS cares nothing for the pollution or dead miners that result from the waste dumping. The Doctor destroys the computer and convinces the United Nations to shut down the company through his ties to U.N.I.T. (The United Nations Intelligence Taskforce).

In "The Invasion of the Dinosaurs" (1974), written by Malcolm Hulke, radical environmental terrorists attempt to reset Earth's history in the hopes of bringing its more verdant past into our present and erasing almost the entirety of human history in the process. The group selects a handful of the wisest and kindest sustainability champions to survive to repopulate the species on a green world. The Doctor stops the plan, but makes it clear to the British authorities that the terrorists are right about the urgency to end the ravages of industrialization before humanity becomes extinct. One of the Doctor's best friends, U.N.I.T. Captain Mike Yates, is even part of the plot because of his fears of imminent environmental catastrophe, validating the perspectives of the episodes' villains more than in any other episode. The next time Yates appears on the series, in "Planet of Spiders" (1974), he is depicted as unambiguously heroic.

In the episode "In the Forest of the Night" (2014), written by Frank Cottrell Boyce, giant trees sprout up all around the Earth in a matter of hours, turning the planet from blue to green. The Doctor notices that a solar flare large enough to engulf the world is forming and surmises, incorrectly, that the trees are calling fire down upon humanity in revenge for years of deforestation. Since he, like most humans, concludes that the trees are hostile, he supports a worldwide effort to use defoliating agents to kill the trees. Then the Doctor encounters fairy-like beings that serve the life force of the planet. They explain that they always grow trees to protect humans from ecological disaster, and saved many lives in the past by growing new trees to blunt the effects of the Tunguska Event and the Curuçá impact. Once the Doctor realizes that the humans will need the trees to protect them from the attacking sun, he hacks into all the cell phones in the world and asks a young girl to plead with humanity not to kill the trees. The solar flare erupts, engulfs the Earth, burns away the newly grown trees, and the force of the blast disperses. No mark is left upon the world. The Doctor concludes that humans should consider being kinder to trees in the future, especially in case trees are needed again to prevent ecological disaster.

In addition to these episodes and serials, other climate fiction adventures include "The Ice Warriors" (1967), "The Enemy of the World" (1967), "Kinda" (1982), and "The Curse of Fenric" (1989).

Ecoterrorist villains notwithstanding, the environmentalist episodes summarized above have a progressive tone that supports sustainability. In keeping with the climate fiction of C. S. Lewis, the villains of these stories are often fascists, settler colonials, and corporate polluters. These factors would all suggest that the show has always been progressive and left-leaning. However, as John Tulloch and Manuel Alvarado argue in *Doctor Who: The Unfolding Text*, the television series' mostly male production team, male star, melodramatic conventions, and Western Christian-centric worldview often make it establishment in tone.

Fig. 3.1. In the episode "In the Forest of the Night" (2014), giant trees sprout up all around the Earth overnight. The Doctor (Peter Capaldi) notices that a solar flare large enough to engulf the world is forming and surmises, incorrectly, that the obviously mystical trees are calling fire down upon humanity in revenge for years of deforestation. BBC.

They do point out that some liberal and anarchic creative influences from scriptwriters, producers, and performers have sometimes pushed the show dramatically into the realm of the subversive and the left-wing (especially, they observed, during periods when the show was most influenced by the writings of science fiction and fantasy novelist Ursula K. Le Guin).[3] Indeed, the show was offensive enough to right-wing tastes that it was the target of semi-regular criticism from Mary Whitehouse's *National Viewers' and Listeners' Association* (now known as *Mediawatch-uk*), a religious pressure group in Great Britain that monitors the mass media for "offensive content" and lodges protest against programs that contain too much sex, violence, profanity, and blasphemy.[4] Paradoxically, Tulloch and Alvarado are correct about the show being Christian in its values systems, just as Whitehouse is correct to assert that it is, at its heart, subversive and atheistic. The series is *both* Christian and secular humanist at the same time. An analysis of the show's appropriations of and rewritings of Lewis's works of speculative fiction is the key to comprehending *Doctor Who*'s complicated attitude toward Christianity.

The 2011 *Doctor Who* Christmas special—"The Doctor, the Widow, and the Wardrobe" written by Steven Moffat—was released the same year as "The Professor, the Queen, and the Bookshop." Its plot concerns war widow Madge Arwell (Claire Skinner) and her children, Lily and Cyril, who travel to their Uncle Digby's house to escape the Blitz. The Doctor is there to play host because he owes Madge a favor: she helped him locate his TARDIS and recover from a desperate injury during a previous adventure. He also knows that the children's father has just been killed in action and that Madge hasn't told them this yet. As his idea of a Christmas gift, the Doctor transports the family to a planet with naturally occurring Christmas trees; evergreens that grow organic ornaments and are adorned with the sparkling lights of the trees' souls.

What the Doctor doesn't know is that his timing for the journey is poor. He has transported the family to this planet on the eve of its harvesting. A conglomerate on

Fig. 3.2. Publicity still from the 2011 *Doctor Who* Christmas special "The Doctor, the Widow, and the Wardrobe," written by Steven Moffat: The Doctor (center, played by Matt Smith) takes war widow Madge Arwell (Claire Skinner) and her children, Lily and Cyril (Holly Earl and Maurice Cole), to a Narnia-like world in an episode that pays tribute to Lewis's environmentalism. BBC.

Androzani Major unleashes acid rain upon the forest from an orbiting satellite, melting down the trees into battery fluid to fuel space travel. The Doctor and the terrified family members take shelter in a lighthouse in the middle of the forest, where they find two sentient wood creatures, the Wooden King and the Wooden Queen. The Dryad-like beings choose Madge to be the repository of the souls of dying trees. She accepts this responsibility, and the lights rise off the trees before the trees are dissolved and pour into Madge's body. The Doctor takes Madge on a voyage into the space/time continuum, where she unleashes the life force of the destroyed forest into eternity. After she is purged of the last tree soul, Madge asks what happened. The Doctor begins to offer what he sees as a scientific explanation, and then switches language to frame it in more religious terms: "The life force of the whole forest has transmuted itself into a sub-etheric waveband of light, which can exist as . . . The-the-the . . . souls of the trees are out among the stars and they're shining, very happy. And you got them there."

Madge understands. Indeed, she is capable of framing events in both religious and scientific terms, and noted at the beginning of the episode that the Doctor seems to be "a space man . . . possibly an angel." When the kids return home to Christmas to find history changed and their father alive after all—thanks to the Doctor's manipulation of the course of their lives and of history—the assessment of the Doctor being both an alien and an angel seems valid. With its inclusion of Dryad-like figures guarding trees, its odd blending of Christian and science fiction themes, its concern for pollution, and its frequent use of motifs from *The Chronicles of Narnia*, the episode is a more apt tribute to Lewis than the comic strip that preceded it. It is also, thanks to Madge Arwell's split perspective on events, both a religious Christian work and a secular humanist one.

Moffat, who is also the series producer and co-creator (with Mark Gatiss) of the BBC show *Sherlock*, revealed in 2013 that he himself sees the Doctor as both alien and angel. That is why, despite surface similarities to Sherlock Holmes, the Doctor is a different character. "The Doctor is the angel who aspires to be human and Sherlock is the human who aspires to be an evil god," Moffat observed.[5] Notably, Moffat created the most famous villains to appear in *Doctor Who* since the Daleks—the Weeping Angels. The Weeping Angels serve as an evil counterpart to the Doctor's good angel. The Weeping Angels use humans as food, transporting them back through time, stranding them, stealing the lives they were meant to have, and vampirically feeding off the lost potential of their intended lives. What they do would be an uncharitable view of the Doctor's penchant to pluck fellow-travelers from among humanity, educate them, and take them around the universe and up and down timelines with little thought of how they might return to a humdrum job and family life on Earth once being exposed to such wonders. Like Sam Gamgee in *Lord of the Rings*, some of the Doctor's former traveling companions can reassimilate to society after their time with the Doctor. Others, like Frodo, cannot.

The notion of the Doctor as an "angel" is worth considering within the context of a *Silmarillion*-like theology. In Middle-earth, the Doctor would be best understood either as a Maia or Vala that loves humans so much that he nurtures and befriends them in much the same manner that Gandalf nurtures and befriends Hobbits. Similarly, the Doctor's childhood best friend, the Master, has pledged himself to evil, and seems much like the dark wizard/angel Saruman of *Lord of the Rings*. Like Saruman, the Master places himself in command of armies of militaristic, hive-mind species, hoping to conquer the Earth and remake it in his own image; instead of Orcs, the Master employs Autons, Cybermen, and Toclafane. Meanwhile, the rest of the Valar of the *Doctor Who* universe, the Time Lords of Gallifrey, spend most of their time pledging not to interfere with the free will and natural development of "lesser species." However, when they do deign to intervene, they behave far more like the Master than the Doctor, and exercise their imperialistic aims instead of seeking justice.

## Is the Doctor John Lennon?

The Doctor has always been frustrated by the Time Lords' tendency toward inertia and horrified by their most imperial and destructive initiatives. Indeed, in "The Trial of a Time Lord: The Ultimate Foe" (1986), the Doctor realizes that the ultimate evil he has fought throughout his life is neither the Master nor the Daleks but the darkness within the hearts of *all* Time Lords, himself included, making Time Lord society's potential for evil outweigh any other evil he has found anywhere else in all of time and space. Long-time series writer Robert Holmes, who wrote adventures for the second through sixth Doctors, portrayed the Doctor's home planet of Gallifrey as a satirical stand-in for everything reprehensible about Great Britain. Gallifrey is a former imperial superpower that simultaneously regrets its past evil deeds and hopes to reclaim the mantle of power and grow more imperialistic than ever. The Doctor shares his people's shame about their imperial past but not their ambition to continue perpetrating war crimes and genocide in the future. Elder Time Lords have tended to regard the Doctor as a softhearted fop and a waste of potential because of his failure to embrace his planet's once and future colonialist destiny. The episode "Listen" (2014) includes a scene set during the Doctor's childhood in which he reacts to his prospective military training with terror and tears, much to his father's chagrin. In "The Deadly Assassin" (1976), the Doctor's maths professor at the Academy, Lord Borusa, tells the Doctor that "you will never amount to anything in the galaxy while you retain your propensity for vulgar facetiousness." In "The Ribos Operation" (1978), the Time Lady Romana boasts of graduating from the Academy with a triple first and then, when the Doctor mocks her for her pride in her grades, she declares, "Well, it's better than scraping through with fifty-one percent at the second attempt." The Doctor's unrealized potential as a gifted maths student and member of the august Prydonian Chapter is reminiscent of Matt Damon's directionless young hero in *Good Will Hunting* (1997). Importantly, both characters are frightened that their intellectual gifts will be harnessed in the service of empire building should they ever decide to "reach their potential."

The Doctor, a fictional character that was created in the 1960s, looks upon his parents—and the Time Lords in general—with much the same moral disgust that one of his real-world inspirations, John Lennon, expressed toward England. The Doctor's childhood is shrouded in mystery, but there is one plausible depiction of what the Doctor and the Master might have been like growing up on Gallifrey that may be gleaned from a scene in *A Hard Day's Night* (1964). In the scene, the Beatles encounter Johnson, a Tory gentleman reading *The Financial Times* in the train compartment they are sharing. He begrudges them opening the compartment window and closes it. When they protest, politely, he gives them a curt reply. When they try to listen to pop music on the radio, he turns it off and quotes his rights to comfort. Paul McCartney protests that they have rights, too.

> JOHN: Knock it off, Paul. You can't win with his sort. After all, it's his train, isn't it, Mister?

> JOHNSON: Don't take that tone with me, young man. I fought the war for your sort.

> RINGO: I bet you're sorry you won.[6]

One of the many things that Johnson implies with his reference to the war is that, should the Nazis ever rise again to menace England, the Beatles and their hippie ilk will be too soft to put up much of a fight. The Beatles are "nicer" than Johnson because they grew up idle and privileged, and did not have to live through World War II. They could content themselves with disdaining the elders who had saved democracy for them so that they could ruin it. Instead of standing firm against fascism, the legacy of the Beatles' generation would be the running of the British Empire into the ground. Johnson's appraisal of the Beatles is the Time Lords' appraisal of the Doctor and the Master. The Doctor's response was to reject all the implications of the criticism and become still more rebellious and antiauthoritarian. In contrast, the Master strove to prove his superiors wrong by becoming a better warmonger and colonialist than they ever could. An actor of Spanish and Belgian descent named Roger Delgado originated the role of the Master in "Terror of the Autons" (1971), and he wore a black goatee, black Nehru jacket, and black leather gloves. Naturally, the Master's physical appearance made him an ideal case study for Edward Said, but his costume cues complicate matters by acting as satirical critiques of British colonial history. A "master" of disguise, the Master has insinuated himself into the clergy as "a rationalist existentialist priest" and has impersonated an intergalactic colonial adjudicator, a retired colonel, a police inspector, and a knight. In the revival series, the Master was even elected Prime Minister of Great Britain in the guise of Harold Saxon and served as a thinly veiled condemnation of Tony Blair. In several episodes, including 1971's "Colony in Space" by Marxist screenwriter Malcolm Hulke, the Master plays the imperialist Weston to the Doctor's indigenous-people's rights advocate Ransom in a revisiting of Lewis's *Out of the Silent Planet*. In all his lives, the Master delights in killing those he need not bother killing, partly just to flabbergast the Doctor. However, the Master's delight in carnage runs deeper than that. It is born of his childhood desire to please the Time Lords. He hopes to amass the largest collection of corpses of indigenous peoples he can to impress the Gallifreyans with the sheer volume of "lesser beings" on countless worlds whose lives he has extinguished. In a sense, the Master grew up to become an Angel of Death—an identity that he wears symbolically in the television series and *literally* in the Big Finish full-cast audio drama "Master" (2003) by Joseph Lidster. Appropriately, since he is the Master's antithesis, the Doctor, during a formative moment, chose the title "The Doctor" for himself because of a "foolish dream"—he "dreamt he could hold back death." Paul McGann's Doctor surmises that this foolish dream is why his friend Grace Holloway became a physician, but he appears to be speaking as much about himself as he is

Fig. 3.3. The Master (in female form, played by Michelle Gomez) retains a twisted affection for her former best friend, the Doctor (Peter Capaldi). In 2014's "Death in Heaven," she begins transforming all of humanity into an army of cybernetic zombies. She then offers the zombie multitude to the Doctor as a gift for his two thousandth birthday so that he can unleash it upon his arch enemies, the Daleks. Here she takes a selfie with him to capture his appalled reaction to the unwanted present. BBC.

about her in *Doctor Who: The Movie*. In a sense, this makes the Doctor the "Angel of Life" and explains his frequent inability to accept it when people he cares about die.

The glimpses we get into the Doctor's formative years suggest a lifetime of unhappiness on Gallifrey, mitigated by his discovery of the Earth religion Buddhism through one of its few Time Lord adherents—an aspect of the Doctor's biography written into the character by Buddhist producer Barry Letts. The non-canonical audio adventure "Auld Mortality" (2003), by Marc Platt, reveals that the Doctor married unhappily and produced an "establishment" daughter who was as mortified by his bohemian temperament as his parents were. However, *her* daughter shared some of his iconoclastic leanings. The Doctor's granddaughter was someone who understood him. *She* might be convinced to flee Gallifrey with him and start anew. Ultimately, the Doctor's granddaughter *did* leave Gallifrey with him, shed her Gallifreyan name, and adopted the identity of Susan Foreman by the time they settled on Earth in the 1960s.

Throughout the series, it is left deliberately unclear whether the Doctor is a thief, con artist, and gadabout who left his home world out of boredom with its stagnant society of "door mice" (see "The War Games") or an aristocrat and co-developer of time travel technology who was exiled from (or fled from) Gallifrey for political reasons (see "An Unearthly Child"—in which Susan explained that she coined the name "TARDIS"—and Marc Platt's "The Beginning" in which Susan said, "At home his views were too disruptive . . . But for grandfather to just sit and watch . . . would have been intolerable"). In some respects, it isn't possible to reconcile these origin narratives, so the information provided by writer Robert Holmes tends to win out over other, contradictory material written for television by Terrance Dicks, Malcolm Hulke, and script editor Andrew Cartmel. In addition to the clues to the Doctor's past provided in the series itself, Eric Saward, Marc Platt, Kim Newman, and an array of writers of non-canonical novel and audio drama tie-in products have crafted several possible "origin" stories for the Doctor set before the first episode. Several of the different narratives contradict one another. Arguably the best of them is Newman's book "Time and Relative" (2002), which focuses on Susan Foreman's life in England before the first episode of the series. The non-canonical audio adventures "Auld Mortality" (2003) and "The Beginning" (2013), by Platt, concern how the Doctor and Susan left Gallifrey. One scholar, Jon Preddle, has come closer than anyone else to providing a comprehensive biography of the Doctor, and history of the *Doctor Who* universe, in *Timelink*, a two-volume tome that strives to resolve all narrative inconsistencies in the series and forge a cohesive series mythology. Combining evidence given in the canonical television adventures and the non-canonical books and audio adventures, some fans speculate that the Doctor's real name is the one given to him by series writers Terrance Dicks and Malcolm Hulke in a non-canonical tie-in book: $\partial^3 \Sigma x^2$. Others speculate that the Doctor grew up named Theta Sigma of the house of Lungbarrow before he took the name of the Doctor. Still others think that his parents named him Basil after Sherlock Holmes actor Basil Rathbone. A minority opinion holds that his mother was human and he always hid his half-human heritage from the Master out of fear of the Master's racism. These differing theories aside, critic Sue Short argues that recent writers Davies and Moffat have revealed far more about the Doctor's past than previous writers and unintentionally changed the nature of the series.[7] Indeed, the 2015 episode "Hell Bent" presents what appears to be Moffat's definitive explanation for why the Doctor fled his home: he learned of a prophecy that he was destined to become a destructive, monstrous force in the universe, and fled home in an *Oedipus Rex*–style effort to avoid seeing the prophecy come true. And yet, the prophecy—which, ironically, he ran *toward* fulfilling, instead of *from* fulfilling—may provide *part* of the answer to the question "Why did the Doctor leave Gallifrey?" although that does not mean it provides the *full* explanation.

## The Daleks: An Iconic, Neofascist Menace

Fan theories and "Hell Bent" notwithstanding, one of the central questions of the series has always been: "What initiating incident inspired the Doctor to steal a Type 40 TARDIS and leave his home world?" Whatever his reasons for abandoning his people, the Doctor chose to steal the TARDIS at around 236-years old and traveled for approximately 189 years before he and Susan decided to build lives for themselves in exile upon the Earth of the 1960s. He was a 425-year-old alien who appeared to be a human in his early sixties (when played by actor William Hartnell). Susan's real age was never disclosed, but she looked sixteen and told humans she met that that was her age.[8] The Doctor chose Earth as his replacement home because he perceived that British humans were enough like the Time Lords that he could relate to them, although he also felt superior to them and harbored racist feelings. When Susan attempted to blend into swinging sixties youth culture by listening to pop music and enrolling in the Coal Hill School in Shoreditch, the Doctor opposed the idea but didn't stop her. Thanks to the relationship he developed with Susan's schoolteachers, Ian and Barbara, the Doctor grew less racist and isolationist over time and interacted more and more with human society. He came to wish that he could find ways to steer humanity away from its self-destructive and warlike impulses, and to prevent humans from becoming as corrupt as the Time Lords. In the process, he would hope to suppress within himself the same streak of fascism that he saw in both humans and Time Lords.

As critic Philip Sandifer has observed, "So much of the early days of *Doctor Who* is bound up in a fear of fascism, not as a political ideology, but as a sort of gravitational tendency to which society succumbs. Stories in *Doctor Who*'s early days aren't just concerned with fascism, but with its ability to creep up into otherwise decent societies. . . . It's important to recognize this as a change in how fascism was thought about. . . . Hitler had been dead for almost twenty-years, and Stalin, the second-choice evil tyrant, had been dead a decade. Totalitarianism was no longer understood as an imminent threat, but an existential one. The question stopped becoming 'how will we fight these specific fascists?' and rather became a concern for how fascism started in the first place, starting from the observation that it was something that appeared in

Germany."[9] This "gravitational tendency" to fascism found in "civilized" countries is the very reason Tolkien was leery of democracies, romanticized rural feudalism in his fiction, and proclaimed himself a philosophical anarchist in his private letters. As Tolkien put it: "I am not a 'democrat,' if only because 'humility' and equality are spiritual principles corrupted by the attempt to mechanize and formalize them, with the result that we get not universal smallness and humility, but universal greatness and pride, til some Orc gets hold of a ring of power—and then we get (and are getting) slavery."[10]

The Time Lords had been fascists once, when the morally ambiguous founder of Time Lord civilization, Rassilon, turned wholly evil, and were always capable of becoming fascists again. Humans were the same. The Doctor feared his own potential to become a fascist. The Daleks, however, were cyborgs from the planet Skaro who were *programmed* to be fascists by their mad creator Davros, so it was natural that they became the Doctor's most hated enemy. Aside from the Great Vampires, a race of beings also much like the Time Lords, the Daleks became the Time Lord's only significant rival for control of the empire of Time itself. Since the Daleks are both a physical, external threat as well as a symbolic and psychological representation of the Doctor's own capacity for evil, they serve the same dramatic function in the *Doctor Who* universe that the Orcs do in the Middle-earth tales. Like the Orcs of Middle-earth and the N.I.C.E. villains of Lewis's *That Hideous Strength*, the Daleks want to remake creation in their image. They are an expansionist culture that believes in converting all life into Dalek life and remaking all natural environments into the all-metal cityscapes they were designed for.

Originally, the Daleks had been human in appearance. When they were the Kaled people of Skaro, they lived in a green world. Tragically, generations of warfare between the Kaleds and the Thals turned Skaro into a radioactive wasteland. The two races reached the brink of extinction, yet both sides continued to court mutually assured destruction by endlessly attacking one another. Considering the possibility that the extreme levels of radiation on the planet would accelerate already-evident extremes of mutation and eventually kill off all his people, the chief Kaled scientist Davros decided to artificially mutate all the surviving Kaleds on his terms. He produced in his lab what he posited would be the ultimate evolutionary destiny of his people—a blobby, tentacled, monoptoid creature. He determined that the weak, sickly mutant he grew in the lab could survive the radiation of Skaro indefinitely if he merged it cybernetically to a tank-like, ambulatory life-support system: the Dalek battle armor and Dalek battle computer. Thanks to Davros's genetic and computer programming, any Kaled mutant placed in the Dalek casing is brainwashed by the battle-computer into embracing a hive-minded form of fascism dreamed up by Davros. The new, cyborg life form produced when mutant meets battle computer instantly loses all compassion, individuality, and—to a large degree—free will. The Dalek is not devoid of emotion. It is devoid of kindness, love, empathy, mercy, irony, and humor. When Davros first planned the design of the Dalek, he determined that he was working toward the preservation of his people, and for their expansion into the stars, so he saw himself as servicing the cause of galactic peace and eternal life. Unfortunately, he felt that the best way to achieve galactic peace was to order the Daleks to conquer all planets and to convert all animal life into Dalek life. All plant life was to be eradicated and all worlds converted into Coruscant- or Cybertron-style all-city, all-metal planets. These themes do not appear in all Dalek stories, but they are prominent in two. In "The Dalek Invasion of Earth" (1964) the Daleks' goal is to destroy "all living matter" and transform the Earth into a pilotable spaceship. In "Revelation of the Daleks" (1985), the Daleks capture humans being held in suspended animation in a pseudo-medical facility and transform them into Daleks; one of their grotesquely mutated victims shouts to his horrified daughter "We shall all become Daleks!" Themes such as these are more frequently explored in stories with the villainous Cybermen, but they are woven into the Dalek mythology as well.

Davros's original plan was for the first few generations of Daleks to remain sequestered in the Kaled capital city and grow accustomed to their new bodies by remaining safely in an indoor habitat ideal for them. The smooth metal floors and walls of the city conducted a static electricity that powered the Dalek exterior and allowed them to glide about effortlessly on obstruction-free surfaces in their salt shaker–shaped tank/wheelchairs. Eventually, they fitted energy-relay satellite dishes to their backs that enabled them to venture outdoors. The natural world that greeted them when they

Fig. 3.4. In "The Daleks" (1963), the Doctor (William Hartnell), his granddaughter Susan (Carole Ann Ford), and their injured friend Ian Chesterton (William Russell) encounter the Daleks for the first time on the planet Skaro. They are expansionist beings who believe in converting all life into Dalek life and remaking all natural environments into the all-metal cityscape habitats they were designed to thrive in. BBC.

finally left the Kaled city irritated them, however. They were unable to move about with ease on Skaro—or on the surface of any other world they found when they developed the capacity for space travel. On whatever world they landed, they were disgusted with the indigenous peoples they met and the natural landscapes they encountered. They could never move with ease over grass, rock, or inside buildings constructed with stairs. The Daleks worked around these problems by developing more sophisticated ways of powering themselves and upgrading themselves to hover in the air. Even with these adaptations, their first instinct was to hate the natural world. They strove to convert each new landscape they encountered into a mirror of their Kaled city back home. Any indigenous persons who welcomed conversion would be turned into Daleks. Any who resisted would be enslaved or exterminated like vermin. In some respects, the Daleks are parodies of the most ruthless Christian missionaries, who used convert-or-die tactics when trying to "civilize" the aboriginal tribes inhabiting colonial lands, and who brought disease, genocide, settler colonialism, and deforestation wherever they went.[11]

## Is the Doctor Running from His Own Fascist Tendencies?

One of the most powerful species in the universe, the Time Lords see themselves as benign rulers, even when they veer between benign neglect and self-serving intervention into the destinies of "lesser" races. Since there is another race of beings in the cosmos that is so evil by its nature, the Time Lords can congratulate themselves that they act as a force for good in keeping the Daleks' evil in check. What the Time Lords do not acknowledge is that, by judging their own worth against the barometer of the Dalek race, they are holding themselves hostage to such low standards that they are not good compared with the Daleks—only marginally less evil. From certain perspectives, the Time Lords are *far more evil*, especially because they are not genetically programmed to be fascists but choose to be fascists with their own free will.

Knowing that the Doctor hates the Daleks more than he hates his own people, the Time Lords have had occasion to call upon him in his adult life—reconnecting with him after his dramatic departure from Gallifrey—to challenge the Daleks on their behalf. On one such occasion, they recruited him to go back in time and prevent their creation ("Genesis of the Daleks"). He agreed to the mission, but found himself unable to blow up the lab in which Davros was transforming the people of Skaro into Daleks. The Doctor felt that he did not have the right to allegorically "kill Hitler as a baby to prevent World War II" because it would be issuing the punishment before the crime was committed. The Time Lords were furious with his soft-heartedness here, but he later halted a Dalek invasion of Gallifrey ("The Apocalypse Element," a 2000 Big Finish audio drama). Furthermore, as the Doctor grew older and more ruthless, he developed fewer qualms about mass-slaughtering Daleks in the name of avenging the genocides that they themselves had carried out—and to prevent future genocides that they planned to commit. In "Remembrance of the Daleks" (1988), the Doctor allows the Daleks to gain possession of dangerous Time Lord technology, the Hand of Omega, because he knows they are too ignorant of its mysteries to operate it properly. When he goads them into attempting to use it before they have had the chance to study it, they accidentally annihilate their entire fleet and their home planet. In doing this, the Doctor smites the Daleks with the same self-righteous wrath that fueled God's wiping away of the Nazis at the end of *Raiders of the Lost Ark* (1981). It is an act appropriate for an incarnation of the Doctor that often hints he is *a* god, if not *the* God (the seventh Doctor, Sylvester McCoy).

Understandably, the writer of "Remembrance of the Daleks," Ben Aaronovitch, shows little sympathy for Nazis, real or fictional, so he grants the Doctor the moral authority to kill Daleks on a grand scale. Other writers who penned adventures for the Doctor were less certain that the Doctor had the right to kill so many Daleks.

In "Dalek" (2005) by Robert Shearman, the Doctor encounters a Dalek that incorrectly believes itself to be the last Dalek in existence. Lost without a military cause to sustain it, the Dalek is uncertain what to do and looks to the Doctor to act as its new commanding officer.

THE DOCTOR: All right then. If you want orders, follow this one: Kill yourself.

DALEK: The Daleks must survive!

THE DOCTOR: The Daleks have failed! Why don't you finish the job, and make the Daleks extinct? Rid the universe of your filth! Why don't you just *die*?

DALEK: [pause] You would make a good Dalek.

Whether the Doctor's ruthlessness when he fights the Daleks—adopting fascist tactics to fight fascism—is an appropriate response to a cosmic-level, Nazi-like menace or a sign of the darkening of the Doctor's character and embracing of Time Lord ways becomes ambiguous in later episodes. Perhaps the Doctor's employment of the Hand of Omega as a honey trap in "Remembrance of the Daleks" would make him worthy of the warrior Time Lord mantle that his parents and professors at the Academy had always hoped he would don for himself. At the age of 953, and in season twenty-five of the original series, he was transforming into more of a warrior than a doctor. By this point in the series, the Doctor's character has come full circle, and he once again risks becoming as cold and ruthless as he was in his early days on Earth. In the seasons in between, he was far more of a hippie figure. But were those kindly sensibilities enough to offer a true challenge to evil? One of the questions that the series *Doctor Who* asks is: What manner of opposition can hippies give to fascists, both homegrown and abroad? Do antifascists all need to change into fascists themselves to more effectively combat fascism?

## Is the Doctor Jesus Christ or Aslan? The Influence of C. S. Lewis

I'm almost 2,000 years old. I'm old enough to be your Messiah.

—The Doctor, "The Zygon Inversion" (2015)

*Doctor Who* posits that it is best to meet the threat of Nazism with the wit, imagination, wisdom, joie de vivre, and secularized version of Christianity that the Doctor represents. The Doctor can inspire viewers to do good in their own lives by modeling goodness for them, and the goodness he represents is a combination of Christian, Buddhist, and secular humanist values mediated through the image of a British intellectual superhero who is an amalgam of Sherlock Holmes, Gandalf, Superman, and Jesus Christ. Several of the regeneration episodes of the series employ Christ symbolism, and none more overtly than the awakening of long-haired Paul McGann's eighth Doctor in a tomblike hospital morgue dressed in a Shroud of Turin–like corpse blanket in *Doctor Who: The Movie*. The Doctor is a Christ symbol—a riff on the "historic Jesus" of the Jesus Seminar who travels through time and space bringing intelligence, humor, and compassion to all he meets. The secular elements of the series mythology make it, in certain respects, an atheist's rewriting of *The Chronicles of Narnia* provided years before Philip Pullman. Therefore, like *His Dark Materials*, the *Doctor Who* narrative exists partly in tribute to Lewis, but partly as a secularized revision of Lewis that Lewis himself would not have appreciated. As John Beversluis argued in *C. S. Lewis and the Search for Rational Religion* (1985), Lewis did not approve of efforts to demythologize Christ in any way, nor did he like efforts to discover the historic Jesus, or attempts to view Jesus as "a great moral teacher" instead of as God.[12] For one thing, Lewis believed that Jesus Christ was, indeed, God, so he regarded any assertion to the contrary as a dangerous error. For another, any view of Jesus as a moral teacher suggests that Christ's overwhelming moral decree that all humans need to love God, love themselves, love their neighbors, love their enemies, and love all plant and animal life on Earth can merely be regarded as *quite good advice* that can be acted upon, discarded, or ignored depending on one's mood. A message such as that given to the world by a mere mortal can be warped and turned into self-serving propaganda instead of followed humbly and religiously and with the full commitment of an honest and faithful heart. This would most likely be Lewis's position on *Doctor Who*—that it would look and feel like a story he would write, but that it would unintentionally support the ideologies his work was crafted to challenge.

In the early 1960s, the many minds behind the development and creation of the series *Doctor Who* did, indeed, read Lewis's works, and they gleaned several tropes and themes from them. However, they made a conscious decision to discard the religious allegory, especially since many of those on the production team were not Christian, and several felt that the Christian content of *The Space Trilogy* was out of place in a science fiction adventure that should, one might think, promote science over religion. "But where ideas were rejected, others were borrowed," Marcus K. Harmes wrote in *Doctor*

*Who and the Art of Adaptation: Fifty Years of Storytelling* (2013). "The original idea of the TARDIS, which from the outset was to be visually manifested as an ordinary and everyday object (hence the use of a police telephone box exterior) was filtered through C.E. Webber's mind as something akin to the 'magic door' in Lewis Carroll's *Alice through the Looking Glass* and the magical portal in the uncle's house in C. S. Lewis' *The Lion, the Witch, and the Wardrobe*. The adaptive influences do not stop there."[13]

One narrative of the birth of the series was written by Mark Gatiss for the docudrama *An Adventure in Space and Time* (2013), starring Jessica Raine and Brian Cox as the co-creators of the series, Verity Lambert (the first producer) and Sydney Newman (the head of BBC drama who commissioned the series, hired Lambert, and exerted a notable degree of creative control). The film suggests that the production team shook up the staid halls of the BBC by creating a subversive television series infused with their own counterculture values. Gatiss emphasizes Lambert's trailblazing role as the BBC's first female producer, Newman's Jewish-Canadian verve and business sense, and the bigotry directed against the gay, British Indian director of the early

Fig. 3.5. Made in celebration of *Doctor Who*'s fiftieth anniversary, the film *An Adventure in Space and Time* (2013) is a "based-on-a-true-story" dramatization of the collaborative creation of the BBC series. The film's narrative concentrates on the life of William Hartnell, the first actor to play the Doctor, as well as depicts the efforts of the series' first producer, Verity Lambert, and first director, Waris Hussein, to launch the unlikely classic. Pictured above: Sacha Dhawan as Hussein and Jessica Raine as Lambert. BBC.

episodes, Waris Hussein. The docudrama intimates that the BBC's WASP establishment marginalized the production team, making them as much maligned outsiders in its halls as the Doctor was among his own people in the fictional universe they created. Some of the docudrama's construction of television production history has been questioned, especially its underrepresentation of the role of scriptwriters such as David Whitaker in creating the series mythology.[14] Though that is a valid complaint, Lambert and Newman deserve a lot of credit for creating the series. When Newman became head of BBC drama in 1962, he brought with him a populist sensibility, a concern that working-class characters be represented sympathetically, and a desire to move away from elitist subjects that lionized the upper classes. All of this inspired him to champion the notion of creating a populist time travel science fiction series that depicted real science and real social history. Alan Kistler writes, "By his own admission to his colleagues, Newman cared little for classic literature anyway, preferring science fiction books, so he decided on [creating] a science fiction program featuring heroic figures. He once stated, 'I love them [science fiction stories] because they're a marvelous way—and a safe way, I might add—of saying nasty things about our own society.' Newman envisioned a show with a broad premise adaptable to practically any kind of story. As many later remarked, he wanted to follow the old BBC adage that broadcast programming was meant 'to inform, educate, and entertain.'"[15]

Newman enlisted the aid of C. E. Webber, who wrote many novel adaptations for the BBC, in researching existing science fiction genre material, including the successful *Quatermass* serial from ten years before, and offered suggestions concerning what kind of series they could produce. At the end of his research, he observed several flaws in the genre that he was eager to avoid reproducing in *Doctor Who*:

1. [Science Fiction] S.F. deliberately avoids character-in-depth. In S.F. the characters are almost interchangeable. We must use fully conceived characters.

2. S.F. is deliberately unsexual; women are not really necessary to it. We must add feminine interest as a consequence of creating real characters.

3. Because of the above conditions, S.F. does not consider moral conflict. It has one clear overall meaning: that human beings in general are incapable of controlling the forces they set free.[16]

The first episode of *Doctor Who*—"An Unearthly Child," written by Anthony Coburn—shows a strong interest in creating a sense of mystery, moral conflict, sharply defined characters, and a notable role for women. The plot involves high school history teacher Barbara Wright becoming concerned that her gifted pupil Susan Foreman is somehow being manipulated or abused by her reclusive, overbearing grandfather. She coaxes her colleague, science teacher Ian Chesterton, to follow Susan to her home—located, somewhat oddly, on the grounds of a junkyard business, I. M. Foreman Scrap

Merchants. The teachers hope to stage a form of intervention in which they hope to pressure Susan's grandfather to afford the young girl more autonomy. While prying into Susan's life, they discover the TARDIS, learn that the Doctor and Susan are aliens, and the Doctor kidnaps them to keep them from alerting the human authorities to his and Susan's presence on Earth. In this first episode, lead actor William Hartnell offers a brilliant portrayal of the Doctor as an antihero, if not a villain. The Doctor's behavior is evocative of the explorers and kidnappers featured in the Lewis novels *Out of the Silent Planet* and *The Magician's Nephew*, and he does not act much like either Aslan or Gandalf in the early Lambert serials.

Susan has cultivated enormous affection for the two schoolteachers she had gotten to know so well while she tried vainly to blend in to native culture during her exile in the 1960s. However, her grandfather is racist against humans and only develops a grudging acceptance of them when they save his life, repeatedly, during the adventures that follow. He is impressed by the bravery they exhibit when he encounters the Daleks for the first time on Skaro. However, the ruthless Doctor is more concerned with his own survival—and with acquiring "fuel" for his TARDIS—than with helping the indigenous peoples of Skaro whom the Daleks are threatening to wipe from existence. It remains troubling viewing for fans that are used to the character often being portrayed as unambiguously good in later adventures. Kistler observes, "The core of the Doctor's character was still being formed. While Sydney Newman did not like the Doctor seeming dangerous, Lambert believed it was an excellent quality. But instead of having him act with deliberate malice, she suggested that the Doctor have obvious character flaws that invited or created danger: insensitivity, overconfidence, a short temper, and an occasionally narrow-minded focus on his goals. She also wanted the character to have a child-like spirit to counter these flaws, believing the paradox of his personality would interest older viewers. 'I rather liked the cantankerous bit,' Lambert told *Dreamwatch* in 2004. 'Getting [people] into terrible scrapes because he wouldn't listen, and always thinking he knew best. But when he was being sweet, he was quite touching and vulnerable.'"[17]

The Doctor's dark side was not the only major point of creative difference between Lambert and Newman. Lambert advocated the inclusion of the Daleks into the series, liking both the commentary they made on fascism and Raymond Cusick's inspired, Art Deco design for the creature's metal, silver and blue, salt shaker–shaped exterior. Newman thought they were ridiculous-looking "Bug-Eyed Monsters" and not educational enough to teach real science or real history. Lambert's view carried the day. The popularity of the Daleks was enormous, ensured the survival of the series, and turned them into British cultural institutions. Meanwhile, in the universe of the series, the Daleks helped Barbara and Ian gradually coax the Doctor into transforming from antihero to hero. The first Dalek-themed serial was followed up with one that would be key in the character development of the Doctor.

Tensions between the Doctor and the kidnapped schoolteachers come to a head in the third adventure, "The Edge of Destruction" (1964), when, in a moment of blind, racist paranoia, the Doctor mistakenly accuses Ian and Barbara of sabotaging the TARDIS to blackmail him into returning them to Earth. The Doctor threatens to eject the teachers into the void of the space/time continuum, killing them, and even coaxes Susan into considering the murder as a wise option. Ian and Barbara are only humans after all. When Barbara explains the real cause of the malfunction, vindicating herself and Ian, she shows the Doctor the error of his ways. Her intelligence, decency, and strength of will shame him into reassessing the humans he was bigoted against. The mistake compels the Doctor to gaze into his own soul, and he dislikes what he sees. He had left his home planet because he was disgusted with Time Lord "superiority" and found that he had brought much of that same superiority with him to Earth and used it as a justification for repeatedly harming Ian and Barbara. Though he has a friendly*ish* rivalry with Ian, he has found himself developing an affection for Barbara and is pained by his constant ill treatment of her. After this point, he makes a genuine effort to become a kinder, less prejudiced person.

Barbara also coaxes the Doctor to become more interventionist in his travels, and not to stand by when he can attempt to educate cultures, improve them, or prevent them being wiped out by an imminent invasion. Initially, he is resistant to the example she sets of humanitarian interventionism. In the sixth adventure, "The Aztecs" (1964), written by John Lucarotti, Barbara is willing to go as far as pose as an Aztec god to convince the Aztec people to give up performing human sacrifices. She posits that, if the Aztecs grow beyond a human sacrifice–based form of worship, they will be too civilized for Hernán Cortés to feel justified in destroying. Her intervention in history *could* prevent their extinction. The Doctor understands her good intentions, objects to her hubris, and declares, "You can't rewrite history! Not one line! Barbara, one last appeal: what you are trying to do is utterly impossible. I know! Believe me, I know!" His allusion to a traumatic event in his past goes unexplained, but Barbara proceeds with her plan, undeterred. When she fails in her endeavor, the Doctor comforts her. He decides from that point forward to do what he can to intervene, but to try not to mimic Barbara's hubris or cultural arrogance. He also finesses his opinion on the potential for changing the course of history in time travel, eventually understanding that time can, indeed, be rewritten, though some points in time, some events, are more fixed than others and harder, if not impossible, to alter.

Since he converted to Barbara's worldview, the Doctor's interventionist actions across all of time and space have had mixed results within the universe of the series, and may be interpreted in a variety of ways by cultural studies scholars. Piers D. Britton and Simon J. Barker have argued that there is a cognitive dissonance between the series' representation of the Doctor as colonial Gothic hero—"a leisured gentleman traveler" and "self-important moral arbiter"—and its preachy moments when it condemns the very "xenophobia, colonialism, and racial intolerance" that the Doctor appears to embody.[18] The scholars point to this problem throughout the series, but they target Jon Pertwee's Doctor as paternalistic—a clever rhetorical strategy since his Doctor is oft regarded by fans as one of the most progressive, so if his politics are reactionary, then the politics of the other lives of the Doctor are still more so. For example, in one poorly written Pertwee-era episode—1974's "Death to the Daleks"—the Doctor encounters the indigenous people of the planet Exxilon, and they are grunting religious fanatics who kill strangers on sight, perform human sacrifices to tribal gods, and persecute and execute religious dissenters. Shortly after the Doctor and the humans have made it clear that they view the Exxilons with utter contempt, the Daleks land on this planet and enslave and exterminate the Exxilons in a troubling segment that evokes sympathy for the Exxilons. One native, Bellal, is an articulate religious dissenter who helps the Doctor; he is a sympathetic enough character but is, essentially, an infantilized local collaborator suffering from a false consciousness. Overall, "Death to the Daleks" is not one of science fiction's better examples of how to portray indigenous peoples in an enlightened manner, even if the narrative condemns the Daleks for slaughtering them.

Britton and Barker are correct about the Doctor's paternalism and the series' divided consciousness concerning the colonial legacy of Great Britain. The writers of the 2005 revival series are aware enough of this critique of the classic series to respond to it by building a deconstructionist take on the character into the revival series' stories themselves, thereby embracing the moral ambivalence as an opportunity for drama. When their scripts work best, they evoke this cognitive dissonance deliberately to excellent effect. When their scripts don't work, the stories collapse into dramatic and ideological incoherence. Much of my reading of the Doctor's internal conflict comes from Moffat's scripts, which exploit the concept that the Doctor is an anticolonialist colonialist and an atheistic Christ figure. The Doctor's ethical code is an uncomfortable hybrid of patriarchal and matriarchal value systems and he vacillates between the two ideological allegiances. Whether his efforts are successful or not, Moffat is engaged in a project of attempting to turn Britton and Barker's indictment of the series and the character in on itself, use it to complicate the series narrative, and transform the series into a more sophisticated iteration of the classic Joseph Campbell "Hero's Journey" motif (by way of *Star Wars*).

## The Last Great Time War and the Wars against Morgoth

Nazis! I *hate* these guys.

—Indiana Jones, *Indiana Jones and the Last Crusade*

One of the central problems the Doctor faces is the question of how violent he should be when protecting innocent people from attacks launched against them by the forces of evil. If he meets violence with violence and uses evil tactics against evil, he could mar his own soul and participate in a conflict that could cause apocalyptic levels of collateral damage—the loss of countless lives and the despoiling of the environment around the battlefield. This moral crisis is one that arises time and again in the works of J. R. R. Tolkien. In Tolkien's universe, evil seems to bring with it environmental degradation and destruction, not just resulting from specific actions but as a hallmark and consequence of the presence of evil itself. Tragically, when forces of good ally themselves to challenge evil and fight it to protect the environment, the resultant war causes additional, often irreparable, environmental destruction. Tolkien's experience in World War I gave him a firsthand perspective of how war can scar the Earth—a theme that appears in his works repeatedly. Tolkien biographer Humphrey Carpenter wrote that Tolkien, a signaler, had expected to contribute to the war effort by sending and receiving critical communiques with functioning equipment far from flying bullets. Instead, he was in the thick of the action, managing barely functioning equipment and carrier pigeons. "Worst of all were the dead men, for corpses lay in every corner, horribly torn by the shells. Those that still had faces stared with dreadful eyes. Beyond the trenches no-man's land was littered with bloated and decaying bodies. All around was desolation. Grass and corn had vanished in a sea of mud. Trees, stripped of leaf and branch, stood as mere mutilated and blackened trunks. Tolkien never forgot what he called the 'animal horror; of trench warfare.' "[19]

Tolkien's depiction of Lucifer is the Vala born with the name Melkor who eventually became known as Morgoth. In the early parts of *The Silmarillion*, the Valar become aware of Melkor's presence on the Earth—which he calls "Arda"—when green and growing things start to wither and die. They feel that they have to combat Melkor to prevent him from devastating Arda, but confronting him causes a military engagement that does still further damage to the planet. The Valar seek Melkor out to drive him from Arda, but he launches an attack before they are ready, and nearly despoils the entire world. He "came suddenly forth to war, and struck the first blow, ere the Valar were prepared; and he assailed the lights of Illuin and Ormal, and cast down their pillars and broke their lamps. In the overthrow of the mighty pillars the lands were broken and seas arose in tumult; and when the lamps were spilled destroying flame was spilled out over the Earth. And the shape of Arda and the symmetry of its lands and waters was marred in that time, so that the first designs of the Valar were never after restored." Almaren, the Valar's first dwelling place, is destroyed. The great landmass is shattered into different continents that become separated from each other; Middle-earth is the largest of these, but across the sea from it is Aman. The Valar cannot pursue Melkor, however, because they must use all their power to stem the tide of destruction and fix the world as best they can. After this apocalyptic clash, the Valar don't want to go to war against Melkor again because the war would do further damage to the world and could prevent the rising of Elves and Men.

Over time, the evils Melkor visited upon the world become so numerous that he earns the name Morgoth, which means "the Black Foe of the World." Finally, centuries later, the Valar come forth to defeat Morgoth once and for all in what is known as the War of Wrath. Morgoth is defeated after forty years of struggle against an alliance of all the Elves of Valinor, the Valar themselves, and many of the Maiar. Morgoth loses, and is chained and cast out into the void, not to return until the Dagor Dagorath, the Battle of Battles at the end of the World. The forces of good prevail against the armies of darkness, but much of the western part of Middle-earth, known as Beleriand, is destroyed.

After the War of Wrath, the Valar decide they cannot go forth to war like that again because of the destruction it wrought upon the world. Consequently, they take a subtler approach to confronting Melkor's chief lieutenant, Sauron, and send the five wizards to intercede, Gandalf included. They do this to avoid a repeat of what has happened in the past every time they went to war. This subtler approach is justifiable because Sauron, even at the peak of his power, is significantly less powerful than Melkor, and most of the deadliest creatures Melkor created, such as Balrogs and Dragons, were destroyed in the War of Wrath, so Elves and Men could fight Sauron and hope to win, while only the Valar could defeat Melkor.

In the universe of *Doctor Who*, the largest conflict ever fought—and the closest parallel to the wars between the good Valar and Morgoth—is the Time War: the conflict between the Time Lords and the Daleks that escalates to end-of-times Biblical proportions. The war had drawn into its scope all races in all time zones and the conflict threatened to set all of creation aflame, rending apart the space/time continuum. In "Night of the Doctor" (2013), a flashback episode with the Paul McGann Doctor, viewers learn that the Doctor had kept out of the Time War as a conscientious objector, but his efforts to save a soldier fighting in it has cost him his eighth life. As he regenerates, he concludes, reluctantly, that it is time he adopted a more ruthless, violent persona in his next life so he can enter the fray and bring the war to a swift and successful conclusion. Unfortunately, his next incarnation, the hitherto unknown War Doctor (John Hurt), fails to do either. The war rages on for far longer and countless lives are lost. When the Daleks again invade Gallifrey, it seems as if the Time Lords will lose the war. It also becomes clear to the War Doctor that, whatever the outcome of the battle, all of creation is doomed. Rather than let this happen, the War Doctor returns to his favorite childhood haunt, a lonely barn on his family land, and unleashes a weapon of mass destruction that destroys Gallifrey, killing every Dalek and taking all the Time Lords with them—except for himself ("Day of the Doctor").

That act of genocide psychologically devastates the Doctor. Even though he was aware of just how evil his people had become, he cannot forgive himself for the sheer number of lives he took with that act, including his own mother (played by Claire Bloom in "The End of Time"), who supported his decision, and the 2.47 billion children of Gallifrey. In the aftermath of the Time War, the Doctor assumes that all his Time Lord family, friends, and enemies are lost. Since the War Doctor was his ninth life and the aftermath of the destruction of Gallifrey has triggered his regeneration into his tenth (Christopher Eccleston), the Doctor is closing in on his final few lives. He is the last of his kind. He will be dead soon and his people will be a memory.

Unlike the Master, who would never accept that he had run out of lives, the Doctor made no attempt to find a magic wand solution to the problem of extending his life cycle or birthing a new generation of Time Lords. Instead, he lied to himself, told little of this to his companions, and continued his travels, convinced that his

Fig. 3.6. In the fiftieth anniversary special "The Day of the Doctor" (2013), the Doctor (John Hurt) concludes that, if the Last Great Time War is allowed to continue to its bitter end, all of creation is doomed. Rather than let this happen, he returns to a lonely barn on his family land and unleashes a weapon of mass destruction that destroys his home planet, Gallifrey, wiping both the Daleks and Time Lords from existence with the press of a button on a seemingly unremarkable box. BBC.

race deserved nothing better than a lonely walk to extinction. The Eccleston Doctor was the first to lie to himself and his companions about his true age and which life he was living, ignoring his War Doctor incarnation and dialing his age back to nine hundred, which was how old he was when he first learned (during "The Trial of a Time Lord") just how evil the Time Lords were. After Eccleston's Doctor died, actor David Tennant played the Doctor's next two lifetimes. In the 2009 adventure "The End of Time," the Doctor regenerated for the twelfth time into his thirteenth life, and Tennant was replaced by Matt Smith. Another sign of the Doctor's lying to himself was his subconscious choice to regenerate into his youngest body yet during his final life, symbolically promising a longevity that was tantamount to a lie. During his final life, the Doctor gradually accepts the inevitability of his death and is bombarded by prophecies of his own demise but keeps his companions unaware that he is dying. He only manages to mention to Clara that he is about to die a permanent death when his final body is old and withered ("Time of the Doctor"). The news is shocking to Clara, but she becomes the vehicle for the magic wand solution that undoes the Doctor's greatest error and results in the recharging of the Doctor's life cycle. In "The Day of the Doctor," fate intervenes and—thanks to the miracle of time travel—the final incarnations of the Doctor find themselves reunited with the War Doctor shortly before he is about to destroy Gallifrey. The War Doctor glimpses his own future and sees the burden of guilt borne by his future lives—which has made these Doctors more manic, childish, and haunted than any of his previous lifetimes' personas. This encounter, plus a timely intervention by Clara, encourages the Doctor's many selves to decide, collectively, to change their personal history and the history of the universe. The War Doctor opts not to destroy Gallifrey after all. Instead, all the Doctor's personas come together to find a way to teleport Gallifrey to another dimension—somewhere even he doesn't know how to reach—placing it out of the reach of the Daleks. The Time War comes to an end with the Gallifreyan retreat.

The resurrected Time Lords thank the Doctor by giving him a new supply of regenerations that may, indeed, be limitless this time. Consequently, when the Matt Smith Doctor dies, he regenerates in the Peter Capaldi Doctor, the fourteenth life that is widely misidentified as the Twelfth Doctor (even by official BBC documentation). This new Doctor is physically older, cantankerous, urbane, unsentimental, scarred by memories of war, and proud of being two-thousand-years old. However, he worries that he can no longer consider himself a good person. He may have undone his most heinous war crime, but there is still much blood on his hands. Capaldi's Doctor has promised himself never to become the War Doctor again, yet worries that he has endless potential to fall from grace.

Considering this extended narrative as a piece, there is both a charitable and an uncharitable way of looking at the Doctor's attitude toward his own impending death, especially during his "final" life as the Matt Smith Doctor. Admirably, the Doctor was willing to allow his final life to expire. He wasn't looking for a way to renew his regeneration cycle, like the vampiric Master has done in the past, but was bowing to the natural order of things in a Tolkienesque manner. For Tolkien, embracing the impermanence of life is one of the essential differences between good and evil. Evil tries to control and shape the world, whether through magic or through industry and technology and the glorification of individual creation over God's creation. That is the nature of Darth Vader's evil in *Star Wars*. It is the nature of Voldemort's evil in *Harry Potter*. To a degree, the Doctor's struggle over whether he is a good or bad person is driven by his unwillingness to give up control. The more he strives to shape things to his own ends, the more he strays from his moral core. So, his decision to accept his own approaching death can be seen almost like a final conversion away from that—an acceptance of the natural order of things. In accepting that—in surrendering the bid for control—he's giving in to nature, because death is a part of nature. For his part, when the Doctor accepts his place, accepts his own approaching death, and puts his faith in the way nature is supposed to unfold, he is in fact rewarded with more lives, which he did not ask for and may not have wanted. Interestingly, Moffat's decision to keep the character alive forever cheapens the Doctor's decision to stop fighting the natural order.

There is also an uncharitable view that might be taken of the Doctor's attitude toward coming to the end of his regeneration cycle during the period between "Rose" and "The Time of the Doctor." By allowing the Doctor to have a magic wand solution to both problems—the destruction of Gallifrey and the end of his regeneration cycle—the series presents a fantasy solution to unsolvable problems. In the real world, actions have consequences and death is final and inevitable. In *Doctor Who*, if you make a mistake, don't worry. If someone you love dies, don't worry. If the planet dies, don't worry. The TARDIS can make it all better. At the least, the unsolvable problems that were "solved" on *Doctor Who* should not have been dealt with so easily and at so little cost to the Doctor. MacGuffins can fix problems in fantasy and science fiction. They don't work so well in reality. Of course, it would be nice to have a magic wand solution to mass extinctions, glacial melt, and the warming of the planet. However, facing humanity's end in the real world will not be so simple. One thing that mitigates the wish-fulfillment absurdity of many of Moffat's scripts—from the resurrection of Madge Arwell's husband in "The Doctor, the Widow, and the Wardrobe" to the return of Gallifrey—is the Doctor's admission in both "The Husbands of River Song" and "Twice Upon a Time" that his victories over Death are destined to only ever be temporary and that he will always outlive those he loves. Another thing that makes some of the undoing/"retconning" of the Doctor's biggest mistakes acceptable is the extent to which the Doctor, the lifelong student with the world's largest undergraduate scarf, does seem to learn something from his past mistakes. What he learns is that war is always futile and wasteful and should always be prevented. And, when he encounters two races set on a seemingly inevitable course of mutually assured destruction (the humans and the Zygons), he explains to them why they need to broker a peace instead of starting a war:

> Every war ever fought . . . is always the same. When you fire that first shot, no matter how right you feel, you have no idea who's going to die. You don't know whose children are going to scream and burn. How many hearts will be broken! How many lives shattered! How much blood will spill until everybody does what they're always going to have to do from the very beginning—sit down and talk! Listen to me, listen . . . I fought in a bigger war than you will ever know. I did worse things than you could ever imagine, and when I close my eyes . . . I hear more screams than anyone could ever be able to count! And do you know what you do with all that pain? Shall I tell you where you put it? You hold it tight . . . Til it burns your hand. And you say this—no one else will ever have to live like this. No one else will ever have to feel this pain. Not on my watch.

In some respects, this monologue is designed to be a final statement for the series, and the episode might well have been a fitting final episode. Of course, the series has continued, and the Doctor's fight for justice rages on—as does the series' moral and political ambivalence.

From a television production history perspective, the real-world motivations behind these storylines go far to explain their epic scope and implausible dramatic leaps. The return of Gallifrey was an epic narrative event that helped celebrate the series' fiftieth anniversary. It also removed from the show's internal history specific creative decisions made by Moffat's predecessor, writer/producer Russell T. Davies, that Moffat seems to have disagreed with: the decision to write Gallifrey out of the series and, in the process, transform the Doctor into one of the worst war criminals in the history of the series. Since returning to television in 2005, the Doctor has seemed a little too overtly evil to be recognizable as the same imperfect moral exemplar Lambert and Newman created him to be. Moffat's vision of the Doctor's heroism is certainly incompatible with the way he was written during the early Time War episodes by Russell T. Davies. So perhaps Moffatt wanted the Doctor rehabilitated to return the character to its more moral roots. Whether or not he saw the Time War story as a mishandling of the character, Moffat used the occasion of the Doctor's fiftieth anniversary to reflect upon his enduring cultural significance and on what moral values the Doctor should, at his best, champion. As Moffat observed in an oft-quoted and circulated internet meme:

> It's hard to talk about the importance of an imaginary hero. But heroes *are* important: Heroes tell us something about ourselves. History tells us who we used to be, documentaries tell us who we are now; but heroes tell us who we *want* to be. And a lot of our heroes depress me. But when they made this particular hero, they didn't give him a gun—they gave him a screwdriver to fix things. They didn't give him a tank or a warship or an X-Wing fighter—they gave him a box from which you can call for help. And they didn't give him a superpower or pointy ears or a heat-ray—they gave him an extra *heart*. They gave him two hearts! And that's an extraordinary thing. There will never come a time when we don't need a hero like the Doctor.

# 4

# Noah's Ark Revisited

## *2012* and Magic Lifeboats for the Wealthy

The apocalypse is not something which is coming. The apocalypse has arrived in major portions of the planet, and it's only because we live within a bubble of incredible privilege and social insulation that we still have the luxury of anticipating the apocalypse.

—Terence McKenna

And God saw that the wickedness of man was great in the earth, and that every imagination of the thoughts of his heart was only evil continually. And it repented the Lord that he had made man on the earth, and it grieved him at his heart. And the Lord said, I will destroy man whom I have created from the face of the earth; both man, and beast, and the creeping thing, and the fowls of the air; for it repenteth me that I have made them. But Noah found grace in the eyes of the Lord. . . . And the Lord said unto Noah, Come thou and all thy house into the ark; for thee have I seen righteous before me in this generation. Of every clean beast thou shalt take to thee by sevens, the male and his female: and of beasts that are not clean by two, the male and his female. Of fowls also of the air by sevens, the male and the female; to keep seed alive upon the face of all the earth. For yet seven days, and I will cause it to rain upon the earth forty days and forty nights; and every living substance that I have made will I destroy from off the face of the earth. And Noah did according unto all that the Lord commanded him. And Noah was six hundred years old when the flood of waters was upon the earth.

—Genesis 6:5–7:6

## The Flood: Tolkien's Recurring Nightmare

During Tolkien's childhood, he enjoyed happy times living with his mother Mabel and brother Hilary in a cottage in Sarehole. Tolkien read stories of dragons, played in the countryside, and loved his family deeply. However, Mabel had been disinherited from her family because of her conversion to Roman Catholicism, and she and the children lived in poverty, barely able to afford food. The daily pressures of caring for her family took a physical and emotional toll on Mabel, and she often looked noticeably ill. Happy as Tolkien was, his happiness was undercut by a sense of foreboding—a fear that he would soon lose his life in the cottage, and his mother to death. These omnipresent anxieties manifested themselves in a series of nightmares about a great flood, which rose to take all he loved away from him, including the trees he adored, his home, and his family. As Tolkien biographer Humphrey Carpenter explained, "The dream was to recur for many years. Later, he came to think of it as 'my Atlantis complex.'"[1]

Tolkien's childhood fears proved apt: he was soon removed from his rural home, and his mother died prematurely. The nightmare "of the ineluctable Wave, either coming up out of a quiet sea, or coming in towering over the green inlands" lingered well past the fulfillment of Tolkien's prophetic visions of personal disaster. Troubling as the dreams were, they were the font of inspiration for one of his most famous narratives, the legend of Númenor found in his deeply personal magnum opus, *The Silmarillion*. "When the [once noble] inhabitants of Númenor are beguiled by Sauron . . . into breaking a divine commandment and sailing West towards the forbidden lands, a great storm rises, a huge wave crashes on Númenor, and the entire island is cast into the abyss. Atlantis has sunk."[2]

Bruce G. Charlton has described Tolkien as a creative genius with an intellectual capacity on the level of Albert Einstein, but he has maintained the importance of keeping in mind Tolkien's devout religion and the mystical and prophetic element of his corpus, especially when contemplating Tolkien's nightmares of the flood and the Númenor stories. As Charlton observed, "For Tolkien, dreams (and creativity in general) are potentially glimpses of divine Truth—in the sense that dreams (and similar experiences of altered consciousness) can be ways that God communicates with a mind that when awake is too-much distracted by the 'noise' and chatter of modern life."[3] Given the urgency, vividness, and recurrence of the flood nightmare, Tolkien may have seen in the dreams a form of prophecy that went beyond a sense of personal foreboding. There may have been, in the dream, a sense that a great flood disaster on the order of Noah's flood was in the Earth's future, should contemporary humans continue to travel down the path of hubris that the Númenoreans trod before them. Of course, there is little to no evidence to suggest that Tolkien's recurring dream was in any way related to fears based in scientific theories about glacial melt and the greenhouse effect. Nevertheless, it is interesting to note that Tolkien's personal, haunting nightmare vision of an apocalyptic-level flood has become an internationally shared recurring nightmare in an age when the disastrous effects of climate change make the fear of the flood into a grim reality, with the great flood disasters of Texas, Florida, and Puerto Rico in 2017 just a few of many that year, all of which herald a new, terrifying normal for island and coastal communities.

## *2012*, Dominion Theology, and Climate Change Denial

Imagine an alternative version of the Noah's Ark narrative in which the waters rise to cover the Earth and drown only the innocent and powerless peoples, while sparing the lives of only the wicked rulers who had summoned the flood waters in the first place. The wicked were those who had made their vast fortunes polluting the planet and financing endless wars, filling their coffers with more than enough booty to build a fleet of arks to protect themselves and their fellow country club associates. They had no more pity for the rest of humanity during this apocalyptic hour than they had before the hour of supreme crisis was at hand, so they took only enough poor people with them to act as their servants and slaves, and not one refugee more. The poor, the sick, and the politically impotent were the ones left to drown. They could not save themselves because they lacked the financing, health, and influence to find ways to do so. This scenario, a possible future repeat of the Noah narrative with a more unjust and horrifying twist, has played out in several speculative climate disaster future narratives, including two written by Mark Millar, *Fantastic Four: The Death of the Invisible Woman* and *Kingsman: The Secret Service*; as well as the French comic book *Snow Piercer* and its film adaptation, *Snowpiercer*, and the movies *Land of the Dead* (2005), *2012* (2009), and *Elysium* (2013). Rising sea levels caused by glacial melt have inspired several revisitings of the Noah's Ark story since World War II, including the novels *The Kraken Wakes* (1953) by John Wyndham, and *Not Wanted on the Voyage* (1984) by Timothy Findley, the comic books *Aquaman: Sub-Diego* (2003) by Will Pfeifer and Patrick Gleeson, and *The Wake* (2014) by Scott Snyder and Sean Murphy, and the film *Noah* (2014), co-written and directed by Darren Aronofsky. The much-reviled Kevin Costner film *Waterworld* (1995) uses a postapocalyptic Earth covered in water as a setting, and the main characters live their lives on boats and floating forts, hoping one day to find a mythical "dry land" that they can plant their feet upon.

The entertaining but deeply flawed film *2012*, co-written and directed by Roland Emmerich, posits that a freak solar flare, not man-made climate change, will raise the sea levels around the world—an unfortunate act of storytelling cowardice on the part of the filmmakers that avoids implementing more accurate climate science so as not to alienate antiscience ticket buyers. In the movie, scientists discover evidence of the impending cataclysm. They convince fictional U.S. president Thomas Wilson (Danny Glover) to join other world leaders in the construction of nine arks to house nine hundred thousand people from the most powerful nations. The wealthy are given the chance to buy seats on the arks for themselves and their family members with a donation of one billion dollars to underwrite construction costs. The film's protagonist is not one of the wealthy

Fig. 4.1. The much-reviled Kevin Costner film *Waterworld* (1995) uses a postapocalyptic Earth covered in water as a setting, and the main characters live their lives on boats and floating forts, hoping one day to find a mythical "dry land" that they can plant their feet upon. Pictured from left to right: Kevin Costner as the Mariner, Tina Majorino as Enola, and Jeanne Tripplehorn as Helen. Universal Pictures.

elect, but one of the insignificant people intended to be "left behind": a middle-class climate fiction novelist (John Cusack) who supplements his meager income as an author by acting as a chauffeur to the wealthy. The film concerns Cusack's discovery of these arks and his efforts to sneak his family onto a refuge intended for the superrich alone.

Significantly, the people of the Republic of the Maldives were not among those selected to be saved in the arks featured in the film because the people of the Maldives are not rich and powerful enough to save. They were not saved in this fictional narrative and it seems likely that they will eventually perish in our own reality should a similar sea rise scenario come to pass. Environmentalist scholar Rob Nixon's narrative voice is at its most compelling when he paints with striking visual language a portrait of the threats posed by climate change, including the danger to this particular tropical nation located in the Indian Ocean. Consider how Nixon begins his epilogue to *Slow Violence and the Environmentalism of the Poor* (2011):

> The Maldives face an incremental threat from rising, warming oceans, a threat difficult to dramatize and even harder to arrest—a form of slow violence

that is rapid in geological terms but (unlike a tsunami) not fast enough to constitute breaking news. In an effort to infuse dramatic urgency into this incremental crisis, the president of the Maldives, Mohamed Nashed, held an extraordinary underwater cabinet meeting in diving gear on October 17, 2009, shortly before the Copenhagen Climate Summit. President Nasheed and his wetsuit-clad ministers convened behind a conference table anchored to the seabed, a Maldive flag planted behind them. Oxygen mask in place, the president signed into law a national commitment to becoming carbon neutral within ten years.[4]

News broadcasters perennially complain that it is difficult to make climate change dramatic and newsworthy because it is so incremental and not remotely visual—a claim that does not ring true when time-lapse photography of melting ice and shots of polar bears swimming where there once was ice (or dying on dry land where there once was ice) have provided ample visual illustration of climate change in documentaries such as *An Inconvenient Truth* (2006), *Planet Earth* (2006), *Chasing Ice* (2012), and *Before the Flood* (2016). However, Nasheed's maneuver was an attempt to provide a climate fiction–style dramatization of a possible future for the Maldives: the Maldives are likely to become the next Númenor. Should the Maldives be drowned by the Indian Ocean, those who had once called the land their home would become refugees elsewhere, seeking shelter, citizenship, and human rights from the very same nations that took little or no action to prevent the drowning of the Maldives in the first place. Indeed, the industrial nations have long been the heart of the problem and have done little of substance to be part of the solution.

For the first time, the COP21, the 2015 United Nations Climate Change Conference in Paris, seemed to offer some measure of hope that the world was ready to act on climate change because, for perhaps the first time, a sitting United States president, Barack Obama, seemed serious about confronting climate change. On December 12, 2015, 195 nations agreed to the contents of the Paris Agreement, a document that called for all participating nations to reduce their carbon emissions as soon as possible to keep global warming "well below 2 degrees C." The agreement—which was inadequate given that island nations like the Maldives could wind up underwater with even one more degree global temperature raise, let alone two—was, nevertheless, hailed as the beginning of a worldwide environmentalist revolution that has the potential to save humanity. Unfortunately, the United States' commitment to reduce its emissions immediately faced a series of legal and political challenges from members of the fossil fuel industry and Republican obstructionists from the Supreme Court on down to the state legislature level. Most infamously, Obama's successor Donald Trump announced the United States' withdrawal from the Paris Agreement in 2017, an action that inspired shock and condemnation worldwide. To a degree, it is understandable why the fossil fuel industry would object to environmental initiatives, but frustrating that the Republican Party has taken so extreme and anti-environmentalist posture when it conceivably could spearhead effective conservative initiatives to combat climate change. The party is comprised of individuals who are, in theory, capable of making up their own minds about important issues. However, there tends to be a uniformity of thought about climate change within the Republican Party because their elected officials have a strong inclination to:

- be hostile to science,

- embrace a pro-pollution form of Christian ethics called Dominionism,

- stand on principle against any form of financial regulation—or any regulation at all,

- and protect corporate profits above all other concerns, come hell or high water.

Also, from the perspective of the average Republican, any initiative undertaken by President Obama, a Democrat, is worth exploding simply because *he* spearheaded it.

To read environmentalist thinker Wendell Berry is, in some ways, to find relief from the endless social stress created by the vanishing ideological middle ground, the endangered species of the political moderate, and the endless gridlock and hyperbole that typifies Republican-versus-Democrat ideological warfare. In "Caught in the Middle" (2013), Wendell Berry laments that, "In the present political atmosphere it is assumed that everybody must be on one of only two sides, liberal or conservative. It doesn't matter that neither of these labels signifies much in the way of intellectual responsibility or that both are paralyzed in the face of the overpowering issue of our time: the destruction of land and people, of life itself, by means either economic or military. What does matter is that a person should choose one side or the other, accept the 'thinking' and the 'positions' of that side and its institutions and be so identified forevermore. How you vote is who you are. We appear thus to have evolved into a sort of teenage culture of wishful thinking, of contending 'positions,' oversimplified and absolute, requiring no knowledge and no thought, no loss, no tragedy, no strenuous effort, no bewilderment, no hard choices."[5]

As a spiritual environmentalist, Berry's frustration with current political discourse is easy to empathize with. For Berry, politicizing everything—including religion and the environmental crisis—is rarely a path that will lead in a fruitful direction. Indeed, the agnostic scientist Neil deGrasse Tyson expressed similar frustration with the politicization of science. Tyson regards science as the search for objective truth and feels that science should not be filtered through a preexisting ideological worldview. Rigid, preconceived ideological assumptions, in Tyson's construction, are the enemies of both science and, in a broader sense, education. As he wrote in a blog post in August 2016, "People who deny human-induced climate change are badly misinformed. This position is neither politically Liberal nor Conservative. It's factual. Although one could argue that all those who want to preserve the environment are the real conservatives in this

Fig. 4.2. Released in 2009 and directed by Roland Emmerich, the film *2012* is a climate change disaster movie thinly (and unconvincingly) disguised as a Mayan Calendar "2012 phenomenon" apocalypse film. Pictured above: the film's poster provides an apt illustration for any discussion of sea-level rise, climate change, and a return to the Noah's Ark narrative. Columbia Pictures.

discussion. . . . [My detractors] use 'Liberal' as a tag to characterize my politics. Since I have no active public political position, that's a hard task to accomplish. Climate change deniers are dangerously misinformed. But so are people who think vaccines gives you autism. . . . These science-denying postures cross political boundaries . . ."[6]

There is no reason that it would logically follow that a conservative person would reject science or that a religious person cannot be an environmentalist, but our cultural moment in America seems to encourage a thinking that there are only two kinds of people: religious people who deny science, are politically conservative, and are not environmentalists versus atheists who are politically liberal, believe in science, and are environmentalists. This form of binary thinking is counterintuitive, absurd, and destructive on every conceivable level. One of the sources of this thinking is a form of conservative Christianity known as Dominionism, which has few numbers that would identify themselves with that label and yet which expresses a worldview that is embraced by a sizable minority of the electorate, clustered primarily throughout the rural regions of the country. Emblematic of this kind of antiscience, Dominionist-in-all-but-name Christian is James M. Inhofe, the Republican senator from Oklahoma who chairs the Senate's Committee on Environment and Public Works. Inhofe is most famous for trying to disprove climate change by tossing a snowball to the Senate floor on February 26, 2015. His argument that the unseasonably cold February faced on the East Coast of the United States somehow made all scientists look foolish is negated by the fact that extreme cold and hot weather patterns add to the evidence of human-caused climate change rather than undermine it.[7] Also, the fact that 2015 had proven to be the warmest year in recorded history seems to have left Inhofe equally unmoved—and that the 2015 record was broken in 2016.[8] In his book, *The Greatest Hoax: How the Global Warming Conspiracy Threatens Your Future* (2012), Inhofe writes that no scientist has the right to assert that the earth is in any danger because the book of Genesis has assured us it is not. He cites as evidence of this claim, Genesis 8:22: *As long as the earth remains/There will be springtime and harvest/Cold and heat, winter and summer.*[9]

Notably, much of the objection to global climate change data is based in religious views, and public skepticism of the motivations of scientists remain rooted in fears of their atheism and adherence to Darwin's theory of evolution. Emblematic of this line of argument is Rush Limbaugh's *The Way Things Ought to Be* (1992). As an unofficial official spokesman of the Republican Party, Limbaugh writes, "My views on the environment are rooted in my belief in Creation. I don't believe that life on earth began spontaneously or as a result of some haphazard, random selection process; nor do I believe that nature is oh-so-precariously balanced. I don't believe that the earth and her ecosystem are fragile as many radical environmentalists do. They think man can come along all by himself, and change everything for the worse; that after hundreds of millions of years, the last two generations of human existence are going to destroy the planet. Who do they think we are? I resent that presumptuous view of man and his works. I refuse to believe that people, who are themselves the result of Creation, can destroy the most magnificent creation of the entire universe."[10]

It is hard to imagine a Christian view of ecology less in sympathy with the principles of Christian Stewardship advocated by Tolkien and Lewis—and by contemporary Christian environmentalist bloggers such as Mark Davies of "One World House"—than those expressed by these Republican stalwarts. The principles of Dominion Theology and Christian Stewardship are opposites. A Dominionist would argue that God gave humans Dominion over the Earth. Humans can do whatever they like to plants and animals. They have no incentive to be environmentalists. If it ever looked as if we were doing real damage to the planet, God would save us, and Heaven awaits us even if we do destroy the world. Environmentalists live in atheistic fear of a Godless world and worship the pagan goddess Gaea. That, in a nutshell, is the Dominionist perspective. In contrast, a Christian Steward would argue God gave us the Earth to take care of. To recklessly destroy all plant and animal life is a sin against the beauty of life and the glory of all of God's Creation. Anyone who places corporate profits over clean drinking water worships money, and Mammon (Matthew 6:24), not Christ. A worship of Mammon is the real heresy, not ecology. The Inklings are Stewards. The modern-day Republican Party is replete with Dominionists, and their thinking bears little to no resemblance to the ecological worldview of the Inklings.

Dominionism is a political and religious worldview associated with Texas senator Ted Cruz and his father that is disdainful of the sciences, the humanities, feminism, multiculturalism, and environmentalism. The movement has grown in influence in the United States since the 1980s. Sociologist Sara Diamond has covered the movement, and writes that "the concept that Christians are Biblically mandated to 'occupy' all secular institutions has become the central unifying ideology for the Christian Right."[11] She also notes that, while there are not many who would label themselves Dominionists, their perspectives inform the thinking of a broad swath of conservative Christians, especially those that have constituted the base of the Republican Party since the rise of the Reagan Revolution. Interestingly, many Dominionists have claimed C. S. Lewis as a champion, assuming that his view that the Earth is "enemy-occupied territory" that needs to be reclaimed by Christians is an appropriate metaphor for reclaiming the United States from liberalism and secular humanism. The question that many might be tempted to ask is, were Lewis alive today, would he still see the world as enemy-occupied territory, and what forces would he regard as being aligned with God and what forces would he see as aligned with the devil? In the era of the *Burwell v. Hobby Lobby Stores, Inc.* Supreme Court case and county clerk Kim Davis's well-publicized refusal to grant marriage licenses to gay couples in Rowan County, Kentucky, in 2015, there is a growing consensus among American Dominionist Christians that the Founding Fathers intended the United States to be a Christian nation and that the political and religious values of the Generation X and Millennial Generations are undermining the original intent of the framers of the Constitution. In the Dominionist view, these rebellious youngsters, and the masses of "Nones" among them who have abjured all organized religion have turned America into a secularist, multicultural wasteland through their economic indolence, mercurial voting patterns, and debauched lifestyles. This Dominionist view of America paints a dark, sinister picture of American progressives, effectively demonizing them as instruments of Satan—and paints anyone who lays claim to the mantle of progressive leadership (such as Obama) as the devil incarnate.

One of the most famous and respected conservative leaders of the Cold War era, Barry Goldwater, warned of the rising influence of problematically religious elements within the Republican Party, including those who could be considered Dominionist politicians. In interviews toward the end of his life, he observed: "Mark my word, if and when these preachers get control of the [Republican] party, and they're sure trying to do so, it's going to be a terrible damn problem. Frankly, these people frighten me. Politics and governing demand compromise. But these Christians believe they are acting in the name of God, so they can't and won't compromise. I know, I've tried to deal with them."[12] He also observed: "When you say 'radical right' today, I think of these moneymaking ventures by fellows like Pat Robertson and others who are trying to take the Republican Party away from the Republican Party, and make a religious organization out of it. If that ever happens, kiss politics goodbye."[13]

While the definition of the term *Dominionist* varies, I will use it broadly to suggest a far-right conservative who argues that America was once a purely Christian nation and should become so again, that Christianity is the only correct religion and that respecting religious freedom is a dangerous cultural policy, whether it is "inferior/irrelevant" Christian sects (such as Pope Francis's species of Roman Catholicism) or, still worse, non-Christian faiths. Dominionists also believe that all American legislation should be gleaned from the Bible, and that secular and multicultural concerns should be driven from government, education, science, and the arts.

Though himself a figure of controversy who has been accused of plagiarism, Chris Hedges makes a strong case that Dominionists (aka Christian Reconstructionists) embody a form of contemporary fascism. He acknowledges that *fascism* is a loaded word, but believes it is appropriate. As he observes in *American Fascists: The Christian Right and the War on America* (2006), the word "evokes a historical period, primarily that of the Nazis, and to a lesser extent Mussolini. But fascism as an ideology has generic qualities. People like Robert O. Paxton in *The Anatomy of Fascism* have tried to quantify them. Umberto Eco did it in *The Five Moral Pieces*. . . . I think there are enough generic qualities that the group within the religious right known as . . . dominionists warrants the word [fascist]. Does this mean that this is Nazi Germany? No. Does this mean that this is Mussolini's Italy? No. Does this mean that this is a deeply anti-democratic movement that would like to impose a totalitarian system? Yes."[14]

Exploring this theme further in a follow-up essay, "The Radical Christian Right and the War on Government" (2013), Hedges wrote:

> U.S. Sen. Ted Cruz—whose father is Rafael Cruz, a rabid right-wing Christian preacher and the director of the Purifying Fire ministry—and legions of the senator's wealthy supporters, some of whom orchestrated the [government] shutdown [of 2013], are rooted in a radical Christian ideology known

as Dominionism or Christian Reconstructionism. This ideology calls on anointed "Christian" leaders to take over the state and make the goals and laws of the nation "biblical." It seeks to reduce government to organizing little more than defense, internal security, and the protection of property rights. It fuses with the Christian religion the iconography and language of American imperialism and nationalism, along with the cruelest aspects of corporate capitalism. The intellectual and moral hollowness of the ideology, its flagrant distortion and misuse of the Bible, the contradictions that abound within it—its leaders champion small government and a large military, as if the military is not part of government—and its laughable pseudoscience are impervious to reason and fact. And that is why the movement is dangerous.

The cult of masculinity, as in all fascist movements, pervades the ideology of the Christian right. The movement uses religion to sanctify military and heroic "virtues," glorify blind obedience and order over reason and conscience, and pander to the euphoria of collective emotions. Feminism

Fig. 4.3. In *Take Shelter* (2011), Curtis LaForche (Michael Shannon) a construction worker and family man from Lagrange, Ohio, is haunted by visions of an imminent apocalypse. He is driven to construct a storm shelter in his back yard, frightening his co-workers, friends, wife Samantha (Jessica Chastain), and deaf daughter, Hannah (Tova Stewart) with his obsessive behavior. Unlike many climate fiction films, *Take Shelter* was released to international critical acclaim and garnered its cast and writer-director Jeff Nichols several science fiction genre awards and film industry honors. Sony Pictures Classics.

and homosexuality, believers are told, have rendered the American male physically and spiritually impotent. Jesus, for the Christian right, is a man of action, casting out demons, battling the Antichrist, attacking hypocrites and ultimately slaying nonbelievers. This cult of masculinity, with its glorification of violence, is appealing to the powerless. It stokes the anger of many Americans, mostly white and economically disadvantaged, and encourages them to lash back at those who, they are told, seek to destroy them.[15]

Whether Hedges's claims are accurate to a degree or are an unfair demonization of a broad swath of the American people, the question remains: Would C. S. Lewis have approved of any religiously informed political movement designed to transform either Great Britain or the United States into a Christian theocracy? The answer, based on Lewis's own writings, is "No." Certainly, Lewis believed that contemporary governments, economic systems, and pride-filled Christian laity tended not to be as informed by Judeo-Christian values as they uncritically assumed they were. Notably, he was deeply skeptical of unrestrained capitalism—especially the use of interest rates and usury to underpin twentieth-century international financial institutions—when the Ancient Greeks, Hebrews, and Medieval Christians uniformly condemned the practice of usury. (Indeed, a reading of Lester K. Little's *Religious Poverty and the Profit Economy in Medieval Europe* would provide well-documented historical context to support Lewis's views of the instinctive Christian theological reaction to the birth of the profit economy.)[16] Lewis, who cannot be easily labeled "liberal" or "conservative" in the contemporary American political sense, wrote:

> [T]he New Testament, without going into details, gives us a pretty clear hint of what a fully Christian society would be like. . . . If there were such a society in existence and you or I visited it, I think we should come away with a curious impression. We should feel that its economic life was very socialistic and, in that sense, "advanced," but that its family life and its code of manners were rather old-fashioned—perhaps even ceremonious and aristocratic. Each of us would like some bits of it, but I am afraid very few of us would like the whole thing. . . . You will find this again and again about anything that is really Christian: every one is attracted by bits of it and wants to pick out those bits and leave the rest. That is why we do not get much further: and that is why people who are fighting for quite opposite things can both say they are fighting for Christianity. . . .

No doubt contemporary "liberal" and "conservative" Christians would read such a passage of Lewis attentively. Lewis himself posits that both Left and Right Christians would be equally troubled by his statements on what a Christian theocracy would look like: "And now . . . I am going to venture a guess as to how this section has affected any who have read it. My guess is that there are some Leftist people among them who are very angry that it has not gone further in that direction, and some people of an opposite sort who are angry because they think it has gone much too far. If so, that brings us right up against the real snag in all this drawing up of blueprints for a Christian society. Most of us are not really approaching the subject in order to find out what Christianity says: we are approaching it in the hope of finding support from Christianity for the views of our own party."[17]

What is important to know about Lewis is that he is a religious Christian, he is a professor of literature, a writer, an environmentalist, and an antifascist. It is far less important to try to get bogged down determining what he may or may not think of contemporary politicians. Indeed, Lewis is at his most valuable when he is read in the spirit of thoughtfulness and evenhandedness that he composed his best works of fiction and theology. It is, perhaps, surprising that someone born in Northern Ireland amid the acrimonious religious sectarianism of the Catholic and Protestant feuding in the region would grow up to express sober and reasonable religious and political perspectives. However, this Ulster Protestant "Home-Ruler" managed to do so despite the sociopolitical context of his early years.[18] Indeed, it is possible his exposure to the religious conflicts in Northern Ireland during his formative years helped encourage him to take a more broad-minded view of Christianity and oppose sectarian conflict. Taking this notion farther, Lewis's species of comparatively even-handed religious writing might well make readers wonder what kind of man Lewis was and what other forces shaped him during his early years.

Lewis biographer Alister McGrath summons two equally compelling images of Lewis in childhood. One posits him living a secluded, almost shut-in life in the home of a bereaved father, with only his brother, some servants, and his books and imagination to keep him company. Readers can picture him exploring the rooms of his family home and imagining fantasy realms in the company of his brother, living a life that seems more than a little like a template of the experience of his later creations, the Pevensie children, occupying themselves scampering about the empty rooms and grounds of Professor Digory Kirke's home. The other representation McGrath offers is of a Lewis who grew to love the beauty of the Irish countryside he was exposed to at an impressionable age—but which he had to leave behind to attend boarding school in England. The Narnia books were his adulthood attempt to recapture the natural beauties of the Ireland of his youth that he had been compelled to abandon. Placed within nature long enough to appreciate its beauty, but living enough of an indoor existence to feel separated from it as well, Lewis's views of nature emerge as partly nostalgic and romanticized.

On the other hand, a reading of Lewis's autobiography *Surprised by Joy* (1955) suggests that some of Lewis's love of nature was due to his immersion in it, not in his feelings of alienation from it. Lewis writes *Surprised by Joy* as a man who eschewed the use of technology and was uniquely positioned to cultivate an appreciation of nature each day he walked instead of drove:

I number it among my blessings that my father had no car, while yet most of my friends had, and sometimes took me for a drive. This meant that all these distant objects could be visited just enough to clothe them with memories and not impossible desires, while yet they remained ordinarily as inaccessible as the Moon. The deadly power of rushing about wherever I pleased had not been given me. I measured distances by the standard of man, man walking on his two feet, not by the standard of the internal combustion engine. I had not been allowed to deflower the very idea of distance; in return I possessed "infinite riches" in what would have been to motorists "a little room." The truest and most horrible claim made for modern transport is that it "annihilates space." It does. It annihilates one of the most glorious gifts we have been given. It is a vile inflation which lowers the value of distance, so that a modern boy travels a hundred miles with less sense of liberation and pilgrimage and adventure than his grandfather got from traveling ten. Of course if a man hates space and wants it to be annihilated, that is another matter. Why not creep into his coffin at once? There is little enough space there.[19]

Lewis's association of the automobile with the death instinct anticipates some of the themes of J. G. Ballard's *Crash* and offers an astute symbol of how humanity's love of technology harbors a secret death wish—as well as how the industrialized culture of the West points inevitably toward death, war, and apocalypse. For Lewis, industrialization, death, and fascism go hand in hand with a materialism and capitalist ethos that is disguised as compatible with Christianity but which is anything but.

Lewis's honesty about the tendency of Christians to selectively read the Bible to support their own natural inclinations—or as a means of validating the traits of the culture and class they were born into—is refreshing to read. It is also refreshing to read works written by someone who does not fall easily into the false dichotomies often employed in the contemporary American mass media, between liberal atheist and conservative Christian, or between pro-science atheist and antiscience spiritualist. Readers may begin reading a work by Lewis expecting him to fall comfortably into those dichotomies, but anyone who reads several of his works in their entirety will find that he does not fit into any of them.

How quaint.

## In a Republican-Controlled America, Is Action on Climate Change Remotely Possible?

Despite the above critique of establishment Republican Party politics, it is important to observe that *some* Republicans have expressed more enlightened opinions concerning climate change, and even acted to mitigate its consequences—most notably Arnold

Schwarzenegger, former governor of California, who was praised for his green initiatives. He also co-produced a documentary with Tom Hanks to educate the public on the issue called *Years of Living Dangerously* (2014). On December 7, 2015, Schwarzenegger wrote a Facebook post called, "I don't give a \*\*\*\* if we agree on climate change." In it, he wrote that even those who don't believe in climate change should be concerned that "every day, 19,000 people die from pollution from fossil fuels" and that, one day, fossil fuels will run out and there is no infrastructure in place yet to adequately replace them. He wrote, "I, personally, want a plan. I don't want to be like the last horse and buggy salesman who was holding out as cars took over the roads. I don't want to be the last investor in Blockbuster as Netflix emerged. That's exactly what is going to happen to fossil fuels. A clean energy future is a wise investment, and anyone who tells you otherwise is either wrong, or lying. Either way, I wouldn't take their investment advice."

Two years earlier, on August 1, 2013, Republicans Christine Todd Whitman, William D. Ruckelshaus, Lee M. Thomas, and William K. Reilly wrote a *New York Times* editorial called "A Republican Case for Climate Action," in which they argued that the science behind climate change is indisputable and the only disagreement is over how bad things will get how quickly if nothing is done. Therefore, they wrote, for the sake of the future survival of humanity, it is the duty of Republicans to demand that President Obama do *more* to stem carbon emissions, not to stonewall him at every turn and stop him from taking the few steps he believes he has the political capital to take.[20] These Republicans represent a minority voice in the party. Far more common are those like Mitt Romney—who, when a candidate for the presidency, derided Obama for protecting America from "the rising of the oceans" instead of focusing on protecting American families. And there is Donald Trump, who has suggested that the concept of climate change is a conspiracy invented by the Chinese to defraud the American people and who has worked tirelessly to derail the Paris Climate Agreement, destroy the EPA, and ban NASA's climate research. With perspectives such as these held by politicians in seats of power across America, several figures in the climate movement have joined Noam Chomsky in arguing that strategic voting is needed to keep climate change–denying Republicans out of offices, as they pose a risk to human and planetary survival.

While such a line of thinking might seem borderline hysterical, the risk of rapid sea-level rise because of global warming has escalated in recent years because of developing nations contributing more pollutants to the atmosphere than ever before. As Naomi Klein explains in *This Changes Everything: Capitalism vs. the Climate* (2014), "It's the fast-rising economies of the Global South—with China, India, Brazil, and South Africa leading the pack—that are mostly responsible for the surge in emissions in recent years, which is why we are racing toward tipping points far more quickly than anticipated. The reason for the shift in the source of emissions has everything to do with the spectacular success multinational corporations have had in globalizing the high-consumption-based economic model pioneered in wealthy Western countries. The trouble is, the atmosphere can't take it. As the atmospheric physicist and mitigation expert Alice Bows-Larkin put it in an interview, 'The number of people who went through industrialization the first time around is like a drop in the ocean compared to the number of people going through industrialization this time.' And to quote President Obama in late 2013, if China's and India's energy consumption imitates the U.S. model, 'we'll be four feet underwater.' "[21]

According to Vermont senator Bernie Sanders, many Republicans do believe that climate change is a real danger to human survival, but they lack the courage to take any action to confront it for fear of losing their campaign funding from the Koch brothers, oil magnates who exert tremendous influence over the entirety of the American political system. On more than one occasion, Sanders has called for a worldwide mobilization for a war on climate change that will be even greater in scope than the mass mobilizing of the Allied nations against the global threat of fascism during World War II.

Despite some promising signs of grassroots and wealthy-donor activisim, the mobilization that Sanders calls for has yet to take full shape. Instead, thanks to the kinds of obstructionism funded by the Koch brothers, right now, a little too much hope is being placed on the idea that a scientific Messiah—or the miraculous free-market economy—will drive innovation and discover a magic wand solution to climate change that the government is too gridlocked to fund. Twenty-sixteen Republican presidential candidate Jeb Bush even posited that one day a scientist working out of a garage might simply solve the problem with a clever invention: a bit of wishful thinking that calls to mind images of teenage scientist Reed Richards in the 2015 *Fantastic Four* film, working in his garage to open a gateway to an upolluted "Earth 2" to colonize. A Miami-based reporter, Kyle Munzenrieder, was particularly aghast at Bush's suggestion, especially since Miami is a coastal community confronting the omnipresent threat of super storms and sea-level rise, "Sure, a lot of companies got their start in garages: Apple, Microsoft, and Hewlett Packard in the tech sector, plus Disney, Barbie, and Nike. Of course, all of those companies started with the ultimate aim of making money, not solving major world problems. Jeb seems to think the person who fixes climate change will end up making lots and lots of money. Granted, that's a fairly common Republican way of thinking. However, because of today's real-estate climate, we wonder if this theoretical hero could even afford a place with a garage (unless this person were living in a garage) and if he/she has enough free time while not working to pay off student debt to devote to world-saving extracurriculars. We can only hope that our garage savior does. Please, person in a garage, save us. You're our only hope."[22]

One of the scientists who is most respected for being an altruistic, self-made man of innovation has also argued that the free market so beloved by Republicans is poorly equipped to solve the climate crisis. In 2015, Bill Gates promised to spend two billion dollars of his money to invest in green energy and expressed his hopes that other private sector billionaires would match his funding of initiatives designed to wean the United States off fossil fuels by 2050.[23] Some wealthy celebrities have made similar pledges, including actor Leonardo Di Caprio, who announced in July 2015 that he was donating fifteen million dollars to a variety of environmentalist causes. Still, Gates argues that the problem would most likely be solved by government research and development, since it has the best track record with fueling scientific innovation: "There's no fortune to be made. Even if you have a new energy source that costs the same as today's and emits no CO2, it will be uncertain compared with what's tried-and-true and already operating at unbelievable scale and has gotten through all the regulatory problems. . . . Without a substantial carbon tax, there's no incentive for innovators or plant buyers to switch." Gates says he proceeds from a position of optimism because he believes that technological innovation of the future will help us mitigate the effects of climate change. However, he worries that—if no scientist ever appears to find the magic-wand solution to the problem—no effective action will be taken.[24] Gates's theory that we will most likely do nothing to combat climate change if the battle to protect the environment is left to corporations alone was proven in the fall of 2015 when the Exxon climate change denial scandal broke. Conclusive evidence culled from internal memos demonstrated that Exxon's own internal research confirmed the apocalyptic-level threat that climate change represents *decades ago*.[25] However, the company funded climate change denial

Fig. 4.4. Co-written and directed by Josh Trank, 2015's *Fantastic Four* film stars Kate Mara as Sue Storm (left) and Miles Teller as Reed Richards (right). Set in the present day, the new origin story shows the members of the Fantastic Four as teenage geniuses engaged in a process of attempting to solve the climate change crisis. Reed begins his journey as a scientist working in a makeshift lab in his garage for years, attempting to open a portal to another habitable world too far for humans to reach by conventionally available space travel technology. When he presents the fruits of his work at a science fair, he is recruited to work at a special think tank tasked with saving humanity. 20th Century Fox.

in the mass media for years to turn the public against environmentalist initiatives, in an effort to protect their profit margins.[26] The Exxon revelations were so shocking that even Bill McKibben, the world's most outspoken environmentalist, was flabbergasted by the scope of the damage Exxon had done. He wrote in an op-ed for *The Guardian* on October 14, 2015:

> To understand the treachery—the sheer, profound, and I think unparalleled evil—of Exxon, one must remember the timing. Global warming became a public topic in 1988, thanks to NASA scientist James Hansen—it's taken a quarter-century and counting for the world to take effective action. If at any point in that journey Exxon—largest oil company on Earth, most profitable enterprise in human history—had said: "Our own research shows that these scientists are right and that we are in a dangerous place," the faux debate would effectively have ended. That's all it would have taken; stripped of the cover provided by doubt, humanity would have gotten to work.
>
> Instead, knowingly, they helped organize the most consequential lie in human history, and kept that lie going past the point where we can protect the poles, prevent the acidification of the oceans, or slow sea level rise enough to save the most vulnerable regions and cultures. . . . No corporation has ever done anything this big and this bad . . . this company had the singular capacity to change the course of world history for the better and instead it changed that course for the infinitely worse. In its greed Exxon helped—more than any other institution—to kill our planet.[27]

Has Exxon repented? No, it is mustering its defense against these charges and trying to discredit those who have exposed them. Perhaps someone should tell the Exxon executives that we all live on the same planet, and if the earth dies, we all die. On the other hand, perhaps the Exxon executives have already created a beautiful bunker that they can retreat to when the end times come, and believe it will keep them safe from the world they have created. Indeed, according to the essays published in *The Secure and the Dispossessed: How the Military and the Corporations are Shaping a Climate-Changing World* (2015), edited by Nick Buxton and Ben Hayes, the wealthy are already making their magic lifeboats all around the world. Certainly, that is what climate fiction tells us the wealthy will do when the eleventh hour arrives.

# Race and Disaster Capitalism in
## *Parable of the Sower*, *The Strain*, and *Elysium*

So far as I know, there are only two philosophies of land use. One holds that the earth is the Lord's, or it holds that the earth belongs to those yet to be born as well as to those now living. The present owners, according to this view, only have the land in trust, both for all the living who are dependent on it now, and for the unborn who will be dependent on it in time to come. . . . The other philosophy is that of exploitation, which holds that the interest of the present owner is the only interest to be considered. The standard, according to this view, is profit, and it is assumed that whatever is profitable is good.

—Wendell Berry, *A Continuous Harmony: Essays Cultural and Agricultural*

## On *Elysium, Daybreakers, The Strain,* and *Pacific Rim*

Simultaneously summarizing and commenting upon the story of *Elysium* (2013), written and directed by Neill Blomkamp, *Telegraph* critic Robbie Collin observed, "In the science-fiction thriller *Elysium*, William Blake's prophesy has come to pass and then some. Not only has mankind built a heaven in hell's despair; they've privatized it. Earth is a toxic dustbowl, but in the sky above hangs the ultimate gated community. Elysium is a space station in the shape of a halo, the inside edge of which is covered with villas, golf courses and serene boating lakes. Within every home is a medical pod that cures all ills and freezes aging. Life there is an infinite retirement, as long as you can afford it. . . . [Blomkamp clearly has many contemporary political] issues on his mind, including faith, capitalism and privatized healthcare. In lesser hands, *Elysium* might have played like a Lib Dem manifesto with extra spaceships, but the South African filmmaker wants to explore ideas, not wave placards, and whether or not you agree with the film's politics, the fire in its belly is catching."[1]

In the film, earthbound factory worker Max De Costa (Matt Damon) falls victim to an industrial accident that bathes him in enough radiation to kill him within the week. He could be cured easily were he a resident of Elysium, but on Earth, the accident is a death sentence because he cannot afford the medical care that will save his life. With nothing left to lose, Max contacts a gangster who runs an illegal immigration space shuttle service in the hopes of sneaking aboard Elysium and stealing access to one of their miracle healing pods. Another *Telegraph* contributor, John Hiscock, profiled the director and examined Blomkamp's motivation for refusing to direct popcorn-fare installments of Disney's revived *Star Wars* series and choosing instead to craft serious science fiction allegories, "Blomkamp's liking for politically provocative stories has its origins in Johannesburg, where he grew up in a middle-class family during the dismantling of apartheid and the skyrocketing violent crime rate that followed. He witnessed violence against blacks, and while a teenager a friend was killed in a carjacking." This biographical background offers the context to explain why Blomkamp strives to make films that are both suspenseful and replete with social commentary. As political as his other films, *Elysium* "touches on issues such as health care, immigration, economic disparities and environmental decay. 'The entire film is an allegory. I tend to think a lot about wealth discrepancy,' says Blomkamp . . . 'People have asked me if I think this is what will happen in 140 years, but this isn't science fiction. This is today. This is now.' "[2] Blomkamp's use of allegory is reminiscent of Lewis's in *The Space Trilogy*. He has disguised a "documentary" about life in contemporary America and Johannesburg as a futuristic science fiction film, making the dark observations about economic and social justice conditions today more palatable by cloaking them in an entertaining science fiction story set in a time and place removed from our own. It is exactly the species of storytelling that the co-creator of *Doctor Who*, Sydney Newman, would also approve of: instruction and cultural criticism disguised as escapist entertainment.

Another, equally political filmmaker who combines entertaining narratives with angry, antifascist social commentary is Guillermo del Toro. Del Toro's *Pacific Rim* (2013) is an ecological science fiction film about Japanese-style giant monsters invading Earth, and these *kaiju* are thinly veiled allegorical representations of climate change run amok. Like Blomkamp, del Toro tries to make his films entertaining enough that his dark political message may be better received: the narrative spoonful of sugar that helps the political medicine go down. What distinguishes his work from Blomkamp's is that del Toro's preferred genres are Gothic horror films such as *Pan's Labyrinth*, *The Shape of the Water*, *Crimson Peak*, and *Cronos* and superhero films such as *Blade 2* and the *Hellboy* series. His most significant work of Gothic horror climate fiction is *The Strain*.

Set in a post-9/11 New York, in the shadow of the 2002–03 Sars outbreak, the Enron scandals, the Rumsfeld torture memos, growing awareness of the threat of climate change, and the wars in Iraq and Afghanistan, *The Strain* trilogy by del Toro and Chuck Hogan (2009, 2010, 2011) concerns a Master vampire's plot to kill off one-third of the human population, turn another one-third into vampires, and force the remaining survivors to live in concentration camps and occupied cities. The heroes of the book series, an unlikely coalition of doctors, gangsters, and blue-collar Everymen, strive valiantly to stave off the impending apocalypse by working together despite their nearly irreconcilable personal differences. The freedom fighters allegorically represent an alliance between the middle and working classes against the top 1 percent that del Toro and Hogan clearly want to see form in the real world, and not just in their climate fiction. These heroes are pitted not only against the Master vampire, but also one of the richest tycoons in the world, the human traitor Eldrich Palmer, as well as the vampire Thomas Eichhorst, who had been, in life, commandant of the Treblinka extermination camp. The books reveal, in a series of flashbacks, that the Master was a regular visitor to Treblinka during World War II, and he fed upon the Jewish prisoners as they slept in their barracks at night. So inspired was he by the ruthless efficiency and inhumanity of the death camp that the Master decided it would be the model for all human society once he assumed control of the planet. These writers draw a direct parallel between Nazis, corporate oligarchs, and vampires. Such a parallel is also clear in villains from

Fig. 5.1. Nazi SS officer Thomas Eichhorst (Richard Sammel), commandant of the Treblinka death camp, before he is turned into a vampire and plots to Terraform the Earth to make its climate more conducive to vampires. Eichhorst is one of the central villains of the FX television series *The Strain* (2014–2017), which is based on a trilogy of climate fiction novels by Guillermo del Toro and Chuck Hogan. The immortal Nazi and his alliance with quisling human robber baron Eldritch Palmer symbolically links the evils of World War II to the corporate evils perpetrated in modern day. FX.

other vampire narratives, such as Russell Edgington, in the television series *True Blood*, who has roots in American slaveowning culture, expresses admiration for Adolph Hitler, and threatens to take over the world to save it from human-caused climate change. Like Edgington, the villains of *The Strain* seem to be, at once, campaigning to seize control of the world while they, in a sense, have always already been in control of the planet behind the scenes.

In the second book of *The Strain* trilogy, when it seems as if the vampires will succeed in their plot, Dr. Ephraim Goodweather of the Centers for Disease Control and Prevention attempts a desperate gambit and tries to assassinate the cloistered, respectable, and well-guarded Eldrich Palmer. After Eph fails to kill Palmer, Palmer decides to amuse himself by having dinner with his would-be assassin. During dinner, Palmer takes the opportunity to gloat over his imminent transformation into a vampire and the almost total success of his plot to enslave the masses. Palmer watches Eph eat, sickened by the sight of Eph's human need for food, and Eph asks if Palmer regards all poor people as little more than animals. Palmer replies:

> "Customers" is the accepted term. But certainly. We, the over-class, have taken those basic human drives and advanced our own selves through their exploitation. We have monetized human consumption, manipulated morals and laws to direct the masses by fear or hatred, and, in doing so, have managed to create a system of wealth and remuneration that has concentrated the vast majority of the world's wealth in the hands of a select few. Over the course of two thousand years, I believe this system worked pretty well. But all good things must end. You saw, with the recent market crash, how we have been building to this impossible end. Money built upon money built upon money. Two choices remain. Either utter collapse, which appeals to no one, or the richest push the pedal to the floor and take it all. And here we are now.[3]

Eph is appalled that Palmer not only wishes to acquire all the world's wealth, but that he is also willing to sell out all of humanity to the Master vampire. Palmer's justification is a harsh, self-serving combination of Darwinian evolutionary theory and social Darwinism: "The planet doesn't care. The entire system is structured around a long-winded decay and eventual rebirth. Why are you so precious about humanity? You can already feel it slipping away now. You're falling apart. Is the sensation really all that bad?"[4]

Del Toro infuses most of his films with an antifascist political subtext that grants dramatic weight to pulp material that might otherwise be considered trivial. In a profile of the director, Mark Kermode observed, "In essence, del Toro is a divided soul, a realist attuned to the strange vibrations of the supernatural, a lapsed Catholic ('not quite the same thing as an atheist') with an interest in sacrifice and redemption who turned down the chance to direct *The Chronicles of Narnia* because he 'wasn't interested in the lion resurrecting.' "[5] Del Toro was, however, interested in writing and directing the film adaptation of *The Hobbit*, but was compelled by endless production delays to leave the project and was replaced by Peter Jackson.

Echoing the central, apocalyptic themes of *The Strain*, the Australian film *Daybreakers* (2009), written and directed by Michael and Peter Spierig, takes place in 2019 in a world where virtually everyone on earth has been transformed into a vampire, and a vampire corporation that provides blood to the masses keeps the few surviving humans in food pens. Unfortunately, the corporation is rapidly running out of blood, as the few remaining humans on earth die in captivity, and the whole vampire population of earth is becoming malnourished and withering into a primal, death-like state as the food is rationed. Faced with rampant rioting and total social collapse, vampire scientist Edward Dalton (Ethan Hawke) seeks a cure for vampirism to end the need for blood, while the corporate head Charles Bromley (Sam Neill) schemes to find new supplies of blood, no matter the cost in human suffering. When Dalton finds a cure for vampirism, Bromley suppresses it, because he knows that a cure would liberate the world from its dependence upon his corporation for sustenance and severely cut into his profits.

The vampires in the film are symbolic representations of wealthy Western nations whose prosperity and social stability is entirely dependent upon finite oil resources. In addition to oil, the blood in the film may also symbolize the dwindling global drinking water supplies that have been quietly bought up and siphoned off by massive private corporations with beloved brand names. The film raises questions about our rapidly depleting natural resource situation that it cannot answer, but it is a warning to viewers to encourage the development of alternative fuels and to embrace the environmental legislation that will protect the world's endangered natural resources and share them equitably worldwide.

The conspiracy-theory nature of the films, books, and television shows discussed above has caused them to be criticized by pundits on television and radio, but it is true that the global supply of oil is finite, especially as the demand for oil from developing superpower nations India and China is exponentially increasing oil use. It is also true that the excavation and burning of fossil fuels is pumping dangerous pollutants into our water supply and our atmosphere. "Peak oil" or "the end of oil" is a phenomenon that worries thinkers such as James Howard Kunstler, who describes the nature of the crisis without resorting to vampire allegory in *The Long Emergency: Surviving the End of Oil, Climate Change, and Other Converging Catastrophes of the Twenty-First Century* (2005).

The social forces that draw the ire of writers such as Blomkamp, del Toro, and the Spierigs are powerful and visible enough that they have inspired the villains of popular nonvampire novels and films. The totalitarian rulers of postapocalyptic America in Suzanne Collins's *Hunger Games* trilogy are not far removed from the vampires of *Daybreakers*, nor are the New Founding Fathers of America in James DeMonaco's *Purge* film series, the "Company" executives of the Weyland-Yutani Corporation in the *Alien* film series and of Omni Consumer Products (OCP) in the *Robocop* series, or the corporate, Nazi, rapist, serial killers Martin and Gottfried Vanger, the main villains of Stieg Larsson's *The*

*Girl with the Dragon Tattoo.* The smaller-scale, "banality of evil" equivalents of these figures could be found in Peter Benchley's 1974 novel *Jaws*, in which the businessmen, gangsters, real-estate developers, politicians, and newspaper owners of Amity, a summer resort beach community on Long Island, are more than willing to sacrifice tourists to a demonic, man-eating Great White Shark before they will even consider closing the beaches to save lives—and risk destroying the local economy for that season. The real-world corporate oligarchs that these books are satirizing have been targeted by the Occupy Wall Street protestors, Carl Gibson's "Shut the Chamber" movement, the activist hacker group Anonymous, and by documentary filmmakers, journalists, and public figures such as Bill Moyers, Naomi Klein, Barbara Ehrenreich, Paul Krugman, Chris Hedges, Michael Moore, and Noam Chomsky. Among the most notable of the documentary films on these themes are *The Corporation* (2003); *The End of Suburbia: Oil Depletion and the Collapse of The American Dream* (2004); *The One Percent* (2006); *Flow: For Love of Water* (2008); *Food, Inc.* (2008); *Inside Job* (2010); *Gasland* (2010); and *Koch Brothers Exposed* (2012). Some of the most notable books describing class warfare in the United States and abroad include Ehrenreich's *Nickel and Dimed: On (Not) Getting by in America* (2001) and *This Land Is Their Land: Reports from a Divided Nation* (2008); Paul Krugman's *End This Depression Now!* (2013); Hedges's *Death of the Liberal Class* (2011) and *Days of Destruction, Days of Revolt* (2012); Moyers's *Welcome to Doomsday* (2006); *Profit Over People: Neoliberalism & Global Order* (2011) by Chomsky and Robert W. McChesney; and *Dollarocracy: How the Money and Media Election Complex is Destroying America* (2013) by John Nichols and McChesney. Not all these authors speak with one voice in diagnosing the social sickness, or on how optimistic or pessimistic they are about how the dangerous social trends we are experiencing now can be mitigated, halted, or reversed. McKibben and Kunstler, for example, would see the energy crisis and the environmental crisis lurking behind the fiscal crisis and overshadowing its importance in *Eaarth: Making a Life on a Tough New Planet* by McKibben (2011) and *The Long Emergency.*

One of the most horrifying exposés concerning corporate profiteering during an era of wars without end and natural disasters is Naomi Klein's *Shock Doctrine: The Rise of Disaster Capitalism* (2007).[6] Klein reveals occasion after occasion where Americans whose homes have been destroyed by natural disaster and forced to become refugees in their own country find themselves robbed instead of assisted by authority figures. While they seek temporary shelter away from the site of the catastrophe, the land they had once lived on is taken from them and converted into luxury homes and vacation resorts and the public schools their children once attended are turned into private or charter schools, Klein writes. Instead of helping American citizens in need, elected officials and corporate lobbyists join the looters pillaging disaster zones, only the looting they do is not limited to a mere television set or fine set of silverware, Klein argues. At the behest of their economic hero, the libertarian Milton Friedman, they take everything, and do it with class and style—not like common, everyday looters. Klein's chief examples of this phenomenon are the corporate land-grabs that followed in the wake of Hurricane

Katrina's devastation of New Orleans and the hotel resort businesses installed in the aftermath of a huge tsunami that ravaged the beaches of Southeast Asia. She also notes the war profiteering characterized by the privatization of the war on terror—with the spoils of the wars in the Middle East going to the oil companies Shell and BP and the military contractors Halliburton and Blackwater. Klein's name for all the above schemes—which are unified by their exploitation of human suffering and placing of profits before people—is "disaster capitalism." All of this can sound a bit far-fetched to those allergic to conspiracy theories. Nevertheless, her works are well documented, and she grounds her argument in recognizable and relatable human drama to demonstrate the on-the-ground, real-life consequences of backroom deals made by men in suits and ties. Take, for example, the slice-of-life tale Klein provides about the victims of Katrina, with which she opens *The Shock Doctrine*:

> The news racing around the [Red Cross] shelter [in Baton Rouge] that day was that Richard Baker, a prominent Republican Congressman from this city, had told a group of lobbyists, "We finally cleaned up public housing in New Orleans. We couldn't do it, but God did." Joseph Canizaro, one of New Orleans' wealthiest developers, had just expressed a similar sentiment: "I think we have a clean sheet to start again. And with that clean sheet we have some very big opportunities." All that week, the Louisiana State Legislature in Baton Rouge had ben crawling with corporate lobbyists helping to lock in those big opportunities: lower taxes, fewer regulations, cheaper workers and a "smaller, safer city"—which in practice meant plans to level the public housing projects and replace them with condos. Hearing all the talk of "fresh starts" and "clean sheets," you could almost forget the toxic stew of rubble, chemical outflows and human remains just a few miles down the highway.
>
> Over at the shelter, [twenty-three-year-old African American Katrina refugee] Jamar [Perry] could think of nothing else. "I really don't see it as cleaning up the city. What I see is that a lot of people got killed uptown. People who shouldn't have died."
>
> He was speaking quietly, but an older man in line in front of us overheard and whipped around. "What is wrong with these people in Baton Rouge? This isn't an opportunity. It's a goddamned tragedy. Are they blind?"
>
> A mother with two kids chimed in. "No, they're not blind, they're evil. They see just fine."[7]

As Klein has observed, one of the factors that made it easier for the investors to seize this land and do with it what they will was the fact that it was land once occupied by a vulnerable population: a poor community with a sizable African American presence. Writing years before this particular disaster, the prophetic African American science fiction writer Octavia Butler dramatized the privatization of major American cities and the transformation of the American people from citizens into "customers" (read: corporate slaves) in her postapocalyptic novel *Parable of the Sower* (1993). The novel's teenage narrator, Lauren Olamina, is a budding religious prophet and the daughter of a minister and a college professor. The family is lower-middle-class—if such a distinction matters much in the walled, fortified suburban enclave of Robledo, California—but they are constantly fearful of losing their income, their home, and all their possessions to the roving, *Mad Max*–style thieves, arsonists, rapists, and murderers who threaten to sneak into their community and destroy it. One evening, a newly corporatized shelter city of Olivar is advertised on television, and Lauren's stepmother Cory is tempted to relocate the family there, while her father is aghast at the suggestion that they should voluntarily surrender themselves to a new form of slavery dressed up to look like liberation by a slick public relations campaign. The corporate land-grab scheme has been facilitated by newly elected American president Christopher Donner, who promised to restore America to its former greatness through a Milton Friedman/Ayn Rand/Ronald Reagan/Donald Trump–style agenda of lower taxes, fewer federal regulations, more privatization, fewer worker protections, and fewer unions. Olamina describes the conquest of Olivar in her diary:

> After many promises, much haggling, suspicion, fear, hope, and legal wrangling, the voters and the officials of Olivar permitted their town to be taken over, bought out, privatized. . . . The company intends to dominate farming and selling of water and solar and wind energy over much of the southwest—where for pennies it's already bought vast tracts of fertile, waterless land. So far, Olivar is one of its smaller coastal holdings, but with Olivar, it gets an eager, educated work force, people a few years older than I am whose options are very limited. And there's all that formerly public land that they now control. They mean to own great water, power, and agricultural industries in an area that most people have given up on. They have long-term plans, and the people of Olivar have decided to become part of them—to accept smaller salaries than their socio-economic group is used to in exchange for security, a guaranteed food supply, jobs, and help in their battle with the Pacific['s rising sea level]. There are still people in Olivar who are uncomfortable with the change. They know about early American Company towns in which the companies cheated and abused people.
>
> But this is to be different. The people of Olivar aren't frightened, impoverished victims. They're able to look after themselves, their rights and their property. They're educated people who don't want to live in the spreading chaos of the rest of Los Angeles County. Some of them said so on the radio documentary we all listened to last night—as they made a public spectacle of selling themselves to KSF. . . . Maybe Olivar is the future—one face of it. Cities controlled by big companies are old hat in science fiction. My grandmother left a whole bookcase of old science fiction novels. The company-city subgenre always seemed to star a hero who outsmarted,

overthrew, or escaped "the company." I've never seen one where the hero fought like hell to get taken in and underpaid by the company. In real life, that's the way it will be. That's the way it is.[8]

Born in 1947 in Pasadena to a shoeshine man and a maid, Butler was raised by her mother after her father's premature death. Butler's mother would bring home books that the families she worked for no longer wanted, and Butler read them voraciously, including science fiction.[9] After college, where she studied with science fiction author Harlan Ellison, she rented a small apartment in Los Angeles, and "rose each day at 2 a.m. to write. She supported herself through a series of dystopian jobs: dishwasher, telemarketer, potato chips inspector."[10] Butler demonstrated that her life prepared her for writing about dystopian worlds and postapocalyptic future, since she saw herself as an outsider and believed that being black in the United States has always been an apocalyptic, dystopian experience.[11] As *Washington Post* editor Ron Charles observed, "White people always think of dystopias as looking forward into this scary future, but black Americans can look back. They've already come through their dystopia. They had 200 years of horror and slavery. All the kinds of things we imagine the future dystopia being like are what black Americans already went through."[12]

Notably, Butler's books include many believable black characters, including strong black women protagonists modeled on herself. Butler's plots and themes emphasize the importance of empathy and community building in an age of austerity and corporate rule that does not value either.[13] Reading Butler alongside Naomi Klein is an object lesson in the real-world applicability of climate fiction, and of the uncanny ability of certain climate fiction authors to anticipate real-world events before they occur. In many significant ways, *Parable of the Sower* anticipates *The Shock Doctrine*. Olivar anticipates post-Katrina New Orleans. In this respect, science fiction novels have much to teach us about science, politics, and society that our establishment, paint-by-numbers news media perennially fails to do.

In Butler's novel, the encroaching seawater pushed the people of Olivar to sell their town to a corporation that could hold the tide back for them. In our own reality, the flooding caused by Hurricane Katrina caused a refugee crisis. Similarly, the potential future drowning of the Maldives would displace all the peoples of that island nation. These are just a few manifestations of a growing refugee crisis that the world faces as the collateral damage caused by climate change escalates. As Al Gore observed in his 2006 documentary film *An Inconvenient Truth*, "The area around Beijing is home to tens of millions of people. Even worse, in the area around Shanghai, there are 40 million people. Worse still, Calcutta and, to the east Bangladesh, the area covered includes 50 million people. Think of the impact of a couple of hundred thousand refugees when they are displaced by an environmental event and then imagine the impact of a hundred million or more. . . . Adding insult to injury, in many parts of Asia, the rice crop will be decimated by rising sea level—a three-foot sea-level rise will eliminate half of the rice production in Vietnam—causing a food crisis coincident with the mass migration of people."[14]

The scenario described by Gore served as the central narrative conceit and initiating incident creating the futuristic America found in Suzanne Collins's *Hunger Games* trilogy: Panem. In the unofficial guide to the series, *The Panem Companion: From Mellark Bakery to Mockingjays* (2012), V. Arrow posits that the transformation of America into Panem began when rising sea levels sent tens of thousands of previously coastal-dwelling American refugees inland seeking new homes.[15] The influx caused those who were already living inland to resent their presence, causing a cultural and legislative backlash against refugees. This backlash was part of a spike in institutional racism and classism along lines similar to the anti-Irish, anti-Italian, and anti-Jewish immigrant sentiments at their height early in the twentieth century, as well as anti-Hispanic and anti-Muslim immigrant sentiment spiking in the West in the early twenty-first century. V. Arrow writes:

> As Glenn Beck put it: "Every undocumented worker is an illegal immigrant, a criminal and a drain on our dwindling resources." Even those born in the United States who share an ethnic background with many illegal immigrants have been treated as criminals without burden of proof; the racial profiling of the mainstream media has given rise to sanctioned government action against an entire racial/ethnic group.
>
> Given the level of immigration that Panem's geological collapse would cause, it is easy to extrapolate that a true chaos of racial targeting and interpersonal distrust would emerge on both civilian and governmental levels. The Capitol might have reacted to this tension by . . . organizing its administrative units by race, ethnicity, and/or culture . . . [segregating and Balkanizing its oppressed and catalogued peoples into Districts ranked by social and economic importance. T]he white-preferential Panem culture [that emerged] still marginalized the specialty-class cultural elements, turning them into markers of lower class and loss of privilege. Nonwhites were displaced, even within the geographical boundaries of each district. . . . It's an all-too familiar process, seen in everything from the rise of the Colonies/United States and the takeover/elimination of Native Americans to England and India, Australia and its aboriginal population.[16]

Collins's trilogy does not dramatize this backstory, as Katniss Everdeen was born after these historical events and was deprived of any substantive education in history. Nevertheless, what Katniss does know of the history of Panem bears out Arrow's extrapolation, and the novel does, indeed, include the critical information that Panem was born from the crisis caused by rising sea levels. One of the central moral themes of *The Hunger Games* trilogy is that the wealthy have no right to ration the last remaining natural resources the way they do, by starving the poor and the ethnic minorities while they live in wealthy excess. Racism and classism justifies the Capital's divvying up of the postapocalyptic world's wealth in this manner, but even in the state of emergency dramatized by Collins, racism and classism remain morally reprehensible and beyond justification. Katniss's first instinct is to focus on her own and her family's survival in this Darwinian universe, yet even she has enough empathy for the suffering of others to see just how immoral the society of Panem is in its construction. When the racially ambiguous heroine (who may be Melungeon) comes face to face with the sufferings of others, even those she is pitted against in a fight to the death during a televised bread-and-circuses event, her first instinct is to show compassion, and the example of her good heart sparks a revolution that shakes the foundations of a racist, classist, and fundamentally evil society.

As the climate crisis intensifies, the best course of action is human solidarity, not a rise in nationalism, racism, classism, and militarism. Tragically, a global crisis tends to exacerbate the human tendency toward tribalism as much as or more than it calls upon humanity's innate reserves of compassion and biological ability to cooperate. In recent years, tribalism has seemed to win out over compassion, and this victory of dark forces over light has inspired great despair from compassionate thinkers and activists.

Consider the assessment of David Niose, who published "Anti-intellectualism is Killing America" on the *Psychology Today* website on June 23, 2015. His pained editorial was written in the wake of Dylann Storm Roof's arrest for the racially motivated murders of nine African American civilians in a mass shooting at Emanuel African Methodist Episcopal Church in Charleston, South Carolina, on June 17, 2015. Niose considered Roof's confession, which revealed that he hoped to ignite a race war by perpetrating the killings, to be a sign that the United States has become so anti-intellectual that it is in danger of total societal collapse. According to Niose:

> America's rates of murder and other violent crime dwarf most of the rest of the developed world, as does its incarceration rate, while its rates of education and scientific literacy are embarrassingly low. American schools, claiming to uphold "traditional values," avoid fact-based sex education, and thus we have the highest rates of teen pregnancy in the industrialized world. And those rates are notably highest where so-called "biblical values" are prominent. Go outside the Bible belt, and the rates generally trend downward. . . .
>
> [C]orporate interests encourage anti-intellectualism, conditioning Americans into conformity and passive acceptance of institutional dominance. They are the ones who stand to gain from the excessive fear and nationalism that result in militaristic foreign policy and absurdly high levels of military spending. They are the ones who stand to gain from consumers who spend money they don't have on goods and services they don't need. They are the ones who want a public that is largely uninformed and distracted, thus allowing government policy to be crafted by corporate lawyers and lobbyists. They are the ones who stand to gain from unregulated securities markets. And they are the ones who stand to gain from a prison-industrial complex that generates the highest rates of incarceration in the developed world.

Americans can and should denounce the racist and gun-crazed culture that shamefully resulted in nine corpses in Charleston this week, but they also need to dig deeper. At the core of all of this dysfunction is an abandonment of reason.[17]

What Niose describes here is *not* a state of affairs that would be endorsed by C. S. Lewis in any way. While Lewis has been dead for fifty years, the evidence of his own writings suggests that, were he alive today, he would be too intelligent and too kind-hearted to recognize his Christianity—or any authentic species of Christianity, for that matter—in the retrograde mindset Niose describes. Unlike Dominionist Christians who fear that education will lead them inevitably down the path of secular humanism, Lewis does not betray a secret dread that his beliefs are untenable and won't stand up to scrutiny or exposure to alien intellectual ideas. Instead, he has the courage of his convictions and can immerse himself in the greatest thoughts of other cultures and religions and not fear being tainted or derailed by them. So, in *A Grief Observed*, Lewis demonstrates greater fear of the demons of Ignorance and Want found in Charles Dickens's *A Christmas Carol* than in the consequences of eating fruit from the tree of Knowledge of Good and Evil in *Genesis*. His faith in the value of education suggests that he sees it as having the potential to help free us from the rule of fascist forces as we live out our lives in enemy-occupied territory.

In his summation of the scholarly and literary legacy of Lewis at the close of his biography of Lewis, Alister McGrath explains that Lewis remains a controversial figure, but an important and beloved one. McGrath argues:

> The volume and tone of the criticism of Lewis from fundamentalisms of the left and right is ultimately to be seen as a reflection of his iconic cultural status, rather than a reliable gauge of his personal and literary defects. Some will doubtless continue to accuse Lewis of writing disguised religious propaganda, crudely and cruelly dressed up as literature. Others will see him as a superb, even visionary, advocate and defender of the rationality of faith, whose powerful appeals to imagination and logic expose the shallowness of naturalism. Some will hold him to defend socially regressive viewpoints, based on the bygone world of England in the 1940s. Others will see him as a prophetic critic of cultural trends that were widely accepted in his time, but are now recognized as destructive, degrading and damaging. . . . Most, however, will see Lewis simply as a gifted writer who brought immense pleasure to many and illumination to some—and who, above all, celebrated the classic art of good writing as a way of communicating ideas and expanding minds.[18]

Lewis believed in knowledge and in love and justice. He was opposed to fascism, imperialism, and institutional racism. Indeed, Lewis warned against the racism and nationalism that arises during periods of crisis, condemning it as evil and unChristian.

Employing Lewis to discuss the problem of white supremacism and ultranationalism in contemporary America, *Washington Post* columnist Laura Turner reviewed Lewis's perspective on nationalism in *The Four Loves* (1960). She quoted Lewis's observation that the love of one's own country "becomes a demon when it becomes a god." For Turner, Lewis's thoughts on the overlap between racist and patriotic sentiments are critical ones to return to in our contemporary political context. "Citing examples of damage done in the name of patriotism, Lewis mentions the trampling of Native American tribes, the gas chambers of Nazi Germany, the sins of apartheid. The love of one's country, driven to the far edge of idolatry, has always led to the enforcement of a fear-based ideology, and often to death. . . . This is not to say that Lewis sees all patriotism as a straight path to racism. We can have a good and natural affection for our particular home, he writes. But we must not let that love of home prevent us from acknowledging the sins of the past. 'The actual history of every country is full of shabby and even shameful doings,' he writes."[19]

In Lewis, contemporary readers may find a soothing antidote to "ugly American"–style patriotism and imperialist Christian theology employed as a weapon of empire building, colonial projects, and racial profiling and subjugation.

As anyone reading this book would have grasped, the possible racist, totalitarian future scenarios illustrated above by Nasheed, Collins, Gore, Lewis, and Arrow are all resoundingly bleak. In these cases, the natural human inclination to tribalism and sorting by kind would be exacerbated by climate change. In addition to looking to our own hearts and challenging our tendencies toward that same tribalism, would it not be a good thing to try to heed the cautionary tales here and either try to halt or slow the sea-level rise, or prepare for it? Little of the above is happening. Too many of our local, national, and international political leaders are too busy pretending that the crisis is not real—or that a magic wand solution will be found by scientists soon—to prevent real sacrifices from being made in the name of the greater good.

Not enough is being done, and time is running short.

## *Snowpiercer*: The Perils of Hacking the Planet as a Last Resort

Several films have been made in recent years that pose the question: What emergency measures could we take to save the world at the very last moment when we have run out of time to act? The answers they suggest are deeply unpleasant. Several such stories concern wealthy scientists who attempt to save the world by sacrificing most of its human population—and electing to rescue a small handful of their own wealthy friends to form the foundation of a new, better, postapocalyptic society. *The Secret Service* (2012) is a comic book that writer Mark Millar collaborated on with artist Dave Gibbons about a megalomaniac Steve Jobs stand-in named Dr. Arnold who has installed a booby trap in each of the cell phones he's distributed that, at his command, will induce a murderous rage in everyone on the planet. The worldwide berserker fit will trigger a holocaust that will decimate the human population, and the only ones who will remain untouched will be those whom he has hand-picked to grant shelter and immunity to. The comic was a revisiting of themes Millar addressed during his work on *The Fantastic Four* comic book *The Death of the Invisible Woman*, a satirical retelling of *Atlas Shrugged* with an inverted moral (examined in greater detail in my 2011 monograph *War, Politics and Superheroes*). *The Secret Service* inspired an adaptation titled *Kingsman: The Secret Service* (2015), directed by Matthew Vaughn and written by Vaughn and Jane Goldman. The film incorporates the climate change crisis themes of the *Fantastic Four* story into its narrative, and the Dr. Arnold character has been changed to Richmond Valentine (Samuel L. Jackson), a composite of Jobs, Spike Lee, and environmentalist James Bond villain Karl Stromberg from the film *The Spy Who Loved Me* (1977). In his version of the classic "Bond villain gives away his evil plan by monologuing," Valentine explains that he will use his cell phone weapon to initiate the cull to save the planet from climate disaster.

> VALENTINE: When you get a virus, you get a fever. That's the human body raising its core temperature to kill the virus. Planet Earth works the same way: Global warming is the fever, mankind is the virus. We're making our planet sick. A cull is our only hope. If we don't reduce our population ourselves, there's only one of two ways this can go: The host kills the virus, or the virus kills the host. Either way—

> ARTHUR: The result is the same: The virus dies.

Valentine's rationale inspires Arthur, the head of a special branch of the British Secret Service called the Kingsmen—to stand down in his efforts to stop Valentine's plot. However, several of the agents under his command, including the working-class Eggsy and the gay, aristocratic "John Steed" character played by Colin Firth, have decided to continue to try to save humanity now and find another way to save the planet later.

Valentine's Malthusian scheme resembles a similar plot carried out by the villains of Dan Brown's fourth Robert Langdon novel, *Inferno* (2013), who seek to sterilize one-third of the earth's populace with a vector virus to save the planet from the consequences of human overpopulation. Additionally, Crake, the corporate ecoterrorist of Margaret Atwood's *MaddAddam* trilogy, wipes out most of humanity by planting a time-release virus in his mass-marketed BlyssPluss pills, which were falsely advertised as the ultimate sex pill—a "silver bullet" drug offering foolproof protection from pregnancy and sexually transmitted disease while enhancing sexual pleasure, virility, and holding back the effects of aging. Naturally, the pill was so popular conceptually, and distributed so strategically in urban centers worldwide, that when the virus was released, the ensuing carnage was impossible to contain.

The fact that variations of the mass-murder-as-solution-to-climate-change evil plan has appeared in several high-profile potboilers of the past several years is a testimony to

Fig. 5.2. In the film *Kingsman: The Secret Service* (2015) ecoterrorist villain Richmond Valentine (Samuel L. Jackson, right), plans to halt climate change by killing off most of the human population. A John Steed–style hero named Harry Hart (Colin Firth, center) and his blue-collar protégé Eggsy Unwin (Taron Egerton, left) are agents of a branch of the British Secret Service investigating Valentine's plan who hope to stop him. In this scene, Harry and Eggsy encounter Valentine unexpectedly while shopping for clothes on Savile Row. 20th Century Fox.

the extent to which ecological anxieties have become more mainstream. The question remains: Does airing these anxieties in the context of thrillers such as *Inferno*, *Kingsman*, and *Avengers: Infinity War* do any good for the cause of environmental justice? Since Valentine is a gay environmentalist, several conservative viewers embraced the movie's message, which they saw as an indictment of the values of President Barack Obama's America, and several Glenn Beck fans gleefully dubbed it the most conservative movie in many years. Fully aware that the film provoked this response, environmentalist Michael Svoboda was appalled by *Kingsman*'s treatment of climate change (and depiction of Valentine) because he believed the film did real damage to the cause of climate advocacy.[20] Svoboda's concerns are understandable, but it seems reasonable to suggest that Valentine's methods are what the film is criticizing, not his message. What Millar does in his comic stories is what Ricky Gervais, Sarah Silverman, and Stephen Colbert often do in their comedy: he pretends to advance a reactionary position while lampooning it through an over-the-top tone and an "if you folks could only hear yourselves" subtext. Millar says he uses this tactic because he feels like "there's nothing duller than some worthy" liberal culture commentary. He is progressive but doesn't think sermons work in fiction, arguing that all thinking people know what is going on in the world and don't need him to set them straight. Satire is both more fun and better storytelling, and it doesn't insult the intelligence of the audience, he feels.[21]

As exploitative as Millar's stories tend to be, they do make one wonder what scientists in the real world are considering doing as a last-minute emergency measure to save us all—hopefully, beyond orchestrating a mass culling of human beings. There are, indeed, several possible plans to "hack" the planet as a last resort, if the need arises. Theoretical physicist Michio Kaku explained in *Physics of the Future: How Science Will Shape Human Destiny and Our Daily Lives by the Year 2100* (2011) that the following radical proposals have been advanced to control greenhouse gases:

- **Launching pollutants into the atmosphere.** One proposal is to send rockets into the upper atmosphere, where they would release pollutants, such as sulfur dioxide, in order to reflect sunlight into space, thereby cooling the earth. In fact, Nobel laureate Paul Crutzen has advocated shooting pollution into space as a "doomsday device," providing one final escape route for humanity to stop global warming. . . . Little is known about how a huge quantity of pollutants will affect the world temperature. Maybe the benefits will be short-lived, or the unintended side effects may be worse than the original problem. . . .

- **Creating algae blooms.** Another suggestion is to dump iron-based chemicals into the oceans. These mineral nutrients will cause algae to thrive in the ocean, which in turn will increase the amount of carbon dioxide that is absorbed by the algae. . . .

- **Genetic engineering.** Another proposal is to use genetic engineering to specifically create life forms that can absorb large quantities of carbon dioxide. . . . Princeton physicist Freeman Dyson has advocated another variation, creating a genetically engineered variety of trees that would be adept at absorbing carbon dioxide. He has stated that perhaps a trillion such trees might be enough to control the carbon dioxide in the air. . . . However, as with any plan to use genetic engineering on a large scale, one must be careful about side effects. One cannot recall a life form in the same way that we can recall a defective car. Once it is released into the environment, the genetically engineered life form may have unintended consequences for other life forms, especially if it displaces local species of plants and upsets the balance of the food chain.

Sadly, there has been a conspicuous lack of interest among politicians to fund any of these plans. However, one day, global warming will become so painful and disruptive that politicians will be forced to implement some of them.[22]

Tolkien devotees might well relish the thought of the creation of Freeman Dyson's super trees as real-world stewards of the planet akin to the Ents. Also, the algae blooms scheme explored above features in Sean Murphy's climate fiction comic book *Punk Rock Jesus* (2012). These climate fiction resonances notwithstanding, Kaku's list of potential last-minute get-out-of-jail-free card schemes seems troubling. Science-based as these ideas are, all of them seem to suggest magic wand solutions to be employed at the last moment, when humanity should take far more thoughtful, far less invasive action far more quickly. Fighting pollution with other forms of pollution, and reversing the effects of meddling with the planet by doing more, slightly different meddling with the planet seems like a dangerously misguided notion. Kunstler and Klein have both condemned the kinds of plans and thinking Kaku explicates above.

Of the above potential doomsday "solutions" to climate change explored by Kaku, perhaps the most alarming one is the idea of hacking the planet by firing enough pollutants into the atmosphere to reflect sunlight off the Earth and cool it. It sounds like a dangerous scheme, indeed, and ideas like it inspired the climate change denial science fiction book *Fallen Angels* (1991) by Larry Niven, Jerry Pournelle, and Michael Flynn. Another climate fiction narrative inspired by such thinking is the 2013 film *Snowpiercer*, directed by South Korean filmmaker Bong Joon-ho, which was based on a French comic book, *Snow Piercer* (by Jean-Marc Rochette, Jacques Lob, and Benjamin Legrand). In the film's prologue, the Earth has reached a tipping point in which a disastrous and endless global warming feedback loop has produced runaway temperature rise that will burn the planet to a cinder. To break free from the feedback loop, world leaders work together to coat the Earth's atmosphere with CW7. Tragically, the CW7 works too well, cutting off so much sunlight from the planet that the global temperature drops precipitously and freezes the world, killing off almost all plant, animal, and human life. Anticipating that the CW7 would have this effect, a billionaire engineer named Wilford creates the Snowpiercer, a "miracle train" conceived as a "luxury locomotive cruise line connecting railways of the entire world into one." Snowpiercer travels 438,000 kilometers a year, circling the Earth once a year, and is "designed to withstand the extreme cold of arctic and scorching heat of African desert." Wilford fortifies the train against all possible climate change scenarios he could envision, "over-engineering and over-equipping" Snowpiercer. As CW7 Doomsday approaches, Wilford invites his wealthiest friends and colleagues onto his train, and it becomes a magic lifeboat for the wealthy in the vein of the Elysium space station and the arks from *2012*. Despite his plans to make the train exclusively for the rich, however, an unruly gathering of poor refugees manages to find passage onto the train. Wilford hoards them into the rear compartments and abandons them there to die without food or water. In short order, the refugees in the rear cabin descend into violent cannibalism and feed off babies and anyone sick, weak, or wounded. This descent into madness is halted when a leader emerges in the rear compartments. Gilliam (John Hurt) cuts off his own arm and offers it to the cannibals intent upon eating a baby. Wilford, who keeps the rear compartments under constant surveillance, is moved enough by Gilliam's sacrifice to order the creation of protein bars comprised of ground-up insects for the stowaways. For a time, a fragile peace settles over Snowpiercer.

Meanwhile, the middle-class passengers at the center of the train serve the wealthiest at the front by cooking gourmet food and performing classical music for them, growing plants in greenhouses, educating the children, maintaining a vast aquarium, and contributing to the maintenance of a self-contained, balanced ecosystem that works well for everyone . . . except those in the rear compartment eating insect protein bars.

As with *Elysium*, *Snowpiercer* is both a reflection of the contemporary state of affairs—the differences between the economic classes within nations and the disparity between rich and poor nations on the world stage—as well as a projection of what might happen if we continue to refuse to take meaningful steps to prevent climate catastrophe. Humanity cannot afford to wait for Exxon, the Supreme Court, or the Republican Party to do the right thing and save our species from extinction. If anything, these establishment organizations have proven that they are interested in quite the reverse—pushing humanity closer to the brink than it already is. No matter what our religion, ethnicity, nationality, political allegiance, socioeconomic class, or occupation, we need to demand better from our leaders. If these plutocrats do not give us better, we need to remove them from power, or force them to get out of our way as we address this global crisis. If we do not, then *Snowpiercer* may well be one of the rosier possible futures awaiting us.

Fortunately, the breadth and depth of climate activism has blossomed in recent years, especially in response to the Keystone XL and Dakota Access Pipeline projects, to the election of Donald Trump to the presidency, and to Trump's choice of ExxonMobil CEO Rex Tillerson (2006–16) as his secretary of state. All these horrifying political and economic developments have enraged environmentalists, water protectors, and indigenous peoples' rights activists and inspired a powerful, widespread, and possibly world-saving grassroots pushback. At a news conference in New York City on December 13, 2016, Hollywood actor and environmental activist Mark Ruffalo made a passionate appeal to fossil fuel investors, arguing for the importance of the fossil fuel divestment movement and supporting the Standing Rock water protectors against the Dakota Access Pipeline (DAPL). His entire statement is worth quoting:

> I want to thank the fossil fuel industry for a hundred years of concentrated carbon fuel to bring us to this place and, through the technological revolution, to give us the technology today to move forward and away from burning carbon, which is killing our planet and our people. This is a twofold approach that you're seeing unfold in front of you. It started with the students. Of course it did, because the students are a moral authority. They haven't been corrupted yet by the influence of money, and so their voices and their hearts are pure. They know what's happening, and it's terrifying to them. And you have a giant social movement starting to blossom in the world today, because the young people know that their lives are at stake, their futures are at stake.

Fig. 5.3. In *Snowpiercer* (2013), the last remaining humans on Earth have survived a freak accident ice apocalypse on a never-ending train voyage. On the train, the wealthy few enjoy luxury in the front cars, the poor are starved and enslaved in the tail section, and the middle-class in the center cars are indoctrinated to love and serve their wealthy "benefactors." CJ Entertainment.

All the money in the world doesn't mean a goddamn thing if the world is burning around them, if they don't have water, if the air isn't clean and if the sun and the elements and the weather become their constant enemy.

So, you have beautiful people in the business sector who hear the call, whose moral vision hasn't been so clouded, that they understand that now is the time to make a move forward to our future. And it's a very beautiful future. It's a future that excludes geopolitical strife. We won't be fighting trillion-dollar wars over energy assets. It's a future that keeps our energy dollars here in the state. It creates 3.5 million net gain of jobs, from the jobs we lose from the fossil industry. It allows people to stay home. They don't have to go to extraction sites and put their lives in danger and put communities in danger, with the crime that comes with it, with that fossil fuel extraction.

Lastly, we have a cultural movement that's arising. And we will keep fighting. What you see happening at DAPL is only the beginning. The 500,000 people that showed up for the climate march is only the beginning. And we are going to keep putting pressure on you businesses and you banks—Citibank, Wells Fargo—to stop poisoning our people and stop financing climate change. And we're not going to stop. If you have your money in fossil fuel industry, you're going to lose it. That's the message coming out of today. That's the message coming out of our youth. That's the message coming out of our technological movement and leaders. Get your money out now, while you can.[23]

# Eden Revisited

## Ursula K. Le Guin, St. Francis, and the Ecofeminist Storytelling Model

I believe that Saint Francis is the example par excellence of care for the vulnerable and of an integral ecology lived out joyfully and authentically. He is the patron saint of all who study and work in the area of ecology, and he is also much loved by non-Christians. He was particularly concerned for God's creation and for the poor and outcast. He loved, and was deeply loved for his joy, his generous self-giving, his openheartedness. He was a mystic and a pilgrim who lived in simplicity and in wonderful harmony with God, with others, with nature and with himself. He shows us just how inseparable the bond is between concern for nature, justice for the poor, commitment to society, and interior peace.

—Pope Francis, "Encyclical Letter, Laudato Si: On Care for Our Common Home"

### Abigail Adams, John Adams, and the Unfulfilled Promise of the American Revolution

On March 31, 1776, Abigail Adams wrote a letter to her husband John, asking for news of the Continental Congress' signing of the Declaration of Independence and urging him and the other founding fathers to remember to fight for rights for women as well as for men in their plans for future governance:

I long to hear that you have declared an independency. And, by the way, in the new code of laws which I suppose it will be necessary for you to make, I desire you would remember the ladies and be more generous and favorable to them than your ancestors. Do not put such unlimited power into the hands of the husbands. Remember, all men would be tyrants if they could. If particular care and attention is not paid to the ladies, we are determined to foment a rebellion, and will not hold ourselves bound by any laws in which we have no voice or representation.

That your Sex are Naturally Tyrannical is a Truth so thoroughly established as to admit of no dispute, but such of you as wish to be happy willingly give up the harsh title of Master for the more tender and endearing one of Friend. Why then, not put it out of the power of the vicious and the Lawless to use us with cruelty and indignity with impunity. Men of Sense in all Ages abhor those customs which treat us only as the vassals of your Sex. Regard us then as Beings placed by providence under your protection and in imitation of the Supreme Being make use of that power only for our happiness.[1]

Abigail Adams's letter protests the imminent formation of the United States as a patriarchal nation in which women lack the right to vote, and she predicts the rise of the feminist movement challenging male societal dominance. The correspondence is forward-thinking in its exhortation to John to consider women's role in the Republic a critical priority; it is also striking in its framing of the enfranchising of women and the treatment of women with respect and compassion as Divinely endorsed causes that are part and parcel of authentic Christianity.

John Adams composed his response to Abigail on April 14, 1776:

As to your extraordinary code of laws, I cannot but laugh. We have been told that our struggle has loosened the bonds of government everywhere; that children and apprentices were disobedient; that schools and colleges were grown turbulent; that Indians slighted their guardians, and negroes grew insolent to their masters. But your letter was the first intimation that another tribe, more numerous and powerful than all the rest, were grown discontented. —This is rather too coarse a Compliment but you are so saucy, I won't blot it out. Depend upon it, we know better than to repeal our masculine systems. Although they are in full force, you know they are little more than theory. We dare not exert our power in its full latitude. We are obliged to go fair and softly, and, in practice, you know we are the subjects. We have only the name of masters, and rather than give up this, which would completely subject us to the despotism of the petticoat, I hope General Washington and all our brave heroes would fight; I am sure every good politician would plot, as long as he would against despotism, empire, monarchy, aristocracy, oligarchy, or ochlocracy.[2]

John Adams's letter is interesting not only for its lighthearted tone and refusal to heed Abigail's warning, but because John perceives the ramifications of her desire to see the democratic principles of the age of Revolution fully realized; if freedom and political power for women is an indisputable good decreed by Providence, then it logically follows that Providence would also approve of the granting of freedom and political power to Indians, negroes, students, and children. To John's mind, the institutional repression of so many disenfranchised peoples was a necessary evil, and the potentially far-reaching scope of Abigail's argument could lead, conceivably, to the end of all such oppression. Consequently, John needed to refuse Abigail's call for women's suffrage because it would open a revolutionary line of thinking that would, inevitably, justify the enfranchisement of the disenfranchised and create an America governed by the tyranny of the great unwashed masses.

If you consider the origins of the practice of the patriarchal oppression of women as explored in *Women's Work, Men's Property: The Origins of Gender and Class* (1986), then it is unsurprising that John Adams would make the rhetorical connections that he does between various potentially revolutionary groupings of people. As the editors of the Verso anthology, Stephanie Coontz and Peta Henderson, wrote in their introduction, "Female subordination actually preceded and established the basis for the emergence of true private property and the state. The historical process involved varied in time and place, but once set in motion, the evolution of sexual and social stratification was closely intertwined. The oppression of women provided a means of differential accumulation among men, which in turn gave some men special access to the labor and reproductive powers of women, as well as to the services of other men. As class stratification became institutionalized, we find that lower-class men were often assimilated to the status of women, while women as a category were assigned to the juridicial status of propertyless in a system increasingly based on private property. . . . [T]he oppression of women was a foundation for a traditional class society . . . [and] sex and class oppression have developed in ways that render them analytically virtually inseparable."[3] Add racial oppression and the exploitation of plants and animals to this discussion and it becomes clear that the ecofeminist view that all oppressions stem from the oppression of the universal "feminine" is strongly justifiable. The sparring match between Founding Mother and Founding Father fought in the pages of their correspondences anticipated a line of thought that has become a foundational idea of ecofeminism. The problems of sexism, racism, slavery, colonialism, and the pollution of the environment are inextricably linked. They are one problem with one solution: a new ethic of respect for all life and a liberation of all life from a tyrannical system.

Ecofeminists are concerned with "the various ways that sexism, hetero-normality, racism, colonialism, and ableism are informed and supported by speciesism and how analyzing the ways these forces intersect can produce less violent, more just practices."[4] One of the unifying tenets of ecofeminism is that the enduring societal preference for the masculine over the feminine has informed the systemic oppression of women around the world. This oppression of women is linked to the oppression of the symbolically "feminized" racial and ethnic minority populations and nonhuman animals that members of the dominant patriarchal culture deem as inferior. In this misogynistic worldview, the correlation between women, ethnic minority populations, and flora and fauna of the natural world are earmarked as united in inferiority. Their inferiority justifies their subjugation, exploitation, rape, and—in many cases—slaughter. The result of "the animalization (to represent *as*, to compare *with*, other animals) of some people in the process of racialization and dehumanization" has led to the development of the institutions of slavery and colonialism, and to ethnic cleansing and genocide movements, including the British Empire's campaigns against the Irish, Indians, and Native Americans, and Nazi Germany's persecution of Jews, gays, blacks, and gypsies.[5] The ecofeminist awareness of the connective tissue between systemic antifeminism, colonialism, and despoiling of the natural world informs their desire to confront all of the above, seemingly separate evils as one great evil—a hatred of the feminine, the maternal, and Mother Nature. Ecofeminist ethics confronts the racist, sexist, and exploitative worldview—that is to say, the *fascist* worldview—with its mirror image: a worldview that fosters a love of the feminine, of feminine values such as education, caregiving, conflict resolution, stewardship of the environment, appreciation of racial and ethnic diversity, and an embracing of gender equality and fluidity. According to ecofeminist Karen Warren, a new form of ethical behavior would include a feminized understanding of interpersonal relations and caregiving. Her conception of feminine "care" is as "a species activity that includes everything that we do to maintain, continue, and repair our 'world' so that we can live in it as well as possible. That world includes our bodies, ourselves, and our environment, all of which we seek to interweave in a complex, life-sustaining web."[6]

As one might expect, the typical arguments leveled against the ecofeminist perspective tend to focus on its essentializing gender norms, all-encompassing scope, embracing of a John Lennon–like idealistic spiritualism that doesn't lend itself to practical action in the real world, and a "good versus evil" worldview. As Lucy Sargisson argued in "What's Wrong with Ecofeminism?" (2001), the utopianism underpinning the ecofeminist worldview is both its strength and its weakness.[7] Sargisson's objections are important to consider, but a philosophy need not be impervious to critique to inspire individuals to do good in its name or to serve as a welcome alternative to the neoliberal socioeconomic program now dominating the globe.

Furthermore, legitimate criticisms notwithstanding, an awareness of the ecofeminist perspective can help illuminate patterns of oppression that might not otherwise be apparent. For example, in the United States, the state of Oklahoma has earned a well-deserved reputation for being hostile to both women's rights and the environmentalist movement. Oklahoma's notorious hostility to these values is related to the conservative brand of Southern Baptist Christianity most prevalent in the state as well as the political and economic power that the oil and natural gas industries hold in the region. Oklahoma Native Alley Agee, author of "Oklahoma's Energy Discourse: An Ecofeminist Rhetorical Analysis," explores the dynamics of Red State politics and explains the seemingly counterintuitive nationwide Republican initiative to pair "extreme reproductive choice restrictions with lax restrictions on fracking and other energy policies." From a libertarian perspective, the pairing of these positions seems hypocritical in the extreme. From the perspective of the patriarchy pitted against ecofeminist values, the two positions make perfect sense, as both involve the subjugation and exploitation of the feminine: the control of the human female body and the violation of the feminine Nature. In a patriarchal worldview, a woman exists solely to be penetrated by the male member and the Earth exists solely to be penetrated by the oil and natural gas industry. God granted men Dominion over the Earth—and over women. Therefore, men have the right to rape women and the Earth however often they wish. As female champion of the patriarchy Sarah Palin said, "Drill, baby, drill." Agee writes:

> Oklahoma has very few regulations on fracking, yet its politicians are some of the loudest voices demanding the federal government leave it up to the states to implement their own regulation. Oklahoma Senators Jim Inhofe and Tom Coburn were key promoters of the FRESH Act, a bill that would have given all control of fracking regulations to the states, and both use Oklahoma as a model example of "safe" and "environmentally friendly" fracking. Unsurprisingly, Oklahoma ranks fourth in natural gas production in the US, and Inhofe and Coburn never fail to point out that the first site for fracking was in Durant, Oklahoma in 1949.
>
> As a Red state with a Republican governor, Republican-controlled Congress, and Republicans holding all other state-wide offices, strict regulations on women's reproductive rights and very little environmental regulation are not surprising. . . . Conservatives use similar practices and arguments to justify the two seemingly opposite positions of extreme regulation and no regulation. For example, in both debates religious conservatives try to de-value or exclude scientific evidence. Despite evidence linking increased earthquakes in Oklahoma to increased fracking, politicians like Jim Inhofe continue to deny legitimacy to these arguments. Inhofe has even criticized the EPA for pursuing studies on fracking, claiming it is unnecessary. Similarly, anti-choice politicians continue to pass legislation that restricts access to birth control despite empirical (and logical) data that proves birth control decreases unwanted pregnancies and thus decreases abortion. Examples like these are endless . . . [and] the question must be asked: are there deeper underlying connections between women and the environment that create the political connections? An ecofeminist would say yes.[8]

Agee's argument resonates with the perspective of the Christian Stewards of the Earth. In contrast, Agee's form of ecofeminism is completely incompatible with the Dominionist Christian view of the relationship between humanity and the planet—and of the relationship between the genders. Indeed, some Dominionist Theologians have argued that the Creation story in the Book of Genesis invalidates Abigail Adams's perspective that God would approve of a women's movement because the Bible dramatizes God's establishment of the patriarchy and of man's right to rule over women and all of Creation.[9] Other explicators of Biblical texts, such as literary critic and religious studies scholar James

Rovira, have argued that Genesis shows that the world as it is constituted now is not what God intended it to be: "Creation narratives articulate primal values for the cultures that they serve. Genesis, for example, not only explains the creation of the universe, but the origin of human suffering and of the differentiation of male and female suffering through its different sources (men in their vocational lives; women in their subjection to men and to pain in childbirth), of meat eating and the estrangement between humans and animals, of the creation of the nation and of its laws and political structure, and even of the origins of local landmarks. In the way that it identifies both meat eating and human suffering as the product of a Fall, it affirms that the world should not be this way, that people should not suffer, that work shouldn't be so hard and unforgiving, and that women should not be subject to men in the ways that they have been and usually still are."[10]

Here again it is useful to turn to C. S. Lewis, who is often understood as a misogynist theologian, yet who is capable of surprising flashes of feminist thought. Lewis was someone who had opposed the creation of female clergy, failed to invite women to any meetings of the Inklings, and expressed disdain for female academics in his unpublished, fragmented Ransom adventure, *The Dark Tower*.[11] However, he included in *A Grief Observed* (1961) a powerful hymn to gender harmony and symbiosis:

> There is, hidden or flaunted, a sword between the sexes till an entire marriage reconciles them. It is an arrogance in us to call frankness, fairness and chivalry "masculine" when we see them in a woman, it is arrogance in them, to describe a man's sensitiveness or tact or tenderness as "feminine." But also what poor warped fragments of humanity most mere men and women must be to make the implications of that arrogance plausible. Marriage heals this. Jointly the two become fully human. "In the image of God created He *them*." Thus, by a paradox, this carnival of sexuality leads us out beyond our sexes.

The above passage represented for critic Ann Loades, "something of a late revolution in his thinking . . . coming close to the end of his life [that is] . . . perhaps all the more impressive and commendable for that."[12] And yet, two decades earlier, Lewis explored this notion of gender-bending and gender fluidity in his rewriting of the Adam and Eve narrative in the second book of his *Space Trilogy*. In *Perelandra* (1943), Professor Ransom prevents the Fall of another Adam and Eve on the planet Venus, thereby creating an opportunity for the inhabitants of Venus to experience a healthier form of gender relations and a more humane attitude toward their home planet.

It is also notable that, as a lay theologian, Lewis exercised restraint when it came to exhorting women to follow a specific moral program regarding their sexual and reproductive lives. Since Lewis made the object of *Mere Christianity* the discussion of tenets that should be considered central and fundamental to all branches of Christianity, he omitted moralizing about female sexuality because he did not see the policing of women's bodies as a key tenet of Christianity. As he put it, "I have said nothing about birth-control. I am not a woman nor even a married man, nor am I a priest. I do not think it my place to take a firm line about pains, dangers and expenses from which I am protected."[13] Lewis also expressed progressive views of premarital sex. In Lewis's mind, cohabiting and exploring one's own personal sexual identity before marriage prevented bad unions from taking place and prevented the breaking of sacred vows. Premarital sex was preferable to divorce.[14]

Furthermore, unlike some of his male theologian comrades, Lewis depicts the female body as good and beautiful and sexuality as natural and not evil. In his *Space Trilogy*, Lewis depicts "female figures as unashamedly unclothed" and "sexual desire" as natural, showing a refusal to embrace "any Gnostic tradition," Matthew Dickerson and David O'Hara explain.[15] "He recognized the fundamental goodness of the physical Earth, including the pleasures of the Earth, such as that of partaking in and enjoying a good harvest. Lewis once said, 'There is no good trying to be a purely spiritual creature. That is why [God] uses material things like bread and wine to put new life into us. We may think this rather crude and unspiritual. God does not: He invented eating. He likes matter. He invented it."[16] For Lewis, the body is good after all. For Lewis, the earth is good after all. Consequently, the human body and the earth should be nurtured and protected, and God has decreed it thus.

Lewis's theological positions on women and human sexuality were a natural extension of his relationships with women in the real world. In *The Oxford Inklings*, Colin Duriez writes an extended passage concerning Lewis's perennially controversial relationships with the women in his life—including Mrs. Moore and Joy Davidman—in terms that are more positive than are often found in other Inklings biographies. It is worth quoting in its entirety:

> On the Western Front C. S. Lewis had lost an army friend named "Paddy" Moore, who was almost exactly his age. Before Paddy's death, Lewis had promised that should anything happen to his friend, he would take care of his mother and younger sister. This brought life-changing complications into Lewis's undergraduate days, and in fact into his entire life up to the early 1950s. Lewis was to help to support Mrs. Janie "Minto" Moore until her death in 1951, and her daughter, Maureen, for many years. Janie Moore was the first woman he self-sacrificingly helped. Much later in life, he was to do the same for the woman he married, who at first needed British citizenship and then succumbed rapidly to terminal cancer—Joy Davidman. The early loss of his mother, whom he had been unable to help, even with his fervent prayers, meant that ever afterwards he reached out when he could to women in great need. Particularly after he became well-known for his writings, this was evident from his conscientious and careful responses to frequent letters from women undergoing many kinds of difficulty and wanting advice.[17]

The pre–Vatican II Roman Catholic Tolkien, like many other more conservative Christians who have followed Lewis's life with careful interest over the years, found

Lewis's relationships with women such as Joy problematic. From a feminist perspective, however, it seems clear that Tolkien's views of women were more problematic than Lewis's. Thanks to the scars he suffered during his formative years, Tolkien had an unfortunate tendency to regard the women in his life as Dryads or Beatrice Portinari figures, and the few women featured in his corpus tend to be cast in the same molds. Furthermore, during his first real conversation with Lewis at a faculty meeting, Tolkien proclaimed that "'[a]ll literature . . . is written for the amusement of *men* between thirty and forty.' Lewis famously concluded his diary record of the meeting with Tolkien thus: 'No harm in him: only needs a smack or so.' "[18]

It is interesting that Lewis felt compelled to observe that Tolkien might deserve a smack for expressing the kinds of opinions that both Lewis's champions and detractors might well assume that Lewis would espouse himself. But Lewis is forever frustrating attempts to earmark him as reactionary with his forward-thinking views. Perhaps most surprisingly of all, considering that he is embraced by the American Christian Right, Lewis espoused tolerant views toward homosexual love as well as heterosexual. In his autobiography, *Surprised by Joy* (1955), Lewis condemned the elitism, violence, and insular thinking of the British boarding school system, painting a picture of the secondary preparatory school he attended, Malvern College, that is as negative as the representation of the British boarding school system found in the Lindsay Anderson film *If . . .* (1968). Like Anderson, Lewis suggests that one of the few redeeming qualities of the boarding school is that some young boys find a rewarding, romantic love between one another that mitigates the experience of having to come of age in such worldly, oppressive, materialistic, and socially stratified surroundings.[19]

Here it would be appropriate to mention another biographical anecdote. As Alister McGrath attests, when Lewis's friend Greeves informed Lewis that he was both gay and in love with Lewis, Lewis responded by letting Greeves down gently. The heterosexual Lewis continued to be friends with Greeves, did not condemn Greeves's homosexuality, try to "cure" Greeves with electroshock treatments (as Mike Pence would have suggested), or insult or oppress Greeves in any manner reflective of how many famous contemporary Dominionists would be likely to have treated Greeves. This acceptance of Greeves is both authentically Christian and emblematic of Lewis's kind-heartedness. Indeed, according to Lewis, the British people were not homophobic because they saw homophobia as mandated by the Bible, but they were homophobic because they feared suffering the same social, political, and criminal disgrace suffered by Oscar Wilde. The fall of Wilde was a trauma that rocked Victorian England and its reverberations were felt for generations.[20] Indeed, Lewis's sober dissection of homophobia in *Surprised by Joy* is emblematic of how intelligently he deconstructs the most controversial issues faced by Christianity in modern times. If Lewis found himself in an intellectual straitjacket, in part because of his faith, he fought to get out of it with the assurance that doing so would bring him to a higher plane of truth and a purer form of Christianity.

All told, it seems clear that Lewis's views on human sexuality, homosexuality, and the place of women in religion and society are not what the stereotypical view of Lewis as stodgy Christian reactionary would suggest they would be. Casual readers of Lewis, including those who have only read *The Lion, the Witch, and the Wardrobe*, would likely be surprised by many of the passages of Lewis quoted in this monograph. One scholar who holds strong views on this subject is Monika Hilder. Hilder feels that Lewis is too often labeled a sexist by public figures such as J. K. Rowling and Philip Pullman, and that these popular writers are poisoning the public's perception of Lewis. Hilder wrote three monographs on the subject of Lewis's relationships to women and depictions of women in his writings: *Surprised by the Feminine: A Rereading of C. S. Lewis and Gender* (2013), *The Gender Dance: Ironic Subversion in C. S. Lewis's Cosmic Trilogy* (2013), and *The Feminine Ethos in C. S. Lewis's* Chronicles of Narnia (2012). In an essay Hilder wrote for the anthology *Women and C. S. Lewis* (2015), she asked:

> [W]hat do Lewis' views of gender have to do with us in the twenty-first century? Everything. Whether the challenge is personal or global, sexism destroys . . . [Lewis] was not a sexist but a seer. . . . [Only half-jokingly, he referred to himself as] the "Old woman of Oxford" . . . As a seer, Lewis fought the "masculine" Superman where "might makes right," predicted Superman's ultimate downfall, and celebrated the feminine, spiritual person whose so-called "weakness" of Christ-like humility and patient endurance overcomes satanic hatred.
>
> Lewis is a prophet whose moral vision potentially transforms our world. As human beings who are "feminine" in relationship to the "masculine" God of the Bible, we are subjects called to reign with justice and mercy, regardless of our gender. In the present world and throughout eternity, receptivity is the proper response to God and to each other—then truth and peace and joy will flourish. For Lewis, *truth*—God's sovereign purpose—will triumph. Meanwhile, Jack's question to us is this: whose side are we on?[21]

It may well be overstating things to contend that C. S. Lewis was an early species of ecofeminist (or a proto-ecofeminist), especially since he still frames God in strongly masculine terms that could potentially validate Dominionist and patriarchal views on religion and society. Nevertheless, echoes of Lewis's perspectives on these issues may be found in contemporary ecofeminist philosophy, fantasy, and science fiction.

## Overlapping Interfaith Perspectives on "The Fall": The Fall is Ongoing; The Fall Can Be Reversed

In the *MaddAddam* trilogy of dystopian novels by Margaret Atwood, pacifist and environmentalist preacher Adam One offers a series of sermons that assert the theological perspective that "the Fall" is not best understood as one moment in time when Adam and Eve shared a forbidden pomegranate. Instead, "the Fall" is something that is ongoing, that occurs every moment of every day in which humans choose—though an active embracing of evil or through an indolent failure to do good—to destroy the natural world, and act cruelly toward humans and nonhuman animals by enslaving, torturing, sexually abusing, murdering, and either causing the suffering of or failing to mitigate the sufferings of others. Each time we do this, we create anew a world that has Fallen away from Eden and ensure that it remains Fallen away from Eden. While these words are placed in the mouth of a preacher of the religious order of God's Gardeners by Atwood, an author who is agnostic, Adam One's message bears striking similarities to the messages of C. S. Lewis and J. R. R. Tolkien. Each time we pollute, harm animals, or harm humans, we ensure—in C. S. Lewis's terms—that the world remains Fallen, enemy-occupied territory. If we, instead, change the narrative, and try to live in a manner designed to reverse the Fall and recreate the world of Adam and Eve before the Fall, we change the narrative arc of the Genesis story and bend it toward the renewal promised by Easter and the Resurrection of Christ, Lewis would assert.

Furthermore, Tolkien's entire project of sub-creating, of writing Middle-earth tales, was an effort to do just this. As he explained, "We have come from God, and inevitably, the myths woven by us, though they contain error, will also reflect a splintered fragment of the true light, the eternal truth that is with God. Indeed, only by myth-making, only by becoming a 'sub-creator' and inventing stories, can Man aspire to the state of perfection that he knew before the Fall. Our myths may be misguided, but they steer however shakily towards the true harbour, while materialistic 'progress' leads only to a yawning abyss and the Iron Crown of the power of evil."[22] Tolkien expressed his religious and environmentalist beliefs in somewhat idiosyncratic terms. However, his questioning of the moral worth of industrial progress and desire to change the narrative arc of the human story, redirecting it back to a newfound appreciation for the beauty of nature, anticipates core ecofeminist writings from multiple faith traditions.

Sallie McFague, a Christian ecofeminist theologian and the Carpenter Professor of Theology at Vanderbilt Divinity School, wrote a vast body of religious literature reconciling Christian theology and scientific evolutionary biology, while advocating that scientific and religious truths are stronger united than they are positioned against one another as opposites. In "Theology of Nature: Remythologizing Christian Doctrine," McFague notes that Christians tend to get bogged down in questions of why or how Creation occurred, and take a backward-looking approach to the world that is overly concerned with discrepancies between the Genesis narrative and Darwinian science. She believes that a more fruitful and crucial project is to cultivate an awareness of where we are now, of "(who) we have become, both in our relations with other life forms (our place in the cosmos) and our special responsibilities." She argues that "within this more practical framework, to say God is creator is not to focus on what God did once upon a time, either at the beginning or during the evolutionary process, but on how we can perceive ourselves and everything else in the universe as dependent upon God now, in terms of our cosmic story. . . . Moreover, and of utmost importance, whatever may have been the mechanisms of evolutionary history in the past, evolution in the

Fig. 6.1. In *Silent Running* (1972), botanist Freeman Lowell (Bruce Dern, pictured in Franciscan-like garb) prepares for his imminent death by programming robots to care for the last surviving indigenous Earth plants as they fly through space in domed habitats. The movie is in the spirit of C. S. Lewis's ecological poetry, features Edenic imagery, and helped inspire the Pixar film *Wall-E* (2008). Universal Pictures.

present and the future on our planet will be inextricably involved with human powers and decisions. Willy-nilly, whether we want it or not, the future of the planet has to a significant degree fallen into our hands."[23]

Since humanity now controls the fate of the world—and this is the case as much in McFague's theological conception of a cosmos with God in it as in more secular models without God in it—then the narrative that humans construct around their relationship to the natural world is of vital significance. Such a narrative would be instrumental in determining how humans will behave toward the cosmos and how humans will shape the future of evolution and of the planet. McFague refers to this narrative as a theological model of behavior that can be shaped, changed, and altered through our perceptions of God and reality and our cosmic role: "If we always and only have constructs with which to interpret reality, then necessarily we have to . . . adopt a model. . . . And if enough of us were to so live, reality would become more like we believe. That is not a vicious circle, but a hope against hope. We can create reality—in fact, we do all the time with the constructs we embrace unknowingly. We can also create reality knowingly—and humanely—by living within models that we wager are true as well as good for human beings and other forms of life."[24]

What is interesting about this line of thought is that it appears not only in McFague's writing, but in the writings of notable Jewish, Catholic, and Muslim thinkers, all of whom have a similar view of the Fall story and its importance to modern ecology. For example, Creation Theology scholar Ellen Bernstein offers a Jewish perspective on the two creation stories in *The Green Bible* (2008), noting that Creation is an ongoing process. Significantly, Bernstein challenges the view that God's granting "dominion" of the Earth to humanity serves as a license to exploit and subjugate it. Advocating a version of the Stewardship of the Earth akin to Tolkien's but rooted in the Jewish tradition, Bernstein notes that the original Hebrew language calls for humanity to "work" (*la-avod*) and "guard" (*lishmor*) the Earth, and to do so with humility, with reverence for God and Creation. The Hebrews are called to observe the Earth and its creatures, help it, and even rest from interacting with it. Consequently, the Dominionist practice of latching onto the word *dominion* and taking its meaning to the extreme is fundamentally misguided, especially since the word is mistranslated from the Hebrew. Like McFague, Bernstein believes that a thoughtful consideration of the ramifications of both Creation Theology and the current ecological crisis necessitates the creation of a new narrative underpinning human interactions with the natural world:

> Creation theology expounds a series of ecological principles, but speaks in a poetic and redolent language to communicate them. As a people rooted in language and story, we must reflect on how our story might provide us the language and perspectives to help us cope with today's mushrooming environmental ills. . . . Creation theology is inherently generative and hopeful. It implies that the way to address the environmental problems and other problems of our world is through our own creativity. It speaks the universal language of sand, stars, earth, and heavens. It provides a common language by which we can express our deepest yearnings, communicate across cultures and beliefs, and work together on the most pressing issues of our day.[25]

Working in yet another faith tradition is Muslim scholar Seyyed Hossein Nasr, who also discusses ways in which humans may recuperate what was lost in the Fall—a more harmonious interaction with nature:

> In the sacred rite of pilgrimage (*al-hajj*) to the house of God in Makka [Mecca], Muslim pilgrims circumambulate around the Kaaba seven times in a counterclockwise direction opposed to the movement of the arrow of

time. The deepest meaning of this aspect of the rite is the undoing of the effects of the Fall of Man and his reintegration into the Edenic state by virtue of which his imperfections and sins are overcome and he regains his state of original purity. One might say figuratively that a similar process has to be taken intellectually, mentally, and psychologically . . . [to make peace between humanity and the world as we know it today][26]

What the Christian McFague, the Jewish Bernstein, the Muslim Nasr, and the agnostic Atwood are all calling for is a paradigm shift away from a model of ecological destruction and toward ecological Stewardship. They express this idea using slightly different language, but there is significant thematic overlap in their respective arguments. Ultimately, they all appear to be saying essentially the same thing, whether their perspective is framed as Jewish Creation Theology, Christian Stewardship, agnostic environmentalism, ecofeminism, or any other ecologically minded theoretical or narrative framework. The fact that such similar arguments have been made by members of different faith communities employing similar narrative and mythological imagery suggests great potential for a united ecological purpose that crosses religious and cultural boundaries and offers hope for alliances between faith communities.

Ecofeminists such as Rosemary Radford Ruether are very interested in building alliances between members of different religious and cultural traditions to work together to restore the planet. Her writings advocate the importance of rethinking the theologies of different faith traditions to "green" them. She promotes taking specific actions to combat pollution and champion environmental justice, shaping a worldview that appears very much compatible with the theological and ecological cosmos of Tolkien and Lewis. In *Integrating Ecofeminism Globalization and World Religions* (2005), Ruether discusses numerous ways in which interfaith ecological activists are already writing new theological tracts within their own, distinct faith traditions to address the climate crisis while working together to make large- and small-scale changes in society, politics, and their home communities. In doing so, they strive to make manifest in the world the changing perspectives they are expressing in their religious narratives. She writes that the many examples she has seen in her activism "of the integration of spirituality, religious vision, and ecological practice express a contagious energy moving around the world. They suggest a new perspective on the dictum of Lynn White in 1967 that 'since the roots of our trouble are so largely religious, the remedy must also be essentially religious.' The vision of a transformed relationship of humanity to each other and to the earth demands new nature-conserving technology and organized political work to reform or shut down oppressive institutions. But the motivation for this work cannot just be anger or hatred. It has to be deeply rooted in joy. It must be integrated with a vision of life-giving community and some actual glimpses of what such community might be like. Ecofeminist rereading of religious traditions, with its vision of humanity as part of one life-giving matrix, offers promises of helping to provide the spirituality for such life-giving community."[27]

The above religious thinkers called for a paradigm shift in the theological conception of the relationship between humans and the earth. A similar paradigm shift also needs to take place in the narratives of literature, film, television, and popular culture writ large. Such a paradigm shift has been advocated by Ursula K. Le Guin, though she frames it in secular, anthropological terms instead of theological, and expresses the paradigm shift as the act of a storyteller or shaman weaving a newer and healthier narrative for us all.

Through her works, Le Guin has become an inspiration to many progressives, a role that she was somewhat uncomfortable with. Indeed, she used self-depreciating humor to denounce herself as an imperfect mouthpiece for socialist and ecofeminist ideals because she was a middle-class hypocrite leading a charmed life. Tongue-in-cheek self-flagellation notwithstanding, Le Guin was an innovative artistic force within the speculative fiction genre and wrote classic novels such as *A Wizard of Earthsea* (1968), *The Left Hand of Darkness* (1969), *The Lathe of Heaven* (1971), and *Lavinia* (2008). A poet, short story writer, critic, and essayist, Le Guin has written about the artistic and social concerns that drive the design of her writing. For Le Guin, the best way to promote a fundamental change in the thinking of the world is to create a truly feminist form of literature that promotes humanitarian and ecological values. In the "The Carrier Bag Theory of Fiction" (1986), Le Guin explains why she avoids following Joseph Campbell's hero's-journey boilerplate in her works. Her objections to the hero's-journey model are aesthetic and political, as well as based in ecofeminism:

> So long as "culture" was explained as originating from and elaborating upon the use of long, hard objects for sticking, bashing, and killing, I never thought that I had, or wanted any particular share in it. . . . Wanting to be human, too, I sought evidence that I was; but if that's what it took, to make a weapon and kill with it, then evidently I was either extremely defective as a human being, or not human at all. That's right, they said. What you are is a woman. Possibly not human at all, certainly defective. Now be quiet while we go on telling the Story of the Ascent of Man the Hero. . . . It is the story that makes the difference. It is the story that hid my humanity from me, the story that the mammoth hunters told about bashing, thrusting, raping, killing, about the Hero. . . . The killer story.
>
> It sometimes seems to me that that story is approaching its end. Lest there be no more telling of stories at all, some of us think . . . we'd better start telling another one. . . . The trouble is, we've all let ourselves become part of the killer story, and so we may get finished along with it. Hence it is with a certain feeling of urgency that I seek the nature, the subject, words of the other story, the untold one, the life story. It's unfamiliar, it doesn't come easily, thoughtlessly to the lips as the killer story does; but still, "untold" was an exaggeration. People have been telling the life story for ages, in all sorts of words and ways. Myths of creation and transformation, trickster stories, folktales, jokes, novels. . . . That is why I like novels: instead of heroes they have people in them.[28]

## Replacing the Killer Story with the Life Story:
## Ecofeminists and Francis of Assisi

In "The Carrier Bag Theory of Fiction," Ursula K. Le Guin notes that she is trying to write new works that recall older works that have fallen out of favor. She is reviving them to pit them against the dominant mode of storytelling: "the killer story." Hers is an ecofeminist ethic, but her reminder that the "life story" is an old tale is significant. It is important, for example, to recall that one of the most notable tellers of the "life story" in the history of Western civilization was the Christian mystic St. Francis of Assisi.

Consider how St. Francis biographer William R. Cook describes the Italian saint, who lived from c. 1181–1226. Cook writes of Francis as a historical figure who retains enormous contemporary sociopolitical and religious influence as someone who has been identified by popes as the patron saint of ecology and animal protection and recognized by Lynn White as a landmark figure in environmentalist thought.[29] Placing Francis in his own historical and theological context, Cook explains the nature of Francis's environmental theology:

> If God is the father of all human beings and indeed of all things that are, then all God's creatures are related by virtue of having the same father—i.e., They are brothers and sisters. Thus, Francis came to understand that God's family included crickets and rocks and sticks as well as fellow humans of all sorts and conditions. . . . When Francis referred to Brother wolf or Sister water, he was not using a clever rhetorical strategy. He meant those titles quite literally. The implications are quite extraordinary for one who takes this brotherhood seriously. What is the proper way to treat a brother or sister? Brothers and sisters are not to be exploited or manipulated; they are loved and respected because of the intimate link between siblings based on their common ancestry. To expand this concept to include everything that exists and to do it seriously leads to some rather startling behavior on Francis' part. . . .
>
> Francis as much as any man who lived took an idea, discovered the implications of that idea, and rejoiced in taking both the idea and the consequences, however radical they were, absolutely seriously. Often when people discover radical implications in something they believe, they adjust their beliefs in such a way as to lessen the consequences for their lives; or they rationalize that the radical implications are not quite as radical as they appear. Francis never adjusted and never rationalized; indeed, he seems to have rejoiced in discovering the most extraordinary consequences of taking his beliefs seriously in his life.[30]

Outside of inspiring his namesake, Pope Francis, to champion the rights of the poor and to take up the fight against climate change as a core religious concern, Saint Francis has not had the influence over Catholic doctrine and the lives of practicing

Catholics that he should have. Nevertheless, Cook believes that Francis will always have the potential to influence the behavior of those alive in the present so long as his history and biography are studied and meditated upon. In the theological context that Cook supplies in his biography of Francis, the rationale behind Francis's famous preaching of the gospel of Christ to the birds and the flowers becomes clear. Similarly, Francis's more ambitious attempts to bring peace to warring factions of humans becomes easier to grasp. As Cook points out, far from being cut off from all human society and living solely among animals, Francis involved himself in the affairs of state. Indeed, Francis "acted in various ways to bring civil peace in Arezzo, Assisi, Bologna, and Siena," and in "settling factional strife in Arezzo" with prayer and "conflicts between ecclesiastical and secular officials in Assisi" with song.[31] Cook notes the counterintuitive thinking inherent in one who would heal political rifts with prayer and song in one set of instances and, in another, draw up a formal peace treaty between humans and the wolf that had been terrorizing the town of Gubbio. "We might have supposed," Cook writes, "that Francis would heal the disputes between rational creatures by means of a formal agreement and the conflict between people and a beast by means of direct prayer or a soothing song. It is always dangerous to assume that Francis would act according to earthly wisdom, for Francis fulfilled in every way St. Paul's image of the fool for Christ. He was always turning the world's standards on their heads."[32]

The story of the wolf of Gubbio is taken from the anonymous, late-fourteenth-century biography of Saint Francis of Assisi, *The Little Flowers of St. Francis* (*Fioretti di San Francesco*). According to this source, sometime in 1220, in the town of Gubbio in northeastern Umbria, a wolf appeared who endangered the livelihood of the local farmers by eating their livestock. When the townspeople attacked and failed to kill the wolf, they enraged it. Behaving much like a vengeful human would, the wolf switched its targets from animal to human prey, ambushing and feasting upon anyone who attempted to leave the city alone. Further efforts to kill the wolf failed, and the people became convinced that the animal was invincible, choosing to sequester themselves within the city walls instead of risking a confrontation with it by venturing outside. At this crisis point, Saint Francis ignored the warnings of the townspeople and led a peace expedition outside to negotiate with the wolf. When the animal came into view, Francis's followers held back, but he walked up to it, unafraid and protected by his faith in God. The wolf charged Francis, its fangs bared, and Francis made the sign of the cross. The gesture halted the wolf's attack, and it placed itself at Francis's feet, nuzzling his hands with its head. According to *The Little Flowers*, the wolf survived two more years in the care of the townspeople, who mourned its passing when it died because of the lessons it had taught them of the glory of God, through the peace treaty with Francis.

The contract between the Saint and the wolf is fascinating for several reasons. First, it shows that Francis respected the wolf as a creation of God and did not want to see it killed. He communicated and negotiated with it as if it had a soul and an intellect and it responded in kind. In offering this respect, Francis was demonstrating Roman Catholic environmentalist values. Also, he was exemplifying, in an intriguing way, a "life story" value system that is in line with his Catholicism and feelings of kinship with all nature. When interpreting this tale, it is also important to remember that each side in any treaty signing takes a risk and invests trust in a current enemy who may live to betray that trust. Consequently, while interpreters sometimes focus on the notion that the people were taking a risk trusting the wolf, it is equally valid to emphasize that the wolf was taking a risk trusting the people of Gubbio, as well as the saint as negotiator. To some degree, the presence of God in the tale suggests that the success of the peace agreement was a foregone conclusion: God was on his side, so Francis was bound to succeed. And yet, that interpretation of the tale downplays much of the dramatic impact of the encounter, and does not serve the spreading of the Christian message of the central importance of peacemaking. St. Francis took an enormous political and social risk attempting to broker such a peace, just as he did when he crossed battlefield lines to meet with the Sultan of Egypt, al-Kamil, in 1219 during the Fifth Crusade.

This tale may strike listeners as too idealistic and too naive about all the forces in nature that are violent, and that support the Darwinian law of the "survival of the fittest" in a "dog eat dog world." And yet, as primatologist Frans de Waal argues in *The Age of Empathy: Nature's Lessons for a Kinder Society* (2009), there are far greater bonds of friendship, empathy, and society within primates, and the broader animal kingdom, than the average person with little knowledge of science realizes. Animals aren't uniformly evil, nor are people, De Waal argues, yet our economic and social systems are based on just such a bleak assumption. His book is as much a social and economic tract as it is a biological science work, and De Waal asserts that humans should look to the empathy and society modeled in the animal kingdom to reimagine our own comparatively cruel human economic and social structures. Too many of us deny scientific Darwinism and embrace social Darwinism, he contends, and that trend needs reversing. De Waal concludes his book by observing:

> One of the most potent weapons of the abolitionist movement were the drawings of slave ships and their human cargo, which were disseminated to generate empathy and moral outrage. The role of compassion in society is therefore not just one of sacrificing time and money to relieve the plight of others, but also of pushing a political agenda that recognizes everyone's dignity. Such an agenda helps not merely those who need it most, but also the larger whole. One cannot expect high levels of trust in a society with large income disparities, huge insecurities, and a disenfranchised underclass. And remember, trust is what citizens value most in their society. . . . We need to rely on our well-developed intellect to figure out how to balance individual and collective interests on [a large scale]. But one instrument that we do have available, and that greatly enriches our thinking, has been selected over the ages, meaning that it has been tested over and over [by evolution] with regard to its survival value. That is our capacity to connect to

and understand others and make their situation our own, the way . . . [that Abraham] Lincoln did when he came eye to eye with shackled slaves. To call upon this inborn capacity can only be to any society's advantage.[33]

De Waal uses scientific and economic arguments to make the same plea to the modern global citizen that St. Francis made to Medieval Europe. Francis is thought of as the patron saint of animals and ecology. He may also be thought of as the patron saint of empathy, in the way that De Waal defines "empathy." In this respect, the story of Francis and the Wolf of Gubbio, and any artistic representation of that narrative, is the most important image of Francis we can carry with us to best internalize his lesson.

Furthermore, from a literary studies and film studies perspective, the story of the Wolf of Gubbio helped establish a literary trope in which those who are willing to make treaties with wolves, befriend them, call them sibling, and love them, dangerous as they are, should be regarded as ecological heroes. Someone capable of befriending a wolf can potentially demonstrate the capacity to treat all animals—and all of nature writ large—with reverence. For example, each of the Stark children in George R. R. Martin's *A Song of Ice and Fire* adopts a wolf of his or her own, and those who develop the strongest bonds with their wolf kin—including Brandon Stark and Jon Snow—are those most likely to be able to attune their senses to the natural order, communing directly with plant and animal life and relating as equals to the indigenous peoples who live beyond the Wall. Finally, and most significantly, the story of the Wolf of Gubbio and the example St. Francis of Assisi sets for Christians, has echoes in Margaret Atwood's ecofeminist climate fiction trilogy *MaddAddam*. These echoes will be explored in the following chapter.

## 7

# *MaddAddam* and *The Handmaid's Tale*

## Margaret Atwood and Dystopian Science Fiction as Current Events

The dogmas of the quiet past, are inadequate to the stormy present. The occasion is piled high with difficulty, and we must rise—with the occasion. As our case is new, so we must think anew, and act anew. We must disenthrall ourselves, and then we shall save our country. Fellow-citizens, we cannot escape history. . . . No personal significance, or insignificance, can spare one or another of us. The fiery trial through which we pass, will light us down, in honor or dishonor, to the latest generation. . . . The world knows we do know how to save it. We—even we here— hold the power, and bear the responsibility. . . . We shall nobly save, or meanly lose, the last best hope of earth.

—Abraham Lincoln, Annual Message to Congress,
December 1, 1862

In the last decades of the twentieth century the major world religions each began to grapple with the possible harm that their traditions may have caused to the environment and to search for the positive elements in their tradition for an ecologically affirming spirituality and practice. Women and men have also extended feminist theologies into a relationship with the earth. They have asked how the hierarchies of gender in religion and culture have been correlated with the hierarchies of human over nature. They have begun to imagine a different way of interrelating human and nature as an interdependent matrix of life.

—Rosemary Radford Ruether, *Integrating Ecofeminism,
Globalization and World Religions* (2005)

## *MaddAddam*, the Great Plains PetroBaptists, and the Return of the Wolf of Gubbio

Margaret Atwood was born in November 1939 to nutritionist Margaret Dorothy Killam and entomologist Carl Edmund Atwood, who operated a forest insect research station in Quebec.[1] "At the age of six months," Atwood explained, "I was carried into the woods in a packsack, and this landscape became my hometown."[2] The spring and summer months of her childhood were spent in the forests of Canada: experiencing nature, reading, drawing comic books, and being disconnected from the media, except for listening to news of the war against fascism on the radio.[3] While Atwood has tended to respond negatively to critics who have employed biographical literary criticism when reading her novels, this sketch of her developmental years includes some clues that point to reasons why Atwood might grow up to become the preeminent ecofeminist novelist of our era, a staunch antitotalitarian, and a polymath who embodies the vast potential of anyone who studies both the humanities and the STEM fields without narrowly choosing only one area of study.

The early years of the Reagan Revolution and the rise of Muslim theocracies in the Middle East alarmed Atwood to such a degree that she was inspired to write her now-classic 1985 novel *The Handmaid's Tale*. The book takes place after pollution and radiation poisoning sterilize much of the American populace, causing the U.S. government to collapse and be replaced by an Old Testament–quoting theocracy. The oligarchic leaders respond to the mass sterilization by ordering the children of single and divorced poor and middle-class women to be legally kidnapped and placed in the adoptive care of childless wealthy households. Fertile women of the lower classes are drafted to become "handmaids" and breed children for rich, childless men whose wives are assumed to be infertile, although the men are the more likely candidates for infertility. These handmaids' entire existence is circumscribed by various forms of patriarchal oppression, as it is forbidden for them to read, speak, or travel alone, and even the most seemingly innocent thoughts, gestures, or attempts at human contact or self-assertion are considered seditious and grounds for swift, cruel punishment. Beyond those quisling women who police their own kind and act as "educators" indoctrinating women into the new world order, no women can have careers or white-collar jobs, and all bank accounts that once belonged to women are frozen and the wealth transferred to their husbands, or—in the case of single women—presumably the state. Meanwhile, the "Unwomen"—political dissidents, gay women, and women unable to procreate—are made to work menial, health-destroying jobs in the Colonies, including handling radioactive waste. As Atwood explained to Bill Moyers on July 29, 2006, "*The Handmaid's Tale* is the answer to the question, 'If you were going to change the United States from a democracy into a totalitarianism, how would you go about doing it?' Well, you . . . [are] likely to say, 'This is the true religion. Follow our flag' . . . If your government says, 'Not only am I your government but I represent the true religion,' if you disagree with it, you are not just of another faction. You're evil."[4]

Fig. 7.1. In Margaret Atwood's book, *The Handmaid's Tale,* fertile women of the lower classes are drafted to become "handmaids" and breed children for rich, childless men whose wives are assumed to be infertile (although the men are the more likely candidates for infertility). In this picture, from the Hulu adaptation by Bruce Miller, the novel's narrator—identified only by her slave name of Offred (Elisabeth Moss)—is pictured literally and metaphorically behind bars. The series won eight Primetime Emmy Awards in 2017, including Outstanding Drama Series. Hulu.

Atwood told Moyers that she had once thought that her early studies in seventeenth-century theology were so esoteric that they would never be of general interest to modern audiences or applicable to modern society; and yet, she explains, it has all become relevant again. She cited as an example the antinomian heresy, which gave its adherents the license to "do all the most atrocious things that you might be inclined to do while still believing that you are justified" because these heretics believed they were destined to be among the elect from birth. Speaking during the height of the Bush-Blair phase of the "war on terror," Atwood observed in an aside that she was concerned about rumors that asserted Tony Blair was an adherent of antinomianism. Whether that was true or not in his case, Atwood felt that too many Christians were prone to embrace sects of Christianity that validated all their worst impulses to self-righteousness, warmongering, racism, sexism, and harsh moral judgment of others. She was displeased with those groups that read the Bible selectively and embraced a heretical form of Christianity that was principally concerned with the coming of the Rapture. Those who await the Rapture, she observed, love the idea of watching other people burn and it never occurs to them that they might not be the ones getting Raptured.

For Atwood, religion is a necessity and a fact of life, and the alternative posed by the secular communist state was hardly better in its record of oppression than religious or capitalist regimes. Consequentially, she is an agnostic who does not argue for the eradication of religion from the world and does not resent the religious faith of others. What she would love to see, in an ideal word, is that religion cease being used as a weapon to persecute others. Atwood observes that the increasing cruelty infecting Christian faith communities in the twenty-first-century United States is a natural consequence of the trying times we live in:

> I think it is the kind of event that replays itself throughout history when cultures come under stress . . . people start looking around for, essentially, human sacrifices. They start looking around for somebody they can blame, and they feel that if only they can demolish that person, then everything is going to be okay, which is never true. . . .
>
> "Things aren't going well, it must be the Communists. Let's have Joe McCarthy. Things aren't going well; it must be them liberals." Whoever it may be . . . [Under these circumstances, civil rights and human rights have a

Fig. 7.2. The white supremacist, fundamentalist dictators of Gilead maintain control of society by denying women all civil and human rights, and they quash potential dissent and revolution by coercing women into policing one another's allegiance to the new social order. In this scene from the 2017 *Handmaid's Tale* series, a social ritual is enacted in which Handmaids publicly shame one of their own who does not "measure up" to the extremist social standards. Hulu.

tendency to vanish in] an almost frighteningly rapid way. Conditions change, there's too much turmoil and that's the point where they will trade their liberties for somebody who comes along and says, "I'm a strong leader. I'll take care of it. The trains will run on time."[5]

As a Canadian, Atwood criticizes America harshly here, but she has the clarity of vision of an outsider and qualifies her remarks to observe that she does, indeed, respect America and care about its fate. From her perspective, America needs to be rescued from its occupation by insurgent right-wing Christian forces working to shatter its democratic and Enlightenment traditions from within. Her advice is that the best thing Americans can do to reclaim their homeland—which has become, to a tragic degree, enemy-occupied territory—is to embrace the Transcendentalist tradition of Henry David Thoreau. Thoreau was a strong opponent of the institution of slavery and of the Mexican American War (1846–48), so he ceased paying tax dollars that he saw as supporting evil enterprises. Because of his conscientious objection, he spent time in jail. Thoreau wrote a justification for his actions, "Resistance to Civil Government" (or "On Civil Disobedience"), which was published in 1849. In her 2006 interview with Moyers, Atwood argued that too few modern Americans have followed Thoreau's example. She suggests that more Americans should, to help steer their country away from the path to totalitarian theocracy and place it back upon the road to a more perfect and more egalitarian democracy.

Atwood's perspective is one of an agnostic and a believer in democracy who seeks to challenge both left- and right-wing forms of totalitarian government, and both secular and religious forms of tyranny. While she does not consider herself Christian, she sees goodness in members of the Christian faith. Her unnamed narrator in *The Handmaid's Tale* remains a religious person despite her persecution at the hands of religious groups. The Constitution of the United States protects religious freedom and prohibits the establishment of a state religion. Atwood would oppose the institution of any state religion. It is untenable and inadvisable. Dante made much the same argument in the early fourteenth century: theocracies serve only to corrupt religious institutions, not elevate to holiness secular ones.

*The Handmaid's Tale* remains Atwood's most famous and respected novel, but the author has also written perhaps the most significant literary work of climate fiction, the *MaddAddam* trilogy. The trilogy includes *Oryx and Crake* (2003), *The Year of the Flood* (2009), and *MaddAddam* (2013). According to Atwood scholar Coral Ann Howells, *Oryx and Crake* works as a literal as well as spiritual sequel to *The Handmaid's Tale*. Read in this fashion, the

> pollution and environmental destruction which threatened one region of North America in the earlier novel have escalated into worldwide climate change through global warming in the latter, and the late twentieth-century Western trend towards mass consumerism which Gilead tried to reverse by

its fundamentalist doctrines and its liturgy of "moral values" has resulted in an American lifestyle of consumerist decadence in a high-tech world which is ultimately death-doomed by one man's megalomaniac project of bioterrorism. . . . [Keeping in mind their original publication dates, b]oth novels are set in the near future in the United States, with the *Handmaid's Tale* scenario occurring around 2005 and that of *Oryx and Crake* around 2025. (The protagonists' birth dates and ages offer clues to the reader. Offred is 33 when she becomes a Handmaid and she must have been born sometime in the 1970s; Snowman is 28 and was born around 1996, though Atwood is deliberately unspecific about precise dates for her dystopias).[6]

The *MaddAddam* series takes place in the years preceding and the months following the outbreak of a deadly virus that wipes out almost all of humanity. Most of the central characters are those who belong to God's Gardeners, a pseudo-Judeo-Christian environmentalist faith founded by a charismatic figure known as Adam One. God's Gardeners are pacifists, vegetarians, conservationists, and anticorporate activists who live in small enclaves based on rooftops, in parks, safe-houses, abandoned box store outlets, and networked apartments. Adam One preaches the importance of the proper stewardship of the Earth, making constant reference to the stories of the Fall and the Flood in Genesis, but infusing them with scientific accuracy and contemporary political urgency. His religion is replete with feast days held in honor of members of the animal kingdom, such as wolves, bees, lions, and (later) the genetically engineered pigoons, celebrated in tandem with a new generation of human saints, including Saints Dian Fossey, Rachel Carson, Sojourner Truth, Shackleton and Crozier, and Karen Silkwood.

Adam One is a complicated figure who regards all those who act out of strict adherence to an honorable, coherent religious code of ethics as demonstrating authentic piety even if they do not experience religion in the form of a lifelong, unwavering faith in the supernatural. He is more than capable of withholding or bending difficult truths, but he is one of the most sympathetically portrayed figures in Atwood's series. Indeed, by the third book, *MaddAddam*, it becomes clear that Adam One is not a character who will be unmasked as a fraud or disgraced. In fact, when his more cynical half-brother, Zeb, relates Adam One's life story to a God's Gardner named Toby, Zeb presents Adam as a bona fide prophet. Zeb contrasts Adam One's genuine faith with the cynical faith of their father, a hypocritical preacher known as "The Rev" who grew wealthy in the years leading up to the apocalypse thanks to owning his own megachurch and allying himself to the fossil fuel industry. Indeed, as Zeb sees it, Adam One grew up to become the legitimate religious leader that their father only pretended to be. Zeb, always a colorful narrator, describes the Rev in these terms:

> The Rev had his very own cult. That was the way to go in those days if you wanted to coin the megabucks. . . . Tell people what they want to hear, call yourself a religion, put the squeeze on for contributions, run your own media

outlets and use them for robocalls and slick online campaigns, befriend or threaten politicians, evade taxes. . . . [T]he Rev had a megachurch, all glass slobbery and pretend oak pews and faux granite, out on the rolling plains. The Church of PetrOleum, affiliated with the somewhat more mainstream Petrobaptists. They were riding high for a while, about the time accessible oil became scarce and the price shot up and desperation among the pleebs set in. A lot of top Corps guys would turn up as guest speakers. They'd thank the Almighty for blessing the world with fumes and toxins, cast their eyes upwards as if gasoline came from heaven, look pious as hell. . . .

The Rev could rave on about the Oleum for hours. "My friends, as we all know, *oleum* is the Latin word for oil. And indeed, oil is holy throughout the Bible! What else is used for the anointing of priests and prophets and kings? Oil! It's the sign of special election, the consecrated chrism! What more proof do we need of the holiness of our very own oil, put in the earth by God for the special use of the faithful to multiply His works? His Oleum-extraction devices abound on this planet of our Dominion, and he spreads his Oleum bounty among us! Does it not say in the Bible that you should forbear to hide your light under a bushel? And what else can so reliably make the lights go on as oil? That's right! Oil, my friends! The Holy Oleum must not be hidden under a bushel—in other words, left underneath the rocks—for to do so is to flout the Word! Lift up your voices in song, and let the Oleum gush forth in ever stronger and all-blessed streams!"[7]

Having inherited his father's skills as an orator, businessman, and figurehead, Adam One embraced his father's best qualities without embracing the worst ones. The religion that Adam One founded, God's Gardeners, grew so successful, however, that the establishment forces began to fear its sociopolitical influence. Consequently, the corporations paid members of street gangs and the privatized police forces to harass, arrest, attack, and kill members of the faith. Unyielding in his pacifism, Adam One refused to use force in retaliation and merely went into hiding with those who maintained their allegiance to him. Zeb, meanwhile, felt that they needed to strike back to protect themselves, especially because the mass media were engaged in a project of convincing the public that the God's Gardeners was a terrorist organization. A schism occurred. Zeb led the more radical offshoot of God's Gardeners, MaddAddam, on an ecoterrorist crusade against the corporate imperialist forces holding the dystopian future America in its iron grasp. This storyline is related in flashback and takes place before humanity is largely wiped from existence by an artificially generated pandemic.

The main arc of the *MaddAddam* trilogy narrative takes place after Crake, a misanthropic corporate scientist, genetically engineers a new species of human beings called "Crakers" and unleashes a deadly virus to wipe out humanity so that his "Crakers" can inherit the Earth. (Most of the scenes in *MaddAddam* that take place before the fall of humanity and the rise of the Crakers are related as memories, journal entries, and historical documents.) The Crakers are part human, part bonobo, and include genetic material from tropical fruits and a variety of other counterintuitive sources. Crake "programs" his new and improved "indigenous" humans to be as innocent as Adam and Eve before the Fall, only more so. To eliminate all human tendency toward violence and destruction of its own habitat, Crake designs the Crakers to subsist entirely on vegetation and their own fecal matter. Consequently, they are in no danger of running out of food and will never fight wars over food or be tempted to turn into hunters or farmers. In addition, Crake strives to drive all desire for private property, religious belief, and interest in making art or music out of the human personality. Perhaps most importantly of all, Crake makes his creations free of all sexual neurosis and feelings of possessiveness toward their mates, which he blames for all violent conflict on domestic and global scales.

Before unleashing the virus, Crake secretly grants his friend Jimmy immunity, hoping that after all other humans are dead, Crake included, Jimmy will be the sole survivor of the original human race and will shepherd the Crakers into a new, more peaceful chapter in human history. Jimmy—a sardonic, womanizing, underemployed college humanities major—finds Crake inscrutable and does not understand what Crake sees in him. Jimmy is not inclined to remember Crake well after experiencing the apocalypse his friend has personally brought about. However, Jimmy follows through with Crake's plan for him to release the Crakers from their artificial habitat in the Paradise Project lab, lead them into the outside world, and guide them through their cultural infancy. Jimmy adopts the name Snowman as something of an inside joke, since snow no longer exists on a warmer Earth and since he, like snow, should no longer exist. His darkly comic mood also inspires him to give the Crakers bizarre names such as Blackbeard, Sojourner Truth, and Abraham Lincoln. For want of anything better to do with his time, Jimmy explains life to the Crakers by designing a religion around their creator Crake. Jimmy unintentionally begins the project of founding a new religion merely by telling the Crakers a broadly accurate story of their creation—simplified and related using symbolic and allegorical language instead of scientific language that is beyond their understanding. As Jimmy and the Crakers discover a handful of other survivors of the plague, including Toby from God's Gardeners and Zeb and several of his MaddAddam followers, these newly discovered survivors soon learn how to continue relating mythic stories to the Crakers. Before long, the most educated of the Crakers, Blackbeard, begins orally telling histories and myths from the Craker perspective, and writing them down in the form of a new Bible for a new society.

By the beginning of the third book in the series, *MaddAddam*, the surviving members of God's Gardeners and MaddAddam take shelter with the Crakers and begin the bizarre process of blending their communities together, developing a common culture, and interbreeding. They had been initially reluctant to blend their disparate communities and genetic materials, but were forced together as allies against two sources of external persecution, barricading themselves in the same community center. Their main enemies were the Painballers, violent human escaped convicts and veterans of televised gladiator matches akin to the Hunger Games depicted in Suzanne Collins's book series of the same name. Driven mad by their experiences in the Painball arena, the Painballers prey upon the Gardeners and MaddAddamites by capturing and gang raping the women and torturing and killing the men that fall into their hands. The other threat to the Craker-MaddAddam community comes in the form of the bizarre, genetically engineered animals that have escaped their cages in zoos and fast food farms, including Rakunks, Wolvogs, Snats, Bobkittens, Pigoons, and Liobambs, which eat their crops and occasionally attack and eat humans. Of these animals, the ones that show the greatest signs of intelligence are the Pigoons, pigs genetically engineered with human stem cells, which have developed a human-level intelligence, culture, and a language that they can use to communicate with one another and their fellow laboratory-born creatures, the Crakers. Once the MaddAddamites shoot and kill the Pigoons that attempt to eat their crops, the Pigoons demonstrate enough intelligence to avoid the guns. The Pigoons also develop a fear of the MaddAddamites who hunt and kill Pigoons, turning their dead into bacon and other pork products. What the Pigoons hate more, however, are the Painballers, who kill Pigoons for sport and then do not eat the flesh afterward. In an unexpected twist, the Pigoons discover that the MaddAddamites hate the Painballers as well, and decide that there is an opportunity to forge a human and Pigoon alliance against the Painballers. They approach the MaddAddamites and attempt to broker a peace using the young, naive Craker "Blackbeard" as a translator.

> "[The Pigoons] are talking, Oh Toby," says Blackbeard. "They are asking for help. They want to stop those ones. Those ones who are killing their pig babies. . . . They want help from you. . . . And in return, if you help them kill the three bad men, they will never again try to eat your garden. Or any of you. . . . Even if you are dead, they will not eat you. And they ask that you must no longer make holes in them, with blood, and cook them in a smelly bone soup, or hang them in the smoke, or fry them and then eat them. Not any more."
>
> "Tell them it's a deal," says Zeb.
>
> "Throw in the bees and the honey," says Toby. "Make them off-limits too."
>
> . . . Something appears to have been concluded. The pigoons, who have been standing with ears cocked forward and snouts raised as if sniffing the words, turn away and head west, back from where they came.[8]

In the Pigoon treaty segment, Atwood is continuing her reflections upon how the Judeo-Christian Bible was probably written, and how we might best read it centuries removed from its composition. In doing so, she suggests sardonically that there may have been some practical historical circumstances that account for some of the Bible's more bizarre prohibitions, including the one against eating pork. She is also, in this scene, referencing the story of the Wolf of Gubbio and showing how her humans are deliberately building a new, postapocalyptic society founded on a more Franciscan respect for animals. Like Francis, who counterintuitively treated animals like siblings and occasionally treated humans like animals, the MaddAddamites ally with genetically engineered pigs over Painballers because the Pigoons, who were created in a lab and not by God, show more soul and humanity than the Painballers do as habitual and unrepentant perpetrators of rape and murder. The Pigoons are worthy of respect. The Painballers are not. Notably, the human and Pigoon Treaty is violated only once in Toby's lifetime—by some young Pigoons seeking autonomy and testing the boundaries of acceptable behavior. The elder Pigoons promise to discipline the young and threaten harsh punishment of their own kind should the treaty be violated again. The humans accept this offer. The incident demonstrates that the treaty is strong enough that the peace is not shattered by this violation—which was, in many ways, excusable given who had perpetrated the crime and why. While the Pigoon treaty segment is bizarre, it works in the confines of the book, especially given the thematic and plot groundwork Atwood lays throughout the series. The segment is illustrative of Atwood's ecofeminist ideals, just as the Wolf of Gubbio story beautifully shows how St. Francis of Assisi was a Christian environmentalist. The overlap between these two stories offers the hope that ecofeminists and Christian environmentalists have a great potential to put their not inconsequential differences aside to work together to find a way to heal the world.

Furthermore, as secular-minded as Atwood's body of work might appear at first glance, it does fit into the broader tradition of religiously concerned climate fiction that Lewis and Tolkien helped establish. In fact, many of the core themes Atwood addresses in *MaddAddam* loom large in the corpus of C. S. Lewis's writings, and have particular resonance in both *The Abolition of Man* (1943)—in which Lewis opposes human genetic engineering because he predicts that it will transform humanity into industrial products—and in the animal rights essay "A Case For Abolition" (1947), in which he opposes animal experimentation because of its inherent cruelty to animals and the Josef Mengele–like precedent it sets for humans experimenting on humans.[9] In this groundbreaking anti–animal experimentation pamphlet, Lewis writes:

> The Christian defender [of vivisection], especially in the Latin countries, is very apt to say that we are entitled to do anything we please to animals because they "have no souls." But what does this mean? If it means that animals have no consciousness, then how is this known? . . . the statement that they "have no souls" may mean that they have no moral responsibilities and are not immortal. But the absence of "soul" in that sense makes the infliction of pain upon them not easier but harder to justify. For it means that animals cannot deserve pain, nor profit morally by the discipline of pain, nor be recompensed by happiness in another life for suffering in this. Thus all the factors which render pain more tolerable or make it less totally evil in the case of human beings will be lacking in the beasts. "Soullessness," in so far as it is relevant to the question at all, is an argument against vivisection. . . .

If loyalty to our own species, preference for man simply because we are men, is not a sentiment, then what is? It may be a good sentiment or a bad one. But a sentiment it certainly is. Try to base it on logic and see what happens!

But the most sinister thing about modern vivisection is this. If a mere sentiment justifies cruelty, why stop at a sentiment for the whole human race? There is also a sentiment for the white man against the black, for a Herrenvolk against the non-Aryans, for "civilized" or "progressive" peoples against "savages" or "backward" peoples. Finally, for our own country, party or class against others. Once the old Christian idea of a total difference in kind between man and beast has been abandoned, then no argument for experiments on animals can be found which is not also an argument for experiments on inferior men. If we cut up beasts simply because they cannot prevent us and because we are backing our own side in the struggle for existence, it is only logical to cut up imbeciles, criminals, enemies, or capitalists for the same reasons. Indeed, experiments on men have already begun. We all hear that Nazi scientists have done them. We all suspect that our own scientists may begin to do so, in secret, at any moment.[10]

Overall, the thematic overlap between these political and theological ideas expressed by Lewis and similar concepts found in Atwood's work is worthy of note and reflection. In "Margaret Atwood and Environmentalism," Shannon Hengen writes:

Nature—physical or human—seen as a commodity always represents a betrayal in Atwood's work, and betrayal has consequences. . . . Not considered a spiritual writer, Atwood nevertheless points towards the soul as a repository of important values, among them a sense of awe at nature's power. The human heart also features significantly throughout her work, as do instinctual drives. Human nature is made as much of reverence, compassion, and the capacity to forgive, as of lust, greed, arrogance, and cruelty. To deny any part is to lessen the whole. As whole creatures we both affect and are affected by the larger environment in which we evolve, and her work asks us to bear that interconnectedness firmly in mind.[11]

## A Message of Hope?

As Atwood's fame and renown increases in the United States, her influence upon its arts and culture has grown. Perhaps the most bizarre and amusing consequence of *MaddAddam*'s publication is the influence it has had upon, of all things, the Scooby-Doo franchise. In 2016, a grim, gritty, and darkly comic Scooby-Doo comic book modeled in equal parts upon *MaddAddam* and *The Mist* was published. In *Scooby Apocalypse*,

Velma Dinkley releases into the world a nanite virus designed to transform selfish, greedy, violent humans into her version of pacifist, environmentalist Crakers. The virus doesn't work as planned. Instead, it transforms most of humanity into classic movie monsters, including vampires, werewolves, gremlins, and Cenobites. Horrified, Velma begins to suspect that her four "Horseman of the Apocalypse" brothers—who are all high-ranking members of the military industrial complex (and one of whom is Donald Trump in all but name)—rewrote the nanite program to deliberately bring about this bizarre apocalypse. The core mystery of the series is: Did her brothers do this and, if so, why? One of the few human survivors of this transformed world, Velma must seek help among other humans who blame her for the end of the world: Shaggy Rogers, Daphne Blake, and Fred Jones, not to mention, of course, Scooby-Doo himself. The parallels to *MaddAddam* are striking: in *Scooby Apocalypse*, Velma and her brothers occupy the position of *MaddAddam*'s Crake, Shaggy is the equivalent of the "Everyman" Jimmy/Snowman, Daphne and Fred are Toby and Zeb, the transformed human populace are the Painballers, and Scooby-Doo and Scrappy-Doo are—very appropriately—the surprisingly intelligent, speaking, genetically engineered Pigoons. As odd as the narrative sounds, *Scooby Apocalypse* is, in some respects, a traditional DC Comic book. It was created by well-known superhero comic creators Jim Lee, J. M. DeMatteis, Keith Giffen, and Howard Porter. It is also plotted as a traditional hero's journey narrative with Velma as the central character. Consequently, despite the noteworthy similarities in theme and character, *MaddAddam* and *Scooby Apocalypse* are starkly different reading experiences. As a work that eschews the hero's journey storytelling model and embraces Ursula K. Le Guin's narrative model, *MaddAddam* bears little resemblance to *Scooby Apocalypse*.

The *MaddAddam* trilogy is not a hero's journey story that celebrates the world-saving potential of Messianic change. Crake thought he was a Messiah, and used a disease to wipe out most of the world's population. Hope should not necessarily be placed in such figures. Many of Atwood's other villains—the Starbucks franchise executives barely disguised as the owners of Happicuppa, and the Secret Burger fast food chain acting as a barely disguised McDonalds—seem much like the same villains found in an over-the-top *Judge Dredd* comic book, but her social satire is too intelligent and incisive to dismiss. Her protagonists can and do use violent means of defending themselves when they are attacked, but they are not superheroes. Consequently, Atwood does not fall into the trap of promoting the myth of the redemptive violence that cli-fi action films such as *Mad Max: Fury Road* do. Instead, she promotes intelligence, learning, compassion, self-awareness, and oneness with nature over mirroring the sins of the oppressors and becoming oneself what one hates the most about others.

Atwood told Bill Moyers in the interview cited above that she would bet against anyone who would argue that *The Handmaid's Tale* "couldn't happen here" in America. However, she has more hope for a brighter future than her observations on the state of contemporary American politics and ecology might suggest. Even though Atwood is by no means averse to confronting the evils of the world, her cli-fi narratives are not uniformly bleak. Atwood's gift is that she maintains her sense of humor in the face of

Fig. 7.3. To appear docile and brainwashed into allegiance to the leaders of Gilead, Offred (Elisabeth Moss) and Ofglen (Alexis Bledel) make regular pilgrimage to "the wall" to contemplate the executed criminals on display—those members of the medical profession and black market who attempted to provide women with illegal birth control and abortions. Hulu.

a darker reality, and works to promote a better future while being honest about the challenges of the present. It is in Atwood's writings, interviews, and efforts to identify and build the canon of cli-fi literature that she has made the most significant contributions to moving the collective human enterprise forward.

Perhaps the most unsettling thing about both *The Handmaid's Tale* and the *MaddAddam* trilogy is the extent to which they appear to be works more about modern America than a future America. Atwood recently joked about hearing reports that librarians across America were moving her works from the science fiction and literature sections to the current events and political science sections because of the way Republican legislatures in particular were moving to ban all forms of birth control in an alarmingly *Handmaid's Tale* manner.[12] "The war on women"—the renewed attack on women's reproductive rights that began in earnest shortly after the passage of Barack Obama's Affordable Care Act and has only escalated since—inspired a spike in the sales of Atwood's novels and the commissioning of television shows based on both of her dystopian sagas.

In a graveyard humor piece for *Vox*, "It's Margaret Atwood's Dystopian Future, and We're Just Living in It" (June 8, 2016), Constance Grady observed that the news media seem to continually demonstrate how Atwood's fictional depictions of the future are accurate representations of the present day. Grady cites as evidence both 2016 U.S. presidential candidate Donald Trump's *Handmaid's Tale*-esque statements on the necessity of punishing women who seek abortions and the news that scientists at the University of California, Davis, have created real-world analogues to the pigoons of *MaddAddam*—"chimeric embryos that carry both human stem cells and pig DNA." (One can only imagine how horrified Grady was when said presidential candidate actually won the 2016 election.)

Many of Atwood's scientific predictions have become reality, demonstrating that she has done her science homework. She has also shown herself to be a perceptive observer of human behavior and societal trends. Still, she is *not* a writer of science textbooks or political science tracts. She is also not writing potboilers, page-turners, or Christopher Vogler–approved narratives. The *MaddAddam* books give primacy to character, theme, and the beauty of the written word, frustrating the expectations of any reader seeking an action story or uniform narrative viewpoint and streamlined, chronological narrative trajectory. These frustrated expectations earmark the books in the trilogy as being written in Le Guin's "carrier bag" mode of storytelling. This mode of storytelling is not often employed in the average bestseller, but is emblematic of literary fiction, making the *MaddAddam* books a challenging read for anyone weaned on the Young Adult equivalents of her works. In theory, fans of *The Hunger Games* should grow up able to appreciate Atwood's dystopian novels because of the thematic overlap between the narratives, although the difference in writing styles between Atwood and Suzanne Collins might prove a stumbling block. Atwood herself was amused to hear of the resonance between her novels and *The Hunger Games*. Still, Atwood was not proprietary about her writing, nor did she assume that Collins had written an intentionally derivative work. (Collins's detractors are perennially accusing her of some form of plagiarism or another, and are convinced that in *The Hunger Games* Collins ripped off the plot of the Japanese multimedia narrative *Battle Royale*.)

One critic who reflected upon the similarities between the two trilogies, Ryan Britt, observed that, "*MaddAddam* is *The Hunger Games* for grown-ups." His observation is a little too dismissive of the merits of *The Hunger Games*, which is often derided because it is a Young Adult book and lacks cultural respectability. However, Britt's disparaging of Collins's books establishes a foundation for him to praise *MaddAddam*'s merits as literature, as brilliant social commentary, and as a work about real science in the real world, "You won't always know who to root for in *MaddAddam*, nor will you be totally satisfied with the direction all the various plot turns take. But you will firmly believe Margaret Atwood is way smarter than you and possibly any other writer working in speculative fiction. Because if there is a master of dystopian fiction which illuminates not only scientific possibility, but also examines the human condition with unflinching and unbiased honesty, then that master is Margaret Atwood."[13]

Indeed.

In a July 14, 2017 interview for *Entertainment Weekly*, Emma Watson asked Atwood directly if the election of Donald Trump and the damage he has done to human rights, democracy, and the environment since assuming office has terrified Atwood and confirmed that the world of *The Handmaid's Tale* is upon us in reality. Atwood replied: "I'm not easily depressed by these sorts of things. It's happened before. If you were born in the '90s, you were born into a world where quite a few rights for various groups had been established, at least in the West, and you thought that was normal. But if you're older than that and you were born into a world in which this was not the case, you saw the fights that went into those rights being established, and you also saw how quickly—in the case, for instance, of Hitler—that you could take a democratically minded fairly open society and turn it on its head. So, it has happened before, but it's also un-happened before, if you see what I mean. History is not a straight line. Also, America is not Germany; America is very diverse; it has a number of different states in it. I don't think America is rolling over in acquiesce to all of this, as you've probably seen from reading the news. You've probably seen that women dressed as Handmaids have been turning up in state legislatures and just sitting there. You can't kick them out because they're not making a disturbance, but everybody knows what they mean." As successful as the Trump administration has been in its unceasing attacks on human rights and the environment, Atwood understandably takes comfort in the solidarity and opposition to systemic, escalated, and omnipresent patriarchal oppression found in the Handmaid's Resistance and in the inspiring and galvanizing 2017 Women's March.

In dark times, hope is crucial.

In dark times, humor is equally crucial.

As many of her interviews demonstrate, Atwood has a sly sense of humor that brings a Jonathan Swift tone to both her public discourse and her dystopian fictions. Her humor, coupled with the beauty of her prose and her ability to create compelling characters, makes reading her novels more of an entertaining experience than their mere plot summaries might indicate. Part and parcel of Atwood's humor is the sense that she is writing these dark stories not mired in hopelessness at the state of our present circumstances, but out of hope that it will be possible for us to change the narrative arc of history and write ourselves a better future than the one she depicts.

Grady notes that "[i]ronically, as more and more of Atwood's dire dystopian predictions enter the realm of real-world possibility, the woman herself seems more optimistic than ever about the future. In 2014, she filed away an unpublished book in an art project known as the 'Future Library.' It will remain in the library, unread, until 2114, when it will be removed from its archival box and printed for readers to consume. For an author who has written more than one apocalypse in her career—and whose apocalyptic visions are growing ever more plausible—it's a hopeful move. It suggests that in 2114, there will still be literate human beings around to read her work."[14] Grady infers that this act on Atwood's part is an act of hope, and the author herself confirmed this in another interview; Atwood does indeed have hope that the human race will survive the climate crisis: "I think hope is among a number of things that are part of the human toolkit. It's built in unless people are suffering from clinical depression. You might even define that state as something's gone wrong with the hope. We are all hopeful in that respect. What was it that Oscar Wilde said about second marriages? A triumph of hope over experience. He was so naughty."[15]

8

# Ur-Fascism and Populist Rebellions in *Snowpiercer* and *Mad Max: Fury Road*

Someone needs to explain to me why wanting clean drinking water makes you an activist, and why proposing to destroy water with chemical warfare doesn't make a corporation a terrorist.

—Winona LaDuke, "Canadian Oil Companies Trample on Our Rights"

Psalm 73

A psalm of Asaph.

1 Surely God is good to Israel,
to those who are pure in heart.

2 But as for me, my feet had almost slipped;
I had nearly lost my foothold.

3 For I envied the arrogant
when I saw the prosperity of the wicked.

4 They have no struggles;
their bodies are healthy and strong.

5 They are free from common human burdens;
they are not plagued by human ills.

6 Therefore pride is their necklace;
they clothe themselves with violence.

7 From their callous hearts comes iniquity;
their evil imaginations have no limits.

8 They scoff, and speak with malice;
with arrogance they threaten oppression.

9 Their mouths lay claim to heaven,
and their tongues take possession of the earth.

10 Therefore their people turn to them
and drink up waters in abundance.

11 They say, "How would God know?
Does the Most High know anything?"

12 This is what the wicked are like—
always free of care, they go on amassing wealth.

13 Surely in vain I have kept my heart pure
and have washed my hands in innocence.

14 All day long I have been afflicted,
and every morning brings new punishments.

15 If I had spoken out like that,
I would have betrayed your children.

16 When I tried to understand all this,
it troubled me deeply

17 till I entered the sanctuary of God;
then I understood their final destiny.

18 Surely you place them on slippery ground;
you cast them down to ruin.

19 How suddenly are they destroyed,
completely swept away by terrors!

20 They are like a dream when one awakes;
when you arise, Lord,
you will despise them as fantasies.

21 When my heart was grieved
and my spirit embittered,

22 I was senseless and ignorant;
I was a brute beast before you.

23 Yet I am always with you;
you hold me by my right hand.

24 You guide me with your counsel,
and afterward you will take me into glory.

25 Whom have I in heaven but you?
And earth has nothing I desire besides you.

26 My flesh and my heart may fail,
but God is the strength of my heart
and my portion forever.

27 Those who are far from you will perish;
you destroy all who are unfaithful to you.

28 But as for me, it is good to be near God.
I have made the Sovereign Lord my refuge;
I will tell of all your deeds.

—*The New Interpreter's Study Bible*

## Umberto Eco's Ur-Fascism in Apocalyptic Narratives

Many notable works of climate fiction depict a world on the brink of an apocalyptic event—or are set in a postapocalyptic future—in which Ur-Fascist forces take control of large pockets of human civilization, seize control of all available food, water, housing, finance, and other natural resources, and imprison the populace in an Ur-Fascist society. These climate fiction narratives are as diverse as *Swastika Night* by Katharine Burdekin (1937); the incomplete *Parable* trilogy by Octavia Butler (1993–98); *MaddAddam* by Margaret Atwood (2003–2014); *The Hunger Games* by Suzanne Collins (2008–10); *The Strain* by Guillermo del Toro and Chuck Hogan (2009–11); the book and film adaptations of J. G. Ballard's *High-Rise* (1975) and Meg Rosoff's *How I Live Now* (2004); *V: The Original Miniseries* by Kenneth Johnson (1983); *V for Vendetta* by Alan Moore and David Lloyd (1982–89); the "A Boy and His Dog" story cycle by Harlan Ellison; and the films *Zardoz* (1974), *Spacehunter: Adventures in the Forbidden Zone* (1983), *Tank Girl* (1995), *Iron Sky* (2012), *Snowpiercer* (2013), and *Mad Max: Fury Road* (2015).

The narratives enumerated above vary vastly in quality, from the canonical classics that are respected by scholars of literature, film, television, and graphic novels to ambivalently embraced cult classics to works so artistically disposable that they barely have champions among those who cherish nerd culture and "trash cinema." Devoting a chapter to such qualitatively uneven works is defensible in terms laid out by I. Q. Hunter, author of *British Trash Cinema* (2013), once the argument is expanded beyond the scope of Britain to include all national cinemas: "Critics have often been at odds with popular tastes, which they cannot police and regularly despair at, and with the even more recherché tastes of cultists and cineastes, who revel in bizarre and undervalued *films maudits* and who, when they notice British films at all, love a different kind of British cinema and perhaps a different version of Britain." Hunter explains that trashy films are culturally and artistically significant because they enable "little stabs of insight into what might grandiosely be described as the Unconscious, even what the Marxist critic Frederic Jameson calls the Political Unconscious, of . . . culture seething with repression and coming apart."[1] The somewhat disreputable films and books considered in this chapter provide more than stabs of insight into the Political Unconscious—they blow the doors off the Political Unconscious, most notably in their exploration of Ur-Fascist villains, feminist heroes, and Marxist ideologies.

As we have seen, fascist villains have been a staple of climate fiction since the birth of the genre. Perhaps most notably, C. S. Lewis's *That Hideous Strength* features the fascist villains of N.I.C.E. who represent a physical threat (they try to kill the heroes), an ideological threat (they try to brainwash all of England through co-opting the mass media), and a spiritual and psychological threat (flawed protagonist Mark Studdock joins N.I.C.E. because his poor self-esteem and weak character predisposes him to embracing fascism). The Daleks, Orcs, and the Empire from *Doctor Who*, *Lord of the Rings*, and *Star Wars* all serve the same narrative function as the Ur-Fascist villains of N.I.C.E. This is no mere lazy genre trope, employing the Nazis and neo-Nazis as pro-forma, *They Saved Hitler's Brain*–style villainy. Fascists are a staple of climate fiction villainy because they are the ideological opposites of environmentalists; they model a fundamentally unhealthy, utilitarian attitude toward the world. Wendell Berry has argued that when we manipulate everything in our environment to service us, we subjugate all forms of life in a fascist-like manner: "This, clearly, is a dictatorial form of behavior, as it is as totalitarian in its use of people as it is in its use of nature. Its connections to the world and to humans and the other creatures become more and more abstract, as its economy, its authority, and its power becomes more and more centralized."[2]

The Ur-Fascist societies depicted in the controversial narratives listed above are oppressive but maintain control by providing an illusion of stability in a world gone mad. The leaders of these societies build religions around themselves, inspiring the worship of those they have subjugated. Their Messianic status grants them the right to persecute and kill anyone who opposes them, and to collect wives, mistresses, and prostitutes around them as trophy-like testimonials to their power. They are also not above incestuous sex. In several of these narratives, charismatic idealists attempt to overthrow the Ur-Fascist overlords by inciting populist uprisings of women and the oppressed working classes in the hopes of forming a more egalitarian society. The villains of these pieces are not only the totalitarian rulers and their militaristic henchmen, but also the cowed members of the middle and lower classes who are too awed by the Messianic veneer of the Ur-Fascist leadership, too enraptured by the prospect of sharing in the pomp and wealth of the ruling classes to want to see those classes humbled, or too afraid of the fruitlessness of the rebellion to help the rebels mount any real challenge to the Ur-Fascists. Each of the narratives identified above depicts slightly different outcomes to the insurgencies, but one consistent theme is the importance of undermining the patriarchal system of thought that validates oppression by giving the villains the tools to cast themselves as Messianic figures or heroes.

In "Eternal Fascism: Fourteen Ways of Looking at a Blackshirt" (1995), Umberto Eco wrote that

> Ur-Fascism is still around us, sometimes in plainclothes. It would be so much easier for us if there appeared on the world scene someone saying, "I want to reopen Auschwitz, I want the Blackshirts to parade again in the Italian squares." Life is not that simple. Ur-Fascism can come back under the most innocent of disguises. Our duty is to uncover it and point our finger at any of its new instances—every day, in every part of the world. Franklin Roosevelt's words of November 4, 1938 are worth recalling: "If American democracy ceases to move forward as a living force, seeking day and night by peaceful means to better the lot of our citizens, fascism will grow in strength in our land." Freedom and liberation are an unending task.[3]

Eco enumerates and explicates a list of fourteen features "typical" of an Ur-Fascism (or "Eternal Fascism") to clarify the connective philosophical tissue between manifestations of fascism in different cultures and historical periods. The following are paraphrased, truncated versions of Eco's fourteen traits of Ur-Fascism, which are presented here for their cultural import as well as their relevance to an understanding of Ur-Fascism in climate fiction. For Eco, Ur-Fascism involves:

1. cult-like reverence for tradition;

2. embracing irrationality and anti-intellectualism;

3. celebration of swift, impulsive, violent action;

4. the view that all dissent is tantamount to treason;

5. belief that dissent suggests a diverse populace, and diversity is evil in this mindset—therefore, Ur-Fascism is implicitly and explicitly racist;

6. rallying the angry feelings of an economically beleaguered middle class;

7. embracing a paranoid form of patriotism in which Ur-Fascists are obsessed with one or many conspiracy theories about subversives or foreigners conquering their beloved homeland;

8. envy of the prosperity of their cultural, ideological, and economic enemies;

9. the view that "life is permanent warfare" and "pacifism is trafficking with the enemy";

10. belief that the masses are weak and contemptible and must be subdued by a strong leader for their own benefit;

11. love of narratives of heroism in which heroes deal out death to vast numbers of enemies before they themselves fall gloriously in battle. (Notably, all citizens are encouraged to emulate these heroic values, and all citizens should consider themselves heroes.)

12. a scenario in which men who are cheated of an opportunity to claim military victory in combat and call themselves heroes transfer their frustrated feelings of aggression to women and "effeminate" men. Consequently, the endless war ethic and hero mentality leads to antifeminist and homophobic attitudes and the exploitation of women and gays in an Ur-Fascist society;

13. an establishment force that uses up-to-date broadcasting technology to create the illusion of populism. In Nazi Germany, radio and film were the most effective means of disseminating Ur-Fascist propaganda. In our present day, cable television, internet sites such as YouTube and Reddit, and social media venues such as Twitter and Facebook join these technologies to present to the public an extremist, minority view as the unified Voice of the People. This niche voice is given the most broadcast attention because it happens to shore up the political power and objectives of the Ur-Fascist rulers;

14. public discourse that is defined by the Ur-Fascist equivalent of Newspeak, including poor vocabulary, syntax, a lack of trust in objective truths or facts, and inability to embrace complex ideas or employ critical thinking skills.

It is of enormous import that the above elements of Ur-Fascism described by Eco are the opposite of the sociopolitical values espoused by environmentalist advocates of ethical stewardship of the planet, point by point. That is why it should be no surprise that Ur-Fascists are the central villains in all the works of climate fiction covered in these pages. The Ur-Fascist ideology is pervasive in climate fiction, as it is in the real world in the twenty-first century, making it worthy of further analysis.

In both climate fiction and reality, Ur-Fascists are revered partly because they make the people they subjugate feel "important" and hint that, one day, one of the worthiest among them might be elevated to a heroic status, if not to the highest status in the land as the next Ur-Fascist leader. This idea is disseminated through propagandistic entertainment, religious and political sermons, heavily biased sources of "news," and in classrooms controlled by teachers who indoctrinate their students instead of instruct them to think for themselves. For example, Margaret Atwood's *The Handmaid's Tale* contains numerous segments in a classroom in which sexually enslaved women are drilled on the honor it is for them to be raped and impregnated by wealthy patriarchs in a dystopian society plagued by widespread sterility.

One of the more memorable film scenes on this theme in recent years is the classroom segment that serves as the thematic centerpiece of *Snowpiercer* (2013). The film's dramatic conceit is that the last remaining humans on Earth have survived a freak-accident ice apocalypse on a never-ending train voyage. On the train, the wealthy few enjoy luxury in the front cars, the poor are starved and enslaved in the tail section, and the middle class in the center cars are indoctrinated to love and serve their wealthy benefactors. At the end of the film's first act, one of the tail sectioners, the young, powerful, and charismatic Curtis (Chris Evans) leads a rebellion in hopes of taking control of the entire train and redistributing the remaining wealth and goods more equitably among the passengers. Curtis calculates that their oppressors ran out of bullets some time ago and lack the capacity to make any new ones. If his theory

Fig. 8.1. Aboard the Snowpiercer, Curtis (Chris Evans) leads a rebellion of enslaved tail sectioners in the hopes of taking control of the entire train and redistributing the remaining wealth and goods more equitably among the passengers. CJ Entertainment.

is true, then the guards have been maintaining control of the train by frightening the tail sectioners with unloaded automatic weapons. The theory appears correct as Curtis and his forces ignite the rebellion and take control of several of the rear cars with relative ease. They face their first, bloody contest as they near the water recycling plant, and win a pyrrhic victory taking that car and capturing Minister Mason (Tilda Swinton) the voice of their oppressive leader, Wilford. Afterward, the hostage Mason leads Curtis and his main supporters on a quest to walk the length of the train and confront Wilford in his office haven in the Engine compartment. On the way, the dirty, bloodied tail sectioner rebels wander into a pristine grammar school classroom overseen by a pregnant, blonde, beaming teacher in an old-fashioned, floral-print dress. Acting as if a rebellion were not in full sway, Teacher begins a film showing the students a hagiographic biography of Wilford, praising him for his forethought in preparing for the apocalypse by designing the Snowpiercer, for his beneficence in hand-picking the survivors of humanity to occupy the train, and for the burden of leadership he has assumed in keeping the train well maintained and impervious to the biting cold. The children then sing a frightening propaganda song in Wilford's honor that sounds much like a church hymn.

> TEACHER: Mr. Wilfred knew that CW7 would freeze the world, so what did the prophetic Mr. Wilford invent to protect the chosen from that calamity?
>
> 10-YEAR-OLD KIDS IN THE CLASSROOM: The Engine!
>
> TOGETHER: Rumble, rumble, rumble, rattle, rattle, it will never die!
>
> TEACHER: [playing organ music and singing] What happens if the engine stops?
>
> KIDS: [singing continuously] We all freeze and die!
>
> TEACHER: But will it stop? Oh, will it stop?
>
> KIDS: No, no!
>
> TEACHER: Can you tell us why?
>
> TOGETHER: The engine is eternal!
>
> Yes!
>
> The engine is forever!
>
> Yes!

Rumble, rumble, rattle, rattle!

Who is the reason why?

Wilfred, yeah!

Wilfred, Wilfred, hip-hip hooray!

This scene was inspired by a similar segment in Vol. 1 of the *Snow Piercer* comic book, in which a tail sectioner is led up the course of the train and stumbles across a frightening religious ceremony hosted by the Brotherhood of the Engine.[4] Transposing the themes and dialogue from a religious ceremony to a grammar school classroom was an inspired decision on the part of the filmmakers. In a chilling (if not subtle) manner, the film evokes the critique of the dehumanizing effects of imperialist education on both teacher and students condemned by Paulo Freire in his educational polemic *Pedagogy of the Oppressed* (1968).

At the song's close, Teacher draws the students' attention to the compartment's windows, knowing that Curtis will look out them as well. Through the windows, onlookers can see ice and snow coating a once great and now dead human civilization. On this part of the Snowpiercer's journey, among the snow-covered wasteland, viewers can make out the frozen figures of seven humans, petrified, mere yards from the train tracks. Teacher tells the gathering that the figures are the members of a failed rebellion, "The Revolt of the Seven," which took place "fifteen years ago, in the third year of the train." The rebels had attempted to stop the train, supposing the Earth had warmed enough that they could survive in the frozen landscape, free of Wilford's tyranny. When they failed to stop the train, they leaped from its safety and tried to find shelter. "There they are, that's how far they made it," Teacher observes smugly. The remark triggers a new religious ritual, in which Teacher and students make knife-handed salutes and chant in observance of Wilford's greatness, and in mockery of those who would seek to escape his domain. The phrases "we all freeze and die" and "we all die" are repeated to underscore this point.

If it isn't already apparent at this point in the film, it becomes clear by the climax that even though this classroom lesson is a ritual and a staple of the children's education, it is being staged at this precise moment to educate Curtis ideologically. Throughout the film, the seemingly absent and disengaged Wilford is slyly instructing Curtis about the folly of rebellion against the status quo while giving Curtis a guided tour of the train. As Curtis moves up the course of Snowpiercer, he develops a sense of the entire contained ecosystem. By the time he reaches the Engine, he has learned enough to be groomed to replace the aging Wilford. The twist is that, while Curtis hopes to *seize* control of the train from Wilford and transform the train into an egalitarian community, what is happening is that Wilford intends to *hand control of the train over to Curtis,* on the condition that Curtis will be neither liberator nor reformer, but the new Ur-Fascist ruler of Snowpiercer.

When Curtis discovers that bullets are not, in fact, extinct, and most of his followers are massacred in a barrage of automatic weapons fire, he begins to realize that his rebellion was not so much successful as it was encouraged and orchestrated by both Wilford and Curtis's tail section mentor, Gilliam (John Hurt), to groom Curtis for leadership. The aging Gilliam, the first leader figure to emerge in the tail section and the hero who had brought an end to cannibal culture there, had long since become a corrupt part of the status quo of Snowpiercer, pretending to oppose Wilford at every turn while secretly talking with Wilford each night on the phone, planning the future of humanity. Between them, the two old men settled on Curtis to take over both roles— leader of the tail section and head of the Engine—because he was young, handsome, intelligent, aggressive, and Caucasian. Other worthy candidates for leadership, such as Tanya (Octavia Spencer) were disregarded based on their race, gender, ethnicity, or the ways in which their impoverished lives marked their physique, deportment, and speaking style. Gilliam and Wilford agree that a shortage of food and other resources warrants a culling of a healthy percentage of the denizens of the tail section, which will be carried out in retribution for a failed rebellion that Gilliam will coax Curtis to orchestrate. Interestingly, while Gilliam betrays Curtis by revealing the most intimate details of their interactions to Wilford, part of him appears to hope that Curtis will succeed in killing Wilford and reforming the culture of Snowpiercer, as he tells Curtis not to listen to Wilford's silver tongue, but to execute him the moment they meet for the first time.

When a captive Curtis does meet Wilford (Ed Harris), he is unable to follow Gilliam's advice. The God of Snowpiercer talks of the burden of leadership and the need to pass the torch onto a worthy successor. It is a lonely job, and filled with grim responsibilities—like orchestrating the occasional culling—but it is a job that he believes a murderer such as Curtis is fit for. The perks involve silence and privacy in the solitude of the Engine room, two things that Curtis has not experienced in almost twenty years. There is also a zaftig bodyguard dressed in yellow who almost never speaks and who serves as a sexual plaything of the God of Snowpiercer. Curtis will inherit her as well. Disenchanted by learning that Gilliam had sold out the tail section at some unknown point in the past, remembering the horrors of life in a cannibalistic society, and furious at the decadence, cruelty, and stupidity he has witnessed on the tour of the train, Curtis wonders if he should not, after all, take this rabble in hand and lead them just as Wilford has. However, he discovers that Snowpiercer's perpetual motion engine is kept running only though the round-the-clock work of enslaved children—the manual labor needed to replace broken parts that could no longer be manufactured in the self-contained world of the train. When Curtis sees the cost of maintaining Snowpiercer, he decides that the train needs to be derailed, as another insurgent, the Inuit Namgoong Minsoo (Kang Ho Song), had insisted earlier. Minsoo is convinced that the snow outside is melting, that the planet was finally warming again, and that the Earth could now sustain life beyond the confines of Snowpiercer. Seeing to the welfare of the children, Curtis does not stop Minsoo from setting off an explosive charge that flips Snowpiercer off its tracks. In the wreck that follows, all the lives aboard Snowpiercer are lost save for

Minsoo's daughter and Tanya's son. The Inuit girl and black boy walk away from the burning train into the snow-swept landscape. They are cold but not freezing to death. In the final shots of the film, they catch sight of a polar bear—the first sign of life they encounter beyond the confines of the train—which offers the hope to this new Adam and Eve that other life lies just over the next snowdrift.

The film was a thematic, not literal, adaptation of the recently reprinted graphic novels *Snow Piercer 1: The Escape* (1982) and *Snow Piercer 2: The Explorers* (1999–2000). Interestingly, the film is different enough from the source material that the comic book creators were able to claim it as part of the series' own continuity—treating it as an adventure that took place on a different Snowpiercer. (There are ten miracle trains, per comic book lore.) Therefore, the graphic novel *Snow Piercer 3: Terminus* by Olivier Bouchet and Jean-Marc Rochette acts as a follow-up to both the film and *Snow Piercer 2: The Explorers* (2016), and reveals the final fate of the film's "Adam and Eve," Tim and Yona.

If one were inclined to be critical of the *Snowpiercer* film and comics, one might suggest that it is a perfect specimen of what Tolkien disliked about the allegory genre. Overt symbolism is rampant. Dialogue is loaded with contemporary political significance. The construction of the world is so ideologically informed and designed to be pedagogical that it feels wholly artificial. It is also, arguably, derivative and contains plot and thematic elements from J. G. Ballard's *High-Rise* transplanted from skyscraper to train. The characters are broadly drawn, representing concepts: rich woman, poor man, and middle-class child. The villains are so operatically evil they are about as intellectually and spiritually nuanced as Orcs or Daleks, yet they are not supposed to be hive-minded automatons. (Of course, this is a deliberate political point the film is making.) Whether one is inclined to consider *Snowpiercer* brilliant or contrived or somewhere in between, the film is noteworthy for having been distributed in America despite its subversive content. As David Denby wrote in *The New Yorker*, "*Snowpiercer*, like *Elysium* and *The Hunger Games* movies, presents a portrait of oligarchical rule and underclass discontent; these films are fueled by disgust for the decadent rich and admiration for the outraged poor. Is revolution being hatched in the commercial cinema?"[5]

## Revolt of the Matriarchs: Octavia Butler's *Parable of the Sower* and *Parable of the Talents*

Unhappy and impoverished people are desperate to see their lot in life improved, and when it seems that hard work is not being rewarded and "the American Dream" is illusory, it is then that a narrative such as *Snowpiercer* is popular. However, would-be revolutionaries such as Curtis—or, perhaps, some viewers of *Snowpiercer*—cannot help but be in awe of the Ur-Fascist ruler and his trappings of wealth and power even as they plot to drag him down from his (Iron) Throne and place his head upon a spike. Indeed, many would-be revolutionaries wonder what it would be like to take the Ur-Fascist's place upon the throne, proving to be poor revolutionaries after all. Gilliam is corrupted in this fashion and Curtis *almost* is. *Snowpiercer* asks us to consider just how invested we are in becoming wealthy and powerful and how much of our feelings of solidarity with the suffering masses is illusory. Do we object to the *concept* of Ur-Fascist oppression or do we only object to being counted among the oppressed? Would our horror at social injustice vanish if we won the lottery and were magically granted a seat at the banquet table with the Ur-Fascists?

When we watch a dystopian film such as *Snowpiercer* or *Hunger Games*, do we think critically about both sides of the dramatized conflict and are we sure which characters we should be sympathetic to and/or rooting for to win? When we watch the cyberpunk film *Blade Runner*, should we feel more empathy for Rick Dekard or Roy Batty? Or does the end of *Blade Runner* suggest that that is not the right question to be asking? When we watch *Snowpiercer*, what character do we find the most compelling and relate to the most: the poor Tanya, who only wants her enslaved son back, or the articulate, polished Wilford, with his fine wine and gourmet steak? When we consider other postapocalyptic scenarios, what characters do we see ourselves in? Most of us probably flatter ourselves that we will be either the Ur-Fascist or the head of the rebellion—Darth Vader or Luke Skywalker, President Snow or Katniss Everdeen. Do we ever see ourselves as the victim of the village massacre on Jakku carried out by Finn's Stormtrooper compatriots in *Star Wars: The Force Awakens* (2015)? Do we see ourselves among the enslaved, like Anakin Skywalker's mother in *Star Wars: The Phantom Menace* (1999)?

Are we more like the brothel owner Littlefinger in *Game of Thrones*, or are we one of his whores? Perhaps one of the reasons why Tyrion Lannister is so popular a character in the universe of Westeros and Shae is so frequently criticized is that Tyrion is the vulnerable but wealthy and clever survivor we would like to see ourselves as and Shae is the pathetic, subjugated prostitute we fear we would be in a "survival of the fittest," pseudo-medieval universe. After all, in the Martin novels, all of the scenes featuring Shae are told from Tyrion's perspective, and she is granted no interiority—her thoughts and feelings are as closed to us as the narrator's of *The Handmaid's Tale* are open to us. When reading the *MaddAddam* trilogy, it might well feel better to readers to relate to Snowman, the fallen-from-grace best friend of the Messianic Crake, than to identify with the child prostitute Oryx, the high-end prostitute Ren, or the rape victims Toby and Amanda Payne. This is also one of the lessons Atwood provides in the epilogue of *The Handmaid's Tale*. When a male historian immerses himself in the heroic, horrifying memoir of a woman who lived as a sex slave in the now fallen civilization of Gilead, he cannot bring himself to research and explicate her story, only strive to find out more about her oppressor, "the Commander." After all, to the male historian, the Commander is a far more interesting subject of study since patriarchs are inherently fascinating and their victims are not.

The problem is that patriarchs are *not* inherently fascinating. They are small. The Commander in *The Handmaid's Tale* has an imposing military title and is one of the founders of the Ur-Fascist regime, but he is ridiculous as a man, looking for constant validation from Offred, the woman he has enslaved, and approval from her for the system he designed that keeps her a slave. Even his real name—Fred—sounds too pedestrian to be the real name of a "Commander." Furthermore, his efforts to coax Offred to fall in love with him instead of just being his slave underline his own insecurity and emptiness as a human being. It is bad enough that he is enslaving Offred; it is still more horrible that he wants to be loved as the slave master. (And he even wants her to *delight in playing Scrabble with him.*) In *A Song of Ice and Fire* by George R. R. Martin, Tyrion makes the same demand of Shae and kills her in part because she refuses to comply with this demand. Her love is an act. Inauthentic. When he realizes this, he feels emasculated and murders her. (Of course, the key phrase above is, "in part," since Tyrion also kills her because she testifies against him during his trial.)

In *The Handmaid's Tale*, what Fred has in his favor is pomp and circumstance and a title—and that is all. His power is all smoke and mirrors and myth: the cult of the wealthy, the Godhood of the Ur-Fascist. Take that mystique away from him and he is ripe for deposing, either by a successor Ur-Fascist or by a mass uprising of those he has subjugated. In the epilogue, readers learn he was likely replaced by still more extremist totalitarians who saw him as having gone soft shortly after the events depicted in Offred's autobiographical account.

When climate fiction such as *The Handmaid's Tale* is told from the perspective of the victims of sexual exploitation, and explicitly condemns the Ur-Fascist antagonist, then they act as a challenge to fascist thinking in the real world. When climate fiction seems to invite audience identification with fascist characters, and depicts scenes of rape from the perspective of the fascist rapist in a manner that makes rape seem somehow justifiable or enjoyable, then the climate fiction is promoting fascist thinking in the real world. Ideally, climate fiction should always challenge fascist thinking. That is its central job in promoting a more ecologically just world.

## The Ur-Fascist as God

In climate fiction narratives set in a postapocalyptic world ruled by Ur-Fascists, the Ur-Fascists maintain their control over the populace by placing a religious gloss over all their activities, whether those activities include feeding and protecting their subjects or raping and executing them. These Ur-Fascists cloak themselves in the robes of godhood and give a ritualistic quality to the moments at which the Ur-Fascists are doing the most to humiliate their subjects. In *Mad Max: Fury Road* (2015), Immortan Joe, the totalitarian ruler of the Citadel, celebrates an unholy mass by appearing upon a balcony high above his emaciated subjects and raining rations of water in one great flood down over their heads, forcing them to crawl over one another and push each other out of the way to catch the water in their mouths and in any makeshift bowl or cup they have handy. He tells them that too much water is no good for them, and not to get addicted to it. If they become too dependent upon water, it is a sign of their weak character. The subjugated peoples fall over themselves thanking Joe for the water with the same gratitude that the Israelites expressed, thanking their God for the manna from Heaven. The implied lesson is that Joe's subjects must never challenge his rule or he will be justly angry—as Gods are wont to become—and the water tap will suddenly find itself shut off. Indeed, in the Arnold Schwarzenegger action film *Total Recall* (1990), the Ur-Fascist ruler of the Earth colony on Mars, corporate CEO and Governor Vilos Cohaagen (Ronny Cox) retaliates against the terrorist insurgents who seek to unseat him by shutting off all the breathable oxygen in the domed neighborhoods he knows are sheltering the rebels. When victory seems assured, "everyman" Messiah Douglas Quaid (Schwarzenegger) yells, "Come on, Cohaagen! You got what you want. Give these people air!" Cohaagen considers the request for a moment and takes another look at the surveillance camera footage of prostitutes, alcoholics, tourists, and members of the working classes suffocating on the floors of the red-light district Venusville. "Fuck 'em," Cohaagen declares, and stops watching the surveillance footage. Characters such as these are portrayed as evil in the movies, but their real-life analogues are more often greeted with respect and are held aloft as models of financial and personal success that everyone should emulate.

American filmgoers are accustomed to rooting against genre villains such as Cohaagen or President Snow in *The Hunger Games* or Lex Luthor in *Batman v Superman* (2016). However, they are more likely to praise, emulate, and vote for the real-world analogues of such figures. Part of our fealty to such figures comes from a lack of knowledge of history. Another part comes from the seductive way figures such as these present themselves in the mass media to an impoverished, uneducated, desperate public. Octavia Butler's prophetic 1998 book *Parable of the Talents* depicts charismatic Texas Senator Andrew Steele Jarret, who mobilizes the racist vote and becomes President of the United States by promising to "Make America Great Again." The following passage from Butler's novel is an excerpt from the personal journal of her heroine, Lauren, dated September 26, 2032:

> [Jarret] wants to take us all back to some magical time when everyone believed in the same God, worshipped him in the same way, and understood that their safety in the universe depended on completing the same religious rituals and stomping anyone who was different. There was never such a time in this country. But these days when more than half the people in the country can't read at all, history is just one more vast unknown to them. Jarret supporters have been known, now and then, to form mobs and burn people at the stake for being witches. Witches! In 2032! A witch, in their view, tends to be a Moslem, a Jew, a Hindu, a Buddhist, or, in some parts of the country, a Mormon, a Jehovah's Witness, or even a Catholic. . . . Jarret condemns the burnings, but does so in such mild language that his people are free to hear what they want to hear. As for the beatings, the tarring and feathering, and the destruction of "heathen houses of devil-worship," he has a simple answer: "Join us! Our doors are open to every nationality, every race! Leave

your sinful past behind, and become one of us. Help us to make America great again." He's had notable success with this carrot-and-stick approach. Join us and thrive, or whatever happens to you as a result of your own sinful stubbornness is your problem . . .

Jarret . . . is a big, handsome, black-haired man with deep, clear blue eyes that seduce people and hold them. He has a voice that's a whole-body experience. . . . It seems inevitable that people who can't read are going to lean more toward judging candidates on the way they look and sound than on what they claim they stand for. Even people who can read and are educated are apt to pay more attention to good looks and seductive lies than they should.[6]

Immediately following Donald Trump's election to the presidency of the United States, George Orwell's *1984* became an overnight bestseller again on Amazon.com. However, Nigerian American fantasy writer Nnedi Okorafor observed that, in many respects, Octavia Butler is the author who most accurately predicted Trump's America, not Orwell. "After everything that happened, I'm not reading *1984*, I'm not reading *Fahrenheit 451*, I'm not reading *The Handmaid's Tale*. I'm reading *Parable of the Sower* [and *Parable of the Talents*] by Octavia Butler. I feel like if we're looking for any answers or where we're going, it's definitely in Octavia's work," said Okorafor.[7]

The passage from *Parable of the Talents* quoted above is insightful in its depiction of the poor and desperate looking for any easily visible peg on which to hang their hopes for survival, no matter how inappropriate. Indeed, as Butler demonstrates, support for fictional characters such as Jarret and their real-life analogues might be explained away by media lionization fueling the fears of a desperate and uneducated public looking for a Messiah figure to save them. However, the historical one-to-one-corollary between divine gods and human demagogues is worth exploring. After all, in the real world, what figure is closer to God the Father than the successful corporate CEO? As theologian and activist Joerg Rieger observed in *Religion, Theology, and Class: Fresh Engagements After a Long Silence* (2013):

From the very beginning, Christian images of God's power . . . [were informed by the example of political power and wealth evident in] the Roman Empire. Consequently, many theological notions of God as king were informed by the power of the upper classes. . . . When contemporary Christians talk of God's power, the power of the CEO of a successful corporation is often what is envisioned. When this definition of power is taken for granted, as it often is, the discussion is confined to an endorsement of such a God by people who consider themselves theists or a rejection by others who claim to be atheists.

Yet what if God's power were not defined in terms of the ruling class but of the working class? The question is not as odd as it may sound, as the

God in the biblical traditions is often described as a worker: in the second Creation account in Genesis 2:4–25, God crafts the human being out of clay and plants a garden. In the creation stories of the Psalms, God's labor is celebrated (Psalm 8:3 describes the heavens as the work of God's fingers, in Psalm 65:9, God is said to water the earth, etc.). And in the first creation account in Genesis, God is said to establish what in capitalist societies was established only by unionized workers: a day of rest after several days of work—that is, the weekend.[8]

Joerg Rieger's theological and political justification for a more egalitarian conception of Christianity is, indeed, compelling. However, it would be understandable if the imperial legacies of Christianity and its historic use as a weapon of the powerful against the weak would make many in our current generation reluctant to strive to reclaim a faith that has been so tainted—even if C. S. Lewis and Pope Francis effectively model how a more loving Christianity might be reclaimed from a more Dominionist form of Christianity. Instead of reforming the old, patriarchal religions, some modern thinkers might be more inclined to advocate the invention of new religions for a new time— and the invention of more female-centric religions to challenge the patriarchy. Octavia Butler dramatizes just such an enterprise in 1993's *Parable of the Sower*.

One of the central themes of Butler's book is the use of religion as a means of responding to periods of extreme personal and social crisis. Her heroine, Lauren, copes with tragedy through creating a new religion called Earthseed that is predicated on the notion that God is the greatest force in the universe: change. Change shapes humanity, and humanity shapes change. As Lauren's lover Bankole explains, the religion is pseudo-Buddhist and pseudo-Deist in its conception of God and in her refusal to provide any strong sense of God (or "Change") as personal, mystical, or Messianic. Derivative or not, Lauren conceived of Earthseed as a commonsense faith and reflection of her direct experience of the real world. In some respects, she is following Ralph Waldo Emerson's call to develop her own relationship to Nature and the Divine through her sense perceptions, rather than have these relationships mediated through texts written by dead prophets. Her enterprise is a classically American transcendentalist one.

In the first book of the incomplete *Parable* trilogy, Lauren uses Earthseed as a tool to boost the morale of the refugees in her charge during their Exodus-like journey to a new home. The minister's daughter aids several lost souls during the book, and the group is notable for its inclusiveness. Lauren offers help to people from a wide variety of ages and races, and a balanced mix of men and women are present. Notably, among those she takes under her wing are former prostitutes and women who have been raped, including one of the widows of a slain, upper-middle-class polygamist; a married female servant of a wealthy man (whose sympathetic wife snuck her out of the house in time to prevent the servant's rape); and a preteen girl who had been a nightly victim of incest by a charismatic relative held blameless by the rest of the family. When Lauren and her followers settle on Bankole's family plot for a destination at the end of the novel, they begin planting the roots of a new kind of humane, matriarchal, agrarian community there called Acorn. While some of Lauren's flock doubt that her vision of a better future will come to anything but death and disaster, Lauren chooses to believe that Earthseed will be the faith that binds them together despite the hardships they will face in the future—and do face in the sequel, *Parable of the Talents*. Certainly, the sense of solidarity the group develops helps them stand together in the face of overwhelming challenges from a hostile environment populated by murderous bands of white supremacists, drug addicts, and cannibals.

(It is important to note here that, even though Butler died before writing her planned third novel, the second book has a strong ending and offers a closer that makes a third novel seem, in many respects, unnecessary. Therefore, no one should be discouraged from reading the two extant books solely because the third doesn't exist.)

In the first *Parable* book, Lauren flees a world overrun with the sort of drug-addled, murderous, cultist villains one might find in a *Mad Max* film, and attempts to found a new society that is safe for women to live and thrive in. Improbably, since it is a well-directed action movie instead of a literary work like *Parable of the Sower*, the

Fig. 8.2. In *Mad Max: Fury Road* (2015), Imperator Furiosa liberates the many "wives" of the water-hoarding Ur-Fascist Immorten Joe, unchaining them from their chastity belts and driving them across perilous desert in an armored oil tanker to take shelter with the feminist Vulvalini. Pictured: Joe (Hugh Keays-Byrne, foreground) and his army of followers are in pursuit. Warner Bros.

fourth film in the Australian, postapocalyptic *Mad Max* series, *Fury Road* (2015), has a similar "story": Imperator Furiosa (Charlize Theron) liberates the Five Wives of the water-hoarding Ur-Fascist Immorten Joe (Hugh Keays-Byrne), unchaining them from their chastity belts and driving them across perilous desert in an armored oil tanker to take shelter with the Vulvalini, a community of women she had been taken from years ago. *Fury Road* and *Parable of the Sower* make an odd pairing, but the thematic similarities between the two are significant.

## Women as Victims and Heroes in the *Mad Max* Series

The first *Mad Max* film (1979), co-written and directed by George Miller, was a science fiction car chase Ozploitation notable for the way it seemed to fit into the mold of the successful Roger Corman B-movie *Death Race 2000* (1975) and took some cues from the satirical British comic book character Judge Dredd (whose first appearance was in the second issue of the periodical *2000 AD* in 1977). Still more notably, *Mad Max* helped launch lead actor Mel Gibson to international stardom, and spawned the sequels *The Road Warrior* (1981) and *Mad Max Beyond Thunderdome* (1985). The first film is about a blood feud between Australian highway patrol officer Max Rockatansky (Gibson) and a biker gang called the Acolytes—a freakish assemblage of psychotic figures dressed in sadomasochistic, tribal, and punk clothing, who appear devoid of all humanity. The Acolytes spend their days terrorizing the small-town communities found dotting the highway. Max and his peers are among the few remaining vestiges of law and order left in the region, and their ability to control the Acolytes gradually slips away. In a humane segment in an otherwise brutal film, Max's partner Goose (Steve Bisley) comforts a woman that the Acolytes have raped (Kim Sullivan), speaking to her in soothing tones, offering her help, and deferring to her at all turns to help her recover a sense of agency. Goose vows to bring her brutalizers to justice, but the system begins to unravel even as he pursues a by-the-book form of justice; he is unable to make arrests permanent or see prosecutions turn into convictions. After the Acolytes murder Goose and run over Max's wife and child, Max hunts down and kills the gang members in revenge and leaves society behind to explore the Australian outback in his black 1973 XB GT Ford Falcon Coupe.

Discussing the film in a recent interview, Gibson explained, "This was the first one of those post-apocalyptic films where you saw the decay and damage of world conflagration and the aftermath, so it was a new notion. It was a revenge story set in a world that was hostile, but underneath it was a scary classic tale that has been told and retold ever since they were painting things on caves and talking across a fire and eating semi-cooked meat on their haunches. . . . It had something mythic at its core that audiences responded to. It is a harbinger of what is to come if we keep destroying our world. We'll see where we end up—with some pretty lawless characters."[9]

The film was not successful in the United States, but *Mad Max 2* was, partly because it had a larger budget, more action, and was marketed as if it were the first film in a new series; it was renamed *The Road Warrior* in the United States. While the circumstances of society's unraveling—and the extent to which human civilization has "ended"—was left unclear in the first film, *The Road Warrior* begins with a narrator offering a vague, mythic sense of post-apocalyptic historical context that appears to describe a civilization-ending war between the United States and the Soviet Union tied to the rapid depletion of the world's remaining oil resources. The narrator is one of many residents of a small, fortified oil refinery settlement whom Max reluctantly saves from being wiped out by a roving band of pirates led by Lord Humungus (Kjell Nilsson). The plot concerns Max's efforts to get the refinery workers and the oil past the pirates to a new settlement, where they will one day become the Great Northern Tribe. At the start of the film, Max is too wounded from the recent loss of his family to consider himself a hero. He comes across and captures a Gyro Captain (Bruce Spence), who leads him to the oil refinery. Max keeps his distance from the settlement, interested in seeing how he can refuel his car, but unwilling to get too close. He knows that the pirates stand between him and the refinery. From their vantage point, Max and the Gyro Captain witness two refinery workers making a vain attempt to leave the settlement. Humongus's men set upon them, raping and murdering the woman and leaving the man for dead. As Max watches, his sympathies are with the woman, who reminds him of both his wife and the other female victims of the Acolytes. For his part, the Gyro Captain relates to the rapists, and wishes that he were getting the "sex" that they were getting. He laments that he doesn't have a "clean woman" of his own and is morally outraged when the rapists kill their victim because he feels that a sex object has been wasted. The rest of the film includes as a comic subplot the Gyro Captain's quest to land himself a "clean woman," and he manages to find one in the end—which is unfortunate given his appalling tendency to empathize with rapists instead of with their victims.

In "Rape Scenes Aren't Just Awful. They're Lazy Writing," (June 30, 2015), *WIRED* columnist Laura Hudson lists a series of ways in which the increasingly frequent depictions of rape in popular culture misunderstand what rape is and seem to justify its being committed. She is particularly concerned with moments when premium channel cable shows such as *Game of Thrones* sometimes blur the lines of what constitutes rape when "rape is rape." As she observes:

> One of the reasons why rape remains so terrifyingly pervasive is far too often, no one is willing to call it what it is. We've generally agreed as a culture that rape is bad, but since people want to continue to commit (and excuse) rape, they resolve that cognitive dissonance by defining rape in incredibly narrow ways that distance it from themselves and the people they know. Behold the rise of euphemisms like "gray rape" and "rape rape" (aka "real" rape).

A small but terrifying study conducted on college-age males earlier this year found that around one in three men said they would be willing to rape a woman if there were no consequences—but only if you didn't call it "rape." For these men, the resistance or disinterest of women was viewed as insincere or inconsequential, and the use of force or coercion was seen as either acceptable, or a nebulous "gray" area—but not "rape rape." That's why definitions of rape and consent are so crucially important: They literally encourage people to commit acts of rape by redefining them into social acceptability. Simply put, any form of media that reinforces any of these ideas actively enables sexual assault.[10]

Also, Hudson explains, rape presented in popular narratives should not be depicted as sexy; should not have to be graphically depicted for the audience to believe it has occurred; and should not be considered shorthand for mature, edgy, or deep storytelling (especially since it is often just the opposite). She adds that female rape victims do not exist solely to motivate men to revenge; rape is not just for women; and not all rapists are mustache-twirling villains, but most often acquaintances, friends of the victim, or romantic partners of the victim.

Hudson concludes by observing, "Yes, there are stories about rape that are worth telling. But without extensive research into the problems, stereotypes, and struggles that rape survivors face—including what makes sexual assault different from other forms of violence—it's too easy for fictional depictions to contribute to those issues rather than combat them. With so many other narrative tools out there, using sexual assault is almost always unnecessary. There are better ways to tell nearly any story, so why use the one that tends to be both the laziest and the most harmful?"[11]

By Hudson's standards, the depiction of rape in the *Mad Max* series is deeply problematic, especially in *The Road Warrior*. Rape is one of the central motifs of *Mad Max*, but the suffering of women is used more as a moral justification for Max's acts of violent aggression against the bikers than it is to tell the story of female exploitation in a postapocalyptic patriarchy. The pain the women experience firsthand is given secondary consideration to the pain that their suffering causes Max vicariously. Their stories become *his* Story. In this context, what makes *Fury Road* so interesting is that, for the first time in the series, the women who are brutalized by the inhuman gangs of men who rule the highways are placed front and center and Max is sidelined. For the first time, their experiences of subjugation, vengeance, and liberation are presented as *their* Story, and Max is brought along for the ride as a witness and male ally. Both he and the filmgoer now know that the women's story is their own, and Max's story is of secondary import.

Since the male chauvinist series star Mel Gibson and the *Mad Max* series are popular with Men's Rights Activists (MRAs), the recasting of Max (now Tom Hardy) and the displacement of the hero in favor of Furiosa in *Fury Road* caused a stir in online forums, with MRAs seeing the shift in principal viewpoint character in this installment of the series as further proof of the unwanted female and multiethnic takeover of the science fiction genre. On the flip side, while the plot was feminist, several critics were quick to point out that Immorten Joe's fugitive Five Wives were all sexy in an undernourished, "lingerie catalogue model" way. In these respects, one might think the film was calculated to please no one: a car chase movie and rape revenge narrative awash in blood-soaked masculine ideals of glorious combat and heroism, yet one that attempts to foreground certain ideas of feminism and critiques of Ur-Fascist culture in unsubtle ways. Improbably, the film has been embraced by critics and fans, dubbed one of the best action films ever made, and was nominated for an Academy Award for Best Picture in 2016.

For all the jokes made at the expense of the sidelined Max character, he is far from inessential. He begins the film so damaged from his experiences in the previous movies, and from being tortured and enslaved in the Citadel at the start of the film, that he is not initially willing to aid Furiosa in her escape efforts. In fact, he is willing to abandon her and the other refugees—including one visibly pregnant woman, the Splendid Angharad (Rosie Huntington-Whiteley)—to die in the desert. However, circumstances compel Max to reconsider his position and he reluctantly allies with Furiosa because he fears Joe more than he dislikes the idea of bearing the responsibility of aiding refugees. Once he

Fig. 8.3. In *Mad Max: Fury Road* (2015), Imperator Furiosa (Charlize Theron) subdues Max Rockatansky (Tom Hardy) before he can steal her water supply and armored oil tanker transport. The liberated "brides" of Immorten Joe look on. Warner Bros.

finds himself caught up in their escape plan, he rapidly becomes emotionally involved in their plight and regains his humanity as his sympathy for the women grows. Max rediscovers the empathy for women that he felt for victimized women in the previous films. The chase they lead Joe and the battles they fight are so intense that Max and Furiosa develop first a wary and battlefield-forged alliance, then mutual respect, then, ultimately, a genuine Platonic affection for one another. During their escape, Furiosa and the Five "Wives" (or "Breeders") benefit from Max's help. He offers key advice. And yet, they do not *need* him to ride in like a white knight to save them. His presence is also instructive to the males in the audience—be careful whom you relate to. As a male, one might expect Max to show more sympathy for Immorten Joe, but he allies himself with Furiosa early on and never rethinks or regrets the decision. Indeed, the film features another, still more dramatic redemption story. One of Joe's most loyal subjects, Nux, is willing to go to his death a hero to help Joe reclaim his brides. When he fails in this task and is abjured by Joe, Nux is shocked into a realization that Joe is not the Godlike figure he thought Joe was, and that if he died fighting for Joe, he would not find himself in Valhalla as promised. Shaken free of the Ur-Fascist ideology Joe had brainwashed him in, Nux helps Furiosa and the others escape. Like Max, Nux sides against the male oppressor and with the women, and is not depicted as a traitor to his gender, but as a champion of freedom. This was a message that, for some reason, offended Men's Rights Activists. Perhaps that fact should not be remotely surprising. Nevertheless, it is more than a little disappointing.

In one of the darkest moments of the film, Furiosa reaches her destination, finds the last few remaining Vulvalini, and realizes that the green paradise she remembered as a child has since withered and died because of climate change. The haven she sought when escaping the Citadel was gone. When she recovers from the shock, she and Max realize that what they need to do is not try to find a new, mythical home, but claim the Citadel for themselves, unseat Joe, and give the water and the greenery within its walls over to Joe's repressed subjects. They turn about and race home, confronting Joe directly on the road back, killing him and his musclebound son and destroying his mobile army. When they arrive at the Citadel with the body of Joe strapped to the hood of Max's car, Joe's remaining lieutenants surrender and hand control of the Citadel over to Furiosa. Since she has experienced suffering, and knows compassion, she will be a benign ruler. She will not become another Ur-Fascist ruler withholding water from the common people. For his part, Max is glad to see Furiosa succeed, but the Citadel is not his home, so he returns to his car to resume his wanderings across the Outback.

The pitched battle over freedom for women and for clean drinking water for citizens has resonance in recent years. The women's rights angle resonates in the era of the war on women's reproductive rights, as well as their rights to receive equal pay and family leave, breastfeed outside the home, be believed when they report sexual abuse, wear yoga pants (or anything flattering to their figures, for that matter), and post cultural criticism of video games on YouTube. Meanwhile, the horrors of the Flint and Detroit, Michigan, water wars; the California drought and its attendant battle between the government and the Nestle corporations for control of the remaining water supply, and the 2016 EPA revelation that hydraulic fracturing poisons local water supplies makes the hoarding and liberating of water motif evocative.

Those interested in exploring greater contemporary cultural context for dystopian climate fiction such as *Fury Road* should consider consulting the following studies: *The Next American Revolution: Sustainable Activism for the Twenty-First Century* (2012) by Grace Lee Boggs and Scott Kurashige; *This Is an Uprising: How Nonviolent Revolt Is Shaping the Twenty-First Century* (2016) by Mark Engler and Paul Engler; and *We the People: Stories From the Community Rights Movement in the United States* (2016) by Thomas Linzey and Anneke Campbell. For histories of similar conflicts, most provocatively in the heart of Oklahoma, read *The Green Corn Rebellion* (2010) by William Cunningham; *The Color of the Land: Race, Nation, and the Politics of Land Ownership in Oklahoma, 1832–1929* (2010) by David A. Chang; and *Agrarian Socialism in America: Marx, Jefferson, and Jesus in the Oklahoma Countryside, 1904–1920* (2002) by Jim Bissett.

As well reviewed as *Snowpiercer*, *Parable of the Sower*, and *Mad Max: Fury Road* have been, none has enjoyed the vast mainstream popularity of *The Hunger Games* or been accorded the smallest percentage of its cultural impact. The following chapter considers *The Hunger Games* saga in detail, the species of populist rebellion against Ur-Fascism that it depicts, and the Tolkien-like Roman Catholic sensibilities underpinning its narrative.

# 9

# Tolkien's Kind of Catholic

## Suzanne Collins, Empathy, and *The Hunger Games*

Corporate globalization represents the dominant system of economic power that has emerged since the Second World War. . . . In the last decade there has emerged increasing protest against this system of power, exposing it as aggravating environmental destruction, disabling authentic democracy, undermining cultural diversity, destabilizing social integrity, and increasing the gap between rich and poor worldwide.

—Rosemary Radford Ruether, *Integrating Ecofeminism,*
*Globalization and World Religions*

We must continue to protest injustice, bad working conditions, and poor wages (which are general now in face of the high cost of living); but our vision is of another system, another social order, a state of society where, as Marx and Engels put it, *"Each man works according to his ability and receives according to his need."* Or as St. Paul put it, "Let your abundance, supply their want."

—Dorothy Day

### Identifying Tolkien's Spiritual Successor

C. S. Lewis biographer Alister McGrath was a believer in the Tolkien-Lewis friendship, despite its ups and downs. Nevertheless, McGrath provides striking anecdotal evidence of tension between the men that might be considered amusing, tragic, or perfectly natural given their dissimilarities. Of course, some of their personal clashes grew out of legitimate differences of opinion on matters of import to them both, including aesthetics and Christian theology. For example, this episode related by McGrath is indicative of Tolkien's reservations about Lewis as the world's foremost Christian apologist:

205

On 8 September 1947, Lewis appeared on the front cover of *Time* magazine, which declared this "best-selling author," who was also "the most popular lecturer in [Oxford] University," to be one of the most influential spokesmen for Christianity in the English-speaking world." [*The*] *Screwtape* [*Letters*] had taken England and America by storm. (America, it must be recalled, had not heard Lewis' broadcast talks on the BBC.) The opening paragraph helps capture the tone of the piece: a quirky and slightly weird Oxford academic—"a short, thickset man with a ruddy face and a big voice"—unexpectedly hits the big time. Were there more bestsellers on the way? Time cautioned its excited readers that they would just have to wait: "He has no immediate plans for further 'popular' books, fantastic or theological."

The *Time* article of 1947 can be seen as a tipping point—both signaling Lewis' arrival on the broader cultural scene, and extending his reach by drawing wider attention to his works. . . . He became the subject of discussion in British newspapers, which often portrayed him in unrecognizable terms. Tolkien was particularly amused by one media reference to an "Ascetic Mr. Lewis." This bore no relation to the Lewis he knew. That very morning, Tolkien had told his son that Lewis had "put away three pints in a very short session." Tolkien had cut down on his drinking, and it was Lent—a time of self-denial for many Christians. But not, Tolkien grumbled, for Lewis.[1]

Tolkien had reservations about the presumptuousness of Lewis's use of the mass media to promote himself and his species of Christianity, differed with Lewis on specific points of doctrine, Lewis's heavy-handed use of allegory in his fiction, and took issues with the discrepancies between Lewis's public persona and the private Lewis that he had developed a close friendship with.[2] Tolkien was more traditionalist than Lewis in terms of specific points of theology, especially regarding human sexuality, and he objected to Lewis's more liberal-minded views on premarital sex, divorce, and remarriage. Their conflict over what might have been a purely "academic" debate about theology gained a sudden personal relevance when Lewis found himself considering getting married to American divorcee Joy Davidman. Lewis was certain that Tolkien would not approve of the union, since Tolkien's Catholicism forbade a single man from marrying a divorced woman. Indeed, Tolkien found Lewis's entire relationship with Joy deeply disconcerting. In *Tolkien and C. S. Lewis: The Gift of Friendship* (2003), Colin Duriez wrote:

> Just how electric this situation was as far as Tolkien was concerned may be seen from his marked differences with Lewis' more liberal theology of divorce. These had come out over certain passages in Lewis' wartime broadcast talks, and were part of Tolkien's reason for his unease about his friend's role as a popular and highly influential lay theologian. . . . Tolkien composed a long letter setting out reasons that he thought his friend's views were mistaken. The letter was never sent, but it is likely that the friends discussed the main

points, and that Lewis was aware of Tolkien's views when he courted and married a divorcee. It is almost certainly the reason that Lewis was reticent about telling him about Joy (so much so that Tolkien didn't learn about the marriage until after the event.)[3]

It seems a shame that Tolkien's views on divorce were so strong that he (possibly) would not have attended his closest friend's marriage even if he had been invited. However, Tolkien biographer Humphrey Carpenter suggests that there were more personal motives in play than merely theological—Tolkien was jealous of the time that Lewis spent with Joy that they weren't spending together, just as Tolkien's wife Edith had once been jealous of his friendship with Lewis. Carpenter makes note of the irony that, before long, Edith and Joy became friends. Furthermore, Tolkien simply didn't take to Joy personally, and that compounded the problem. According to Joy's biographer Abigail Santamaria, Joy's aggressive speech style and New York mannerisms "almost disgusted him," and the unorthodox nature of the Lewis-Joy association made Tolkien "concerned for the university" being tainted by a sex scandal.[4]

To be fair to Tolkien, in addition to his reservations about divorce and remarriage, it seems likely that he would never understand the notion of marrying someone you are not in love with at the time of the wedding, as was the case with Lewis and Joy. The film and television versions of *Shadowlands* dramatize the courtship of Lewis and Joy and the narrative of their short marriage, which culminated in the death of Joy in 1960 and a crisis of faith for Lewis. *Shadowlands* paints the love story in tragic and romantic colors while still being quite clear that Joy was the one aggressively pursuing Lewis—and that it took her some time to succeed in seducing him. Even so, the Santamaria book goes into far more lurid and specific detail than *Shadowlands* does about Joy's earliest, failed attempts to have intercourse with Lewis, notes the timeframe when she succeeded, and describes what the sex was like when it finally happened. As Joy wrote to her ex-husband William Lindsay Gresham, "in a characteristically inappropriate aside," American "assumptions about the 'intellectual Englishman's supposed coldness' were pure bunk. 'The truth about these blokes . . . is that they are like H-bombs; it takes something like an ordinary atom bomb to start them off, but when they are started—Whee! See the pretty fireworks! He is mucho hombre, my Jack.' "[5] After reading a passage such as the preceding one, it seems fairly self-evident why Lewis would find Joy a delightful, electrifying person to be around, and why Tolkien would find her obnoxious in the extreme. Both reactions to the sort of person who would plant such a passage in a letter to an ex-husband seem entirely understandable.

In contrast to both *Shadowlands* and Santamaria's accounts, Lewis biographer McGrath suggests that Joy may have seduced Lewis into marrying her in a civil service in 1956 *primarily* because she was a Jewish socialist fleeing from anti-Semitism and anticommunist sentiments during the Second Red Scare (1947–1957) in the United States and was a morally compromised opportunist eager to emigrate to England.

While McGrath offers excellent textual support for this claim, he overstates his case in a protracted analysis and seems somewhat inclined to harbor personal dislike for Joy. In contrast, Santamaria offers a far more sympathetic and complex portrait of Joy in *Joy: Poet, Seeker, and the Woman Who Captivated C. S. Lewis*—one that won over longtime Davidman skeptic (and Lewis's personal secretary) Walter Hooper, transforming his once cold view of Lewis's wife into genuine affection.

Offering further criticisms of *Shadowlands'* depiction of the romance, McGrath also posits that Lewis had mysterious motives in marrying Joy, since his private papers and letters indicate that he was not in love with her at the time of their marriage, but only fell in love with her later when she was diagnosed with bone cancer. It was then that Lewis sought to sanctify the marriage in a religious service, and he only succeeded in getting one by cajoling and coercing his friend Reverend Peter Bide into marrying them while Joy was in Oxford's Churchill Hospital on March 21, 1957. By the time of her death, Lewis was so in love with Joy that her passing was a keenly felt blow that shook his religious faith and resulted in his writing and anonymously publishing *A Grief Observed* (1961) about his dark night of the soul.

In the end, Lewis did, indeed, love Joy. Tolkien would not have been likely to have predicted that events would unfold in quite that manner, especially given the odd circumstances of their courtship. Tolkien's own love story was far more graspably "romantic" than Lewis's more unusual one. Following his mother's death, Tolkien and his brother became wards of a Roman Catholic priest. At sixteen, Tolkien fell in love with a nineteen-year-old Anglican named Edith, who was a fellow lodger in the boarding house he and his brother lived in after his mother's death. She was pretty, musically inclined, sewed a lot, and bonded with Tolkien quickly. They developed a whistle-signal to one another when it was time to skulk out of the boarding house and meet in secret at neighborhood tea shops, away from the prying eyes of other residents of the boarding house—although not out of sight of other spies. Tolkien's guardian, Father Francis Xavier Morgan, discovered the relationship and forbade Tolkien courting Edith because she was not a Catholic. This was a decree that Tolkien followed despite "accidentally" crossing paths with Edith repeatedly for some time before Francis's spies—and his growing rage—made even these briefest of encounters impossible. The forbidden-fruit quality of the romance helped it survive the extended period the two spent apart, and the moment Tolkien was free to do so, he proposed to Edith, when he came of age on his twenty-first birthday. Edith became a Catholic. They married in 1916, shortly before he was deployed to the front. Morgan's opposition to the romance had softened by this time. Later, Tolkien would artfully comment upon Morgan's role in their love story by depicting the priest as King Thingol, the patriarch in the tale of Beren and Lúthien.

Tolkien returned from the Western Front suffering from "trench fever"—an illness that began as a seemingly mild case and then snowballed alarmingly. He spent a year recovering from the physical and mental wounds he suffered on the battlefields of France. On one morning, Edith took Tolkien to a woodland glade in Yorkshire and worked to lift his spirits by singing and dancing for him. Her dance among the trees moved him so strongly that he perceived her as the most beautiful elf princess who ever lived. As Tolkien recalled, "Her hair was raven, her skin clear, her eyes bright, and she could sing—and *dance*."[6] The moment, which left an indelible impression upon Tolkien, inspired the very first of his Middle-earth stories: the love story of the elven princess Lúthien and her heroic human lover, Beren, which served as the centerpiece tale of *The Silmarillion*. Tolkien's trip to "a small wood with an undergrowth of hemlock" located "near Roos," where his wife "sang and danced for him," also inspired the love story of Arwen and Aragorn.[7] Tolkien may have disliked allegory, but it is probably difficult for any reader of the tale familiar with the details of Tolkien's life to not think of him and Edith when reading his account of Beren laying eyes upon Lúthien for the first time. In *The Silmarillion*, the battle-weary traveler "Beren came stumbling into Doriath grey and bowed as with many years of woe, so great had been the torment of the road. But wandering . . . in the woods of Neldoreth he came upon Lúthien, daughter of Thingol and Melian, at a time of evening under moonrise, as she danced upon the unfading grass in the glades beside Esgalduin. Then all memory of his pain departed from him, and he fell into an enchantment; for Lúthien was the most beautiful of all the Children of Iluvata. . . . [A]nd suddenly she began to sing. Keen, heart-piercing was her song as the song of the lark that rises from the gates of night and pours its voice among the dying stars . . . and the song of Lúthien released the bonds of winter, and the frozen waters spoke, and flowers sprang from the cold earth where her feet had passed." In this moment, Beren's "trench fever" melted away, and there are several other moments in the story when he is grievously wounded, and the healing power of Lúthien's love saves his life.

Why did Tolkien's romantic moment in the woods with Edith—who "was (and knew she was) my Lúthien"—mean so much to him?[8] Think of it from his perspective. He had just returned from the war to end all wars, wracked by "trench fever" and horrified by the knowledge that most of his friends had been killed and had joined both his parents in death. There seemed little left in life to bring him joy. And yet, at that moment, he experienced the love and beauty of his wife in a verdant, peaceful setting, basking in the spirit of romance and reveling in the beauty of the natural world he so cherished. Following a tour of duty in one of the worst wars in human history, the permanently scarred veteran found a perfect moment of peace and domestic bliss in a woodland with his lifelong love. The emotional, spiritual, romantic, and creative significance of this moment is incalculable, both to Tolkien and to the evolution of climate fiction. When Tolkien died in 1973, he was buried with his wife, who preceded him in death by two years. Their shared tombstone was marked with both their own names and the names of Beren and Lúthien.

With this kind of romance in his life, it is little wonder that Tolkien found Lewis's seemingly politically calculated marriage to Joy odd. What kind of Christian man would marry primarily to offer political sanctuary to a refugee from Joe McCarthy's America? Odd.

What these biographical stories suggest is that, in many ways, Tolkien was a gentle, warm-hearted individual. They also suggest that he had Victorian views of religion and romance that earmark him as an old-fashioned, if not deeply conservative person. When one considers this side of his personality, then it becomes understandable that the writers of *Doctor Who* would have the fictional Amy Pond refer dismissively to Tolkien as "misery guts." Tolkien's stodgy streak has also made it easier for contemporary Opus Dei–species Catholics to lay claim to him as one of their own, and to cite *Lord of the Rings* as a classic Christian fundamentalist text. It was, indeed, true that Tolkien was a devout Catholic. He was upset by Lewis's not embracing Catholicism, just as he was disappointed whenever Edith struck him as drifting from the faith. However, Tolkien's apparent rigidity is best understood in terms of his own personal history—especially in the story of his mother's conversion, persecution as a member of the Catholic faith, and eventual death.

According to biographer Humphrey Carpenter, Tolkien's mother Mabel converted to Roman Catholicism in 1900, following the death of her husband Arthur, and began taking her sons, [J.] Ronald [R. Tolkien] and his younger brother Hilary, to St. Anne's Catholic Church in the slums of Birmingham. "Immediately the wrath of the family fell upon [Mabel, and her sister, May, who had also converted]. Their father, John Suffield, had been brought up at a Methodist school and was now a Unitarian. That his daughters should turn papist was to him an outrage beyond belief."⁹ Mabel's brother-in-law Walter Incledon had provided her financial support since Arthur's death. He withdrew this support upon learning of the conversion. Mabel also faced hostility from the "Tolkiens, many of whom were Baptists and strongly opposed to Catholicism."¹⁰ The strain took a toll upon her health as well as her finances, but she raised both boys Catholic.

Mabel died young. The technical cause of her death was complications from diabetes, but Tolkien considered her death a martyrdom to Catholicism. Clearly, he felt she would have lived a longer, healthier life if her family had not retaliated against her for her new faith. Mabel's death inspired Tolkien to rededicate himself to the two things his mother had encouraged him to embrace: Roman Catholicism and the study of languages. He transferred the affection he felt for her to these pursuits. The trauma he suffered from her loss also cleaved his personality in half, creating both an "outgoing" and a "reserved" Tolkien that were not wholly reconciled. Carpenter described the two Tolkiens as his public and private personas. "He was by nature a cheerful almost irrepressible person with a great zest for life. He loved good talk and physical activity. He had a deep sense of humor and a great capacity for making friends. But from now onwards there was to be a second side, more private but predominant in his letters and diaries. This side of him was capable of bouts of profound despair. More precisely, and more closely related to his mother's death, when he was in this mood he had a deep sense of impending loss. Nothing was safe. Nothing would last. No battle would be won forever."¹¹ This public, funny Tolkien seems to be more like the light-hearted Bilbo Baggins, while the private, heavy-hearted Tolkien bears more in common with Frodo Baggins. According to Carpenter, Edith had a strong preference for the Bilbo side of his personality and was easily ruffled when his Frodo side emerged.

This more reserved, deeply sad aspect of his personality accounts, to a large degree, for the image of Tolkien as archconservative that surfaces frequently in the broader public's stereotyped perception of him. The rot has settled into this stereotype, and—though there are elements of truth to it, as the above stories suggest—the stereotype demands to be challenged and qualified. Indeed, while it is possible to view Tolkien as stodgier and ideologically crueler than Lewis, Ursula K. Le Guin would argue that, in fact, an immersion in the works of both Inklings reveals that Tolkien had the more open-hearted and open-minded worldview:

> J. R. R. Tolkien, Lewis' close friend and colleague, certainly shared many of Lewis' views and was also a devout Christian. But it all comes out very differently in his fiction. Take his handling of evil: his villains are Orcs and Black Riders (goblins and zombies: mythic figures) and Sauron, the Dark Lord, who is never seen and has no suggestion of humanity about him. These are not evil men, but embodiments of evil *in* men, universal symbols of the hateful. The men who do wrong are not complete figures but compliments: Saruman is Gandalf's dark-self, Boromir Aragorn's; Wormtongue is, almost literally, the weakness of King Theoden. There remains the wonderfully repulsive and degraded Gollum. But nobody who reads the trilogy hates, or is asked to hate, Gollum. Gollum is Frodo's shadow; and it is the shadow, not the hero, who achieves the quest. Though Tolkien seems to project evil into "the others," they are not truly others, but ourselves; he is utterly clear about this. His ethic, like that of a dream, is compensatory. The final "answer" remains unknown. But because responsibility has been accepted, charity survives. And with it, triumphantly, the Golden Rule. The fact is, if you like the book, you love Gollum. In Lewis, responsibility only appears in the form of the Christian hero fighting and defeating the enemy: a triumph, not of love, but of hatred. The enemy is not oneself but the Wholly Other, demoniac. . . . Give me Gollum any day.[12]

Le Guin's critique of Lewis caricatures him somewhat and doesn't account for his deftly portrayed analogues to Gollum—Edmund Pevensie, Eustace Scrubb, and Mark Studdock—all of whom are more overtly redeemed than Gollum. Her perspective is worth contemplating nevertheless, especially in regards to Lewis's troubling views of female academics and his highly problematic depiction of Jane Tudor Studdock in *That Hideous Strength*. Perhaps most intriguingly, Le Guin's view demonstrates how Tolkien may be regarded in a more positive light than Lewis when both are evaluated by her feminist, pacifist, and socialist moral standards.

In recent years, the film adaptations of *Lord of the Rings* and of Lewis's works, *The Chronicles of Narnia*, have encouraged many Americans to consider both Inklings paragons of religious Christian conservatism. Like Lewis, Tolkien does not fit easily into this prefabricated mold. In the cultural context of the Bush-Blair war on terror, it is hardly surprising that *The National Review* included the recent Tolkien and Lewis "action movie" film adaptations on their list of "The Best Conservative Movies of the Last 25 Years." *The Lord of the Rings* (2001, 2002, 2003) appears as number 11 on the list and *The Chronicles of Narnia: The Lion, the Witch, and the Wardrobe* (2005) comes in at number 17. As Tolkien and Lewis found renewed fame among neoconservatives and conservative Christians following the release of these film adaptations, they faced repudiation from some of the same species of liberal literati who had once embraced their writings. This was especially true in the case of Tolkien, who had always been more beloved of "hippies" than his more overtly Christian colleague, Lewis.

A McSweeney's column by Jeff Alexander and Tom Bissell effectively summed up the twenty-first-century leftist academic case against Tolkien by dramatizing an invented conversation between two anti-imperialist thinkers. The column was called "Unused Audio Commentary by Howard Zinn and Noam Chomsky, Recorded Summer 2002, for *The Lord of the Rings: The Fellowship of the Ring* DVD (Platinum Series Extended Edition), Part One." This excerpt is emblematic of its contents:

> CHOMSKY: The film opens with Galadriel speaking. "The world has changed," she tells us. "I can feel it in the water." She's actually stealing a line from the nonhuman Treebeard. He says this to Merry and Pippin in *The Two Towers*, the novel. Already we can see who is going to be privileged by this narrative and who is not.
>
> ZINN: Of course. "The world has changed." I would argue that the main thing one learns when one watches this film is that the world hasn't changed. Not at all.
>
> CHOMSKY: We should examine carefully what's being established here in the prologue. For one, the point is clearly made that the "master ring," the so-called "one ring to rule them all," is actually a rather elaborate justification for preemptive war on Mordor.[13]

In this reading of *Lord of the Rings*, Gandalf is Dick Cheney and the ring is the nonexistent "yellowcake" that led America into war with Iraq under false pretenses. This satirical text takes aim at Zinn and Chomsky as well as Tolkien, and cleverly mocks the cultural studies school of literary criticism that this monograph belongs to. Since the McSweeney's piece is spot-on political satire (and funny), one might easily miss that the interpretation of *Lord of the Rings* is a bit oversimplified and hostile to the source text. Even though it is intended as humor, this piece represents a view of Tolkien and *Lord of the Rings* that has become somewhat common: it is a proto-neoconservative text. This mockery of both Tolkien's original text and Jackson's adaptations as neoconservative classics stands in contrast with the perspective of scholars and fans who have a more broad and apologetic view of Tolkien, including Brian Rosebury and Stephen Colbert.

Rosebury has an impatience with some of the new historicist and cultural studies scholarship that considers Tolkien and his works as essentially imperialist, racist, and endorsing far-right-wing political movements. Rosebury is particularly troubled when interpreters try to find the one true meaning of *Lord of the Rings* and simplify it into an allegorical work of conservative propaganda, against the explicit wishes of the author. Rosebury explains that

> unsympathetic commentators on Tolkien, sensing his non-subscription to the secular-left consensus, have found construing his work as a coded right-wing polemic even more helpful. To Nick Otty, for example, Mordor simply is "Wiggan or Sheffield in the 1930s," while Aragorn is "like a Tory cabinet minister." To John Carey . . . the Hobbits are "gentlemen" and the Orcs "working class." Germaine Greer picked this theme up in her televised outburst that the villains of *The Fellowship of the Ring* (movie version) are "the Dwarves," who live in mines and "actually do the work," while the Hobbits are "a leisured class." All these readings exemplify a tendency endemic in twentieth-century literary criticism, with its unresolved confusions over meaning and authorial intention: the tendency to use the license of the critical reader ("what it means to me") to assign a crass and reductive meaning to a text, and then to hold the author responsible for having written a crass and reductive work. Greer's remark is particularly sad . . . because so ideologically aware a critic ought to be capable of recognizing in Tolkien's invention, even if she disagrees with it, an attitude to work which is close to John Ruskin's, and not too remote from Marx's.[14]

Rosebury's frustration is easy to understand. He published *Tolkien: A Cultural Phenomenon* in 2003, during the height of the popularity and power of the Bush administration, and left-leaning cultural critics of the time seemed prone to transferring their anger for the members of that administration over to Tolkien. Rosebury, like other Tolkien fans, felt that the deceased author should not be held responsible for how the American political Right was appropriating his life's work after his death. Rosebury is an academic defender of Tolkien. In the mainstream media, unabashed Tolkien aficionado and devout Roman Catholic Stephen Colbert frequently presents Tolkien's works and worldview in a positive light. Indeed, Colbert paid tribute to the outgoing host of *The Daily Show*, Jon Stewart, during Stewart's final episode as host on August 6, 2015, by comparing Stewart to Frodo. As Colbert explained, Stewart was called upon, not fully by choice, to bear the weight of the responsibility of representing truth and fighting for progressive causes in the political wasteland of Washington, D.C. (read: Mordor). In making this analogy, Colbert again demonstrated that the forces of Saruman and what they represent may be interpreted in a variety of different ways. In this case, Colbert suggested that the Orcs are a hive-minded mob of neoconservatives rampaging through American democracy.

Colbert's boundless enthusiasm for Tolkien and his works is widely known. He frequently inserts sudden, rapid-fire monologues about some of Tolkien's most arcane *Silmarillion* mythology into *The Late Show with Stephen Colbert*, and once seemed on the verge of stopping the natural flow of an episode to regale his audience with the story of how "Lúthien freed Beren from the dungeons of Sauron." In addition, Colbert is known for challenging audience members, academics, actors, and even Peter Jackson to Tolkien trivia battles and emerging triumphant. Indeed, Jackson declared Colbert the biggest Tolkien geek he has ever met, and granted the comedian a cameo appearance as a Lake-town spy in *The Hobbit: The Desolation of Smaug* (2013). Colbert himself revealed on a December 9, 2015, episode of *The Late Show with Stephen Colbert* that *The Silmarillion* is "my favorite book, even if it's the one no one reads." He also said, "I spent my entire teenage years reading *all* of Tolkien, not just *The Hobbit* and *The Lord of the Rings*. I'm talking 'Farmer Giles of Ham,' *Smith of Wootton Major*, 'Leaf by Niggle!' . . . [I chose to] ignore all my classwork, abandon sports, and achieve a paleness I have yet to shake off." He has jokingly suggested that his immersion in Tolkien was not just the act of an obsessed fan, but a means of "preparing myself for something important . . . to arm myself for a moment of heroism. And now that moment has arrived!"

Perhaps Colbert's grandest moment of Tolkien heroism came in his confrontation with Stephen Bannon over who best understands Tolkien and who owns the author's legacy. In early 2017, while he was still President Trump's chief strategist and senior counselor, Bannon proudly compared the supporters of the Trump administration to "the working-class hobbits" of Middle-earth, depicting them as heroic and denigrating liberal Americans as representing the forces of Sauron. Bannon's assertion that he and Trump were for the meek and humble flew in the face of the Trump administration's authoritarian, corporate, and theocratic legislative agenda. Before, during, and after his affiliation with the Trump administration, the conservative Roman Catholic Bannon has consistently advocated the implementation of a steady stream of policies and executive orders that strip away many of the rights of freedom of speech and freedom of religion afforded to the American people by the First Amendment. Bannon also tried to silence members of the press who were critical of Trump by ordering them to shut their mouths and listen to Trump for a while. Bannon did all of this in the name of supporting blue-collar American Hobbit Trump voters. On a January 30, 2017, episode of *The Late Show*, a visibly angry Colbert replied to Bannon's employment of Tolkien mythology in the service of Trump's political agenda by saying:

> Hey! Now you've gone too far. You might be the dark media genius behind the biggest electoral upset in American history, you might be playing footsie with neo-Nazis, but now we're talking Tolkien, and that's a subject I happen to know just a little bit about. There is no "working class" in Hobbiton—it's an agrarian society. The only "working-class" citizen of Hobbiton is Ted Sandyman, the miller, and he's the bad guy—he scoffed at Samwise Gamgee, said Bilbo was cracked, and allied with Saruman in "The Scouring of the Shire." So, Steve Bannon, when it comes to Hobbits, maybe you should shut your mouth and listen for a while.[15]

Well known as a Tolkien fan, Colbert is equally well known for being an openly religious Roman Catholic. Colbert acknowledges that it is rare to find a devout Catholic like himself in the entertainment industry, as he explained to Terry Gross in an interview on NPR's *Fresh Air*. "I still go to church, and my children are being raised in the Catholic Church. I was my daughter's catechist last year for first communion, which was a great opportunity to speak very simply and plainly about your faith without anybody saying, 'Yeah, but do you believe that stuff?' which happens a lot in what I do." Gross then asked him how he deals with contradictions between the Church's teachings on social issues and his own personal and political values. He replied, "Well, sure, that's the hallmark of an American Catholic is the individuation of America and the homogenation of the Church in terms of dogma. I love my church. I don't think that it makes zombies or unquestioning people. I think it is a church that values intellectualism."[16]

While Colbert has been willing to criticize his own church, he has also been vocal criticizing conservative Christians who embrace libertarian economic policies that he believes Ayn Rand would celebrate but Jesus Christ would find abhorrent. Whenever Christian politicians who describe themselves as fiscal conservatives cut taxes for the wealthy and fund those tax cuts by slashing funding for social programs that help the poor, women, and children, and that support education, the environment, and health care, Colbert is inevitably one to criticize them for not behaving authentically Christian. As he sees it, these fiscal conservatives trumpet the notion that America is a Christian nation while passing deeply unChristian legislation modeled more on *Atlas Shrugged* and *The Klansman* than on the Bible. As Colbert observed, "If this is going to be a Christian nation that doesn't help the poor, either we have to pretend that Jesus was just as selfish as we are, or we have got to acknowledge that He commanded us to love the poor and serve the needy without condition and then admit that we just don't want to do it."[17]

To a degree, the fact that both the liberal Roman Catholic Colbert and the conservative Roman Catholic Bannon enjoy Tolkien and seek to claim him as a political ally speaks to the broad appeal of Tolkien in the United States. Many of Tolkien's readers would like to think he would be on their "side" and vote their way. Paul E. Kerry, editor of *The Ring and the Cross: Christianity and The Lord of the Rings* (2010), has observed that "[i]t may be precisely a religious sensibility that makes Tolkien so compelling for so many, including Americans. In speaking with my colleagues at Villanova University—a university engaged in Augustinian renewal—they note that many times Catholic students are unaware that Tolkien was in fact Catholic, but that once they realize this new, deeper ways of understanding his and other major Catholic contributors to what Goethe called 'world culture' become apparent. Yet, readers of other faiths or those who profess none have read and enjoyed Tolkien. But isn't that a part of what Catholicism is able to do, that it is be universal? Certainly, the translations into which Tolkien has been translated attest that there is an enormous intercultural appeal."[18]

It is possible to celebrate this broad appeal of Tolkien's while still lamenting it when his works are weaponized by right-wing ideologues and employed to justify elective warfare and the persecution of women and racial, ethnic, and religious minorities. It is also important to try to evaluate Tolkien's ideological positions soberly and fairly. One scholar who has taken a particularly evenhanded approach to the fraught question of Tolkien's contemporary political relevance is Regina Bennett, who asked in 2003, "What kind of car would Tolkien drive?" in honor of a then-recent Evangelical Environmentalist campaign against SUVs branded with the question "What Would Jesus Drive?"[19] Bennett discovered, through consulting Humphrey Carpenter, that Tolkien owned two Morris Cowley automobiles between 1932 and the beginning of World War II. Tolkien nicknamed his first car "Jo" and careened recklessly around the countryside in it, terrifying Edith to the point that she refused to ride with him for a time. Tolkien gave up his second car "when Petrol rationing made it impractical to keep it. By this time, Tolkien perceived the damage that the internal combustion engine and new roads were doing to the landscape, and after the war he did not buy another car or drive again."[20] Bennett was aware of the more conservative strain in his religious and political thinking and was hesitant to grant him an anachronistic or misleading political label. However, she argues that we should all take it very seriously that Tolkien did, indeed, give up driving to take up bicycling in the name of protecting the environment. For Bennett, Tolkien's actions are what we should grant the greatest weight to—and emulate—when considering Tolkien's relevance today.[21]

As Bennett has noted, in the cold light of reason it is apparent that, religiously and politically, Tolkien indeed holds some conservative views. Perhaps most problematically, he isn't entirely free of a Rudyard Kipling–style set of "white man's burden" assumptions about the role of the British Empire in the world. Indeed, much of his motivation in creating the Middle-earth mythology appears to have been to create a prehistoric mythology for the "superior" cultures of Northern Europe, whose knowledge and culture is descended from the Elves and High Men. On the other hand, the downfall of Númenor story may be read as anticolonialist. Númenor starts out as a peaceful, artistic, and intellectual culture, but gradually transforms into an imperialist power that effectively colonizes much of the coastal regions of neighboring Middle-earth. The subjugated, "lesser" people of Middle-earth regard Númenor's King Ar-Pharazôn as the greatest tyrant since Morgoth. In the version of the narrative featured in *The Silmarillion*, Tolkien uses the word *dominion* repeatedly, like a refrain, explaining that the Númenóreans sought *dominion* over the "lesser peoples," *dominion* over Valinor, and *dominion* over death itself. The word is emblematic of their corruption, and the fall of Gondor tale related to Frodo by Faramir in *Lord of the Rings* (see chapter 1) mirrors the moral of this tale. Both narratives seem designed to warn England away from its grand imperial project—meaning that Tolkien wrote his version of *Out of the Silent Planet* after all.

Tolkien's Victorian opinions and the debate concerning his views of colonialism notwithstanding, it seems fair to say that the environmentalist, egalitarian-leaning Tolkien has far more in common with Catholic social justice warrior Dorothy Day (1897–1980) than he does contemporary American corporatocrat Roman Catholics such as Paul Ryan, John Boehner, and Rick Santorum. Much has been written in conservative online blogs attempting to group Tolkien in with modern-day right-wing Catholics. Less has written about the synchronicity between Tolkien and more left-leaning Catholics. That omission needs to be rectified. Consider how the political and religious sentiments of Dorothy Day resonate with Tolkien's writings. A member of Alice Paul's suffragist movement who was imprisoned for protesting in 1917, Dorothy Day was a lifelong champion of human rights—including labor rights, women's rights, and civil rights for African Americans—and, with Peter Maurin, founded the Catholic Worker Movement during the 1930s. She was still actively protesting well into her seventies, and getting arrested for challenging establishment forces. Her socialistic brand of Roman Catholicism could always be regarded as a niche species of Catholicism, but she and fellow liberal Catholic Thomas Merton enjoyed a wider appeal in the early days of the Second Vatican Council. However, the template of the "liberal Roman Catholic" or member of the "Christian Left" fell out of favor during the reign of Pope John Paul II, who encouraged Catholics to look to more conservative Catholics for inspiration regarding what social and political values to champion. (John Paul II was deeply anticommunist and a supporter of Ronald Reagan and the American CIA's efforts to undermine Catholic Liberation Theology and social justice movements throughout South America.)[22] In recent years, the pontificate of Francis has encouraged some Catholics to revisit Day's writings in light of Francis's interest in environmentalism and the plight of the poor. Other Catholics, who prefer to remain faithful to Pope John Paul II's staunchly antisocialist version of Roman Catholicism, hold fast to their resistance to embracing Day's Catholicism, the ethos of Vatican II, and the legacy of Liberation Theology. None of these forms of Catholicism appeal to conservative Catholics such as Bannon, who have Opus Dei sympathies and want to see the liberal, 1960s-style ideas and initiatives of Vatican II purged from the Church.

Day wrote in 1972 of the Catholic Worker Movement's objection to traditional capitalism. She explained that capitalism pits individuals against one another in an unChristian manner, creating systemic injustice and social instability. "Since the aim of the capitalist employer is to obtain labor as cheaply as possible and the aim of labor is to sell itself as dearly as possible and buy the products produced as cheaply as possible there is an inevitable and persistent conflict." Day also wrote that capitalism views people only as commodities—obedient workers and potential consumers but not complete human beings with souls: "Capitalist society fails to take in the whole nature of man but rather regards him as an economic factor in production. He is an item in the expense sheet of the employer. Profit determines what type of work he shall do. Hence, the deadly routine of assembly lines and the whole mode of factory production."[23] Capitalism turns working people into cogs in giant profit-making machines—a consequence of industrial capitalism that Day lamented. According to Day, capitalism pits workers against one another, creates conflict between workers and their employers, and divides and conquers entire communities. Consequently, Day found traditional capitalism to be wholly incompatible with Christianity.

Dorothy Day's views on capitalism are not dissimilar to those of another famous Roman Catholic, the Victorian social satirist Oscar Wilde, who was born in 1854 and died in 1900, three years after Day's birth. A Roman Catholic novelist, poet, playwright, and author of children's fairy tales, Wilde saw the values of Christianity as existing in conflict with the values of industrialization and capitalism. However, Wilde saw the progressive potential of technology so long as it was used as a Christian socialist means of liberating the masses. Unlike Marx, Wilde did not see Christianity and socialism as antagonistic opposites; Wilde was a socialist who saw in Jesus Christ the embodiment of proto-socialist values, as Day did years later.[24]

In *The Soul of Man Under Socialism* (1891), Wilde wrote, "Socialism, Communism, or whatever one chooses to call it, by converting private property into public wealth . . . will restore society to its proper condition of a thoroughly healthy organism, and ensure the material well-being of the community."[25] Wilde believed that socialism would foster a liberating environment in which people will not be coerced into doing meaningless and oppressive labor merely to serve an indolent establishment and the interests of the grinding machine of industrial capitalism. Indeed, Wilde saw the industrial society of his day, and the machines used by the labor force, as oppressive, but he envisioned a time when technology might be a source of liberation for the oppressed masses. In the same essay, Wilde wrote an extended passage in which he expressed the hope that machines might eventually eliminate the menial, mindless, and physically debilitating occupations foisted upon the working class:

> Up to the present, man has been, to a certain extent, the slave of machinery, and there is something tragic in the fact that as soon as man had invented a machine to do his work he began to starve. This, however, is, of course, the result of our property system and our system of competition. One man owns a machine which does the work of five hundred men. Five hundred men are, in consequence, thrown out of employment, and, having no work to do, become hungry and take to thieving. The one man secures the produce of the machine and keeps it, and has five hundred times as much as he should have, and probably, which is of much more importance, a great deal more than he really wants. Were that machine the property of all, everybody would benefit by it. It would be an immense advantage to the community. All unintellectual labor, all monotonous, dull labor, all labor that deals with dreadful things, and involves unpleasant conditions, must be done by machinery. . . . At present machinery competes against man. Under proper conditions machinery will serve man.[26]

At the time this passage was published, it would have been understandable for some readers to dismiss this vision of the future as being as plausible as the development of an invisibility formula or time travel technology seen in a novel by H. G. Wells. There is humor in this essay, but the core argument is serious. As early Wilde critic

Holbrook Jackson observed in *The Eighteen Nineties*, Wilde's "intellectual playfulness destroyed popular faith in his sincerity, and the British people have still to learn that one can be as serious in one's play with ideas as in one's play with a football."[27] Jackson sees in Wilde a kindred, Fabian socialist spirit, and notes that Wilde's sympathy with the disenfranchised and the socialist and anarchist movements of the period are present in Wilde's work as a subtext masked by "his lambent humor."[28]

Arguably the earliest modern-day critic to treat Wilde's socialism seriously, Regenia Gagnier explained in *Idylls of the Marketplace: Oscar Wilde and the Victorian Public* (1986) that Wilde's "aestheticism was an engaged protest against Victorian utility, rationality, scientific factuality, and technological progress—in fact, against the whole middle-class drive to conform—but the emphasis is on *engaged*."[29] Unfortunately, Wilde was a proto-modernist living in the Victorian age, and was participating in a limited discourse. Therefore, so many of his most insightful social criticisms, funny as they were, were dismissed as insincere showmanship. However, one may be funny as well as correct, as many contemporary social satirists working in comedy demonstrate daily.

While the Roman Catholic Church took a decidedly conservative turn during the 1980s and 1990s under the leadership of Pope John Paul II and Pope Benedict XVI, their predecessors, John XXIII and Paul VI were theologians more in line with Dorothy Day's thinking. The current pope, Francis, is as well, and he has given many homilies in the spirit of Day—and even Oscar Wilde. Of course, it is Francis's liberal bent that has inspired Steve Bannon to commit himself to supporting Opus Dei priests in efforts to undermine Francis's authority and depose him.[30] Why is Bannon so committed to destroying Francis's papacy? Francis's Catholicism is simply too kind, too loving, and too multicultural by half for Bannon. As *Washington Times* journalist Cheryl K. Chumley reported on May 22, 2013, Pope Francis began his tenure as pontiff by urging a global move away from material gain and toward charity. Lambasting the "dictatorship of the economy" and the "cult of money," Francis observed that, "A savage capitalism has taught the logic of profit at any cost, of giving in order to get, of exploitation without thinking of people . . . and we see the results in the crisis we are experiencing."[31]

Furthermore, while some Christians believe that only those who follow a specific Christian sect are allowed access to Heaven, other prominent Christian theologians would argue that Jesus promises access to Heaven to all who do good in the world. Pope Francis is one such theologian. Time and again, he has argued that Jesus prefers atheists who model loving kindness in the world to phony, wealthy Christians who often boast of being pious Catholics on television while exploiting the poor, oppressing women and minorities, selling weapons, and polluting the planet. In a homily in February 2017 that appeared specifically calculated to condemn the pseudo-Christian values of Bannon and the Trump administration, Pope Francis lambasted fake and hypocritical Christians. The pope posited what would happen if a Christian robber baron presented himself at the gates of Heaven saying, "Here I am, Lord! . . . I went to Church, I was close to you, I belong to this association, I did this. . . . Don't you remember all the offerings I made?" The pope then imagined Jesus replying: " 'Yes, I remember. The offerings, I remember them: All dirty. All stolen from the poor. I don't know you.' That will be Jesus' response to these scandalous people who live a double life." Elaborating on this point, the pope said, "To be a Christian means to do: to do the will of God—and on the last day—because all of us we will have one—that day what shall the Lord ask us? Will He say: 'What you have *said* about me?' No. He shall ask us about the things we *did*."[32]

This more recent homily appears to be continuing a similar theme found in a 2013 homily. In that address, Pope Francis suggested that Heaven is open to people of all faiths, and that Christians should not fall into Lucifer's sin of pride by congratulating themselves for their piety at the expense of people of other faiths. Instead, Christians should work together with people of other faiths to do good in the world. The pope said, "The Lord has redeemed all of us, all of us, with the Blood of Christ: all of us, not just Catholics. Everyone. 'Father, the atheists?' Even the atheists. Everyone! . . . We must meet one another doing good. 'But I don't believe, Father, I am an atheist!' But do good: we will meet one another there."[33] While such open-mindedness might scandalize doctrinaire Christians, it is in the spirit of Jesus, who related a parable about a "good Samaritan" who was, ironically, a better Jew than most Jews. This tale shocked Jesus's audience because Samaritans were considered archenemies of the Jewish people and the Jews were convinced that their God had cursed all Samaritans on their behalf. It is hard to imagine any parable of Jesus being more offensive to a Jewish audience of that time than one praising a Samaritan, and the "good Samaritan" parable suggests that God's love extends far beyond his chosen people to those they would deem political and cultural enemies who practice a false religion. Francis, like Day, Wilde, and Tolkien, represents a more authentically loving Catholicism than Opus Dei's. Their Catholicism is the Catholicism of Suzanne Collins.

Suzanne Collins's *Hunger Games* trilogy is steeped in the Catholic labor rights advocacy of Dorothy Day, the socialist Catholicism of Oscar Wilde, and the Catholic environmentalism of Tolkien. Like Tolkien's apocalyptic, three-volume fantasy saga, Collins's apocalyptic three-volume science fiction saga is Catholic without being overtly Catholic, keeping it free of the readily translated allegory and preachiness that Tolkien objected to in Lewis. Collins depicts war and the devastation of nature much as Tolkien does (see chapter 3). She is a private Catholic as opposed to a public preacher, like Lewis. She seeks inspiration for her narratives from mythology, as Tolkien does. Finally, her works have a Catholic sensibility—a longing for a world that is purer and more beautiful than it can ever be. Her *Hunger Games* saga has much the same quality that writer and poet Charles A. Coulombe sees in *Lord of the Rings*: "It has been said that the dominant note of the traditional Catholic liturgy was intense longing. . . . It is a longing for things that cannot be in this world: unearthly truth, unearthly purity, unearthly justice, unearthly beauty. By all these earmarks, *Lord of the Rings* is indeed a Catholic work, as its author believed: But it is more. It is this age's great Catholic epic, fit to stand beside the Grail legends, *Le Morte d'Arthur* and *The Canterbury Tales*."[34]

This sense of "intense longing . . . for unearthly justice" is found in *Hunger Games* protagonists Katniss, Peeta, and Haymitch, and permeates the entire text of the books themselves. Tonally, thematically, and theologically, *The Hunger Games* is much like Coulombe's representation of *Lord of the Rings*. As readers of *The Hunger Games* books can attest, Collins is—in several key respects—someone who more closely follows the theology and the aesthetics of Tolkien than Lewis did. Her ability to subtly weave Catholic sensibilities throughout her books without telegraphing them, her more private public persona, her environmentalist and Catholic Worker–style Christianity, her lament for the death and destruction caused by war, revisiting of ancient mythological texts, and embracing of a Franciscan love of all life tie her closely to the tradition of Catholic speculative fiction that Tolkien epitomizes. In this respect, Collins is Tolkien's clearest ideological and aesthetic analogue in the halls of contemporary climate fiction. It also appears likely that Tolkien would have enjoyed Collins's novels far more than he did Lewis's. Collins seems to be very much Tolkien's kind of Catholic.

## *Spartacus* and the Roman Empire,<br>*The Hunger Games* and the United States

Suzanne Collins's climate fiction trilogy—comprised of the books *The Hunger Games* (2008), *Catching Fire* (2009), and *Mockingjay* (2010)—is a futuristic reimagining of the classic Spartacus tale, presented as a stealth political satire of American imperialism and social Darwinism during the Bush administration. Here, the reluctant Spartacus figure is a female gladiator, Katniss Everdeen, who shows mercy to her enemies and extreme reluctance to participate in the titular free-for-all fight-to-the-death melee broadcast live to all inhabitants of a futuristic America called Panem. Katniss's visible distaste for President Coriolanus Snow's totalitarian regime and her sadness at the deaths of several of her would-be killers have a startling effect on viewers in every district across Panem. Her obvious humanity, even in the context of the dehumanizing games she's been compelled to fight in, makes the inhumanity of Panem's upper classes even more apparent, creating a sense of shared purpose between previously competing impoverished districts and sparking a society-wide class war.

Thanks to the antiestablishment nature of the series, it has been embraced by both the libertarians who supported the Oregon militia group that occupied the Malheur National Wildlife Refuge as well as by liberals who opposed the Iraq invasion, the Rumsfeld torture memos, and the passing of the Patriot Act. In addition, the strong central female character has broad, apolitical appeal to readers of young adult novels more accustomed to seeing male heroes such as Harry Potter dominate popular multibook sagas. Its greater emphasis on action and social commentary has made it a tonic in comparison to the abstinence-advocating Mormon romance series *Twilight* (2005–08). The series *does* feature a love triangle, but its significance is primarily psychological; whether Katniss chooses to accept the love of militant terrorist Gale Hawthorne or of comparatively humane and idealistic Peeta Mellark will determine to what extent she will be able to recover from the crippling post-traumatic stress she suffers after living through two Hunger Games and a war of rebellion against the Capital.

A religious Catholic who appears to have a worldview that exists in sympathy with Tolkien's, Collins indicates that Katniss's only hope of recovering from her "trench fever" will be to one day allow herself to fall in love, have a family of her own, and settle into comfortable civilian life. In choosing a family and dropping out of the world of the Capitol, Katniss will finally free herself of the political intrigue and death dealing that have plagued her formative years thanks to the Hunger Games. In Collins's worldview, Katniss's stepping away from endless participation in the Hunger Games—be it the arena combat of the Hunger Games proper or the calculated inauthenticity of a (for want of a better term) political "game of thrones" that dominates her time between military engagements—would be a good thing. Indeed, it would be a good thing no matter how unpalatable the thought of a female "superhero" hanging up her bow for domestic bliss seems at first glance to the series' readership. If Katniss is unable to find peace of mind in her post–Hunger Games life, she risks going mad like Johanna Mason, becoming a war criminal like Gale, descending into alcoholism like Haymitch Abernathy, or embracing cynical political wheeling and dealing like Plutarch Heavensbee. Perhaps worst of all, Katniss risks transforming into yet another Ur-Fascist ruler like Snow—Collins's analogue of real-life authoritarian president George W. Bush—or his would-be successor, the equally evil Alma Coin.

(As a note of significant historical and political interest, Coin is clearly Collins's commentary on hawkish New York senator Hillary Clinton, who appeared to be on the verge of succeeding President Bush in the White House when the books were being written. Collins appears to have regarded Clinton as a Goldwater Republican disguised as a Democrat—a perspective on Clinton that many progressives have shared with Collins, and one that helped prevent her from winning the presidency during two successive campaigns. Those who would take umbrage with Collins's depiction of Clinton here would find the former first lady more sympathetically portrayed in 2017's *Star Wars: The Last Jedi*. That film's thinly veiled Hillary Clinton is the tragically misunderstood Vice-Admiral Amilyn Holdo. Meanwhile, its analogue to Katniss Everdeen—that is to say, its analogue to "Bernie or Bust" and Jill Stein voters—is the recklessly unreasonable leftist rebel Poe Dameron.)

Anita Sarkeesian is one of several feminist commentators who has objected to the significance of the Katniss-Peeta-Gale love triangle, and to Katniss's story arc. Some fans have also lamented that Katniss becomes less of a strong heroine and less adept at combat as the series progresses thanks to her increasingly potent Post Traumatic Stress symptoms. However, it is possible that sometimes these commentators fail to ponder what Collins is arguing "a strong female hero" should be like. For Collins, a "strong female hero" is not the world's best gladiator but someone who is defined by compassion, intelligence, integrity, and a desire to live life in peace rather than eternal conflict. Her position in life after the war of the rebellion ends is akin to Samwise after the War of the Ring and the Scouring of the Shire, or of the Studdocks at the end of *That Hideous Strength*. From an Inklings worldview, there is no shame in Katniss becoming like Samwise or the Studdocks at the end of *Mockingjay*.

Collins herself is known for leading a quiet life. She has not interacted much with the press and what readers do know of her inspiration for the book series comes from a statement she provided for the publisher: "One night, I was lying in bed, and I was channel surfing between reality TV programs and actual war coverage. On one channel, there's a group of young people competing for I don't even know; and on the next, there's a group of young people fighting in an actual war. I was really tired, and the lines between these stories started to blur in a very unsettling way. That's the moment when Katniss's story came to me. When I was a kid, my dad fought in Vietnam. He was gone for a year. Even though my mom tried to protect us—I'm the youngest of four—sometimes the TV would be on, and I would see footage from the war zone. I was little, but I would hear them say 'Vietnam,' and I knew my dad was there, and it was very frightening. I'm sure that a lot of people today experience that same thing. But there is so much programming, and I worry that we're all getting a little desensitized to the images on our televisions. If you're watching a sitcom, that's fine. But if there's a real-life tragedy unfolding, you should not be thinking of yourself as an audience member. Because those are real people on the screen, and they're not going away when the commercials start to roll."

Collins's interest in depicting the emotional scars experienced by war veterans, inspired by her father's experience in Vietnam, exists in strong sympathy with Tolkien's depiction of the psychological effects of warfare on his heroes in *Lord of the Rings* in an obvious allusion to his own traumatic experiences in World War I. Time and again, *The Hunger Games* revisits the core themes of *Lord of the Rings* without pilfering its plot points or borrowing its dwarves and elves, repurposed and repackaged to make a new, Tolkien-derived speculative world. Instead of creating her own "Middle-earth," Collins was inspired to set her commentary on war, which took in both her father's Vietnam service and the current war on terror, within the context of the myths of the Roman Empire she embraced as a child—especially the myth of Theseus and the minotaur. Collins relocated the Roman Empire to a future America ravaged by climate change. In her speculative future, sea-level rise covers much of the United States, kills off most of the populace, and the remaining survivors experience social division by class and race. The wealthiest create an enclave for themselves in District One and divvy up the remaining regions of the former America by resources—the aquatic region characterized by fisheries, the woodland region occupied by loggers, the coal regions occupied by miners, and so on. The Capital maintains its control over the poorer, harshly subjugated districts through exercises of ruthless power, a crack force of "Peacekeepers," and by exhibiting the pomp and circumstance of the Roman Empire, going so far as to assign the members of the Capital names culled from Roman histories.

In addition to linking the books to the Theseus myth and Spartacus, Collins achieves another subtle goal by drawing comparisons between Panem, contemporary America, and ancient Rome. The comparison suggests that America has all the decadence we have seen in depictions of Ancient Rome in films like *Caligula* (1979) or television shows such as *Rome* (2005–07) and may be even more decadent. Consider theologian

Fig. 9.1. *Hunger Games* heroine Katniss Everdeen lives in a futuristic, dystopian United States called Panem. To feed her starving family, she becomes a poacher. Jennifer Lawrence was cast as Katniss in the four *Hunger Games* films (2012–15) after playing a remarkably similar working-class heroine in *Winter's Bone* (2010). Lionsgate Films.

Joerg Rieger's assessment of the moral ramifications of income inequality in contemporary America:

> In the United States, such a severe polarization between the classes has not been seen since the Great Depression. It is considerably greater than class polarization in the Roman Empire. In Ancient Rome, the top 1 percent controlled 16 percent of the society's wealth, compared to 40 percent in the contemporary United States. Ironically, while many believe that class is less a hurdle in the United States than elsewhere, past or present, the opposite is the case. The gaps between the classes are tremendous and in terms of income inequality the United States ranks behind any of the other wealthy nations, slightly ahead of Hong Kong and Singapore. Unemployment is at record levels and affects even those in the middle class who had assumed their positions to be secure; minority groups are even more heavily affected. The official data, which underestimates the real numbers, state that the unemployment was at 7.4 percent for whites, 14.4 percent for African Americans, and 11 percent for Latinos and Latinas in July 2012. Furthermore, the option to move up

the ladder—the so-called American Dream—is less an option although many people hold onto it. In these matters, the United States is behind England, hardly a country known for its reputation of social mobility. However, although almost everybody agrees with the popular sentiment that "the rich are getting richer and the poor are getting poorer," and the numbers confirm it, there is little examination of what this means and even less investigation of what the root causes are.[35]

As a theologian interested in issues of class, Rieger believes that a truly Christian ethic would fight such stark social divisions. For Rieger, Jesus is a figure who sides with working people and the poor, not a champion of free-market capitalism, and would approve of socialist efforts to raise the quality of life of the suffering poor in America and throughout the world. His view of Christian ethics is not a common one, but it has parallels in Liberation Theology. Though Rieger is not himself Catholic, he has views similar to Roman Catholics such as Dorothy Day and Oscar Wilde. The Opus Dei branch of Roman Catholic thinking, in contrast, repudiates the progressive iterations of Catholicism advanced during Vatican II and explored in Liberation Theology. Indeed, Opus Dei Catholics would see less merit in Collins's progressive Catholicism as it is expressed in *The Hunger Games* series, and be more inclined to ignore it, repudiate it, or perhaps not even perceive it. This was why several conservative Catholic commentators had difficulty fairly or effectively interpreting Collins's trilogy as the work of a devout Catholic when the books were first published.

In "What We Missed in *The Hunger Games*" (2013), Ellen Finnegan castigated Collins's fellow Roman Catholic critics and theologians for depoliticizing Collins's trilogy. According to Finnegan, these Catholic critics first dismissed *Hunger Games* as an escapist potboiler and then privileged an Ancient Rome–to–Panem comparison while foregoing a Panem-to-contemporary-America comparison. For Finnegan, Catholics Monica Mullen and Father Barron, both from *The National Review*, demonstrated that they are desensitized to violence and unwilling to ponder the profound moral questions raised by a society engaged in a project of endless, borderless global warfare. As she argues, the teenage readership who grew up during the war on terror have embraced the books not because they don't know any better and have poor taste in literature, but because the books speak to their experience of life in twenty-first-century America. Consequently, Finnegan portrays these teenage *Hunger Games* fans as more literate, socially aware, and *better Catholics* than the veteran Catholic journalists she quotes, including Steven D. Greydanus of *The National Catholic Reporter* and John Mulderig of the Catholic News Service. Finnegan then makes explicit the parallels between America and Panem that the Catholic critics failed to: "When I watch a video that compiles reactions to Osama Bin Ladens' reported death, I'm in Panem. When I go to a sports stadium and hear the Star-Spangled Banner and watch fighter jets fly overhead and hear the crowds roar and the fireworks explode, I am in Panem. When I can't board a plane without getting a photograph taken of my naked body, when I read about the NSA's Prism program or the purchasing of military-grade weapons and equipment by local police departments with grants from the Department of Homeland Security, when I think about all of the ways the government has managed to shred the Bill of Rights in the past ten years, using the War on Terror as an excuse, there is no doubt in my mind that these wars are being used to manipulate and dominate the populace."[36]

The problems posed by inadequately thoughtful reader responses to the books were compounded by the problematic film adaptations, which encouraged still more pernicious misreadings than the ones Finnegan decries. Anita Sarkeesian offers one of the most articulate assessments of how and why Collins's intended message fails to be conveyed by the film adaptation during key moments. In the Feminist Frequency video, "The *Hunger Games* Movie vs. the Book," Sarkeesian describes observing the first film in a packed movie theater and being disturbed that the gladiator combat scenes depicted in Collins's books, which were designed to horrify the reader with its depictions of children fighting and killing one another, played on screen as merely exciting and entertaining to most people in the theater with her. She says:

> Here is the problem: we as the audience are watching a story in which a fictional Capitol audience in turn is watching and deriving pleasure from the death of children. So, understandably, you and I are supposed to be horrified by the whole media spectacle of The Hunger Games. But when Clove's head is bashed in and her lifeless body is thrown to the ground, the real audience in the theater I was in actually cheered and gained satisfaction from her death. Ironically, we are encouraged by the filmmakers through the construction of the scene to behave in the same way that the Capitol audience does. . . . This is an utter failure on the part of the filmmakers to be consistent about portraying the horror of the death of children.[37]

Sarkeesian further criticized the films for failing to cast an olive-skinned actress as Katniss—and for refusing to audition non-Caucasian actresses—as well as for portraying the Capitol villains as effeminate and homosexual, suggesting that that is why the people in the Capitol are evil—they are not manly enough—instead of portraying the evil of the Capitol as deriving from the Capitol's economic and military exploitation of the poor and minority populations. The errors made by the filmmakers that Sarkeesian points out were compounded by marketing campaigns attached to the sequel film adaptations, *Catching Fire* and *Mockingjay*. In 2013, *CoverGirl* launched a makeup line tie-in to the film series encouraging women to buy makeup designed to make them look like residents of the Capitol. Cosplay—dressing up as characters from popular franchises—is indeed an increasingly popular and socially acceptable means of showing a fan's affection for a fictional universe, but the corporate product tie-ins in this case promote the choice of relating to the oppressors onto impressionable young fans the products were marketed to.[38] Considering how effectively Collins's narrative has been undermined and coopted by journalists, filmmakers, and advertisers, the only way to reclaim the text effectively is to return to it and to read it carefully as it was intended to be read—as a mature work of antiwar fiction and an ecofeminist Catholic parable, not a piece of Young Adult tripe.

## Katniss Everdeen and a Revolution of Empathy

At the start of the first *Hunger Games* book, readers learn that Katniss is the daughter of a coal miner who died in an underground explosion and a mother who suffered a complete emotional collapse afterward. Consequently, Katniss becomes head of the Everdeen family at eleven years old and, functionally, a single mother raising her younger sister/daughter Primrose. To feed them all, she becomes a poacher, hunting game in the fenced-off forest land on the outskirts of her home in the impoverished District 12—in what was once the coal mining regions of Appalachia. If she does not kill too much game, the Peacekeepers turn a blind eye to her poaching because she shares the fruits of her hunts with them and sells them at market. It is also significant that she hunts with only a bow and treats nature respectfully. She does not kill more game than she needs to feed her family and make just enough profit to buy essential household goods. As feminist cultural critic Valerie Estelle Frankel observes, the forest is Katniss's image of Eden, "It is also an American fantasy, as literature by James Fenimore Cooper, Washington Irving, and Henry David Thoreau focuses on the retreat into the forest, the quest for a return to nature. It offers simplicity, endless bounty, and safety from the agendas of others. But the forest remains a fantasy or only a momentary sanctuary."[39] And yet, the forest has greater significance. Its fenced off parameters and the bounty of food found within it underscore that Katniss lives in a world in which the poor have been cut off from a privatized food source and are unable to feed themselves or participate equitably in the distribution of food. The very districts that produce the food for the wealthy and the urban areas of Panem are those that see the most starvation. Brianna Burke explores how well this metaphor serves as an indictment of big agriculture's dominance of the global food market in our own corporate-dominated present in " 'Reaping' Environmental Justice Through Compassion in *The Hunger Games*," an article in the Summer 2014 issue of *Interdisciplinary Studies in Literature and Environment*. Burke writes, "Katniss' life is not unlike the billions of poor people around the globe who simply cannot afford food. As numerous food-politics writers point out, globally we produce enough calories per person to feed everyone in the world, but hunger is not about insufficient production, *it is structurally created*. Well-known sociologist Harriet Friedman argues that 'food politics are an aspect of class politics' and, I would add, globally entrenched politically sanctioned racism, which together make unequal access to food an environmental justice issue. Often, we do not think of food as an environmental justice issue, but if environmental justice is defined as the equal distribution of environmental benefits based on race, class, or gender, healthy nutritious organic food is an environmental 'benefit' that the poor too frequently cannot afford."[40]

The alienation between even rural people and their own land—created by the industrial world, modern trade practices, and institutional racism and classism—was something that Lewis and Tolkien addressed in their conversations, though they framed their discussions of these issues in religious and anthropological terms rather than in the politicized terms Burke employs. Nevertheless, the fact that the Inklings discussed the concept of eating locally and respecting nature and being aware of how food is distributed internationally is worthy of note in this discussion. In a 1930 letter to Arthur Greeves, Lewis wrote, "Tolkien once remarked to me that the feeling about home must have been quite different in the days when a family had fed on the produce of the same few miles of country for six generations, and that perhaps this was why they saw nymphs in their fountains and dryads in the wood—they were not mistaken for there was in a sense a *real* (not metaphorical) connection between them and the countryside. What had been earth and air & later corn, and later still bread, really was in them. We of course who live on a standardized international diet (you may have had Canadian flour, English meat, Scotch oatmeal, African oranges, & Australian wine today) are really artificial beings and have no connection (save in sentiment) with any place on earth. We are synthetic men, uprooted. The strength of the hills is not ours."[41]

One of the things that makes Katniss heroic is that she is "of the hills." She is not a synthetic person. As a hunter, and as someone who walks in nature, loves nature, and may hail from a Native American background with a tradition of reverence for nature, Katniss has recovered the sense of "home" that Lewis argues the modern human has, essentially, lost. Thanks to the stresses of Katniss's domestic life, she is only at peace—and at home—when she is in the forest, hunting, resting, or singing her father's old, mournful folk tunes to the animals. She is linked to the natural world time and again throughout the books. Her surname, Everdeen, is a playful corruption of Evergreen, and her trademark symbol as a rebel hero is the Mockingjay, a songbird that lives among the trees and is associated with freedom, antiestablishment sentiment, and subversive ideals. Given her ties to the "outdoors," it is thematically significant that, in the final book, *Mockingjay*, Katniss is forced to hide in a subterranean bunker city with the "underground" rebel movement. During her time underground, her distance from the sun wilts her. When the rebels are bombarded in an aerial attack by Capital forces and they survive the bombardment unscathed, the leader of the rebellion, Alma Coin, declares the moment a great victory. Afterward, Coin grants Katniss leave to explore the area above ground, assess the damage, and hunt again. Katniss emerges into the sunlight to find the forest above a smoldering, decimated ruin. She comes across the corpse of a deer that she had spared just the other day because it had been too beautiful to kill. Seeing the devastation, she cannot bring herself to share Coin's cold calculation that "victory" was achieved that day. Appropriately enough, while Katniss is associated with nature, her main enemies—Snow and Coin—have surnames symbolizing death and greed.

Katniss is more than willing to kill, but she does it in self-defense and when she is protecting and avenging civilian lives. Her preference is to not fight or kill at all. During the first Hunger Games gladiator match, she abstains from participating in the combat for as long as possible—hiding in trees, eating their fruit, and moving about

Fig. 9.2. Donald Sutherland plays President Coriolanus Snow, the Ur-Fascist ruler of futuristic Panem, in the film series based on Suzanne Collins's *Hunger Games* book trilogy. Lionsgate Films.

in their branches so she will not be seen. When she is forced to kill in self-defense, she uses the weapons provided by her natural surroundings—a nest of genetically modified yellowjackets (trackerjackers), poisonous berries, and a simple bow and arrow. Her compassion for her adversaries is awakened at the sight of another girl who, like Prim, has no business participating in the Hunger Games due to her age. Rue, a twelve-year-old black girl from the forest-covered logging District 11, travels among the trees like Katniss does. The two bond, even though Katniss is either an ethnic white, Native American, or a Melungeon and, technically, of a different "race." But what are racial differences when solidarity is required to survive the Hunger Games? When the other gladiators kill Rue, Katniss gives the fallen girl an emotional burial. The affection of an olive-skinned girl from one District for a fallen black girl from a rival District helps inspire racial solidarity between members of different races who were culturally conditioned to despise one another. Immediately after Rue's funeral is broadcast live, an uprising occurs in Rue's district that sparks a Panem-wide rebellion uniting all the poor districts against Snow.

By book two of the series, *Catching Fire*, readers learn that Peeta's love for Katniss—and his refusal to kill her even in a melee in which only one survivor is allowed—further inspires rebellion and heroic status for himself and Katniss. He has a common decency (even in a death arena) and a recognizable humanity (even living in an Ur-Fascist society) that Katniss wants to emulate. Some of the most cynical Capital dwellers want to as well, and several defect to District 13 after seeing Katniss and Peeta survive the first Hunger Games. By book three, *Mockingjay*, the gentle Peeta is so scarred by what he sees of war that he begins to question the moral and practical necessity of the rebellion. He hates fascism and wishes Snow could be overthrown, but he is concerned that the price of war is too high. He sees the few surviving humans in a post-apocalyptic world running the risk of killing themselves off altogether in a bloody, merciless conflict. He sees natural resources being polluted and destroyed because of the rebellion, and he wonders if there will be anything left alive—plant, animal, or human—after the war ends to celebrate "victory." Certainly, if Peeta were a character in *Snowpiercer*, he would disagree with the Namgoong Minsoo's contention that derailing Wilford's train and risking killing off almost all of humanity would constitute a good game plan for an uprising.

When President Snow captures Peeta, he tortures and brainwashes the boy against Katniss and the rebellion. Snow takes advantage of Peeta's misgivings about the war, sharpens and redirects those misgivings, and uses Peeta as a propaganda tool of the Capitol against the rebellion. Snow broadcasts a series of public service announcements in which a mind-controlled Peeta presents Snow as a protector of the peace, savior of humanity, and holy steward of the Earth's last remaining natural resources. In turn, Peeta and Snow argue that District 13 will lead humanity to extinction if their rebellion refuses to stand down. Like many Satanic figures, Snow makes a series of true statements to help his listeners come to a false conclusion. He is using Peeta's Tolkienesque misgivings about war and the ecological damage it causes to argue for a peace that is equivalent to capitulation and slavery. Katniss's rebel allies see Peeta's television broadcasts as the ravings of a traitor, and they will admit no truth to his claims that the war could end humanity before it saves it from fascism. Since Coin herself is eager to become the new Ur-Fascist leader of Panem, in violation of all the principles of egalitarianism and feminism, she sees no virtue in Peeta's argument whatsoever. (Indeed, as critic Anthony Pavlik noted in "Absolute Power Games," Coin is already the Ur-Fascist ruler of District 13, and she demonstrates Eco's point that Ur-Fascism can be found "in the most innocent of guises").[42] Peeta's thoughtful, compassionate assessment of the situation—warped as it is by Snow's drugs and evil influence—should garner more sympathy from Coin than it does. Katniss remains one of the only ones in District 13 to see the real Peeta under the brainwashing.

Indeed, when the rebels ask Katniss to try to shake off her post-traumatic stress symptoms and take a more active role in the rebellion, she continually refuses by saying variations of the same thing: "Where is Peeta? I will not help you until I see him here." Those who are inclined to be impatient with Katniss, including several of the rebels who don't understand the full ramifications of what she is saying, think she is a lovesick child who wants her boyfriend rescued from Snow, no matter the cost. They think she is willing to put puppy love before the sacrifices they all must make for the rebellion to be successful. It is true that she wants to see Peeta rescued from his torturers, but something more is going on. When she asks where Peeta is, she is *really* asking why the rebels, as an austere, underground, militaristic culture, show no signs of Peeta's love of nature or compassion for his enemies. She is really asking, "Where is Peeta's kind sensibility among you rebels who claim you are about to transform Panem for the better? I don't see it, which is why I don't trust you." There is so little evidence of Peeta's Tolkienesque traits among the rebels, Katniss wants to know why she should fight hard to unseat the Capital and Snow, to replace it with a new regime that is just as heartless as the old one. Here again, her instincts are proven correct by the end of the series.

The theme of rape does not saturate *The Hunger Games* series to the same degree that it does the *Mad Max* films or the Westeros saga. However, it is present, most especially in the character of Finnick Odair. A former Hunger Games champion, he had hoped to retire from the public sphere, marry fellow champion Annie Cresta, and raise a family to put his life as a gladiator past him. Unfortunately, he was perceived as sexy by wealthy viewers of the Games, so Snow ordered that Finnick be farmed out as a sex toy and stud to any rich person who wanted to use him in that way. When Finnick

Fig. 9.3. Alma Coin (Julianne Moore, right) hopes to ride the revolutionary wave of Katniss Everdeen's populist appeal into the presidency of Panem. Posing as a progressive social reformer, Coin secretly wants to replace President Snow's decadent totalitarian regime with her own, more austere form of totalitarianism. From *The Hunger Games: Mockingjay—Part 1* (2014). Lionsgate Films.

first meets Katniss, he is attracted to her, but she smells the "sex" upon him and is offended by what she perceives to be his promiscuousness. Her own sexual immaturity prevents her from seeing him for what he is—a victim of rape. When the rebellion rescues him from Snow and grants him haven in District 13, he reveals to them all the dirty secrets he learned in the bedrooms of the wealthy, including enough dirt on President Snow to ensure his political assassination. Once Katniss learns of Finnick's painful history, she feels compassion for him and corrects her perception of what his seemingly tainted sexuality represents. In making the primary victim of rape in the series a male, Collins challenges reader expectations of gender roles and representations. She asks male readers who might not be inclined to sympathize with female rape victims to wonder what it would be like to be a male forced into prostitution. Also, Collins reminds readers that to be male is not necessarily to be a patriarch. There's only ever one Ur-Fascist dictator and a handful of oligarchs. The rest of us, male or female, black or white, are, to one degree or another, servants and slaves of the Ur-Fascists. That Alma Coin, a female politician, cannot see this is a dark mark against her character. That she would aspire to become the next Ur-Fascist leader of Panem earmarks her as a symbolic rapist and dictator.

When it becomes clear to Katniss that Coin is going to succeed Snow as a new dictator, Katniss assassinates Coin. Katniss is captured and sequestered out of sight to give the political firestorm that follows time to die down. Then she is returned to her burnt-out District 12 to live a quiet life in exile from all future political concerns. She had become an embarrassment to most of her allies, but—had she pushed to become Coin's successor—she might have had support. However, Katniss had no ambition to become the new Ur-Fascist dictator of Panem. Instead of becoming a dictator, Katniss embraces a life of quiet seclusion, and starts a family with Peeta. The wounded veteran retreats to domestic life and parenthood, living close to nature, and doing what she can to experience the kind of peace that Tolkien experienced with Edith in the woodland grove near Roos as he recovered from his "trench fever." She would be Tolkien, and Peeta would be a slightly less idealized Edith.

On the one hand, the results of Katniss's interventions in the political and revolutionary arena appear positive. There are indications that Coin's successor is more humane than either Coin or Snow, ushering in an era characterized by peace and the discontinuation of the Hunger Games. On the other hand, the nature of Coin's evil and her near-success paint a grim picture of the likelihood of populist rebellions succeeding only in replacing one form of oppressive government with another—replacing a decadent tyrant with an austere one. Collins's novels, therefore, question the notion that large-scale social change, and regime change, can ever bring about the more humane society that kindhearted revolutionaries hope it will. Instead, the best thing any good person can do, like Peeta or Katniss, is to be good on a domestic level—not a political one. In the powerful epilogue to the book *Mockingjay*—which falls flat and feels tacked on at the end of the film adaptation—Katniss regards her children and wonders how she can break their hearts by telling them her war stories, or by letting them read the written account of her life—literally, the text of the three *Hunger Games* books:

> The questions are just beginning. The arenas have been completely destroyed, the memorials built, there are no more Hunger Games. But they teach about them at school, and the girl knows we played a role in them. The boy will know in a few years. How can I tell them about that world without frightening them to death?
>
> My children . . . don't know they play on a graveyard.
>
> Peeta says it will be okay. We have each other. And the book. We can make them understand in a way that will make them braver. But one day I'll have to explain about my nightmares. Why they come. Why they won't ever really go away.
>
> I'll tell them how I survive it. I'll tell them that on bad mornings, it feels impossible to take pleasure in anything because I'm afraid it could be taken away. That's when I make a list in my head of every act of goodness I've seen someone do. It's like a game. Repetitive. Even a little tedious after more than twenty years.
>
> But there are much worse games to play.[43]

In this epilogue, Collins seems to be painting an autobiographical portrait—only, she is the child and her father, the scarred Vietnam veteran, is Katniss. That is why this scene rings so true and is so powerful and loving and imbued with meaning. One might reasonably assume that this was the scene Collins most looked forward to writing and that this was, in some respects, the most important scene in the series to her. That is why any intimation that the epilogue is somehow "a let-down" as an end to a hero's journey narrative is so disappointing. This epilogue is the "Return" stage of Campbell's hero's journey, which is so often underestimated and misunderstood. That is why the assessment of filmgoers that the film version of this epilogue should have been omitted is so frustrating.

In another interesting point of connection between Tolkien's writings and Collins's, Tolkien had written an epilogue to *Lord of the Rings* about Samwise relating his war stories to his daughter, Elanor, revealing the final fates of most key members of the Fellowship, and showing her the Red Book of Westmarch, which includes the text of *The Hobbit* by Bilbo Baggins and *The Lord of the Rings* by Frodo Baggins and Sam himself. Sam does not show the book to his youngest children: Goldilocks, Ham, Daisy, and baby . . . *Primrose*. Tolkien was attached to the idea of including this idyllic family scene as an aftermath of the great war, but observed in a letter to Naomi Mitchison on April 25, 1954, that the epilogue, "has been so universally condemned that I shall not insert it. One must stop somewhere."[44] Christopher Tolkien has published the epilogue alongside "The Notion Club Papers" in *Sauron Defeated* (1992).[45]

Like "The Scouring of the Shire," the closing passages of *The Hunger Games* are essential to understanding the moral of *The Hunger Games* trilogy, and demonstrate why the book, in the end, will always best the film as a work of art and as a pedagogical tool to teach the audience compassion and respect for all life, human and nonhuman. The moral found in the epilogue is one that the conservative Catholic critics of the book utterly failed to grasp, as Finnegan rightly argued. It is also a moral that a great many Millennial fans of the series intuit when reading the book on their own, for pleasure, and one that they understand still better when they discuss the book in a college course in the eco-humanities.

Brianna Burke teaches *The Hunger Games* in an environmental literature class at Iowa State University. Burke notes that the open ending of the book means that "evil" is not vanquished with the deaths of Coin and Snow and a world filled with hunger and poverty remains. Consequently, the ending refuses to give readers easy "solutions" to the complex social problems explored by the book series—the same social problems we face in the world today. Burke challenges the students with the question, "Can empathy be taught?" After much consideration, they answer that it can. Collins is striving to teach empathy through her books, and Burke works to facilitate Collins's work. Burke notes that the books promote the ecofeminist values of Vandanna Shiva's Earth Democracy and "transform the spiritual teachings of the Dali Lama into narrative."[46] The golden age that Katniss fails to truly usher in through her participation in a violent rebellion in Panem and via the assassination of Coin is not the true revolution Katniss ignites as "The Girl Who Was on Fire," either within the confines of the book series or beyond the scope of its pages. Instead, Katniss's real revolution is one of compassion. Her acts of empathy, televised by mistake, inspire a ripple effect of other compassionate gestures, made by Peeta, Cinna, Rue, and Haymitch, and moving outward from her immediate circle of friends to inspire a revolution of compassion and empathy throughout the cynical and inauthentic Panem. Katniss leads by example in the world of fiction. Burke strives to use Collins's books to stoke the same revolutionary sentiments in the college classroom in the real world. The story's accessibility and popularity, normally considered blights upon its literary merit, are the virtues it needs to educate Millennials about the problems of war, class, hunger, and environmental injustice, and offer them a possible solution to those same problems. Burke writes that "Collins proposes a simple but radical solution for large-scale social change: to practice compassion when faced with need, each time we see it, in whatever way we are able, even if that action seems too small. . . . [After reading the books in class, the students agree that] if we act against oppression in any way we can, however small, it is enough to start a revolution. That is hopeful and profound, indeed."[47]

# 10

# The Cowboy and Indian Alliance

## Collective Action against Climate Change in *A Song of Ice and Fire* and *Star Trek*

You can't shoot the financial meltdown in the head—you can do that with a zombie. . . . All the other problems are too big. As much as Al Gore tries, you can't picture global warming. . . . But you can picture a slouching zombie coming down the street.

—Max Brooks

In the enjoyment of a great myth we come nearest to experiencing as a concrete what can otherwise be understood only as an abstraction.

—C. S. Lewis, "Myth Becomes Fact"

[The Children of the Forest] made their homes simply . . . resided in the woods, in crannogs, in bogs and marshes, and even in caverns and hollow hills. It is said that, in the woods, they made shelters of leaves and withes up in the branches of trees—secret tree "towns" . . . It was the children who carved the weirwoods with faces, perhaps to give eyes to their gods [or to their wise men, the greenseers]. . . . [The] First Men believed this; it was their fear of the weirwoods spying upon them that drove them to cut down many of the carved trees and weirwood groves to deny the Children such an advantage.

—George R. R. Martin, Elio M. Garcia Jr., and Linda Antonsson,
*The World of Ice and Fire: The Untold History
of Westeros and the Game of Thrones*

## Winter *Isn't* Coming: Ice Zombies as an
## Allegory for Climate Change

During a question-and-answer session at Dymock's Literary Luncheon in Sydney, Australia, on December 13, 2013, a fan of George R. R. Martin's *A Song of Ice and Fire* novels asked the author something surprising: "J. R. R. Tolkien strenuously denied that his books were in any way an allegory for World War II. Have you ever been accused of writing about climate change by proxy? You know, it being a bit of a thing in your works, the long Winter?" Martin replied, "No, I haven't, not until now." He added, "Like Tolkien, I do not write allegory—at least not intentionally."[1] Despite being taken aback by the question at the time it was asked, Martin appears to have grown supportive of the idea that some critics and fans categorize his Westeros Saga as part of the climate fiction genre. Indeed, during at least one interview, Martin advanced the environmentalist interpretation of *A Song of Ice and Fire* himself as a means of understanding the contemporary relevance of his escapist saga (see the Introduction).

Fig. 10.1. "The Children of the Forest," are the indigenous peoples of Westeros who were displaced north of the Wall by settler colonialism. The First Men hunted the Children to near-extinction in a genocidal campaign that also resulted in the destruction of the Children's most sacred trees. *Game of Thrones* episode 6.5. "Door" reveals that "Leaf"—a matriarch of the Children of the Forest (pictured second from the left and played by Kae Alexander)—created the White Walkers as a doomsday weapon to defend her people from the First Men. "Door" premiered on May 22, 2016. HBO.

The grand narrative of *A Song of Ice and Fire* has, thus far, played out over the course of five novels: *A Game of Thrones* (1996), *A Clash of Kings* (1999), *A Storm of Swords* (2000), *A Feast for Crows* (2005), and *A Dance with Dragons* (2011). Martin plans to write two more novels, which should finish the series: *The Winds of Winter* and *A Dream of Spring*. He has raised the possibility of there being *three* more, which would not be surprising, as he initially intended the story to be a trilogy, and the tale grew in the telling. The concluding books are expected to be released sometime over the course of the next decade, though fans and members of the press harass Martin to hasten his writing pace lest he die before he completes the story, as Octavia Butler died before completing her *Parable* series, Tolkien died before finishing *The Silmarillion*, and Robert Jordan died before finishing *The Wheel of Time*. Unlike Tolkien and Jordan, Martin has revealed that he has no son (like Christopher Tolkien) or collaborator (like Brandon Sanderson) on hand to finish the book series in the event of his death. Whether or not Martin appoints his own official successor to write the final books, the story will have an ending, thanks to its immense popularity. In fact, it already has several endings. Impatient to see the narrative reach a conclusion, some fans have written their own endings to the series and published them online as works of fan fiction. Some of these alternate endings reportedly have a measure of literary merit and compare well to Martin's writing style, but Martin has found their existence an irritant and has said he will not read them.

As much consternation as Martin's writing pace has caused readers of the books, *A Song of Ice and Fire* has inspired the highly successful HBO television adaptation *Game of Thrones* (2011–), which finished adapting the material from the extant novels during its sixth season. Once it became clear that the television series will outpace Martin and reach its conclusion before the final book has been either written or published, the producers pressed Martin to reveal his master plan for the end of the tale. (He had kept much of it to himself during the first several seasons of the show's production.) At this point, producers David Benioff and D. B. Weiss have an outline of the broad sweep of the remaining books and have managed to wheedle out of Martin the final fates of all the characters that have found their way from the books into the television series. Unless Martin's writing pace quickens exponentially, the producers will finish his story for him on television, during the eighth season of the show. Given this state of affairs, Martin has promised to make reading his books worthwhile to those who have seen the saga end on television first by adjusting his master plan, if not crafting an entirely different ending for the books than the one he gave Weiss and Benioff.

However the Westeros story ends, its vast scope and enormous cast of characters make it open to a wide array of interpretations, and different fans latch onto different elements of the story. Some are focused primarily on its representation of Machiavellian court intrigue and its application to contemporary, real-world politics in which, as Cersei Lannister observes in the first book, "When you play the game of thrones, you win or you die." Others critics and fans are concerned with Martin's representations of gender, especially where he draws the thin, permeable line between hero and murderer (Arya

Stark), and between benevolent queen and proto-fascist dictator (Daenerys Targaryen). The fate of women in an uncivilized age makes the books difficult to read (and the series difficult to watch) as even more women are raped and murdered and turned into prostitutes in this universe than meet the same fates in the world of *Mad Max* (which is really saying something). Only the political wheeler-dealer matriarchs, the magical queens with dragons for bodyguards, and the young, savage female knights fare even remotely well in Westeros, and none of them are ever safe for a single moment. Finally, the zombie storyline, and the oft-quoted Stark family motto, "Winter is Coming," appeals most to those fans of the books and television series inclined to interpret the story as a climate change narrative. While all the above narratives seem incompatible, they do, in fact, weave together well, and the climate fiction reading works best as the lynchpin interpretation.

Some of the most notable characters in the grand, multimedia Westeros story include the Brothers of the Night's Watch. The Brothers are pardoned criminals, gadabouts, political exiles, and starving men who renounce family ties and dedicate their lives to guarding the Wall, a mammoth ice structure reminiscent of Hadrian's Wall, the Great Wall of China, or—unfortunately—the Wall Donald Trump pledged to build across the U.S.-Mexico border during his 2015–16 presidential campaign. The Wall divides the mainland of Westeros from the bitterly cold regions beyond where the

Fig. 10.2. A White Walker: a member of an ancient and powerful race of beings thought to be mere myth by most of the people of contemporary Westeros. The Walkers have the seemingly limitless power to raise the dead and place them in their thrall, creating a potentially boundless army of "wights." Casual fans of the book series *A Song of Ice and Fire* and the television adaptation *Game of Thrones* (from which this publicity photo is taken) refer to the combined forces of the White Walkers and the wights as "the unstoppable army of ice zombies." HBO.

zombie forces lurk and gather strength, waiting for their chance to strike down the Wall and sweep southward. (In the universe of the books, the creatures counted among the zombie hordes are identified as the Others, the wights, and the White Walkers.) By the fifth book in Martin's series, *A Dance with Dragons* (2012), Jon Snow, newly minted Lord Commander of the Night's Watch, begins to fear that the Wall doesn't so much protect those on his side as it does condemn to a horrific death the indigenous peoples trapped on the same icy terrain with the zombies on the other side. Snow wonders if he should grant haven to these refugees before they, too, become ice zombies and go from potential allies to invincible enemies. However, when Snow follows through with his proposal to grant haven in Westeros to the very same "Wildlings" that his fellow Night's Watch members have fought and died to keep out of their side of the Wall, he faces an assassination attempt led by Bowen Marsh. Like Ser Alliser Thorne, Marsh had always been a bitter malcontent envious of Snow's position and fearful that Snow's soft heart would doom both the Night's Watch and the entire kingdom. Once Snow opens the massive gates at the base of the Wall, letting legions of Wildlings into Westeros, the horrified conservative wing of the Night's Watch membership comes to agree with Marsh: Snow has betrayed the fraternity's sacred mission of protecting the lands of Westeros from *all* incursions from beyond the Wall, both zombie *and* Wildling. Enraged, they surround Snow and stab him to death, proclaiming "For the Watch!" with each stab.

Notably, the last *A Song of Ice and Fire* novel Martin completed ends with the assassination of Jon Snow and Daenerys's reunion with the Dothraki after fleeing an assassination attempt in Meereen, so any events that take place afterward in the series have no direct analogue in the novels. Therefore, all discussion of events that take place after Jon's death in this chapter are, naturally, discussions of events depicted in the HBO series *Game of Thrones*.

According to the mythology of *Game of Thrones*, the zombie menace can be traced back thousands of years to the violent clashes between the First Men (who migrated to Westeros from other lands twelve thousand years before the events of *A Song of Ice and Fire*) and the indigenous peoples of Westeros. Called the "Children of the Forest" because of their diminutive height and cherubic faces, these indigenous Westerosi were mature and wise adults infantilized by the First Men's name for them. While not elves in the Tolkien sense, the Children of the Forest occupy a close relationship to Nature evocative of his elves' respect for the natural world. They are also reminiscent of the Wolfriders and other tribes of elves from *Elfquest* by Wendy and Richard Pini. Nevertheless, Martin resists dubbing them "elves" because he sees "elves" as a clichéd and overused staple of the fantasy genre. A still better reason to avoid dubbing them "elves" is the fact that they are better understood not in mythological terms, but as an indigenous people displaced by settler colonialism. They are the victims of the First Men's genocidal campaign which has all but wiped them out and turned them into figures of long-lost legend in the eyes of modern humans.

During a time-travel segment in the HBO series episode "Door," Bran Stark learns that the Children of the Forest created the White Walkers as a doomsday weapon to defend themselves against the First Men. A matriarch among the Children of the Forest whom Bran has nicknamed "Leaf" is revealed to be the ancient magician who created the first White Walker. After the time-traveling Bran witnesses Leaf's past self performing the spell to unleash the weapon upon humanity, the Leaf of the present day explains to Bran that—at the time—she felt as if she had no choice but to create the zombie horde.

LEAF: We were at war. We were being slaughtered. Our sacred trees cut down. We needed to defend ourselves.

BRAN: From whom?

LEAF: From you. From men.

At this moment, Bran occupies a privileged position of knowledge. He is one of the only living humans to know the secret of the creation of the White Walkers. He is also one of the few who knows for certain that the White Walkers and the Children of the Forest not only really did exist in ancient times, but still walk the earth in modern times. For most other modern, cynical Westerosi, all talk of such creatures is fanciful and should be discredited. Certainly, any assertion that the Brothers of the Night's Watch should be well funded and their mission to guard the Wall from the White Walkers should be taken seriously is dismissed out of hand by almost anyone in the cosmopolitan city of King's Landing.

In the books and the television adaptation, it is Jon Snow who sees the threat posed by the zombies clearly and correctly identifies the opportunities presented by allying with the Wildlings. Other characters do not have Snow's vision. Some of the Westerosi doubt the existence of the ice zombies and joke that if zombies are real, so must "grumkins and snarks" also be real. (They aren't.) Others, such as Thorne, admit that the zombies pose something of a threat but don't see the need to confront the menace by changing society or by making former enemies into new allies. Thorne is only interested in seeing more money invested in fortifying the Wall and more men recruited to guard it. Other characters, including Cersei, pay lip service to the importance of defending Westeros but regard all warnings of an imminent zombie apocalypse as the ravings of alarmist and uneducated members of The Night's Watch. Cersei would also be unlikely to ever make alliances with enemies of her family, even if the end times are near, because she is so obsessed with protecting the Lannister clan above all other concerns. Furthermore, she is exactly the sort of character who would sequester herself in the Red Keep atop Aegon's Hill when the zombie hordes grow nearer, complacent in her belief that she will be safe in her "magic lifeboat for the wealthy."

Aside from characters such as Cersei, there are the members of the Night's Watch who are terrified of the zombies but certain that the Wall can contain the threat that they represent. These "reasonable" men call for a calm and measured response to the zombie menace, but are not so much reasonable as they are protectors of the status quo. They are complacent in their belief that the Wall will keep them safe from the threat posed by the climate-changing zombies because contemplating any other eventuality would compel them to consider making sacrifices they are not emotionally prepared to make in the name of protecting the kingdom. Naturally, there is no way the Wall will ever keep the zombies at bay forever, whatever they think. Indeed, *they think they know everything*. In contrast, Snow knows only one thing: that he knows nothing. This hard-won self-awareness has made Snow one of the wisest man in Westeros, and he is clearly the one everyone else needs to listen to. Provocatively, in what he refers to as "a sad irony," the actor who plays Jon Snow on *Game of Thrones*, Kit Harrington, found himself sounding very much like Snow when he warned about climate change in the real world in an *Entertainment Weekly* interview on June 29, 2017. He explained that the show's production team had a frighteningly difficult time finding snow-blanketed winter locations to film the series in, making climate change shockingly real for him: "We went to Iceland to find snow, because winter is [there]. . . . We got there and we

Fig. 10.3. Jon Snow (Kit Harrington), Lord Commander of the Night's Watch, fears that the massive ice Wall on the northern border of Westeros will not keep his home safe from an imminent ice zombie invasion. Snow considers granting safe haven to the Wildling refugees living on the other side of the Wall before they, too, become zombies and go from potential allies to implacable enemies. Here Snow is pictured approaching the Wildling encampment at Hardhome by boat, accompanied by the red-bearded Wildling leader Tormund Giantsbane (Kristofer Hivju). HBO.

were lucky to get the snow we did because, in our world, winter is definitely not here. It's this weird parallel, the opposite parallel [to the unnaturally cold world of *Game of Thrones*]. We go out there this year, and the glacier that me and [former co-star Rose Leslie] filmed on four years ago, I saw it and it has shrunk. I saw climate change and global warming with my own eyes, and it is terrifying."

In the fictional world of Westeros, there are three main characters that offer some hope Snow will eventually receive the aid he needs. Early in book two, Tyrion Lannister heeds the call of the Brothers of the Night's Watch for more men, and offers them support covertly while publicly pretending to laugh off the warning of the dead rising. In book three, thanks to the wise counsel of his trusted advisor, Davos Seaworth, King Stannis Baratheon gives credence to the tales of the zombies before the other pretenders to the Iron Throne and sends his forces to fortify the Wall against both the zombies and the Wildlings. Finally, some of the people of Westeros hope for salvation from Queen Daenerys Targaryen, who will come from the East with her dragons and bring a liberating thaw that will drive back the cold and the zombies and return spring to Westeros.

Charli Carpenter, who wrote "*Game of Thrones* as Theory" for the online journal *Foreign Affairs* on March 29, 2012, perhaps put it best when she wrote,

> [In *Game of Thrones*, t]he slogan "Winter is coming" is meant literally as well as metaphorically: planetary forces are moving slowly but inexorably toward climatic catastrophe as the infighting among kings and queens distracts them from the bigger picture. This is a collective action story, with the Night's Watch issuing increasingly desperate alarms yet receiving indifferent shrugs. The wight [zombie] menace gives the term "human security" a new meaning, presenting Westeros with a common threat against which it might ally, but even so cooperation is difficult. The answer will eventually come from alliances with northern barbarian hordes, fringe populations who are the first victims of environmental change, and with these alliances will come dramatic tradeoffs in political culture, as newcomers bring with them distinct ideas about politics, society, and religion. The argument seems clear: if existing governance structures cannot manage emerging global threats, expect them to evolve or fall by the wayside.[2]

Carpenter's real world–centric interpretation of the Westeros saga is rich in its potential implications, and anyone who wishes to read further works of nonfiction confronting similar political, ecological, and indigenous themes should consult research in the field, including the texts: *An Indigenous Peoples' History of the United States* (2015) by Roxanne Dunbar-Ortiz; *Climate Refugees* (2010) by Collectif Argos; *Mohawk Interruptus: Political Life across the Borders of Settler States* (2014) by Audra Simpson; and *Indigenous Peoples and the Collaborative Stewardship of Nature: Knowledge Binds and Institutional Conflicts* (2011) by Anne Ross, Kathleen Pickering Sherman, Jeffrey G. Snodgrass, Henry D. Delcore, and Richard Sherman.

While the television series has not always been good at dramatizing the book series's most pointedly ecology-themed segments, its finest hour was, in fact, a "climate fiction"–themed episode that was written specifically for the show and has no concrete analogue in the books. The *Game of Thrones* television series episode "Hardhome" dramatizes a siege that is referenced but not depicted in Martin's novels. The script, written by Benioff and Weiss, features a conversation between Snow and the Wildlings living in a settlement north of the Wall called Hardhome. Snow offers an alliance and shelter south of the Wall to any Wildling who allies with the Brothers of the Night's Watch against the zombies. The conversation is peppered with proud tribal affiliation labels and derisive nicknames; the Wildlings refer to themselves as Free Folk and to their enemies, the Brothers, as "Crows." These labels underscore how difficult it is for Snow and his chief Wildling ally, Tormund, to forge an alliance between former enemies who have a long history of animosity toward one another, shedding the blood of one another's friends and family. Snow also has the unenviable task of winning the trust of the Wildlings when he was the one who executed the Wildling's beloved leader, Mance Rayder. The political and climate change resonances of the conversation are clear:

JON: We're not friends. We've never been friends. We won't become friends today. This isn't about friendship. This is about survival. This is about putting a 700-foot wall between you and what's out there.

KARSI: You built that wall to keep us out.

LOBODA: Since when do the Crows give two shits if we live?

JON: In normal times, we wouldn't. But these aren't normal times. The White Walkers don't care if a man's Free Folk or Crow. We're all the same to them. Meat to their army. But together we can beat them . . .

KARSI: I lost my father, my uncle, and two brothers fighting the damn Crows.

JON: I'm not asking you to forget your dead. I'll never forget mine. I lost fifty brothers the night that Mance attacked the wall. But I'm asking you to think about your children now. They'll never have children of their own if we don't band together. The Long Night is coming and the dead come with it. No clan can stop them. The Free Folk can't stop them. The Night's Watch can't stop them. And all the southern kings can't stop them. Only together, all of us, and even then, it might not be enough, but at least then we'll give the fuckers a fight.[3]

These reluctant peacemakers are talking about fighting zombies together. They are also, very clearly, talking about surviving climate change. The fact that the conversation can be interpreted so easily both ways, literally and symbolically, means that *Game of*

*Thrones* works well as an allegory in the spirit of C. S. Lewis. It is a work of speculative fiction. It is a work of climate fiction. It is also a covert "documentary" about climate change. The climate fiction interpretation of *Game of Thrones/A Song of Ice and Fire* echoes a jeremiad issued in a nonfiction book by a chronicler of climate change consequences. In 2008, Canadian science journalist Marq De Villiers wrote *The End: Natural Disasters, Manmade Catastrophes, and the Future of Human Survival* and warned that the time for ideological conflict, family feuds, the clashing of political parties, useless wars, and battles of religion has long since come and gone. Humanity has bigger problems to solve as a species:

> [The debate over the truth of evolution is] of all of the quarrels of our time perhaps the most deeply irrelevant, joined in its fatuity only by religious quarrels over, well, nothing—Protestant against Catholic, Old Believers versus New, Sunni versus Shia. Perhaps five angels, or fifty can dance upon the point of a needle, but none of their dancing will affect the course of the tsunami that will be rolling someone's way quite soon. Or the hurricane that will be coiling its deadly way across the Caribbean this summer. Or the earthquake that will tumble down cities. Or the volcano fire that will spread its pall of ash and destruction across towns and villages not yet known. Or the rising sea levels that will swamp coastal communities. This is surely where our attention must be focused. . . . Earth has time. But we don't. There would be life, but it wouldn't be our life, or even life as we more or less know it. The planet won't die, but the version of the planet that makes our existence agreeable or even possible could do so with ease. Either human-caused or natural calamities or both in concert could make it happen. This is the vulnerability we need to confront and then devise policies that would maximize our chances of keeping ourselves alive and well. It remains possible. We are an inventive species as well as a destructive one. We now need to invent not just new science but a new politics. We are doing plenty of the first. And we are beginning to do the second, with climate change the engine that's driving us.[4]

Sectarianism and family feuds that last for generations distract the characters in Martin's story from being adequately aware of the menace that lurks north of the Wall, and the implication is that the Westeros saga echoes De Villiers's sentiment. Characters in the present are still furious over events that took place during Robert's Rebellion, and Oberyn Martell's righteous indignation over the fate of his sister and her children drives him into a singleminded quest for vengeance that ends in his untimely death. Other characters, such as Arya Stark, are so scarred by a tragedy they witnessed in childhood that they spend their lives seeking reparations for the event. The zombies north of the wall are all "more important" than these personal tragedies, and Oberyn and Arya are warnings to readers not to waste their lives perpetuating an endless cycle of violence and revenge, of repeating the errors of their forebears, and of living in the past.

Fig. 10.4. Arya Stark, played by Maisie Williams on *Game of Thrones*, is one of several "strong female characters" in George R. R. Martin's Westeros saga. She is obsessed with obtaining revenge against all the heads of the Lannister and Frey families for betraying and butchering most of her family members—and trains with a league of assassins to become a killer deadly enough to achieve her goals. HBO.

The upper-class characters of Westeros also place too much importance upon their noble houses, fetishizing their allegiance to House Stark, House Lannister, House Martell, and others. On the one hand, the feudal-like system seems in keeping with a medieval configuration of power in our world and oaths of allegiance to feudal lords. Still, the characters in *A Song of Ice and Fire* place too much emphasis upon their house's sigil, motto, and fight songs, such as the Lannister's mocking and triumphalist ballad "The Rains of Castamere." Some characters pay lip service to the honor they owe the house they serve, but there is still a sense in which house allegiance comes at too high a price in Westeros. The political fragmenting of Westeros along cultural lines, family houses, religious belief, and feuds that go back multiple generations are reminiscent of the bitter, personal conflicts that divided the families of Florence in Dante's *Divine Comedy*. Ostensibly, the families of Florence feuded over the lofty cause of whether they were Guelphs and Ghibellines, and whether they threw their political support behind the secular ruler, the Holy Roman Emperor, or the religious authority of the pope. And yet, to a significant degree, they were really fighting over personal slights and long-term family grudges. One slight in particular—a wedding between the two families that was unexpectedly, violently called off—sparked a particularly long and bloody chapter in the Guelph and Ghibelline feud, as Dino Compagni's *Chronicle of Florence* (1280) explains. The years of family feuding, bloodshed, acrimony, scheming, exile, and murder that grew out of the abortive matrimonial union is worthy of the Starks and the Freys. Compagni was highly critical of that state of affairs in his history, as Dante was in his epic poem. Dante placed Farinata degli Uberti, leader of the Florentine faction of the Ghibellines, in the circle of the heretics in Hell, in part for denying the existence of the afterlife, but also for placing the importance of his family and political party over his allegiance to God; he had made idols of politics and bloodline, and worshipped them as his true Gods, instead of the Judeo-Christian deity.

The wheel of political fortune in our world mirrors the wheel of political fortune in Westeros. As Daenerys Targaryen said in the series *Game of Thrones*, "Lannister, Baratheon, Stark, Tyrell . . . they're all just spokes on a wheel. This one's on top and that one's on top and on and on it spins, crushing those on the ground. We're not going to stop the wheel. I'm going to break the wheel." It sounds so wonderful, but there is the question of how she hopes to achieve this end. There is the possibility that her solution to the problem is more frightening and devastating than the problem itself. Or she may bring real change for the better.

In Martin's world, placing love of family over love of country and love of truth is a sign of moral corruption. Jon Snow's willingness to sacrifice his family obligations to his greater duty is demonstrated early on when he refrains from seeking to avenge the murder of the man who raised him, and instead keeps his oath to stand and guard the Wall. Snow was no heretic in a Farinata sense, and kept his oath and his honor. Snow's difficult decision laid the groundwork for his later choice of the greater good—an alliance between his men and the Wildlings that was desirable to preserve all human life in the world—over his sectarian duty to the Brotherhood. His worldview is informed by his duty to protect the people of Westeros. He interprets that duty by being consistently true to the spirit of the laws he has sworn to protect, and avoids making false choices by sacrificing that duty to the letter of the law, or to smaller, more personal and political concerns. In a sense, Snow's morality is not worldly at all, but exists in the realm of idealism and true faith, and that appears to be the reason that he could return from the dead to continue the fight against the zombies even after his assassination. Snow was Christ-like in his worldview even before his resurrection.

And yet, a seemingly "true" faith and a knowledge of the threat represented by the zombies does not necessarily mean that a given character knows how best to face that threat, or to behave in a consistently honorable fashion. The Red Priests and Red Priestesses who worship R'hllor, the Lord of Light, know of the White Walkers and have directed all the practitioners of the faith to devote their full attention to protecting the world from the Walkers. Unfortunately, while the Red Priests and Priestesses can accurately perceive the threat posed by the Walkers, their religion is one of the most intolerant, and demands that they burn all practitioners of other faiths at the stake, because all other religions are regarded as being in league with the Great Other, the god of the zombies. Also, the priests believe that the best way to fight the zombies is to summon into existence a new generation of dragons. The spell to create dragons requires the human sacrifice of those with royal blood. This means that the seemingly "good" members of the religion of the Lord of Light are the ones who are most often trying to slaughter innocent royal children. Consequently, the Red Priests and Priestesses are among the most frightening and ruthless in the saga, if among the most aware of the supernatural climate menace.

A character such as Melisandre, Red Priestess of R'hllor, is problematic because she is responsible for assassinating the pretender king, Renly Baratheon, and human sacrificing the young Princess Shireen Baratheon, one of the kindest and most innocent characters in *Game of Thrones*. Also, Melisandre is often at odds with one of the most consistently wise and moral characters in the story, Ser Davos Seaworth. Her killing of Shireen proves fruitless and she falsely identifies King Stannis Baratheon as humanity's chosen messiah in the war against the White Walkers. Many of these plot and character points suggest that Melisandre is a villain, and yet it is *her* spell that brings Snow back

Fig. 10.5. Melisandre, Red Priestess of the Lord of Light (played by Carice van Houten), burns the leader of the Wildlings, Mance Rayder (Ciarán Hinds), at the stake. Melisandre knows that the zombie threat is real, and performs powerful spells to help the cause of humanity against the supernatural menace, but her methods are so ruthless and destructive that she is a deeply problematic figure. HBO.

from the dead. Martin has noted enigmatically that Melisandre is the most consistently misunderstood character in his series. Like Tyrion, she is one of the morally grey characters capable of great acts of both good *and* evil that seem to engage so much of Martin's interest as a storyteller.

"One has to imagine that Melisandre is surprised at the mismatch between the victories she's seen in her flames and those she's witnessed in real life," critic Andrew Zimmerman Jones has observed. "When she does finally let her air of confidence slip, she justifies the failure of the world to match up to her prophecies by placing the blame not on her perfect Lord of Light, but upon herself. 'The vision was a true one. It was my reading that was false. I am as mortal as you, Jon Snow. All mortals err.' "[5]

Until the saga ends and her fate becomes clear, it seems reasonable to assert, at this juncture, that Melisandre represents a warning to those who believe in climate change—you can be right about the threat and wrong about how to face it. Melisandre may offer any of the following warnings to climate champions: Don't turn away would-be allies because of their ideological or religious labels; don't use ruthless tactics in desperate maneuvers when you are uncertain what the consequences will be; do not be so righteous that you do not build humility into your character and worldview; don't place too much of your faith in messianic figures; and do not place too much of your faith in magic wand solutions to problems. In short, it is a nice thing to be "right" about something. That does not mean you are always doing the "right" thing. That does not mean you are always on the "right" side. Be careful. Even if she is capable of the occasional stunning feat of goodness, it is unwise to be too much like Melisandre.

Melisandre also acts as a warning to more traditional religious ideologues. While some devout Christian fans of the Westeros saga might content themselves that Melisandre is a pagan character and may in no way reflect badly upon Christianity, it is inescapably true that she behaves like a member of the Inquisition—burning heretics and insisting upon doctrinaire beliefs. One of the great ironies of the history of Christianity is that hive-minded thinking, violent torture and oppression, and ideological and political tunnel vision have so often been employed in the name of Jesus of Nazareth, the Prince of Peace.

While the vision of Jesus as a warrior and persecutor of heretics is a popular one in America, in *Profiles of Jesus* (2002) the Jesus Seminar provided a variety of other ways of thinking of (and following) Jesus based on their own textual interpretations of the Gospels. One of the most compelling essays in this anthology is "Jesus as Peasant Artisan," by Arthur J. Dewey. Dewey portrays Jesus as a "crafty" wordsmith who employs "humorous exaggeration" and a narrative "double focus" to discourage dogmatic thinking and collapse either/or choices and good/bad distinctions in on themselves.[6] Consequently, Jesus's parables and aphorisms confound his audiences by making listeners ponder the ever-expanding ramifications of what he has said. Jesus employed his narrative brilliance and pedagogical skill to teach his audiences about social injustice in first-century Palestine. Dewey offers as an example, the ever-expanding ramifications of Jesus's exhortation to love *everyone*:

The aphoristic command "Love your enemies" (Luke 6:27b; Matt 5:44b) also plays upon a double-perspective. First, it disputes the conventional wisdom that enjoins primary concern for those within one's social group. Second, it admits the alienation in Palestinian society (village feuding, opposition by the rich, Roman occupation). The audience could easily identify their enemies. Third, it challenges the listeners to replace a simplistic obedience with a radical reconfiguration of their societal categories. As the Seminar rightly puts it in *The Five Gospels*, "Those who love their enemies have no enemies." The challenge of the aphorism is clear: can you imagine acting differently towards those outside the circle of your people? The saying has a concussive effect; it keeps echoing in the resisting areas of the listeners' hearts.[7]

While it may seem far-fetched to suggest this, given that *A Song of Ice and Fire* is an incomplete, seemingly misanthropic narrative, there is textual evidence to suggest that, on some level, Martin is arguing for the importance of Jesus's worldview (as explicated

Fig. 10.6. Tyrion Lannister (Peter Dinklage) is one of the few people of influence to use his political power to help the Night's Watch shore up its defenses against the gathering wight forces. A wealthy intellectual who believes that "a mind needs books like a sword needs a whetstone," Tyrion speaks in epigrams and prods members of the ruling classes to treat the poor more justly. He sees himself as having spent his entire life on trial for being a dwarf and is deeply bitter about never finding genuine romantic love. However, his actions often justify his claim that he has "a tender spot in [his] heart for cripples and bastards and broken things." HBO.

by Dewey) as a corrective to the dominant, war-torn culture of Westeros. Indeed, to some degree, Tyrion the sly wordsmith is a wealthy, cynical counterpart to Arthur Dewey's characterization of Jesus as a raconteur and rhetorical wizard. Significantly, Tyrion attempts to broker a peace treaty between freed slaves and their former masters in the HBO adaptation. When the liberated slaves object that the former masters are their hated enemies, Tyrion patiently reminds them that one only ever makes treaties with enemies, not with friends. Furthermore, Tyrion proudly states that he has "a tender spot in [his] heart for cripples and bastards and broken things." Tyrion speaks the truth. He does, indeed, have this soft spot; so, too, does Jesus. Ironically, in Martin's universe, the drunken, whoring, murderer Tyrion is a closer analogue to Jesus than Melisandre, because he is not a doctrinaire thinker, he does not persecute those who think differently or pray differently, and—arrogant as he is—he is aware of his own faults. Melisandre only learns humility after she murders a child by mistake. All of this should provide food for thought for the devout who are most certain that their intentions are pure, actions are pure, and place in heaven is secure.

It would be appropriate here to consider Lewis's portrayal of Jesus in the form of Aslan, especially how Aslan demonstrates love for the unlovable and forgives the unforgivable, modeling a Christian environmentalist ethic in the process. As Matthew Dickerson and David O'Hara wrote, "To explore the expressions of love, mercy, and grace in Lewis's writing . . . we really need look no farther than the character of Aslan, who in mercy toward Edmund and love for Narnia gives up his own life to save not only Edmund but all of Narnia: its animals, trees, and rivers; the creatures who love him, and even those who don't. The vices behind the worst environmental damage— greed, lust, hoarding, selfishness—are those at the exact opposite of love. Thus, love may be the greatest environmental virtue. It is love that is most able to prompt one to act for the good of others, rather than always seeking one's own benefit. Wendell Berry . . . comments on Lewis's portrayal of love as a discipline and as a practice, and how it contrasts sharply with modern ideas. 'Well, we've degraded the word "love" to mean simply feeling. Which is alright except you don't feel loving all the time, you know. And what Lewis is saying is love is a practice—it is something you *do*. Whether you feel like it or not, like milking your cows. And you understand that, well, that's painful.'"[8]

This is clearly the moral of Lewis's corpus. How odd is it that such sentiments also appear to underpin the blood-soaked, rape-filled narrative of George R. R, Martin's Westeros saga? Improbable as this sounds, if this theory is true, it means that Martin's narrative has the aesthetics of Robert E. Howard's *Conan* stories, the tropes of the Inklings novels, and the morality of Ursula K. Le Guin's *Earthsea*. That is a challenging notion worth meditating upon.

## George R. R. Martin's Inspirations for *A Song of Ice and Fire*

George R. R. Martin grew up immersing himself in the extant body of fantasy literature and was inspired to create his own fictional universe when he read those created by

Edgar Rice Burroughs, J. R. R. Tolkien, and Robert E. Howard. Martin said that he was drawn to fantasy as a child because he lived in a circumscribed world. Isabel Berwick, columnist for Britain's *Financial Times* observed that Martin grew up in Bayonne, New Jersey, the son of a longshoreman. Martin's family didn't have the money to travel, so he read extensively to travel in his mind. The apartment they lived in didn't allow dogs or cats for pets, so he purchased six "dime store" turtles and kept them in the courtyard of a tin toy castle he had set up near his bed. Because he kept them in a castle, he decided they must be knights and royalty and created a mythology around them based on the notion of a turtle kingdom. Unfortunately, the tin castle was not the best habitat for the turtles, and some of them died within the castle, while others escaped and died in other parts of the house. Martin found one dead under the refrigerator a month after it disappeared. Since he had already chosen to understand the turtles within the context of a speculative fiction kingdom narrative, he began to wonder if the turtles were killing one another off in a plot to claim the tin throne. This musing was the earliest inspiration for *A Song of Ice and Fire*, and it is the reason he wears the sigil of a turtle on his cap.

Martin has told interviewers that the long Winter from his book series was inspired by a bitterly cold semester he spent at Northwestern University as an undergraduate. Furthermore, Martin has explained that he first began plotting the events of the series around 1990. That would have been before the publication of Al Gore's widely derided *Earth in the Balance* (1992), a period when climate change was not foremost on the minds of the masses but when the cultural anxieties surrounding the fall of the Berlin Wall on November 9, 1989 were still part of the zeitgeist.

In addition to the events and millennial apocalyptic fears headlining the last decade of the twentieth century, the Inklings appear to have been an important formative influence upon Martin and his work. Martin would acknowledge many of these influences, but he doesn't like it when they are overstated, especially in the case of Tolkien, "There were thousands of years of fantasy before Tolkien, but the way it is shaped as a modern commercial publishing genre and the fantasy books that have been written in the past half century have all been influenced by Tolkien. So, [Tolkien] still sort of defines the playing field."[9]

Some of Martin's references to Tolkien are playful and seem peppered throughout the narrative for fans to discover and wink at. For example, Martin named his character Marillion the bard after Tolkien's *Silmarillion*. There are other notable nods to Tolkien, just as there are in-joke references to other classic fantasy novels, such as William Goldman's 1973 novel *The Princess Bride* and its 1987 film adaptation (e.g., Prince Oberyn Martell appears to be a more somber version of Inigo Montoya). Most readers see more of Tolkien in Martin than Lewis, but Lewis does appear to be the greater influence. Perhaps it is odd thinking of *A Song of Ice and Fire* as a profane retelling of *The Chronicles of Narnia*, though the idea is not unprecedented, as one might argue that the director's cut of the Ridley Scott film *Legend* (1985) was a similarly provocative revamping of Lewis for a more adult audience. Odd as it may seem, some of the most important thematic elements in *A Song of Ice and Fire* echo Lewis's writings: the frost

Fig. 10.7. On the HBO television series *Game of Thrones*, Emilia Clarke plays Daenerys Targaryen, the Mother of Dragons, who may be Westeros's last hope for salvation—or yet another false and unstable potential Messiah figure. HBO.

that comes to Westeros bears a strong resemblance to the eternal winter that the White Witch (aka Jadis, Queen of Charn) brings upon Narnia in *The Lion, the Witch, and the Wardrobe* (1950), and the problematic Messianic figure Queen Daenerys seems to have inherited and expanded upon a brief slave-liberation storyline that underscored the heroism of King Caspian in *The Voyage of the Dawn Treader* (1952). Furthermore, the devastated world and the magical tree from *The Magician's Nephew* both show up in the form of an abandoned city that Daenerys discovers during an Exodus across the desert in *A Clash of Kings*. Depending on how Martin chooses to end the unfinished book series, Daenerys, Brandon Stark, and Jon Snow all have the potential to act as a secularized commentary on the liberation the Christ-figure Aslan brings to Narnia when he thaws the frozen damned with his holy breath and brings rebirth to Narnia. It is also notable that Tyrion Lannister's name seems to be taken from the last king of Narnia, Tirian.

However, Tyrion's personality and story arc do not come from Lewis.

Tyrion is Martin's reimagining of the title character of *I, Claudius* (1976), the classic, critically beloved BBC miniseries adaptation of Robert Graves's 1934 novel *I, Claudius* and its sequel, 1935's *Claudius the God*. Claudius (Derek Jacobi) is physically handicapped, underappreciated by his family, underestimated by his enemies, brilliant, and tormented by the women in his life—including a wife who is far taller than he. Indeed, there is a broad correlation between most of the plot elements of *I, Claudius* and the King's Landing storyline in *A Song of Ice and Fire*, just as there are virtual one-to-one correspondences between characters in each. King Robert Baratheon and Queen Cersei Lannister were inspired by barrel-chested Caesar Augustus and his wife Livia Drusilla, the great poisoner of Ancient Rome. The mad, murderous Caesar Caligula is a clear influence upon Joffrey Baratheon. Patrick Stewart's scheming, aspirational villain Lucius Aelius Sejanus has an analogue in Littlefinger, and both villains transfer their affections from mother to daughter as their fortunes rise. The idealistic and murdered Agrippa Postumus seems to have inspired Ned Stark, Emperor Tiberius inspired King Stannis, and there is even a character named Arria, whose name Martin spells "Arya." The connections between Westeros and Ancient Rome suggest that the politics of Westeros are as bloodthirsty, dynastic, and antipopulist as those of ancient history in our world, and the parallels between Westeros and contemporary American politics further make one wonder if there is a one-to-one correlation between American elected officials and the likes of Caligula. Indeed, Martin himself has identified Donald Trump as alarmingly similar to Westeros's answer to Caligula, the evil child-king Joffrey Baratheon. Though the comparison is clearly uncharitable, Martin has qualified it by observing that growing old has not made Joffrey/Trump any wiser, kinder, or saner. Ultimately, in *A Song of Ice and Fire*, as in *The Hunger Games*, the parallels drawn between the United States and the decadence of Ancient Rome are both direct and indirect, and apt.

On the one hand, the description of the pet turtle carnage inspiring the saga in the first place validates the idea that *A Song of Ice and Fire* and *Game of Thrones* is, first and foremost, a fantasy retelling of *I, Claudius* used to comment on contemporary American politics and draw the same parallel between American decadence and the decadence of Rome. The parallels can be drawn easily and the television series is adept at dramatizing the brutal nature of Martin's universe and the Machiavellian politics of the seven kingdoms. And yet, Martin points to the idea that this central question of the main narrative, "Who will sit upon the Iron Throne?" is a red herring. The real response might be: "Who cares? What about the zombies?" Readers of the books seem to understand this readily, though the viewers of the television show are growing savvier as the series progresses and have begun to ask the same question.

Weiss and Benioff have professed enormous respect for their source material, and have tried to include as many of the small details, subplots, and characters from the novels as they can. As of the writing of these words, they have omitted some significant characters from the books that have had small parts, and other minor characters have had their storylines reassigned to more major characters. There have also been several small but striking improvements upon the novels, most notably the inspired decision to have Arya serve as Tywin Lannister's cup-bearer at Harrenhal, which resulted in a segment with far greater dramatic weight than its equivalent in the books. However, the biggest challenge facing the showrunners is how to include information about the universe that the characters would know and take for granted—whether it is the history and geography of Westeros, the myths of the dragons, the theologies of the invented religions, the mystery of Jon Snow's parentage, or any other information provided in the book by a narrator or an inner monologue. The series tends to provide this information in a series of monologues that tend to take place in brothels or during sex scenes. Information about the extinction of all dragons, which appears in a moody scene in the novel *A Game of Thrones* when Tyrion stares upon the empty eye sockets of the skull of a dead dragon with a flickering torch, is provided in an absurd hot-tub dalliance between Viserys Targaryen and a servant girl. Moments like this, dubbed "sexposition" online, are intended to kill two birds with one stone—make the executives and marketing mavens at HBO happy by inserting the requisite number of nude scenes, and find a way to deal with the absence of interior monologue and narration. The sexposition is such a staple of the series that it has become a running joke in fandom and popular culture, especially since it is so clearly included because of a corporate directive from HBO executives (who obviously make similar demands of other producers who work on their other shows). Comedians Keegan-Michael Key and Jordan Peele mocked the frequent inclusion of gratuitous nudity in HBO shows during a two-hander routine in the first season of *Key & Peele*. Peele noted that it is difficult for him to watch an HBO show with his girlfriend because the nudity designed to pander to men is supposed to elicit an erotically charged response from him while he is sitting on a couch beside the woman he's supposed to show more erotic interest in than the nude women on television.[10]

In addition to its overreliance on sexposition—and the often-discussed shocking, offensive, and culturally destructive rape scenes—the show is also not always adept at bringing to the screen the ecological themes from the book. In material mostly excluded from the second season of the television series, Arya spends dozens of pages of a *Clash of Kings* traveling across Westeros. She surveys destroyed towns, burned-out lands, and spoiled food stocks in segments that might seem gratuitous to the average reader until it becomes clear how vital they are. War is sung about and romanticized, but the real cost of war is an entire green country turned to ashes. The television adaptation never comes close to adequately dramatizing these Arya segments.

Another frequently omitted major theme of the books is food scarcity and the unfair distribution of food. George R. R. Martin dedicates multiple, extended prose passages in his novels to describing the food that his characters eat, especially during dining room scenes and banquet segments. The members of the Night's Watch consume copious amounts of mulled wine and salt beef, while the aristocrats of King's Landing ate seventy-seven lavish courses at the wedding of King Joffrey to Margaery Tyrell. Comparing the food at this wedding to the food available to the poor of Westeros is much like comparing the food available in the front and rear compartments of Snowpiercer or the feasts served in the Capitol to the meager scraps available to the poorest districts of Panem. In a scene written for the series, Tyrion comments archly on the immorality and the wastefulness of such extravagance and Lady Oleanna Tyrell talks of the value of pomp and circumstance in keeping the masses in awe and in their places. As good as that new scene is, the conversation in question doesn't resonate as much as do the book passages about food. During the first book, these multiple, extended passages might be perceived as a means of setting up the world of Westeros. The catalogue of mundane visual details would serve the dual purpose of setting the scene and helping readers suspend their disbelief in visiting a world of dragons and zombies. As the books progress, however, and the food catalogues remain a fixture, readers might be forgiven for finding the catalogues gratuitous. Indeed, many readers might begin to skim past them, or wonder if they had been included in error. In certain cases, the extended descriptions of food have been used as part of an overall suspense-building strategy, as in the subtly ominous—and protracted—descriptions of the festivities unfolding during a wedding at Walder Frey's Twins. However, it becomes clear that there is more to the food cataloguing than either suspense or verisimilitude. As the books go on, the catalogues of food grow gradually shorter as provisions vanish and the long winter draws near. By the fifth book in the series, winter finally comes, and food shortages have hit the Wall, leaving the members of the Night's Watch with virtually no food stocks to speak of to feed themselves, let alone the Wildling refugees that have come to flee the incursion of undead into their lands. Consequently, the catalogues that have seemed irksome to many readers have an unexpected and vital thematic importance. In Westeros, and in our world, we are wasting food, wasting lives, and wasting time with endless wars, pointless political infighting, and bitter family feuds while the climate is changing. This is a moral the books make clear. The show is getting better at doing this, but didn't start off adept at conveying this message. Indeed, the Honest Trailer satire of *Game of Thrones* deftly points to the core reader misdirection strategy of the books: it doesn't matter whether the Starks defeat the Lannisters, or which would-be monarch sits upon the Iron Throne of Westeros; all that matters is the importance of dealing with the coming climate disaster. As the narrator of the Honest Trailer intones in a comic-ominous voice, "Watch as everyone fights to sit in the world's most uncomfortable chair, while completely ignoring an invasion of ice zombies that threatens to kill them all. Seriously, someone should really get on that!"[11]

The "Hardhome" episode of the series finally brought this message to the fore, undoing some of the damage to the central theme of the books the showrunners had done unintentionally by failing to find a way to successfully include Martin's subtlest narrative touches: the food catalogues and the repeated descriptions of the devastation Arya encountered on her long journey across Westeros. These missing subtle touches are part of why an adaptation, even one as excellent as *Game of Thrones*, can hit all the right beats, have all the major scenes, and all the major characters played by some of the best actors of our generation and still feel wrong to those who love the books.

## "Jim . . . they're *dying*":
## Making Peace with the Klingons in *Star Trek*

In the world of Westeros, the Brothers of the Night's Watch may be interpreted as the equivalent of "cowboys" guarding a fort from the equivalent of "Indians" in the form of the Wildlings. When Gene Roddenberry crafted *Star Trek* (1966–69) to be a science fiction western in the 1960s, it didn't take long for the series to develop its own "cowboy and Indian" conflict—hero cowboy Captain Kirk and his U.S. Cavalry comrades-in-arms in the United Federation of Planets versus their Indian equivalents in that speculative fiction universe, the Klingon Empire. It was a classic western movie conflict transposed to the science fiction genre and set in space, "the final frontier." Since the series was a Cold War–era form of popular entertainment, the reading of the episodes concerning the conflicts between Starfleet and the Klingons were just as easy to interpret as an allegorical depiction of the clash between the United States and the communist nations—especially the Union of Soviet Socialist Republics and the People's Republic of China. The saga of Captain Kirk (William Shatner) and his logical Vulcan science officer Mr. Spock (Leonard Nimoy), and their exploration of the far reaches of space aboard the Starship Enterprise was chronicled on three seasons of a live-action television show, an animated cartoon scripted by writers of the original series, a line of comic books, movies, video games, novels (by authors such as Diane Carey, Diane Duane, J. M. Dillard, and Peter David), and a series of films starting with *Star Trek: The Motion Picture* (1979) and culminating in *Star Trek VI: The Undiscovered Country* (1991). The sixth movie was designed both to end the series in celebration of its twenty-fifth anniversary and provide a fitting retirement from the franchise for the aging original cast members.

Like the Orcs, the Klingons are multivalent symbols that may stand in for a variety of real-world peoples, but they are consistently symbolic of cultures that the United States is currently involved in either a cold or hot war with—usually, communist societies such as Russia or China. They have also been evocative of members of African or Middle Eastern nations, as well as served as "Indians." The Klingons have been presented, throughout the history of *Star Trek*, as variously good, evil, tragic, honorable, terroristic, and morally complex. They tend to be portrayed most sympathetically during periods of time when U.S.-Russia relations are positive and as more villainous when those relations are more strained, if not overtly hostile.

(As an important side-note, a prequel series that premiered on CBS All-Access in 2017, *Star Trek: Discovery*, concerns a catastrophic outbreak of war between the Klingons and the Federation. The series is clearly written to echo themes from *Undiscovered Country*, and quite deliberately begins the epic twenty-third-century story that will end with that film.)

*Star Trek VI: The Undiscovered Country* was written during a period of easing tensions between the United States and Russia, between the United States and antagonistic regimes in the Middle East, and between Native Americans and the white communities

Fig. 10.8. The logical Vulcan scientist Mr. Spock (Leonard Nimoy) in *Star Trek II: The Wrath of Khan* (1982). In movie appearances and episodes of *Star Trek: The Next Generation*, the character strove to make peace between the Klingons and the Federation and between the Romulans and the Vulcans. In the real world, actor Leonard Nimoy wrote and directed stories for *Star Trek* that promoted ecology and argued allegorically for the brokering of peace between the Israelis and the Palestinians. Paramount Pictures.

that live near them. It is a story of peace. Sadly, watching the film in modern times is a more emotionally challenging prospect, especially now that fears of Vladimir Putin's Russia, violent flare-ups between indigenous peoples and settler colonials, and increased tensions between Western nations and the peoples who practice Islam tragically problematize the film's pacifistic and idealistic message. Indeed, it is no accident that the current *Star Trek* series, *Discovery*, is set during a time of war between the Klingons and the Federation at what has often been euphemistically called "this particular political moment." And yet, *Discovery* notwithstanding, perhaps these rising tensions between so many global, tribal, and nationalistic communities make it even more urgent that we take *Star Trek VI*'s moral message seriously. There may be no morally "bad" time to watch and contemplate this film.

Putting aside for a moment the sequel series *Star Trek: The Next Generation*, its spinoffs, and the J. J. Abrams original series reboot, *Star Trek VI: The Undiscovered*

*Country* is the perfect ending to the *Star Trek* saga because it depicts what would happen if the "Cold War" between the United Federation of Planets and the Klingon Empire came to an end. Indeed, the idea for the plot came from Leonard Nimoy, who suggested that the film's writer-director Nicholas Meyer should design the plot around the question "What would happen if the Berlin Wall came down in space?" The initiating incident in the film is an ecological catastrophe that makes the Klingons rethink their commitment to waging a Cold War against the Federation and redirect their focus to caring for their own planet's environment. A Cherynobyl-style disaster on the Klingon moon Praxis "caused by over-mining and insufficient safety precautions" has caused "a deadly pollution of their ozone" and the Klingon homeworld will have run out of oxygen within fifty years, Spock reports to a top-secret meeting of Starfleet brass, noting that "due to their enormous military budget, the Klingon economy does not have the resources to combat this catastrophe." The forward-thinking Chancellor of the Klingon High Council, Gorkon, receives Spock's request to open peace negotiations favorably, and the two plan to begin negotiations for the dismantling of Federation military outposts "along the Neutral Zone, an end to almost seventy years of unremitting hostility with the Klingons, which the Klingons can no longer afford."

Nimoy was an actor in a science fiction franchise, but he was also a teacher. He and Meyer intended the final *Star Trek* story to be a commentary on the fall of the Berlin Wall. It was also a thinly veiled political allegory that served as joint statement by two Jewish storytellers delivered to those on both sides of the Arab-Israeli conflict: now that the Cold War is ending, let us also end our conflict and bring peace and stability to the Middle East. Just as the aging character of Mr. Spock worked to broker peace between the Federation and the Klingons and between the Vulcans and the Romulans, Nimoy never gave up on the possibility of helping to broker peace in the real world between Arabs and Jews. He set his hopes for achieving the real-world peace by advocating a two-state solution to the Arab-Israeli conflict in which, from his perspective, each side might enjoy the security of its own, autonomous homeland. In an open letter addressing the issue, Nimoy wrote:

> I reach out to you as someone who is troubled to see the conflict between Israelis and Palestinians continue apparently without an end in sight.
>
> In fact, there is an end in sight. It's known as the two-state solution—a secure, democratic Israel as the Jewish State alongside an independent Palestinian state. Even Israel's nationalist Prime Minister Binyamin Netanyahu has come to see this as the shape of the future. The problem is how to reach that end point. It's something we should be concerned about—not only as world citizens, but as Americans.[12]

While Nimoy's views on the Arab-Israeli conflict have been depicted as a rarity among Jewish social commentators, perspectives akin to his may be found represented in texts such as *Essays* (2010) by Wallace Shawn and *Not the Israel My Parents Promised Me*

(2014) by Harvey Pekar and J. T. Waldman. Historically, plans to partition the contested lands into cleanly delineated Jewish and Arab territories have been advocated by the Peel Commission in 1937, by the United Nations' Resolution 181 in November 1947, and even, quite reluctantly, by Chaim Weizmann, the first president of the State of Israel.

In addition to advocating for peace in the Middle East, Nimoy was an environmentalist who directed the film *Star Trek IV: The Voyage Home* (1986), which argued that in both foreseeable and unforeseeable ways humanity was sowing the seeds of its own annihilation through whaling, overfishing, and pollution. For Nimoy, endless wars were luxuries we could no longer afford in an age of mass extinction of animal life and global climate change. An actor, storyteller, and prophet, Nimoy spoke through the fictional world of *Star Trek* to craft sociopolitical science fiction allegories that asked viewers to join him in the effort to turn the imperfect real world into the more utopian future *Star Trek* represented. However imperfect a model *Star Trek* may be as a utopian future to strive for, its idealistic, multiethnic hippie/cowboy narrative and iconography was useful as a teaching tool in the manner that Nimoy used it during his lifetime, for the reasons discussed here. As a species, Nimoy preaches, we need to leave war behind and try to realize the utopia that *Star Trek* strived for throughout its narrative and only achieved at the end of *The Undiscovered Country*.

The promise of a utopian peace is achieved in this film but it takes enormous effort to forge. Spock strives to convince Kirk and the warrior class of the Klingon Empire to turn their swords into ploughshares and work together to make war obsolete—and, in the process, make their roles as warriors obsolete as well. For most of the film, Kirk positions himself against Spock's peace initiative, siding with the most militarist and conservative elements of the Federation. Gorkon has announced his intention to end the conflict between the Klingons and the Federation, but his people have been, traditionally, so militarily aggressive that the normally more level-headed Kirk greets their peace overtures with paranoia and bitterness. After all, he has spent his life fighting the Klingons, and they have only recently murdered his son, Dr. David Marcus (during the events depicted in the 1984 film *Star Trek III: The Search for Spock*). When Federation Admiral Cartwright learns of Spock's peace initiative, he cuts off the Vulcan's idealistic report angrily:

> CARTWRIGHT: I must protest. To offer the Klingons a safe haven within Federation space is suicide. Klingons would become the alien trash of the galaxy. And if we dismantle the fleet, we'd be defenseless before an aggressive species with a foothold on our territory. The opportunity here is to bring them to their knees. Then we'll be in a far better position to dictate terms.

Cartwright's remarks were written during a time when Israel was considering ceding lands to the Palestinians that would give them a home while also making Israel itself smaller and more vulnerable to attack from hostile Palestinians should the peace break down. In the intervening years, his remarks seem only more relevant, as his argument against offering safe haven to refugees has been used by those throughout the West who have opposed granting haven to Syrian refugees in the recent diaspora crisis. It is exactly the sort of pessimistic, cynical argument one would expect the idealistic 1960s hero Captain Kirk to refute in a passionate, humanist speech. Surprisingly and heartbreakingly, the elderly and bitter Kirk joins the chorus of skeptical voices by making this argument, "The Klingons have never been trustworthy. I'm forced to agree with Admiral Cartwright. This is a terrifying idea."

Spock replies, "It is imperative that we act now to support the Gorkon initiative, lest more conservative elements persuade his Empire that it is better to attempt a military solution and die fighting."

After the meeting concludes, Kirk privately expresses his outrage that Spock volunteered him and the crew of the Enterprise to act as Gorkon's security escort during the next phase of negotiations.

SPOCK: There's an old Vulcan proverb: "Only Nixon could go to China."

KIRK: You know how I feel about this. They're animals!

SPOCK: Jim, there is an historic opportunity here.

KIRK: Don't believe them! Don't trust them!

Fig. 10.9. A friendship divided by politics. In *Star Trek VI: The Undiscovered Country* (1991), Spock seeks to forge a lasting peace between the Klingon Empire and the United Federation of Planets, a secret political initiative that his best friend, Captain Kirk (William Shatner), sees as a treasonous betrayal of Earth and devastating breach of their trust. The two lifelong friends were never farther apart. Paramount Pictures.

SPOCK: They're dying.

KIRK: Let them die!

In *Game of Thrones* terms, Kirk is taking Bowen Marsh's position on the Klingon/Wildling refugee issue and Spock is stating Jon Snow's political perspective. At no point does Kirk shout, "For the Federation!" and stab Spock to death, but there are moments early in the film where he seems to be considering it. *Entertainment Weekly* columnist Darren Frainch observed in "*Star Trek VI: The Undiscovered Country* Is a Masterpiece until It's a Franchise Movie" (2016) that genre films made in recent years have taken pride in being "dark," and in dramatically pitting heroes against one another (i.e., *Batman v. Superman* or *Captain America: Civil War*), often using murky political commentary as an artificial pretext for the broken friendship and action movie mayhem. And yet, Frainch writes, a low-budget *Star Trek* film from the 1990s starring aging actors is far darker and offers far more incisive political commentary: "*Undiscovered Country* is clear on its politics. . . . Spock believes the point of war is peace; Kirk thinks war ends when there's only one side left. . . . [Consequently] minutes into *Undiscovered Country*, Captain Kirk hates Mr. Spock."[13] Frainch is also struck by the brazenness with which the film presents the Klingon martyr Gorkon as far more sympathetic than Kirk, who comes off as a petulant child refusing to participate in a conversation between adults—Spock and Gorkon:

> You may dislike how completely *Undiscovered Country* rips its central story from the headlines, you may yearn for science fiction with a less clear allegory, but the joy of this film is how it makes the Klingons Soviet only to make some of the most convincing, fully-fleshed-out, three-dimensional Soviet characters ever to appear in a Hollywood entertainment. Consider that, circa 1991, the Russian bad guy was merely being pushed into a new phase—now renegade Cold Warriors instead of official party members—and consider how, up until this point of the movie, the most likable character [Gorkon] has been the onscreen symbol of everything our heroes used to fight against.[14]

William Shatner, who played Kirk throughout the original *Star Trek* adventures, had reservations about his character turning so racist and expressing hateful opinions throughout the beginning of the film, even with the audience being aware that he was a man grieving for his murdered son. After all, Kirk is supposed to be a hero and a role model. And yet, Kirk is the villain of the first act of this film and Spock the hero. Kirk's position in this film is the exact opposite of the one he took in the 1968 *Star Trek* television series episode "Day of the Dove," in which he was the one who made overtures of peace to a female Klingon named Mara, urging her and her people to team up with the crew of the Starship Enterprise against a greater alien menace. In a memorable exchange, Kirk asks for an end to fighting between humans and Klingons, at least until an immediate crisis passes. Mara and the Klingons do come around to his way of thinking, after offering up some initial resistance to the idea of peace:

MARA: We have always fought. We must. We are hunters, Captain, tracking and taking what we need. There are poor planets in the Klingon systems. We must push outward if we are to survive.

KIRK: There's another way to survive. Mutual trust and help.

For all of Shatner's reservations about Kirk's racism in the "final" Star Trek story, *Star Trek VI: The Undiscovered Country*'s message is powerful and eternally relevant: even the most honorable heroes can turn evil if they grow too bitter; even the revered veterans of long-standing conflict must beware of demonizing their opponents and growing so racist that the very thought of peacetime is anathema to them. Of course, since it is a *Star Trek* narrative, Kirk does not stay a villain for long. His hate is eclipsed by the hate of others. He is frightened and appalled by the insane level of racism the Federation villains exhibit; their horrifying example shows him the folly of his own, initial reaction. In contrast, the central villains of the film—the racist reactionaries and members of the military-industrial complex on both sides who want to perpetuate never-ending warfare—do not soften or repent as Kirk does. Instead, the right-wing Klingons and right-wing members of the Federation conspire with one another to shatter the fragile peace being brokered by the left-wing Klingons and the left-wing Federation

Fig. 10.10. Newly arrived on the U.S.S. Enterprise and flanked by a cohort of his fellow Klingons, Chancellor Gorkon (David Warner) warmly greets his dinner hosts. Spock offers a genuine welcome in return, while Kirk attempts to disguise his mistrust and displeasure. Paramount Pictures.

members. The conspirators assassinate Gorkon and frame both Kirk and his hapless friend Dr. McCoy for the assassination in the hopes of igniting one last war between the Klingons and the Federation. Their goal is to make the universe safe for endless warfare and limitless industrial pollution.

Fortunately, detective work by Spock exonerates Kirk and McCoy from the crime and they expose the conspiracy before it claims the life of the liberal president of the United Federation of Planets. Once the conspiracy is thrown into the light of day, the progressive elements on both sides recommit themselves to peace, and a treaty is signed. The treaty restores Kirk's faith in peace, in the potential of Klingons to be good and wise, and in the belief that the universe, and history, will unfold as it should. Notably, in an earlier draft of the script, Kirk was shot and killed by a right-wing Federation Admiral shortly after succeeding in preserving the peace he had started out so skeptical of. It would have been a bittersweet, operatically heroic end to the character of James T. Kirk, and a more fitting death than the one he was granted at the end of the first motion picture with Captain Picard, *Generations* (1994). While that might have been a good ending to the saga of the original crew, and to Captain Kirk's story, the version that was ultimately filmed worked very well. Indeed, when one views *Star Trek VI* today, one might argue that there could have been no more appropriate ending to a Cold War saga that was always, on some level, a covert prayer for a future without war buried under the trappings of an escapist action narrative and American patriotic sentiment.

Towards the end of the film, when they are en route to confront the conspirators and save the president, Kirk and Spock reflect upon their heated conversation in the briefing room at the beginning of the film. Each has regrets. Spock is angry with himself for forcing Kirk to do the right thing instead of having faith that Kirk, given time and respect, would have come to the negotiating table of his own accord. He says, "It was arrogant presumption on my part that got us into this situation. You and the Doctor might have been killed." Kirk, for his part, regrets that his anger over his son's death made him forget his most cherished personal values and pushed him to take the side of some of the worst warmongers on Earth. Kirk says, "You're a great one for logic. I'm a great one for rushing in where angels fear to tread. We're both extremists. Reality is probably somewhere in between us. . . . I couldn't get past the death of my son. . . . Gorkon had to die before I understood how prejudiced I was." Here, the logical Spock strikes a note of bitterness, "Is it possible that we two, you and I, have grown so old and so inflexible that we have outlived our usefulness? Would that constitute a joke?"

Spock is speaking in character, as a Federation representative wrestling with the new reality of a Federation facing the potential for universal peace, but Nimoy is speaking as a Baby Boomer trying to make sense of living in a world that has moved beyond the Cold War into a new and uncertain political era. Times of political change are stressful to live through and require flexibility, compassion, and the ability to imagine many possible futures that might grow out of an uncertain present. The older and more inflexible and bitter we grow, the harder it is to imagine possibilities, to be truly flexible, and to feel compassion and empathy for those in the other political camp. As difficult as it is, Nimoy urges us to always leave room for hope, compassion, and many possible futures. That is the moral of *Star Trek VI*, and it is the perfect moral to end the *Star Trek* saga on. A similar moral would make an apt coda to *Game of Thrones*, though it is not yet clear that such will be the moral, or that its end will be half so optimistic as the end of *Star Trek*.

As columnist Salena Wakim wrote on February 27, 2015, the day after Nimoy's death: "For many of [Nimoy's] young fans, [Spock's] voice of reason, always calling for a 'logical' look at any given situation, made a huge impression. In 2010, Nimoy was named as the recipient of the Douglas S. Morrow Public Outreach Award, by the Space Foundation, for 'creating a positive role model that inspired untold numbers of viewers to learn more about the universe.' Even he had often noted that his biggest contribution to the various fields of science was probably the number of people he had inspired to become scientists. . . . To be true to his legacy, it is important that the world continues to care as much as about the world as he did during his time on this planet. Only then will we, and all the other species on this planet, have any hope of being able to truly 'Live Long and Prosper.' Rest in peace Leonard Nimoy, you will be greatly missed."[15]

## The Cowboy and Indian Alliance

Night gathers, and now my watch begins. It shall not end until my death. . . . I shall wear no crowns and win no glory. I shall live and die at my post. I am the sword in the darkness. I am the watcher on the walls. I am the fire that burns against the cold, the light that brings the dawn, the horn that wakes the sleepers, the shield that guards the realms of men. I pledge my life and honor to the Night's Watch, for this night and all nights to come.

—The Oath of the Brothers of the Night's Watch

"The Curse of Fenric" (1989) is a *Doctor Who* serial written by Ian Briggs that is set during World War II on a British military base in Northumbria. In the story, the insane Commander Millington has developed a biochemical weapon that he hopes to use to kill the Russians after the war, when they stop being allies and start being a threat to global democracy. Millington expects the weapon to kill all the Russians but not spread beyond their shores to the rest of the world. He is wrong, but when he begins to suspect the truth, he pushes on with his plan anyway. A closet Nazi sympathizer, Millington has read his Norse mythology and the idea of igniting Ragnarök appeals to him. As the Doctor investigates mysterious occurrences on the base camp, he discovers that Millington is working for an evil, disembodied intelligence. Millington calls it Fenric, after Fenrir, the son of Loki, but the Doctor knows it as an all-powerful alien life form.

The Doctor has also seen evidence of an alternate future Earth in which Millington's plan succeeds—an Earth populated only by mutant vampires created by the biochemical weapon. The Doctor urges Millington's soldiers to release Russian spies being held in the stockade and join forces with them against Millington to prevent that dark vision of Earth's future from coming to pass. To convince the British and the Russians to embrace solidarity, the Doctor and his friend Ace use a chess metaphor: black pawns and white pawns need to break the rules of the game, join forces, and work together to save humanity from the mad white king. The threat posed by the insane Millington is, indeed, so great that former adversaries—British soldiers and Russian soldiers, capitalists and socialists, Christians and atheists—put aside their differences, forge a truce, and stand together against a lunatic tyrant bent on the destruction of the whole world. It is a compelling portrait of collective action against a grand, global threat.

Leonard Nimoy, Marq De Villiers, George R. R. Martin, and Ian Briggs all tell stories of peace initiatives of vast historic scope and import. These initiatives involve a rapprochement between bitter enemies in the interests of taking collective action in the face of an apocalyptic-level ecological crisis. These peace overtures, between warring religious factions in the real world discussed by De Villiers, between the Klingons and the Federation in *Star Trek*, and between Jon Snow and the Wildlings in *A Song of Ice and Fire* all have much to teach us about what we should be doing in the real world, and what is already being done. Indeed, Naomi Klein depicts several such collective actions taken against the fossil fuel industries to prevent them from continuing to poison water supplies and pollute the lands and the air. She chronicles several key initiatives in her book *This Changes Everything* (2015), as well as the documentary film based upon it, and one of the most striking initiatives is the "cowboy and Indian alliance" against the Keystone XL pipeline. Here, again, Klein is quoted for several paragraphs, but those who read through them without skimming will be struck by the parallels between her real-world reporting and the worlds of both *Game of Thrones* and *Star Trek VI*:

> It was Keystone that provoked that historic wave of civil disobedience in Washington D.C. in 2011, followed by what were then the largest protests in the history of the U.S. climate movement (more than 40,000 people outside the White House in February 2013). And it is Keystone that brought together the unexpected alliance of indigenous tribes and ranchers along the pipeline route that became known as "the Cowboy and Indian alliance" (not to mention unlikely coalitions that brought together vegan activists who think meat is murder with cattle farmers whose homes are decorated with deer heads). In fact, the direct action group Tar Sands Blockade first coined the term "Blockadia" in August 2012, while planning what turned into an eighty-six-day tree blockade challenging Keystone's construction in East Texas. This coalition has used every imaginable method to stop the pipeline's southern leg, from locking themselves inside a length of pipe that

had not yet been laid, to creating a complex network of treehouses and other structures along the route.[16]

The activists and water protectors who line Blockadia fortify themselves for the extended conflict by cloaking their movement in political imagery, traditional protest songs, mythic narrative, and social media hashtags. These efforts gird them against implacable opposition from the fossil fuel industry, media blackouts and efforts to demonize them as violent rabble-rousers in the press. This common mythic imagery helps solidify the various peoples engaged in the same protest, making them think of themselves as the many working together for a united purpose.

Spend enough time in Blockadia and you start to notice patterns. The slogans on the signs, "Water is life," "You can't eat money," "Draw the line." A shared determination to stay in the fight for the long haul, and to do whatever it takes to win. Another recurring element is the prominent role played by women, who often dominate the front lines, providing not only powerful moral leadership but also some of the movement's most enduring iconography. In New Brunswick, for instance, the image of a lone Mi'kmaq mother, kneeling in the middle of the highway before a line of riot police, holding up a single eagle feather went viral. In Greece, the gesture that captured hearts and minds was when a seventy-four-year-old woman confronted a line of riot police by belting out a revolutionary song that had been sung by the Greek resistance against German occupation. From Romania, the image of an old woman wearing a babushka and holding a knobby walking stick went around the world under the caption: "You know your government has failed you when your grandma starts to riot". . . .

Something else unites this network of local resistance: widespread awareness that the climate crisis, and the understanding that these new extraction projects—which produce far more carbon dioxide, in the case of the tar sands, and more methane in the case of fracking, than their conventional counterparts—are taking the entire planet in precisely the wrong direction. These activists understand that keeping carbon in the ground, and protecting the ancient, carbon-sequestering forests from being clear-cut for mines, is a prerequisite for preventing catastrophic warming. So while these conflicts are invariably sparked by local livelihood and safety concerns, the global stakes are never far from the surface.[17]

The widespread protests Klein describes, especially those that defend indigenous tribes from their final displacement—and from seeing the last of their lands stolen from them and destroyed—have garnered high-profile support from Hollywood actors and activists such as Robert Redford, Mark Ruffalo, and Leonardo DiCaprio. On January 10, 2016, DiCaprio won an Academy Award for Best Actor for his performance in the historical drama and wilderness survival film *The Revenant*. He used the occasion of his award to address his feelings about both climate change and the rights of indigenous peoples in his acceptance speech. He said, "Making 'The Revenant' was about man's relationship to the natural world. A world that we collectively felt in 2015 as the hottest year in recorded history. Our production needed to move to the southern tip of this planet just to be able to find snow. Climate change is real. It is happening right now. It is the most urgent threat facing our entire species, and we need to work collectively together and stop procrastinating. We need to support leaders around the world who do not speak for the big polluters, but who speak for all of humanity, for the indigenous people of the world, for the billions and billions of underprivileged people out there who would be most affected by this. For our children's children, and for those people out there whose voices have been drowned out by the politics of greed. I thank you all for this amazing award tonight. Let us not take this planet for granted. I do not take tonight for granted."[18]

Political speeches at the Academy Awards are often met with impatient groans and scoffs, not only from conservative pundits but from average viewers who don't like being preached to. However, the truth and urgency of DiCaprio's words made them well worth saying, despite the criticism he invited for being the umpteenth Hollywood liberal to play the prophet. He is advocating for strengthening and empowering the same collective action against climate change championed by Jon Snow and Mr. Spock in the realm of climate fiction and described by Klein as already taking place in the real world. DiCaprio may have been playing prophet, but his speech had a quantifiable impact on the public. In the wake of the address, "tweets and Google searches about the topic were enormous and, at least in the case of tweets, appear to have set a new record based on analyses between 2011 and the present. 'A single speech, at a very opportunistic time, at the Oscar ceremony, resulted in the largest increase in public engagement with climate change ever,' says John Ayers of San Diego State University, who completed the work with colleagues from the University of California San Diego, the Santa Fe Institute, and other institutions."[19] The positive repercussions of the Oscar speech testify to the effectiveness of a high-profile figure bringing attention to the issue, even if he was "only" a Hollywood actor talking about a movie, and neither scientist nor politician. Even if he did not have the "right" to discuss climate change in such an "inappropriate" forum, the aftermath of his speech, and its positive results, validate his decision to act.

The next step, beyond raising awareness of the climate crisis and calling for solidarity with native peoples, is to move beyond symbolic solidarity and to stand with them. As the conflict between native tribes and the fossil fuel industry surrounding the construction of the Dakota Access Pipeline grew in intensity, Native American poet, musician, and author Joy Harjo of Mvskoke Nation posted on her Facebook page on September 4, 2016, at 11:13 a.m. a lament that the largest earthquake in the history of Oklahoma had rocked her home in Tulsa the day before—even as Native American protestors at Standing Rock were attacked with tear gas and police dogs. Harjo's spirits were low because she felt that the news media was not adequately covering the pipeline conflict. Furthermore, her attempts to bring the issue to the attention of the public caused a noticeable plummet in the number of people who followed her on social media, making her feel punished for her pro–clean water, anti-human-made-earthquake activism. She wrote, "My generation participated in the Wounded Knee of the seventies. We know what the state and U.S. governments are capable of when it comes to dealing with Native people who come in peace. See also Sand Creek. We do not want that to happen. Please help."[20]

Harjo covered the conflict closely on her social media page, registering developments that both elevated and dashed her spirits. She described the Native Americans as "protectors" of the Earth instead of "protestors"—a word that has almost uniformly negative connotations and is deeply inadequate to the task of describing the scope of what she saw was at stake in the conflict, popularly known as #NoDAPL. Assistance and solidarity did eventually come, in the form of financial donations and fossil fuel divestment initiatives. These initiatives were co-organized domestically by reporter and Black Lives Matter activist Shaun King, but money came from a multitude of sources worldwide, buying food, shelter, transport, and legal aid for the water protectors. The Native Americans dug in en masse near the site of the pipeline construction, willing to camp out through a long, bitter winter to protect their lands and water. Winter had come to Standing Rock, and the water protectors were prepared to face it. Meanwhile, a bank divestment campaign advocated by Jane Fonda and Lily Tomlin was undertaken to punish banks that funded the project. Environmentalist politicians such as Bernie Sanders and Jill Stein visited Standing Rock camp in solidarity. Most surprising of all was the support that came from environmentalist and Native American rights activist military veterans. Americans tend to expect Hollywood actors, hippies, members of Greenpeace, and activist reporters such as Amy Goodman to make a political fuss over environmental issues, but they don't generally expect to see veterans stand in solidarity with legions of protestors.

Wesley Clark Jr. was one of four thousand veterans who acted as unarmed human shields for the Native Americans, who with little or no provocation had been drenched by massive hoses in freezing temperatures and fired upon with rubber bullets by the police. The arrival of the veterans helped give the protestors a brief reprieve from overt militarized police harassment. Shortly after their arrival, Barack Obama's presidential decree on December 4, 2016 temporarily halted construction of the pipeline. None of the activists believed that the pause in the construction would last long, especially given the upcoming installation of Donald J. Trump in the White House. On December 5, Clark and several of his compatriots celebrated the temporary victory and participated in a rapprochement ceremony between the veterans and tribal elders, who included Chief Leonard Crow Dog, a Lakota, and Phyllis Young, of the Standing Rock Sioux. Standing in formation, Clark and the veterans knelt before the tribal leaders, apologizing for the injustices heaped upon the indigenous peoples of the United States by government and military authorities.

Clark said, "Many of us, me particularly, are from the units that have hurt you over the many years. We came. We fought you. We took your land. We signed treaties that we broke. We stole minerals from your sacred hills. We blasted the faces of our presidents onto your sacred mountain. When we took still more land and then we took your children and then we tried to eliminate your language that God gave you, and the Creator gave you. We didn't respect you, we polluted your Earth, we've hurt you in so many ways but we've come to say that we are sorry. We are at your service and we beg for your forgiveness."[21] Speaking on behalf of the Native peoples, Chief Leonard Crow Dog granted Clark and the other veterans forgiveness. Crow Dog offered up hope for a lasting peace between the indigenous peoples and settler colonials of the world. "We do not own the land; the land owns us." Young, a Sioux, added a sobering note to the celebration. "The black snake has never stopped and if they didn't stop at desecrating our graves of our ancestors, they'll stop at nothing. . . . So there will be a motion filed by the Energy Transfer today to continue the pipeline. . . . We are a peaceful movement, but we may have to make a move to protect our territory."[22]

Young here cites an oft-employed environmentalist image of the pipeline as a "black snake." Such an iconic image is clearly Tolkienesque. The pipeline is a snake. It is a wyrm. It is a dragon. It is Smaug, the personification of greed, pride, mercilessness, the hoarding of resources, the burning of the earth, and the wasteful loss of life and mass devastation wrought upon the land during the unnecessary World War I. At Standing Rock, the Sioux and the veterans stood together, a Tolkien-like fellowship united in opposition against the Desolation of Smaug. Former enemies, united by a new peace treaty, standing together against an evil ideology of endless "extractivism"—an ideology with seemingly limitless power to corrupt, but one which needs to be confronted, as peacefully, resiliently, and implacably as possible. Of course, surprising no one, the newly minted president Donald Trump wasted no time overturning his predecessor's executive order, issuing his own order to reactivate both the Dakota Access Pipeline project and the Keystone XL Project that had so inspired entrenched global resistance for so long. Trump's executive decree his first week in office in January 2017 was a dark day for the environmentalist movement and for believers in Native American rights. It was a dark day that everyone knew was coming. On September 10, 2016, Harjo posted a spiritual mission statement for all protectors of the Earth that beautifully sums up the main argument of this monograph: it doesn't matter what our religion is, our politics, our gender, our nationality, or our race, class, or ethnicity. Using terminology that has appeared throughout this book in Catholic, Protestant, Jewish, Muslim, and ecofeminist contexts, this Native American artist expresses that we should all be stewards of the Earth instead of viewing the Earth as being in our dominion. Appropriately, Harjo ends her mission statement using the Mvskoke word for "love":

The original peoples of the Americas are the caretakers of these lands, just as the original peoples of Africa, Europe, Asia . . . all lands, are charged with taking care of their earthly homes. This does not mean caretakers have

Fig. 10.11. In this evocative poster for *The Hobbit: The Battle of Five Armies* (2014), Bard of Laketown (Luke Evans) stands alone against the dragon Smaug. Tolkien imagery has been evoked by many environmental activists and indigenous peoples in their struggles against the fossil fuel industry, corporate greed, runaway pollution, and climate change. Still, one of the lessons of the Standing Rock Protests is that the peoples of the world should not look to a solitary hero, such as Bard, to stand between them and the desolation of Smaug—the personification of Greed, Death, and Destruction. Instead, we should all stand together before Smaug, and face the threat side by side, in solidarity. Warner Bros.

dominion. It means we act humbly and respectfully as we move about and share in what is given to us for sustenance. We do not take more than we need. We do not destroy to steal. We do not neglect. Nor do we proudly claim ownership. We are here as stewards. We share. Our words and actions lift each other up. Even the land and all beings of the land share in personhood. We are essentially one person. As original caretakers, it is our responsibility to stand up when the actions of others endanger life for all of us in our earthly place. The stand of the original peoples of the Americas has been predicted by those who see and know things. We have no other choice. Everyone will come home. We are always headed in that direction, no matter where we are in our journeys. In the place of home we remember these things. We remember *vnokeckv*.[23]

# 11

# What Next?

## Robert Crumb's "A Short History of America" and Ending the Game of Thrones

Do not be daunted by the enormity of the world's grief. Do justly now. Love mercy now. Walk humbly now. You are not obligated to complete the work, but neither are you free to abandon it.

—The Talmud

### How Will It All End?

Robert Crumb, underground comix innovator and creator of *Fritz the Cat*, is a frequent, savage satirist of contemporary culture, and environmentalist themes permeate his body of work. One of his most famous comic strips, "A Short History of America," first appeared in 1979 in the *Co-Evolutionary Quarterly* ecological magazine. It is a drawn, "time-lapsed" series of snapshots of the same strip of unspoiled native land, which grows more and more industrialized and polluted with each panel, culminating in the "progress" of a typical twentieth-century American urban scene. In 1988, Crumb returned to the strip and drew an epilogue entitled "What Next?" comprised of three horizontal panels depicting that same stretch of land in three alternative possible futures. Crumb's first prophetic scene is labeled "Worst case scenario: ecological disaster." It depicts a sun burning hotter than ever, baking the ground to a crisp, with no sign of human life occupying a decrepit, collapsing main street intersection. The second projected future is called, "The FUN Future: Techno Fix on the March," and is reminiscent of the predictions Michio Kaku makes in *Physics of the Future* (2011), in which the miraculous discovery of fusion technology grants us a world of flying cars and motorcycles and the ability to use high-tech magic wands to clean up the world and make society something akin to *The Jetsons* or *Star Trek*. In the third scenario, "The Ecotopian Solution," humans live in a small-town environment with homes built in and around a forest scene, something of a cross between the Ewok tree houses on the forest world of Endor in *Return of the Jedi* and life in *Little House on the Prairie*, where people walk or ride bikes rather than drive and where the slowed pace of life makes it possible to enjoy living and being one with nature. The tone of a given work by Crumb is notoriously difficult to pin down, but one gets the feeling that he not only prefers the final panel, but believes it is the only way we really can proceed from here. His three projected futures are three possible next chapters in the future of human civilization and a prophecy outlining the rest of the twenty-first century. It is a very useful, moral, and instructive cartoon from a controversial and important figure in the history of comic books.

Robert Crumb's concerns about the fate of humanity and the fate of nature reflect the concerns of other artists and storytellers whose views are explored in this book. The works of mythmakers C. S. Lewis, J. R. R. Tolkien, Margaret Atwood, George R. R. Martin, Suzanne Collins, Octavia Butler, Philip Pullman, and the nonfiction authors Naomi Klein and Chris Hedges, among others, give us passionate, political, spiritual, and humanistic calls to action on climate change. Some of these figures are Christian. Some are atheist. Some are agnostic. Among the ecological storytellers are those who are American, Canadian, British, Australian, and Korean. Some advocate violent action in defense of the environment. Some argue that nonviolent civil disobedience is always the best way to bring about change. Some see capitalism as a tool to help fight pollution. Others see capitalism as the chief cause of pollution. All these perspectives are valuable to contemplate. The issue of climate change is depressing and difficult to understand. The science is hard for Americans who lack a solid educational foundation in the sciences to grasp. It is also difficult to gauge how the planet is faring and how the effort to go green globally is going when most sources of news are replete with corporate propaganda and are wholly unreliable for much beyond sports scores. Also, Donald Trump has worked overtime to prevent new, accurate scientific studies from reaching the American people and has muzzled NASA and the EPA. In this absurd contemporary culture, learning about climate change from *Lord of the Rings* or *Snowpiercer* is arguably better than learning about climate change from an EPA run by corporate shill Scott Pruitt.

The global social, economic, and environmental crisis we face has had one notable consequence: the rise of nationalism and the resurgence of far right-wing ideologies throughout Europe and the United States. As resources dwindle, racial purity movements have emerged demanding that their people get their share of the remaining resources first. Little to no sympathy is shown to refugees of military and ecological conflicts, and these and other marginalized figures are demonized as less than human or branded as leeches and potential terrorists. In this political context, it is more important than ever to remember that C. S. Lewis, a writer respected by readers from a broad variety of political and religious backgrounds, had nothing but condemnation for racist and ultranationalist sentiment.

Let us assume that we, as readers, are inclined to look to authors of climate fiction such as Lewis and Tolkien for a better model for real-world action than the one that world leaders such as Donald Trump provide. What practical advice for confronting climate change can be gleaned from works as fantastical as those found in the climate fiction genre?

Climate fiction is designed to address the most pressing issues of our time. Some narratives are more like *Star Wars* in their conception, depicting an apocalyptic war between green forces and industrialized forces, and hoping for a peaceful aftermath and a greener future after victory is achieved (*Snowpiercer*, *Princess Mononoke*, *Mad Max: Fury Road*). There are other, more pacifistic cli-fi narratives, and they are rarer. Some of the closest examples of these works are by ecofeminist science fiction and fantasy writers, including Margaret Atwood's *MaddAddam*, Octavia Butler's *Parable of the Sower*, and C. S. Lewis's *Space Trilogy*. All these texts help readers wrestle with Robert Crumb's vitally important question: Is humanity destined for self-destruction, or can we imagine a better future? Can these narratives push us more toward one fate than another? Which ones should we take the most to heart?

Tolkien certainly felt that there were moral and immoral narratives, and it was up to us to tell the correct stories. He wrote:

> Fantasy can, of course, be carried to excess. It can be ill done. It can be put to evil uses. It may even delude the minds out of which it came. But of what human thing in this fallen world is that not true? Men have conceived not only of elves, but they have imagined gods, and worshipped them, even worshipped those most deformed by their authors' own evil. But they have made false gods out of other materials: their notions, their banners, their monies; even their sciences and their social and economic theories have demanded human sacrifice. *Abusus non tollit usum*. [Abuse does not cancel use.] Fantasy remains a human right: we make in our measure and in our derivative mode, because we are made: and not only made, but made in the image and likeness of a Maker.[1]

We are all potential storytellers and we are all engaged in the collective writing of the story of human history.

As of the writing of this monograph, fans of George R. R. Martin's *A Song of Ice and Fire* remain in suspense over what possible ending he might write for his epic narrative. Meanwhile, humanity waits in suspense to determine just how rapidly the climate crisis will escalate, how grave the threat it poses is—not just to humanity but to all life on Earth—and to what degree humans can do anything to slow or halt, if not reverse, the calamitous global consequences of industrialization. It is beyond the scope of this book to speculate on any of these matters, and it is inappropriate to strike too hopeful or too dire a note in these closing passages, which will carry enormous narrative weight coming, as they do, at the end of this book.

We do not know how long human civilization has left. We do not have full control over what humanity, as a species, will or will not rise to do to meet the gravest challenge of the twenty-first century. We do, however, have some sense of how many years remain of our own lives. We do boast a measure of control over what kinds of lives we live. We have some say in what ethical codes we choose to embrace: what kind of family members we are, what kind of friends we are, and how we behave in our respective occupations. We can take some control over our own actions as members of our respective civic communities, faith communities, and even as members of one global community. We should also acknowledge that most of us can do better than we have been doing. However kind we may be already and however activist we may be already, we can all do better to at least some degree. We can be better citizens, better stewards of nature, and better human beings.

Mere hours before he was shot and killed, John Lennon offered a final interview in which he expressed reservations about the popularity of *Star Wars* and the lessons that it taught the young about the inevitability of warfare. Whether it took place "a long time ago" was not relevant to his overall point, which was that combat-centric science fiction and fantasy prodded Americans to content themselves with imagining futures for humanity that were as dark and combat-filled as our present. He explained to a perceived skeptical audience that what he and Yoko Ono were striving to do with their antiwar activism, performance art, and idealistic song lyrics was to

project . . . the future in a positive way. And people said, "You're naive, you're dumb, you're stupid." It might've hurt us on a personal level to be called names, but what we were doin'—you can call it magic, meditation, projection of goal—which business people do, they have courses on it. The footballers do it. They pray, they meditate before the game. They visualize themselves winning. Billie Jean King visualizes [in advance] every move . . . on the court. . . . People project their own future. So, what we wanted to do was say, "Let's imagine a nice future."

[Yoko's] right, the males like even Aldous Huxley and George Orwell who produced *1984* . . . even now—I think these people that project these space fantasies are projecting war in space continually, with women in mini-skirts, available sexual objects, men with super-macho John Wayne guns on their hips. I'm sayin' it's time for the people to get hip to that, man. Because they're projecting our future.

Do we want to go . . . our children to be out in space, or our grandchildren fighting—maybe not Russians—but Venusians in space? You see? If it works for a football player and a tennis player it can work for all of us. We have to project a positive future.

I mean I think that's what Christ and Mohammed and those people were saying in their way in their time for their society.[2]

The above quote is somewhat free-form because it is from an interview and spoken extemporaneously. Nevertheless, climate fiction is designed to address the very issues that John Lennon discusses.

Similarly, in composing a new preface for the fortieth anniversary of her utopian feminist novel *Woman on the Edge of Time* (1976), Marge Piercy explained that she wrote the book during "the heyday of the second wave of the women's movement" as part of a "desire to imagine a better society when we dared to do so." In the years since, the Reagan Revolution and its seemingly endless legacy of right-wing rule has brought setback after setback for the causes of economic and social justice, making the possibility of even imagining a feminist utopia, let alone fighting for one and creating one seem more and more remote. As Piercy explains, "When our political energy goes into defending rights, and projects we won and created are now under attack, there is far less energy for imagining fully drawn future societies we might wish to live in." Nevertheless, Piercy maintains that the feminist utopian enterprise remains a critical one in the battle for the future of American society. The stories we tell ourselves, fiction and nonfiction, help shape our collective values, understand our past, and plan for our future. Like Octavia Butler—and other ecofeminist authors such as Le Guin—Piercy found herself impatient with histories and fictions that lionized powerful white men and left women out of the narrative altogether. Like Butler, like LeGuin, Piercy has worked to change the narrative and write herself, and women, and figures from a diverse range of backgrounds, into central roles in the story. As she explains, "We need a past that leads to us. Similarly, what we imagine we are working toward does a lot to define what we will consider doable action aimed at producing the future we want and preventing the future we fear."

This monograph began with the observation by Gus Speth that the biggest problem facing the world is not a lack of scientific knowledge, but a lack of any form of ethical sense. As Speth has observed, "The top environmental problems are selfishness, greed, and apathy, and to deal with those we need a spiritual and cultural transformation." A spiritual and cultural transformation begins with at least one individual making the decision to transform on a personal level. What follows then is the hope that many more will, of their own accord, make the same or similar decision. We cannot control how others act, but we can choose how *we* will act and transform our own relationship to Nature and to other people. We can decide to imitate the kinds of ethically and spiritually transformative behaviors of the real-life Joy Harjo and the fictional Jon Snow: we can join forces with members of other cultures and faith communities—even those we have previously experienced religious, cultural, racial, and political tensions with—to stem the efforts of big polluters to hasten the degradation of our ecosystem. We can—either like Katniss Everdeen in the epilogue to *Mockingjay* or like the faith community of St. Anne's in *That Hideous Strength*—choose to live sustainable lives off the grid and let the vast political and military fights going on in the world play out without our participation. In that configuration, our goal would be to "do no harm," first and foremost. Such a course of action may not directly result in the overthrow of any Ur-Fascist dictators or determine the outcome of any critically important battle in a grand ecological war. Nevertheless, the decision to merely not participate in the active destruction of the planet made by enough individuals has the potential to do much good for the world. These are just some ideological positions we might embrace and some actions we might take, when many more are possible.

Alternatively, a broad variety of actor-network theory texts—which are especially prominent in the fields of sociology and rhetoric—might provide roadmaps for concerned citizens and activists to follow. The writings of Bruno Latour and Deleuze and Guattari may be particularly salient here, as well as the work of Dipesh Chakrabarty and additional scholarship on intersectionality and assemblage theory. There are many possible paths that we may follow, each according to our own particular gifts, cultural values, Myers-Briggs/Buzzfeed/Big-Five personality types, and central causes for concern.

All of us can choose to immerse ourselves in environmental activist texts such as those explored in this volume, and look to them for models of more ethical behaviors than the kind we have enacted in our lives thus far. As Elizabeth Ammons writes, "Liberal activist texts have transformative power. They play a profound role in the fight for human justice and planetary healing that so many of us recognize as the urgent struggle of our time. Words on the page more than reach our minds. They call up our feelings. They call out our spirits. They move us to act."

The works of climate fiction examined in these pages are not necessarily perfect works of art. They are not always free of unfortunate ideological sentiments, problematic racial or gender stereotypes, or even the glorification of violence and warfare. Problematic as they may be, these books, and their authors, raise important questions about whether we want to respond to the challenges of our time with anger, ultranationalism, and militarism or whether we want to embrace ethical stewardship of the planet and try to find common ground with different cultures and religions (and even political enemies) to put an end to unnecessary wars and the exploitation of women and ethnic minorities. These books suggest that we need to take serious steps toward creating a more humane society in a vitally important effort to do better to help make life worth living for ourselves, our families, our friends, and even our enemies, for however much time we all have left in our lives. The alternatives to this kind of utopian thinking are terrifyingly dystopian: we can, on an individual level, choose to take part in the march toward global totalitarianism, apartheid, endless war, and extinction. That drummer is always there to march to and those forces are always looking for recruits. That side tends to pay better as well, and often provides excellent dental benefits and retirement plans. Nevertheless, we cannot make decisions that will lead us toward dystopia when we can, instead, make conscious decisions that will lead us away from a dystopian society.

We live in stressful times and none of us are as politically and economically powerful as we would like to be, but we can do what we can, where we can, to try to help. Like the Hobbits, we are only very little people, but we can try, and perhaps we can do more than we think we can to make the world a better place, as Bilbo and

Frodo and Sam did. Even if we are, on some level, doomed to failure in this idealistic enterprise, we must at least try. It is our duty to do so. However daunting that enterprise may sound, we need to undertake it on behalf of ourselves, our families, our friends, and our enemies.

And here I would like to end in the very same way I ended chapter 1: with a reminder of the very apt words of J. R. R. Tolkien. At the beginning of *The Fellowship of the Ring*, Gandalf tells Frodo of the grave times they are living in and explains the necessity of the Hobbits coming out of their protected, provincial bubble to face up to the challenges that lie ahead, for the sake of all the peoples of the world. The news of this crisis is devastating to Frodo. He doesn't want any part of this conflict, though he understands what he needs to do.

"I wish it need not have happened in my lifetime," says Frodo.

"So do I," said Gandalf, "and so do all who live to see such times. But that is not for them to decide. All we have to decide is what to do with the time that is given us."[3]

# Epilogue

## Who Owns the Legacy of J. R. R. Tolkien?

There are two novels that can change a bookish fourteen-year old's life: *The Lord of the Rings* and *Atlas Shrugged*. One is a childish fantasy that often engenders a lifelong obsession with its unbelievable heroes, leading to an emotionally stunted, socially crippled adulthood, unable to deal with the real world. The other, of course, involves Orcs.

—John Rogers

In 1965, a bootlegged, mass market edition of *Lord of the Rings* found widespread popularity within the United States, especially on college campuses, among comic book geeks, antiwar activists, and environmentalists. The book was a worldwide phenomenon for the first time, ten years after its initial release as a modestly successful, prestige format publication with a high cover price demanded by its length. Incredibly, the same young activist reading audience that had embraced Holden Caulfield and LSD had flocked to an epic narrative penned by a gentle, Roman Catholic, British academic. Tom Shippey commented upon this ironic state of affairs, and explicated the potential reasons for Tolkien's popularity among the young Left: "Perhaps one could say he offered a 'mellow' kind of heroism, which he was convinced was also old, familiar, and natural. And also, the students of the 1960s were perfectly well able to see that through the metaphor, Tolkien was writing about real life: the connection to Vietnam and the military-industrial complex (Mordor and Saruman) was obvious—though not intended."[1]

Tolkien himself was confused and bemused by experiencing for the first time the extreme notoriety he had been so envious of Lewis achieving as far back as 1947. Tolkien observed: "Being a cult figure in one's own lifetime I am afraid is not at all pleasant. However, I do not find that it tends to puff one up; in my case at any rate it makes me feel extremely small and inadequate. But even the nose of a very modest idol cannot remain untickled by the sweet smell of incense."[2]

Tolkien's newfound fame brought flocks of counterculture fans to his front door, eager to make a pilgrimage to his humble suburban home, whether or not he and Edith were eager to entertain the steady stream of disciples. Some, like his future biographer, Humphrey Carpenter, met an embarrassed and awkward Tolkien in his makeshift Middle-earth library, located in his home's repurposed garage. In the early years of his writing, Tolkien had had to contend with the fan devotion of C. S. Lewis, who had been inspired by the Middle-earth writing to try his own hand at works in a similar vein. Tolkien had not responded well to the derivative result. Then Tolkien had to contend with numerous offers to adapt his works into films and radio programs, plays and board games. He was often distressed by the plans presented to him, feeling that they failed to reflect the true core of his life's work. It is also clear that he was not enthralled by the quality of the journalistic and literary assessments of his work, or some of the alarmingly pro-war sentiments of some of the American fans who liked *Lord of the Rings* principally for its battle scenes. Tolkien's rejection of most of these "uses" of his works—and sometimes misguided or plagiaristic "tributes" to them—might make him seem overly negative, but he always had a good reason to be troubled by efforts to appropriate and rewrite his words and change them into something different than he intended.

Since his death, legions of fan, pulp, and literary writers have appeared to write new genre works in imitation of *Lord of the Rings*. Stephen King's *The Dark Tower* series is one of the more popular works written in overt tribute to Tolkien. The underrated television series *Babylon 5* (1993–98) is at once a faithful science fiction remake of *Lord of the Rings* and creator J. Michael Straczynski's deeply personal antifascist manifesto. Among the writers who have clearly followed in Tolkien's footsteps are those who have taken the trappings and tropes of Tolkien's genre fiction, but have (consciously or unconsciously) not mirrored Tolkien's writing style, religious sentiment, critique of mechanized warfare, or environmentalist values. Some writers, such as Suzanne Collins, have penned works sufficiently in the spirit of Tolkien that one could conceivably imagine him approving of their efforts. More often, however, one might well imagine Tolkien being appalled by the Peter Jackson film adaptations of his novels (as film critic Roger Ebert suggested he would have been, had he seen them), or by the profane, ultraviolent, and rape-saturated *Game of Thrones* television show. The depiction of Earthseed in Octavia Butler's apocalyptic works would have troubled him, as would many of the sentiments and incidents depicted by Margaret Atwood in her novels. Of course, Tolkien should not be taken as the final arbiter of literary quality, and the works that he himself would not have liked that I have discussed in these pages should be judged on their own terms. Indeed, I would argue that the ecofeminist genre writers examined in this book are the true inheritors of the "spirit" of Tolkien, and of his efforts to portray a world in which Nature is re-sacramentalized and the values of Eden are brought back into the corrupt present to redeem it. Meanwhile, those authors who imitate the "letter" of Tolkien—the R. A. Salvatores of the world—write multibook narratives with elves and dragons and plot points taken from *Lord of the Rings*, but don't craft a story that has Tolkien's values, intellect, or soul.

However, the question remains: Of all of Tolkien's fans and imitators, which ones would he most approve of? Who owns the legacy of J. R. R. Tolkien? Fans as diverse as C. S. Lewis, Gary Gygax, Peter Jackson, and Steve Bannon have all staked claim to be legitimate participants in Tolkien's literary and ideological mission and inheritors of Tolkien's legacy. To one degree or another, all these claims may be considered problematic. In his lifetime, however, Tolkien offered a clue as to what kind of reader he most valued: it was the reader who best appreciated his environmental vision, and who pledged to join the Hobbits in their opposition of industrial pollution, endless warfare, and the relentless felling of trees.

Before becoming a full-blown counterculture cult hero, Tolkien still enjoyed enough international fame to be invited to a "Hobbit Dinner" hosted by Het Spectrum, his Dutch publisher, and the bookseller Voorhoeve & Dietrich on March 28, 1958. The dinner took place at the Twaalf Provinciën Huis assembly hall, where Tolkien made a speech in playful imitation of Bilbo Baggins's mischievous birthday oration. His final statement was a toast to all his environmentalist readers, who he hoped to see rising to challenge the legions of real-world polluters who despoiled our Earth as relentlessly as Saruman polluted Middle-earth. He said, "[I]t is now exactly twenty years since I began in earnest to complete the history of our renowned hobbit-ancestors of the Third Age. I look East, West, North, South, and I do not see Sauron; but I see that Saruman has many descendants. We Hobbits have against them no magic weapons. Yet, my gentlehobbits, I give you this toast: To the Hobbits. May they outlast the Sarumans and see spring again in the trees."[3]

That, indeed, is a toast worth drinking.

# Notes

## Introduction

1. Ullrich, J. K. "Climate Fiction: Can Books Save the Planet?" *The Atlantic*, August 14, 2015. Accessed August 14, 2015. http://www.theatlantic.com/entertainment/archive/2015/08/climate-fiction-margaret-atwood-literature/400112/.

2. Gerry Canavan and Kim Stanley Robinson, eds., *Green Planets: Ecology and Science Fiction* (Middletown, CT: Wesleyan University Press, 2014); Chris Baratta, *Environmentalism in the Realm of Science Fiction and Fantasy Literature* (Cambridge: Cambridge Scholars Publishing, 2012); Elizabeth K. Rosen, *Apocalyptic Transformation: Apocalypse and the Postmodern Imagination* (New York: Lexington Books, 2008); Adam Trexler, *Anthropocene Fictions: The Novel in a Time of Climate Change* (Charlottesville: University of Virginia Press, 2015).

3. Ed Finn, "An Interview With Margaret Atwood," *Slate*, February 6, 2015. Accessed December 2, 2015. http://www.slate.com/articles/technology/future_tense/2015/02/margaret_atwood_interview_the_author_speaks_on_hope_science_and_the_future.html.

4. Rio Fernandes, "The Subfield That Is Changing the Landscape of Literary Studies," *The Chronicle of Higher Education*, March 21, 2016. Accessed April 6, 2016. http://chronicle.com/article/The-Subfield-That-Is-Changing/235776?cid=rc_right.

5. Ibid.

6. Ibid.

7. Ammons, 103–104.

8. Alister McGrath, *C. S. Lewis—A Life: Eccentric Genius, Reluctant Prophet* (Colorado Springs: Tyndale House, 2013), 376.

9. Farah Mendlesohn, "Thematic Criticism," in *The Cambridge Companion to Fantasy Literature* (Cambridge: Cambridge University Press, 2012), 125–26.

10. Ibid.

11. Ibid., 132.

12. Cheryll Glotfelty, "Literary Studies in an Age of Environmental Crisis," in *The Ecocriticism Reader: Landmarks in Literary Ecology*, ed. Cheryll Glotfelty and Harold Fromm (Athens and London: The University of Georgia Press, 1996), xviii.

13. Ibid., xxii.

14. Ibid., xxi–xxii.

15. Finn, "An Interview with Margaret Atwood."

16. Octavia E. Butler, *Parable of the Sower* (New York, Boston: Grand Central Publishing, 1993), 337–38.

17. Andrew Simms, "Philip Pullman: New Brand of Environmentalism," *The Telegraph*, January 19, 2008. Accessed July 9, 2015. http://www.telegraph.co.uk/news/earth/3322329/Philip-Pullman-new-brand-of-environmentalism.html.

18. Ibid.

19. C. S. Hughes, "George R. R. Martin: On the End of Thrones," *Nerdalicious*, Dec. 13, 2013. Accessed October 16, 2015. http://nerdalicious.com.au/books/george-r-r-martin-on-the-end-of-thrones/.

20. David Shuster, "George R.R. Martin talks to David Shuster," *Al-Jazeera America*, November 13, 2014. Accessed November 17, 2015. http://america.aljazeera.com/watch/shows/talk-to-al-jazeera/articles/2014/11/13/george-rr-martintalkstodavidshuster.html.

21. Bethan Forrest, "Cli-Fi; Climate Change Fiction as Literature's New Frontier?" *Huffington Post*, July 23, 2015. Accessed October 11, 2015. http://www.huffingtonpost.co.uk/bethan-forrest/climate-change-fiction_b_7847182.html.

22. *The Golden Compass*, written and directed by Chris Weitz. DVD. New Line Home Video, 2008.

23. Sam Rigby, "Peter Capaldi, David Tennant and Maisie Williams want to Save the Arctic with Greenpeace," *Digital Spy*, July 14, 2015. Accessed October 16, 2015. http://www.digitalspy.com/celebrity/news/a658261/peter-capaldi-david-tennant-and-maisie-williams-want-to-save-the-arctic-with-greenpeace.html#ixzz3orQViFDG.

24. Ibid.

25. J. K. Ullrich, "Climate Fiction: Can Books Save the Planet?" *The Atlantic*, August 14, 2015. Accessed August 14, 2015. http://www.theatlantic.com/entertainment/archive/2015/08/climate-fiction-margaret-atwood-literature/400112/.

26. Ursula K. Le Guin, "Introduction," in *The Left Hand of Darkness* (New York: Ace Books, 2003).

27. Ullrich, "Climate Fiction."

28. Ellen Briana Szabo, *Saving the World One Word at a Time: Writing Cli-Fi* (Charleston: CreateSpace, 2015).

29. J. R. R. Tolkien, "Foreword to the Second Edition," in *The Lord of the Rings: 50th Anniversary One-Volume Edition* (Boston and New York: Houghton Mifflin, 2004), xxiv.

## Chapter 1. *Star Wars*, Hollywood Blockbusters, and the Cultural Appropriation of J. R. R. Tolkien

1. Doug Williams, "Not So Long Ago and Far Away: *Star Wars*, Republics, and Empires of Tomorrow," in *The Science Fiction Film Reader*, ed. Gregg Rickman (Milwaukee: Limelight, 2004), 229–54.

2. Kate Aronoff, "*Rogue One* May Be the Most Leftist Star Wars Film Yet," *In These Times*, December 16, 2016. Accessed March 1, 2017. http://inthesetimes.com/article/19744/the-rogue-one-may-be-the-most-leftist-star-wars-film-yet.

3. Williams, "Not So Long Ago."

4. Joseph Campbell and Bill Moyers, *The Power of Myth* (New York: Doubleday, 1988), 146–47.

5. Ibid.

6. Paul Hiebert, "Are All Movie Heroes the Same Person?" *P-S. Pacific Standard*, June 20, 2014. Accessed June 14, 2015. http://www.psmag.com/books-and-culture/movie-heroes-person-joseph-campbell-monomyth-83796; Ryan O'Hanlon, "Formula for a Hollywood blockbuster," Salon, May 7, 2013. Accessed June 14, 2015. http://www.salon.com/2013/05/07/formula_for_a_hollywood_blockbuster_partner/; Blake Snyder, *Save the Cat!: The Last Book on Screenwriting You'll Ever Need* (Studio City, CA: Michael Wiese Productions, 2005); Peter Suderman, "Save the Movie!" *Slate*, July 19, 2013. Accessed June 14, 2015. http://www.slate.com/articles/arts/culturebox/2013/07/hollywood_and_blake_snyder_s_screenwriting_book_save_the_cat.single.html.

7. Joseph Campbell, *The Hero with a Thousand Faces* (Princeton: Princeton University Press, 1972), 193.

8. Marina Warner, "Boys will be Boys: The Making of the Male," *The Independent*, February 2, 1994. Accessed: April 20, 2016. http://www.independent.co.uk/life-style/the-reith-lectures-1994-boys-will-be-boys-the-making-of-the-male-marina-warner-in-the-second-lecture-1391550.html.

9. Gina Salamone, "James Cameron on 'Avatar': Fox wanted me to take out 'tree-hugging,' 'FernGully crap,' " *New York Daily News*, February 18, 2010. Accessed September 19, 2015. http://www.nydailynews.com/entertainment/tv-movies/james-cameron-avatar-fox-wanted-tree-hugging-ferngully-crap-article-1.171225.

10. Theodor W. Adorno, "The Schema of Mass Culture. The Culture Industry," ed. J. M. Berstein (New York: Routledge, 2001), 67.

11. Max Horkheimer and Theodor W. Adorno, "The Culture Industry: Enlightenment as Mass Deception," in *Dialectic of Enlightenment: Philosophical Fragments*, ed. Gunzelin Schmid Noerr, trans. Edmund Jephcott (Stanford: Stanford University Press, 2002), 106.

12. Ian Adams, *Ideology and Politics in Britain Today* (Manchester: Manchester University Press, 1999), 328.

13. J. R. R. Tolkien, *The Letters of J. R. R. Tolkien*, 270.

14. Tom Shippey, "Another Road to Middle-earth: Jackson's Movie Trilogy," in *Understanding* The Lord of the Rings*: The Best of Tolkien Criticism*, ed. Rose A. Zimbardo and Neil D. Isaacs (Boston and New York: Houghton Mifflin, 2004), 236–37.

15. "J. R. R. Tolkien: The Mind of a Genius: Special *Newsweek* Edition," *Newsweek*, April 22, 2017, 86.

16. Ibid., 88.

17. J. R. R. Tolkien, *The Hobbit, or There and Back Again* (Boston and New York: Houghton Mifflin, 1997), 134–36.

18. From a digital transcription of the original text found online at http://www.ae-lib.org.ua/texts-c/tolkien__the_silmarillion__en.htm.

19. Tim Robey, "Viggo Mortensen Interview: Peter Jackson Sacrificed Subtlety for CGI," *The Telegraph*, May 14, 2014. Accessed December 14, 2015. http://www.telegraph.co.uk/culture/film/10826867/Viggo-Mortensen-interview-Peter-Jackson-sacrificed-subtlety-for-CGI.html.

20. Tolkien, *The Lord of the Rings: 50$^{th}$ Anniversary One-Volume Edition*, 679.

21. Ibid., 681.

22. Loren Wilkinson, "Tolkien and the Surrendering of Power," in *Tree of Tales: Tolkien, Literature, and Theology* (Waco, TX: Baylor University Press, 2007), 80, 83.

23. Matthew Dickerson and Jonathan Evans. *Ents, Elves, and Eriador: The Environmental Vision of J. R. R. Tolkien* (Lexington: The University Press of Kentucky, 2006), 260.

24. Kristen M. Burkholder, "Dreaming of Eggs and Bacon, Seedcakes and Scones," in *The Hobbit and History*, ed. Janice Liedl and Nancy R. Reagin (New York: Wiley, 2014), 86–87.

25. Hugh T. Keenan, "The Appeal of *The Lord of the Rings*: The Struggle for Life," in *Tolkien and the Critics: Essays on J. R. R. Tolkien's The Lord of the Rings* (Notre Dame: University of Notre Dame Press, 1968), 66–67.

26. Ibid., 75.

27. Ibid., 68–70.

28. Ibid.

29. C. S. Lewis, "The Dethronement of Power," in *Understanding* The Lord of the Rings: *The Best of Tolkien Criticism*, ed. Rose A. Zimbardo and Neil D. Isaacs (Boston and New York: Houghton Mifflin, 2004), 12.

30. Dickerson and Evans, *Ents, Elves, and Eriador*, 282.

31. Tolkien, *The Letters of J. R. R. Tolkien*, 37.

32. Ibid.

33. Christine Chism, "Middle-earth, the Middle Ages, and the Aryan Nation: Myth and History in World War II," in *Tolkien the Medievalist*, ed. Jane Chance (London: Routledge, 2003), 63.

34. Anderson Rearick III, "Why Is the Only Good Orc a Dead Orc? The Dark Face of Racism Examined in Tolkien," *Modern Fiction Studies* 50 (Winter 2004): 4.

35. Kristen Whissel, *Spectacular Digital Effects: CGI and Contemporary Cinema* (Durham: Duke University Press, 2014), 70.

36. Ibid., 68.

37. Ibid., 81–82.

38. Timothy Morton, *Ecology Without Nature: Rethinking Environmental Aesthetics* (Cambridge: Harvard University Press, 2007), 97–98.

39. John Elder, "Foreword," in *Ents, Elves, and Eriador: The Environmental Vision of J. R. R. Tolkien*, ed. Matthew Dickerson and Jonathan Evans (Lexington: The University Press of Kentucky, 2006), x–xi.

40. Tolkien, *The Lord of the Rings: 50th Anniversary One-Volume Edition*, 741–42.

41. Dickerson and Evans, 240–41.

42. Tolkien, *The Lord of the Rings: 50th Anniversary One-Volume Edition*, 60.

## Chapter 2. Of Treebeard, C. S. Lewis, and the Aesthetics of Christian Environmentalism

1. Anne C. Petty, *Tolkien in the Land of Heroes* (New York: Cold Spring Press, 2003), 219–20.

2. Ibid.

3. Humphrey Carpenter, *J. R. R. Tolkien: A Biography* (Boston and New York: Houghton Mifflin, 1977), 40.

4. Ibid., 30.

5. Daniel Helen, "Tolkien's Favourite Tree to Be Cut Down," *The Tolkien Society*, July 30, 2014. Accessed September 29, 2015. http://www.tolkiensociety.org/2014/07/tolkiens-favourite-tree-to-be-cut-down/.

6. C. S. Lewis, "The Dethronement of Power," in *Understanding* The Lord of the Rings: *The Best of Tolkien Criticism*, ed. Rose A. Zimbardo and Neil D. Isaacs (Boston and New York: Houghton Mifflin, 2004).

7. Carpenter, *J. R. R. Tolkien: A Biography*, 198.

8. David C. Downing, *Planets in Peril: A Critical Study of C. S. Lewis' Ransom Trilogy* (Amherst: The University of Massachusetts Press, 1992), 127.

9. James Waterman Wise Jr., "Fascism in America," *The Christian Century* 53 (February 5, 1936) (Chicago: Christian Century Foundation): 245.

10. C. S. Lewis, *The Chronicles of Narnia (with illustrations by Pauline Baynes)* (New York: HarperOne, 2005), 677.

11. Hugh T. Keenan, "The Appeal of *The Lord of the Rings*: The Struggle for Life," in *Tolkien and the Critics: Essays on J. R. R. Tolkien's The Lord of the Rings* (Notre Dame: University of Notre Dame Press, 1968), 65.

12. C. S. Lewis, "That Hideous Strength," in *The Space Trilogy: Out of the Silent Planet, Perelandra*, and *That Hideous Strength* (New York: HarperOne, 2013), 139–40.

13. Ibid., 412.

14. Downing, *Planets in Peril*, 53–54.

15. Kathleen Norris, "Preface," in *Mere Christianity* (New York: HarperOne, 2000), xvii–xix.

16. Lewis, "That Hideous Strength," 427.

17. Henry A. Giroux, *University in Chains: Confronting the Military-Industrial-Academic Complex* (London: Routledge, 2007); Colleen Flaherty, "Prioritization Anxiety," *The Chronicle of Higher Education*, August 16, 2016. Accessed September 5, 2016.

18. McGrath, *C. S. Lewis—A Life*, 376.

19. Matthew Schmitz, "Ayn Rand Really, Really Hated C. S. Lewis," *First Things*, March 27, 2013. Accessed October 6, 2015. http://www.firstthings.com/blogs/firstthoughts/2013/03/ayn-rand-really-really-hated-c-s-lewis.

20. Lewis, "That Hideous Strength," 436–37.

21. Tolkien, *The Lord of the Rings: 50th Anniversary One-Volume Edition*, xxiv.

22. Roland Barthes, "The Death of the Author," in *Image-Music-Text* (New York: Hill and Wang, 1978).

23. Tolkien, *The Letters of J. R. R. Tolkien*, 121.

24. See Salwa Khoddam, "The Book of Revelation, Ragnarök, and the Narnian Apocalypse in C. S. Lewis' *The Last Battle*," in *C. S. Lewis and the Inklings: Discovering Hidden Truth*, ed. Salwa Khoddam, Mark R. Hall, Jason Fisher (Newcastle: Cambridge Scholars Press, 2012); and Marjorie Burns, *Perilous Realms: Celtic and Norse in Tolkien's Middle-earth* (Toronto: University of Toronto Press, 2005).

25. Joseph Loconte, *A Hobbit, a Wardrobe, and a Great War: How J. R. R. Tolkien and C. S. Lewis Rediscovered Faith, Friendship, and Heroism in the Cataclysm of 1914–1918.* (Nashville: Thomas Nelson, 2015).

26. Ethan Gilsdorf, "J. R. R. Tolkien and C. S. Lewis: A Literary Friendship and Rivalry," *The Literary Traveler*, October 1, 2006. Accessed August 1, 2015. http://www.literarytraveler.com/articles/tolkien_lewis_england/.

27. Ibid.

28. Ibid.

29. "J. R. R. Tolkien: The Mind of a Genius: Special *Newsweek* Edition," *Newsweek*, April 22, 2017, 24.

30. McGrath, *C. S. Lewis—A Life*, 178–79.

31. Perry C. Bramlett, *I Am in Fact a Hobbit: An Introduction to the Life and Work of J. R. R. Tolkien* (Macon, GA: Mercer University Press, 2003), 80–81.

32. Colin Duriez, *The Oxford Inklings: Lewis, Tolkien, and Their Circle* (Oxford: Lion Hudson, 2015), 125.

33. Ibid., 152–53.

34. Ibid., 54.

35. Ibid., 18, 45.

36. Ibid., 113.

37. Ibid., 156.

38. Ibid., 130.

39. J. R. R. Tolkien, "The Notion Club Papers," in *Sauron Defeated. The End of the Third Age: The History of the Lord of the Rings—Part IV* (New York: Houghton Mifflin Harcourt, 1992), 249.

40. Bruce G. Charlton, "A Companion to J. R. R. Tolkien's Notion Club Papers," *Tolkien's* The Notion Club Papers, July 27, 2012. Accessed April 23, 2017. http://notionclub-papers.blogspot.com/2012/07/a-companion-to-jrr-tolkiens-notion-club.html.

41. Duriez, *The Oxford Inklings*, 217.

42. Sources referenced: William S. Baring-Gould, *Sherlock Holmes of Baker Street: A Life of the World's First Consulting Detective* (New York: Random House, 1995); Win Scott Eckert, "An Expansion of Philip José Farmer's Wold Newton Universe," *PJFarmer.com*, January 24, 2010. Accessed October 4, 2015. http://www.pjfarmer.com/woldnewton/Pulp.htm; Dwayne McDuffie, "Six Degrees of St. Elsewhere (aka The Grand Unification Theory)," Dwayne McDuffie (1962–2011), October 17, 2011. Accessed: October 4, 2015. http://dwaynemcduffie.com/?p=47; Alan Moore and Kevin O'Neill, *League of Extraordinary Gentlemen Omnibus* (New York: DC Comics, 2011); Kim Newman, *Anno Dracula* (London: Titan Books, 2011); Jon Preddle, *Timelink: The Unofficial and Unauthorised Guide to the Continuity of Doctor Who* (Prestatyn, Denbighshire: Telos, 2006).

43. Lewis, "That Hideous Strength," 345–46.

44. Ibid., 616–21.

45. Tolkien, "Letter #169," in *The Letters of J. R. R. Tolkien*, 224.

46. Diana Pavlac Glyer, *The Company They Keep: C. S. Lewis and J. R. R. Tolkien as Writers in Community* (Kent, OH: Kent State University Press, 2007), 98 n. 29.

47. J. R. R. Tolkien, *Sauron Defeated: The History of The Lord of the Rings, Part Four*, ed. Christopher Tolkien (New York: Houghton Mifflin, 1992), 153.

48. Alejandro Dávila Fragoso, "The Planet Is Going Through A 'Catastrophic' Wilderness Loss, Study Says," *Think Progress*, September 8, 2016. Accessed September 9, 2016. https://thinkprogress.org/most-wilderness-is-gone-thanks-to-humans-ad828409f4b6#.n1vlxbh7m.

49. Ibid.

50. Downing, *Planets in Peril*, 145.

51. Ibid., 144.

52. Matthew Dickerson and David O'Hara. *Narnia and the Fields of Arbol: The Environmental Vision of C. S. Lewis* (Lexington: University Press of Kentucky, 2008), 233.

## Chapter 3. The Time Lord, the Daleks, and the Wardrobe

1. Kim Newman, *Doctor Who: BFI TV Classics Series* (London: BFI, 2005), 3.

2. James Whitbrook, "This Quote from Peter Capaldi Totally Nails the Appeal of *Doctor Who*," *IO9*, November 22, 2016. Accessed February 3, 2017. http://io9.gizmodo.com/this-quote-from-peter-capaldi-totally-nails-the-appeal-1789281392.

3. John Tulloch and Manuel Alvarado, *Doctor Who: The Unfolding Text* (New York: St. Martin's, 1983), 8.

4. Ibid., 3.

5. See Dan Wilson, "Doctor Who and Sherlock Holmes: Are they Really 'Opposites'?" Metro.co.uk, Thursday 22 Aug 2013. Accessed October 20, 2015. http://metro.co.uk/2013/08/22/doctor-who-and-sherlock-holmes-are-they-really-opposites-3934458/#ixzz3oyRKlFpl.

6. George Garrett, O. B. Hardison, and Jane R. Gelfman, eds., *Film Scripts, Volume 4: A Hard Day's Night, The Best Man, Darling—Classic Screenplays* (New York: Applause Theatre and Cinema Books, 2013), 49.

7. Sue Short, *Cult Telefantasy Series: A Critical Analysis of* The Prisoner, Twin Peaks, The X-Files, Buffy the Vampire Slayer, Lost, Heroes, Doctor Who, *and* Star Trek (Jefferson, NC: McFarland, 2011), 171.

8. Philip Sandifer, *TARDIS Eruditorum: An Official History of Doctor Who—Volume One: William Hartnell*, 2nd ed. (San Antonio: Eruditorum Press, 2013), 419.

9. Ibid., 7.

10. Brian Rosebury, *Tolkien: A Critical Assessment* (London: Palgrave, 1992), 149.

11. William Cronon, *Changes in the Land: Indians, Colonists and the Ecology of New England* (New York: Hill and Wang, 1983).

12. John Beversluis, *C. S. Lewis and the Search for Rational Religion* (Grand Rapids: Eerdmans, 1985).

13. Marcus K. Harmes, *Doctor Who and the Art of Adaptation: Fifty Years of Storytelling* (Lanham, MD: Rowman and Littlefield, 2014), 6.

14. Critic and historian Sue Short has argued that Newman garners too much credit for commissioning the series when he built upon notes and treatments for a potential science fiction series written the year before he was hired by several BBC staff members, including Eric Maschwitz, Donald Bull, Alice Frick, John Braybon, and Donald Wilson. Short, *Cult Telefantasy Series*, 171.

15. Alan Kistler, *Doctor Who: A History—Celebrating Fifty Years* (Guilford, CT: Globe Pequot Press, 2013), 3.

16. Ibid., 5.

17. Ibid., 13.

18. Piers D. Britton and Simon J. Barker, *Reading between Designs: Visual Imagery and the Generation of Meaning in* The Avengers, The Prisoner, *and* Doctor Who (Austin: The University of Texas Press, 2003), 137, 145.

19. Carpenter, *J. R. R. Tolkien: A Biography*, 91.

## Chapter 4. Noah's Ark Revisited

1. Carpenter, *J. R. R. Tolkien: A Biography*, 31.

2. Ibid., 173.

3. Charlton. "A Companion to J. R. R. Tolkien's Notion Club Papers."

4. Rob Nixon, *Slow Violence and the Environmentalism of the Poor* (Cambridge/London: Harvard University Press, 2011), 263–64.

5. Wendell Berry, "Stuck in the Middle," in *Our Only World: Ten Essays* (Berkeley: Counterpoint, 2015), 73–74.

6. Walter Einenkel, "Conservative Talk Show Host Pens Attack on Neil deGrasse Tyson—Tyson Goes Supernova on Him," *Daily Kos*, August 23, 2016. Accessed September 2, 2016. http://www.dailykos.com/story/2016/8/23/1563180/-Conservative-talk-show-host-pens-attack-on-Neil-deGrasse-Tyson-Tyson-goes-supernova-on-him.

7. "It's Cold and My Car is Buried in Snow. Is Global Warming Really Happening?" *Union of Concerned Scientists*, December 17, 2015. Accessed February 25, 2016. http://www.ucsusa.org/global_warming/science_and_impacts/science/cold-snow-climate-change.html#.Vs9J0za9jzI.

8. "NASA, NOAA Analyses Reveal Record-Shattering Global Warm Temperatures in 2015," NASA, online, January 20, 2016. Accessed February 25, 2016. http://www.nasa.gov/press-release/nasa-noaa-analyses-reveal-record-shattering-global-warm-temperatures-in-2015.

9. Ryan Grim, "Senator Who Cited Snowball in Climate Change Debate Cites Scripture To Back Himself Up," *The Huffington Post*, March 6, 2015. Accessed July 11, 2015. http://www.huffingtonpost.com/2015/03/06/jim-inhofe-genesis_n_6815270.html.

10. Rush Limbaugh, *The Way Things Ought to Be* (New York: Pocket Books, 1992), 152.

11. Sara Diamond, *Spiritual Warfare: The Politics of the Christian Right* (Boston: South End Press, 1989), 138.

12. John W. Dean, *Conservatives Without Conscience* (New York: Penguin Books, 1994).

13. Lloyd Grove, "Barry Goldwater's Left Turn," *The Washington Post*, July 28, 1994. Accessed February 22, 2016. http://www.washingtonpost.com/wp-srv/politics/daily/may98/goldwater072894.htm.

14. Chris Hedges, *American Fascists: The Christian Right and the War on America* (New York: Free Press, 2006), 265.

15. Chris Hedges, "The Radical Christian Right and the War on Government," *Truth-Dig*, October 6, 2013. Accessed February 22, 2016. http://www.truthdig.com/report/item/the_radical_christian_right_and_the_war_on_government_20131006#14506663780421&action=collapse_widget&id=0&data=.

16. Lester K. Little, *Religious Poverty and the Profit Economy in Medieval Europe* (Ithaca: Cornell University Press, 1983).

17. Lewis, *Mere Christianity*, 84–85, 87.

18. Duriez, *The Oxford Inklings*, 58.

19. C. S. Lewis, *Surprised by Joy: The Shape of My Early Life* (New York: Harcourt, Brace, Jovanovich, 1966), 156–57.

20. William D. Ruckelshaus, Lee M. Thomas, William K. Reilly, and Christine Todd Whitman, "A Republican Case for Climate Action," *The New York Times*, August 1, 2013. Accessed April 26, 2016. http://www.nytimes.com/2013/08/02/opinion/a-republican-case-for-climate-action.html?_r=0.

21. Naomi Klein, *This Changes Everything: Capitalism vs. the Climate* (New York: Simon and Schuster, 2014), 412.

22. Kyle Munzenrieder, "Jeb Bush Thinks Climate Change Will Be Fixed By 'A Person in a Garage Somewhere," *Miami New Times*, July 9, 2015. Accessed November 6, 2015. http:// www.miaminewtimes.com/news/jeb-bush-thinks-climate-change-will-be-fixed-by-a-person-in-a-garage-somewhere-7739675.

23. Tom Cahill, "Bill Gates: Only Socialism Can Save the Climate, 'The Private Sector is Inept,'" *U.S. Uncut*, October 26, 2015. Accessed November 6, 2015. http://usuncut.com/climate/bill-gates-only-socialism-can-save-us-from-climate-change/.

24. James Bennet, "We Need An Energy Miracle," *The Atlantic*, November 2015. Accessed November 6, 2015. http://www.theatlantic.com/magazine/archive/2015/11/we-need-an-energy-miracle/407881/.

25. Neela Banerjee, Lisa Song, and David Hasemyer, "Exxon: The Road Not Taken—Exxon's Own Research Confirmed Fossil Fuels' Role in Global Warming Decades Ago—Top Executives Were Warned of Possible Catastrophe from Greenhouse Effect, Then Led Efforts to Block Solutions," *Inside Climate News*, September 16, 2015. Accessed November 6, 2015. http://insideclimatenews.org/news/15092015/Exxons-own-research-confirmed-fossil-fuels-role-in-global-warming.

26. Kate Jennings, Dino Grandoni, and Susanne Rust, "How Exxon Went from Leader to Skeptic on Climate Change Research," *Los Angeles Times*, October 23, 2015. Accessed November 6, 2015. http://graphics.latimes.com/exxon-research/.

27. Bill McKibben, "Exxon's Climate Lie: 'No Corporation Has Ever Done Anything This Big or Bad,'" *The Guardian*, October 14, 2015. Accessed February 11, 2016. http://www.theguardian.com/environment/2015/oct/14/exxons-climate-lie-change-global-warming.

## Chapter 5. Race and Disaster Capitalism in *Parable of the Sower*, *The Strain*, and *Elysium*

1. Robbie Collin, "Elysium, review," *The Telegraph*, August 21, 2013. Accessed February 10, 2016. http://www.telegraph.co.uk/culture/film/filmreviews/10258064/Elysium-review.html.

2. John Hiscock, "Neill Blomkamp Interview: 'Elysium Isn't Science Fiction. It's Now,'" *The Telegraph*, August 19, 2013. Accessed February 10, 2016. http://www.telegraph.co.uk/culture/film/10244979/Neill-Blomkamp-interview-Elysium-isnt-science-fiction.-Its-now.html.

3. Chuck Hogan and Guillermo del Toro, *The Strain Book II: The Fall* (New York: HarperCollins, 2012), 218.

4. Ibid., 219.

5. Mark Kermode, "Pain Should Not Be Sought—But It Should Never Be Avoided," *The Guardian*, November 5, 2006. Accessed September 12, 2016. https://www.theguardian.com/film/2006/nov/05/features.review1.

6. Naomi Klein, *The Shock Doctrine: The Rise of Disaster Capitalism* (New York: Alfred A. Knopf, 2007).

7. Ibid., 3–4.

8. Butler, *Parable of the Sower*, 118–28.

9. Margalit Fox, "Octavia E. Butler, Science Fiction Writer, Dies at 58," *New York Times*, March 1, 2006. Accessed April 26, 2016. http://www.nytimes.com/2006/03/01/books/01butler.html?_r=0.

10. Ibid.

11. Ibid.

12. Nnedi Okorafor, "*Parable Of The Sower*—Not *1984*—Is the Dystopia for Our Age," *Modern Ghana*, February 17, 2017. Accessed February 21, 2017. https://www.modernghana.com/news/756213/parable-of-the-sower-not-1984-is-the-dystopia-for-our-ag.html.

13. Fox, "Octavia E. Butler."

14. Al Gore, *An Inconvenient Truth*, dir. Davis Guggenheim, 2006, as quoted in V. Arrow, *The Panem Companion: From Mellark Bakery to Mockingjays—An Unofficial Guide to Suzanne Collins' Hunger Games* (Dallas: SmartPOP, 2012).

15. V. Arrow, *The Panem Companion: From Mellark Bakery to Mockingjays—An Unofficial Guide to Suzanne Collins' Hunger Games* (Dallas: SmartPOP, 2012), 21–26.

16. Ibid., 24–26.

17. David Niose, "Anti-intellectualism Is Killing America," *Psychology Today*, June 23, 2015. Accessed July 13, 2015. https://www.psychologytoday.com/blog/our-humanity-naturally/201506/anti-intellectualism-is-killing-america.

18. McGrath, *C. S. Lewis—A Life*, 378–79.

19. Laura Turner, "C. S. Lewis Predicted Donald Trump," *The Washington Post*, March 31, 2016. Accessed April 7, 2016. https://www.washingtonpost.com/news/acts-of-faith/wp/2016/03/31/c-s-lewis-predicted-donald-trump/.

20. Michael Svoboda, "Climate Change at the Movies: A Summer 2015 Update," *Yale: Climate Connections*, August 12, 2015. Accessed November 8, 2015. http://www.yaleclimateconnections.org/2015/08/climate-change-at-the-movies-a-summer-2015-update/.

21. Marc DiPaolo, *War, Politics, and Superheroes* (Jefferson, NC: McFarland, 2011), 34.

22. Michio Kaku, *Physics of the Future: How Science Will Shape Human Destiny and Our Daily Lives by the Year 2100* (New York: Anchor, 2012), 268–72.

23. " 'You Are Hurting Future Generations': Mark Ruffalo's Message to People Profiting from Fossil Fuels," *DemocracyNOW!*, December 13, 2016. Accessed February 3, 2017. https://www.democracynow.org/2016/12/13/you_are_hurting_future_generations_mark.

## Chapter 6. Eden Revisited

1. "Letter from Abigail Adams to John Adams, 31 March–5 April 1776," *The Adams Family Papers: An Electronic Archive of the Massachusetts Historical Society.* Accessed April 26, 2016. https://www.masshist.org/digitaladams/archive/doc?id=L17760331aa.

2. Philip B. Kurland and Ralph Lerner, eds., "Document 10: John Adams to Abigail Adams, 14 Apr. 1776," *The Founder's Constitution* (Chicago: University of Chicago Press), online ed. Accessed April 26, 2016. http://press-pubs.uchicago.edu/founders/print_documents/v1ch15s10.html.

3. Stephanie Coontz and Peta Henderson, "Introduction," in *Women's Work, Men's Property: The Origins of Gender and Class*, ed. Stephanie Coontz and Peta Henderson (New York: Verso, 1986), 37.

4. Carol J. Adams, *Ecofeminism: Feminist Intersections with Other Animals and the Earth* (London: Bloomsbury, 2014), 1.

5. Ibid., 195.

6. Karen Warren, *Ecofeminist Philosophy: A Western Perspective on What It Is and Why It Matters* (Lanham, MD: Rowman and Littlefield, 2000), 140.

7. Lucy Sargisson, "What's Wrong with Ecofeminism?" *Environmental Politics* 10, no. 1 (2001).

8. Ally Agee, a graduate student working toward an MA in communications at the University of Utah, sent me a copy of this unpublished paper when she heard of this book project.

9. Hedges, "The Radical Christian Right and the War on Government."

10. James Rovira, "*Ex Machina*: Girlbots vs. Geekboys and Creation Anxiety in the New *Frankenstein*," Sequart, January 10, 2016. Accessed September 5, 2016. http://sequart.org/magazine/62406/ex-machina-girlbots-vs-geekboys-and-creation-anxiety-in-the-new-frankenstein/.

11. Ursula K. Le Guin, "Reviews: *The Dark Tower* by C. S. Lewis," in *Dancing at the Edge of the World: Thoughts on Words, Women, Places* (New York: Grove Press, 1989), 243–44.

12. Ann Loades, "On Women," in *The Cambridge Companion to C. S. Lewis* (New York: Cambridge University Press, 2010), 171.

13. Lewis, *Mere Christianity*, xii.

14. Duriez, *Tolkien and C. S. Lewis: The Gift of Friendship* (Santa Monica: HiddenSpring, 2003). Also, Marc DiPaolo, "Meeting Madonna and C. S. Lewis Again, For the First Time," in *Unruly Catholics from Dante to Madonna* (Lanham, MD: Scarecrow, 2013).

15. Dickerson and O'Hara. *Narnia and the Fields of Arbol*, 59.

16. Ibid.

17. Duriez, *The Oxford Inklings*, 65.

18. Ibid., 98.

19. Lewis, *Surprised by Joy*, 108–109.

20. See DiPaolo, *Unruly Catholics*, xl–xli.

21. Monika Hilder, "Jack, the 'Old Woman; of Oxford': Sexist or Seer?" in *Women and C. S. Lewis*, ed. Carolyn Curtis and Mary Pomroy Key (Oxford: Lion Books, 2015), 173.

22. Carpenter, *J. R. R. Tolkien: A Biography*, 151.

23. Sallie McFague, "Theology of Nature: Remythologizing Christian Doctrine," in *Collected Readings*, ed. David B. Lott (Minneapolis: Fortress Press, 2013), 96–97.

24. Ibid., 105–106.

25. Ellen Bernstein, "Creation Theology: A Jewish Perspective," in *The Green Bible: New Revised Standard Version* (San Francisco: HarperOne, 2008), 55–57.

26. Seyyd Hossein Nasr, "Religion and the Resacralization of Nature," in *Many Heavens, One Earth: Readings on Religion and the Environment*, ed. Clifford Chalmers Cain (New York: Lexington Books, 2012), 86–87.

27. Rosemary Radford Ruether, *Integrating Ecofeminism Globalization and World Religions* (New York: Rowman and Littlefield, 2005), 177–78.

28. Ursula K. Le Guin, "The Carrier Bag Theory of Fiction," in *The Ecocriticism Reader*, ed. Cheryll Glotfelty and Harold Fromm (Athens and London: The University of Georgia Press, 1996), 151–53.

29. William R. Cook, *Francis of Assisi: The Way of Poverty and Humility* (Eugene, OR: Wipf and Stock, 1989), 52.

30. Ibid., 53–57.

31. Ibid., 63.

32. Ibid.

33. Frans De Waal, *The Age of Empathy: Nature's Lessons for a Kinder Society* (New York: Three Rivers Press, 2009), 224–25.

## Chapter 7. *MaddAddam* and *The Handmaid's Tale*

1. Robert Potts, "Light in the Wilderness," *The Guardian*, online. Accessed April 26, 2016. http://www.theguardian.com/books/2003/apr/26/fiction.margaretatwood.

2. Ibid.

3. Ibid.

4. Margaret Atwood and Bill Moyers, "Bill Moyers on Faith and Reason," *Moyers and Company*, July 29, 2006. Accessed November 23, 2015. http://www.pbs.org/moyers/faithand reason/portraits_atwood.html.

5. Ibid.

6. Coral Ann Howells, "Margaret Atwood's Dystopian Visions," in *The Cambridge Companion to Margaret Atwood*, ed. Coral Ann Howells (Cambridge: Cambridge University Press, 2006), 161, 163.

7. Margaret Atwood, *MaddAddam* (New York: Anchor Books, 2013), 111–12.

8. Ibid., 269–71.

9. C. S. Lewis, "A Case for Abolition," in *Animals and Christianity: A Book of Readings*, ed. Andrew Linzey and Tom Regan (Eugene, OR: Wipf and Stock, 2007), 160–65.

10. Ibid.

11. Shannon Hengen, "Margaret Atwood and Environmentalism" in *The Cambridge Companion to Margaret Atwood*, ed. Coral Ann Howells (Cambridge: Cambridge University Press, 2006), 84.

12. Jennifer Vineyard, "Margaret Atwood on *Payback, The Handmaid's Tale* as Current Events, and *The Hunger Games*," *Vulture*, May 1, 2012. Accessed September 2, 2016. http://www.vulture.com/2012/05/margaret-atwood-payback-interview.html.

13. Ryan Britt, "Margaret Atwood's *MaddAddam* is *The Hunger Games* for Grown-Ups," *Tor.com*, September 18, 2013. Accessed September 2, 2016. http://www.tor.com/2013/09/18/margaret-atwoods-maddaddam-is-the-hunger-games-for-grown-ups/.

14. Constance Grady, "It's Margaret Atwood's Dystopian Future, and We're Just Living in It," *Vox.com*, June 8, 2016. Accessed September 2, 2016. http://www.vox.com/2016/6/8/11885596/margaret-atwood-dystopian-future-handmaids-tale-maddaddam-pigoons.

15. Finn, "An Interview With Margaret Atwood."

## Chapter 8. Ur-Fascism and Populist Rebellions in *Snowpiercer* and *Mad Max: Fury Road*

1. I. Q. Hunter, *British Trash Cinema* (London: BFI and Palgrave Macmillan, 2013), vii.

2. Wendell Berry, *Bringing it to the Table: On Farming and Food* (Berkeley: Counterpoint, 2009), 7.

3. Umberto Eco, "Eternal Fascism: Fourteen Ways of Looking at a Blackshirt," in Chris Hedges, *American Fascists: The Christian Right and the War on America* (New York: Free Press, 2008), xi.

4. Jacques Lob and Jean-Marc Rochette, *Snow Piercer, Vol. 1: The Escape* (London: Titan Books, 2014), 47–49.

5. David Denby, "Endgames," *The New Yorker*, July 7, 2014. Accessed April 26, 2016. http://www.newyorker.com/magazine/2014/07/07/endgames.

6. Octavia E. Butler, *Parable of the Talents* (New York, Boston: Grand Central, 1998), 19–20.

7. Nnedi Okorafor, "*Parable Of The Sower*—Not *1984*—Is The Dystopia For Our Age," *Modern Ghana*, February 17, 2017. Accessed February 21, 2017. https://www.modernghana.com/news/756213/parable-of-the-sower-not-1984-is-the-dystopia-for-our-ag.html.

8. Joerg Rieger, *Religion, Theology, and Class: Fresh Engagements After a Long Silence* (New York: Palgrave Macmillan, 2013), 6–7.

9. "Mad Max: The Film Phenomenon," *Mad Max*, Blu-ray Disc Special Feature, Scream Factory, 2015.

10. Laura Hudson, "Rape Scenes Aren't Just Awful. They're Lazy Writing," *WIRED*, June 30, 2015. Accessed July 9, 2015. http://www.wired.com/2015/06/rape-scenes/.

11. Ibid.

## Chapter 9. Tolkien's Kind of Catholic

1. McGrath, *C. S. Lewis—A Life*, 239–40.

2. Duriez, *Tolkien and C. S. Lewis*, 156.

3. Ibid.

4. Abigail Santamaria, *Joy: Poet, Seeker, and the Woman Who Captivated C. S. Lewis* (New York: Houghton Mifflin Harcourt, 2015), 279, 303.

5. Ibid., 310–11.

6. Carpenter, *J. R. R. Tolkien: A Biography*, 105.

7. Ibid.

8. Ibid.

9. Ibid., 31.

10. Ibid., 32.

11. Ibid., 39.

12. Le Guin, "Reviews: *The Dark Tower* by C. S. Lewis," 243–44.

13. Jeff Alexander and Tom Bissell, "Unused Audio Commentary by Howard Zinn and Noam Chomsky, Recorded Summer 2002, for The Lord of the Rings: The Fellowship of the Ring DVD (Platinum Series Extended Edition), Part One," in *Created in Darkness By Troubled Americans: The Best of* McSweeney's *Humor Category*, ed. Dave Eggers, Kevin Shay, Lee Epstein, John Warner, and Suzanne Kleid (New York: Random House, 2005), 73.

14. Brian Rosebury, *Tolkien: A Cultural Phenomenon* (New York: Palgrave Macmillan, 2003), 160–61.

15. Jamie Lovett, "Stephen Colbert Schools Stephen Bannon On *Lord Of The Rings*," *Comic Book.com*, January 31, 2017. Accessed February 10, 2017. http://comicbook.com/popculturenow/2017/01/31/stephen-colbert-schools-stephen-bannon-on-lord-of-the-rings/.

16. Terry Gross, *Fresh Air: Stars: Terry Gross Interviews 11 Stars of Stage and Screen*. Audiobook, HighBridge Company, February 1, 2007.

17. Stephen Colbert, "Jesus Is a Liberal Democrat," *The Colbert Report*, December 16, 2010. New York: Comedy Central. http://www.colbertnation.com/thecolbert-report-videos/368914/december-16-2010/jesus-is-a-liberal-democrat.

18. Sean McGuire, "An Interview with Paul E. Kerry, editor of *The Ring and the Cross: Christianity and The Lord of the Rings*," *Ignatius Insight*, May 23, 2011. Accessed February 6, 2017. http://www.ignatiusinsight.com/features2011/pkelly_tolkienintvw_may2011.asp.

19. Regina Bennett, "What Would Tolkien Drive? Ecopolitics in The Lord of the Rings," *5th Annual C. S. Lewis and the Iklings Conference: The New MythMakers*, Oklahoma City University, Saturday, April 5, 2003. Unpublished essay.

20. Carpenter, *J. R. R. Tolkien: A Biography*, 159.

21. Bennett, "What Would Tolkien Drive?."

22. Amy Goodman, "Fascism in the Church: Ex-Priest on 'The Pope's War,' Clergy Abuse and Quelling Liberation Theology," *Democracy NOW!* February 28, 2013. Accessed March 1, 2017.

23. Dorothy Day, "Catholic Worker Positions," *The Catholic Worker*, May, 1972. Accessed February 6, 2017. http://www.catholicworker.org/dorothyday/daytext.cfm?TextID=519/.

24. DiPaolo, *Unruly Catholics*.

25. Oscar Wilde, "The Soul of Man Under Socialism," in *The Collected Works of Oscar Wilde* (London: Wordsworth Editions, 1997), 1042.

26. Ibid., 1050–51.

27. Holbrook Jackson, *The Eighteen Nineties* (New York: Capricorn Books, 1966), 77.

28. Ibid., 89.

29. Regenia Gagnier, *Idylls of the Marketplace: Oscar Wilde and the Victorian Public* (Stanford: Stanford University Press, 1986), 3.

30. Emma-Kate Symons, "How Pope Francis Can Cleanse the Far-Right Rot From the Church," *The Washington Post*, February 9, 2017. Accessed March 1, 2017. https://www.washingtonpost.com/news/global-opinions/wp/2017/02/09/how-pope-francis-can-cleanse-the-far-right-rot-from-the-catholic-church/?utm_term=.7869155b98ef.

31. Cheryl Chumley, "Pope Francis Attacks 'Savage Capitalism' in Call for Charity," *Washington Times*, May 22, 2013. http://www.washingtontimes.com/news/2013/may/22/pope-francis-attacks-savage-capitalism-call-charit/.

32. Daniel Burke, "Pope Suggests It's Better to Be an Atheist than a Bad Christian," *CNN*, February 24, 2017. Accessed February 28, 2017. http://www.cnn.com/2017/02/23/world/pope-atheists-again/index.html?sr=fbCNN022317pope-atheists-again0400PMStoryLink&linkId=34805927.

33. Ibid.

34. Quoted in Joseph Pearce, "J. R. R. Tolkien: Truth and Myth," *Catholic Authors*, 2005. Accessed February 6, 2017. http://www.catholicauthors.com/tolkien.html.

35. Rieger, *Religion, Theology, and Class*, 8.

36. Ellen Finnigan, "What We Missed in *The Hunger Games*," *LewRockwell.com*, December 11, 2013. Accessed September 2, 2016. https://www.lewrockwell.com/2013/12/ellen-finnigan/what-catholics-got-wrong-about-the-hunger-games/.

37. Anita Sarkeesian, "The Hunger Games Movie vs. the Book," *Feminist Frequency*, April 12, 2012. Accessed June 14, 2015. https://www.youtube.com/watch?v=3AilblBXIWU.

38 Casey Cipriani, "Easy, Breezy, Brutal: CoverGirl Gets *The Hunger Games* Wrong," *Critic Behind the Curtain*, November 22, 2013. Accessed June 15, 2015. https://criticbehindthecurtain.wordpress.com/2013/11/22/easy-breezy-brutal-covergirl-gets-the-hunger-games-wrong/.

39. Valerie Estelle Frankel, "Reflections in a Plastic Mirror," in *Of Bread, Blood, and* The Hunger Games: *Critical Essays on the Suzanne Collins Trilogy*, ed. Mary F. Pharr and Leisa A. Clark (Jefferson, NC: McFarland, 2012), 56.

40. Brianna Burke, " 'Reaping' Environmental Justice Through Compassion in the Hunger Games," *Interdisciplinary Studies in Literature and Environment* 22, no. 3 (Summer 2015): 547–48.

41. C. S. Lewis, *The Collected Letters of C. S. Lewis, Volume 1. Family Letters: 1905–1931*, ed. Walter Hooper (New York: Harper, 2004), 909.

42. Anthony Pavlik, "Absolute Power Games," in *Of Bread, Blood, and* The Hunger Games: *Critical Essays on the Suzanne Collins Trilogy*, ed. Mary F. Pharr and Leisa A. Clark (Jefferson, NC: McFarland, 2012), 33–34.

43. Suzanne Collins, *The Hunger Games Trilogy—Book III: Mockingjay* (New York: Scholastic Press, 2010), 389–90.

44. Tolkien, *Sauron Defeated. The End of the Third Age*, 132.

45. J. R. R. Tolkien, "The Second Version of the Epilogue," in *Sauron Defeated. The End of the Third Age: The History of the Lord of the Rings—Part IV* (New York: Houghton Mifflin Harcourt, 1992), 121–28.

46. Burke, " 'Reaping' Environmental Justice," 562.

47. Ibid., 560, 563.

## Chapter 10. The Cowboy and Indian Alliance

1. C. S. Hughes, "George R. R. Martin: On the End of Thrones," *Nerdalicious*, December 13, 2013. Accessed October 16, 2015. http://nerdalicious.com.au/books/george-r-r-martin-on-the-end-of-thrones/.

2. Charli Carpenter, "Game of Thrones as Theory," *Foreign Affairs*, March 29, 2012. Accessed July 9, 2015. https://www.foreignaffairs.com/articles/2012-03-29/game-thrones-theory.

3. D. B. Weiss and David Benioff, "Hardhome," *Game of Thrones* (Season Five, Episode Eight), transcribed online May 31, 2015. Accessed April 26, 2016. http://genius.com/Game-of-thrones-hardhome-script-annotated.

4. Marq De Villiers, *The End: Natural Disasters, Manmade Catastrophes, and the Future of Human Survival* (New York: Saint Martin's Press, 2008), 324, 322–23.

5. Andrew Zimmerman Jones, "Of Direwolves and Gods," in *Beyond the Wall: Exploring George R.R. Martin's* A Song of Ice and Fire (Dallas: SmartPOP, 2012), 115.

6. Arthur J. Dewey, "Jesus as a Peasant Artisan," in *Profiles of Jesus*, ed. Roy W. Hoover (Santa Rosa, CA: Polebridge Press, 2002), 77–79.

7. Ibid., 80.

8. Dickerson and O'Hara, *Narnia and the Fields of Arbol*, 82.

9. Isabel Berwick, "Lunch with the FT: George RR Martin," *Financial Times*, June 2, 2012. Accessed April 26, 2016. http://www.ft.com/cms/s/2/bd1e2638-a8b7-11e1-a747-00144feabdc0.html#axzz1wYzURCl0.

10. Keegan-Michael Key and Jordan Peele, "Episode 5: Dueling Magical Negroes," *Key & Peele: Season One*. DVD. New York: Comedy Central, 2012.

11. "Honest Trailers—Game of Thrones," *Screen Junkies*, April 1, 2014. Accessed June 27, 2015. https://www.youtube.com/watch?v=SVaD8rouJn0.

12. Juan Cole, "Leonard Nimoy to Palestinians and Israelis: Live Long and Prosper in Two States," Informed Comment Posted Online June 8, 2011. Accessed April 26, 2016. http://www.juancole.com/2011/06/leonard-nimoy-to-palestinians-and-israelis-live-long-and-prosper-in-two-states.html.

13. Darren Frainch, "*Star Trek VI: The Undiscovered Country* Is a Masterpiece until It's a Franchise Movie," *Entertainment Weekly*, June 7, 2016. Accessed November 24, 2016. http://www.ew.com/article/2016/06/07/star-trek-vi-undiscovered-country-geekly.

14. Ibid.

15. Salena Wakim, "What Leonard Nimoy's Death Means to the Environment," Examiner, February 28, 2015. Accessed April 26, 2016. http://www.examiner.com/article/what-leonard-nimoy-s-death-means-to-the-environment.

16. Klein, *This Changes Everything*, 301–304.

17. Ibid.

18. Leonardo DiCaprio and Kadeen Griffiths, "Transcript of Leonardo DiCaprio's Oscars Acceptance Speech Gets Political about Climate Change—VIDEO," *Bustle*, February 28, 2016. Accessed April 26, 2016. http://www.bustle.com/articles/144803-transcript-of-leonardo-dicaprios-oscars-acceptance-speech-gets-political-about-climate-change-video.

19. Chris Mooney, "People Really Do Pay Attention to Climate Change—When Leonardo DiCaprio Talks about It," *The Washington Post*, August 5, 2016. Accessed September 9, 2016. https://www.washingtonpost.com/news/energy-environment/wp/2016/08/05/the-leo-effect-when-dicaprio-talked-climate-change-at-the-oscars-people-suddenly-cared/?utm_term=.bbdc9f211159.

20. Joy Harjo, "Yesterday Was Rough," *Facebook*, September 4, 2016, 11:13 a.m. Accessed September 5, 2016. https://www.facebook.com/joyharjopoetsax/posts/10153743781611837?pnref=story.

21. Vanessa Willoughby, "U.S. Army Veterans Apologized to Native Americans at Standing Rock," *Teen Vogue*, December 5, 2016. Accessed February 4, 2017. http://www.teenvogue.com/story/us-army-veterans-apologized-to-native-americans-at-standing-rock.

22. Charlie May, "'We Beg for Your Forgiveness': Veterans Join Native Elders in Celebration Ceremony," *Salon*, December 5, 2016. Accessed February 4, 2017. http://www.salon.com/2016/12/05/we-beg-for-your-forgiveness-veterans-join-native-elders-in-celebration-ceremony/.

23. Joy Harjo, "The Original Peoples of the Americas," *Facebook*, September 10, 2016, approximately 8 a.m. Accessed September 10, 2016. https://www.facebook.com/joyharjopoetsax/posts/10153757986091837?pnref=story.

## Chapter 11. What Next?

1. J. R. R. Tolkien, "On Fairy Stories," *The Rivendell Community*, December 13, 2015. Accessed February 3, 2017. http://www.rivendellcommunity.org/Formation/Tolkien_On_Fairy_Stories.pdf.

2. "John Lennon's Last Interview, December 8, 1980." Beatles Archive. Posted online December 21, 2013. Accessed April 26, 2016. http://www.beatlesarchive.net/john-lennons-last-interview-december-8-1980.html.

3. Tolkien, *The Lord of the Rings: 50th Anniversary One-Volume Edition*, 60.

## Epilogue

1. Michael Foster, "An Unexpected Party," *Christianity Today* 78: *J. R. R. Tolkien & Lord of the Rings*, 2003. Accessed April 8, 2017. http://www.christianitytoday.com/7812?type=issueNext&number=15&id=7824.

2. Ibid.

3. "Hobbit Dinner in Rotterdam," *Tolkien Gateway*. Accessed April 8, 2017. http://tolkiengateway.net/wiki/%22Hobbit_Dinner%22_in_Rotterdam.

# Bibliography

Adams, Abigail. "Letter from Abigail Adams to John Adams, 31 March–5 April 1776." The Adams Family Papers: An Electronic Archive of the Massachusetts Historical Society. Accessed April 26, 2016. https://www.masshist.org/digitaladams/archive/doc?id=L17760331aa.

Adams, Carol J. *Ecofeminism: Feminist Intersections with Other Animals and the Earth.* London: Bloomsbury, 2014.

Adams, Ian. *Ideology and Politics in Britain Today.* Manchester: Manchester University Press, 1999.

Adorno, Theodor W. "The Schema of Mass Culture. The Culture Industry." Edited by J. M. Berstein. New York: Routledge, 2001.

Alexander, Jeff, and Tom Bissell. "Unused Audio Commentary by Howard Zinn and Noam Chomsky, Recorded Summer 2002, for The Lord of the Rings: The Fellowship of the Ring DVD (Platinum Series Extended Edition), Part One." In *Created in Darkness by Troubled Americans: The Best of* McSweeney's *Humor Category*, edited by Dave Eggers, Kevin Shay, Lee Epstein, John Warner, and Suzanne Kleid, 73. New York: Random House, 2005.

Ammons, Elizabeth. *Brave New Words: How Literature Will Save the Planet.* Iowa City: University of Iowa Press, 2010.

Aronoff, Kate. "*Rogue One* May Be the Most Leftist Star Wars Film Yet." *In These Times.* Posted online December 16, 2016. Accessed March 1, 2017. http://inthesetimes.com/article/19744/the-rogue-one-may-be-the-most-leftist-star-wars-film-yet.

Arrow, V. *The Panem Companion: From Mellark Bakery to Mockingjays—An Unofficial Guide to Suzanne Collins' Hunger Games.* Dallas: SmartPOP, 2012.

Atwood, Margaret. *The Handmaid's Tale.* New York: Anchor Books, 1998.

———. *MaddAddam, Book I: Oryx and Crake*, Anchor Books, 2004.

———. *MaddAddam, Book II: The Year of the Flood.* Anchor Books, 2010.

———. *MaddAddam, Book III: MaddAddam.* New York: Anchor Books, 2013.

———, and Bill Moyers. "Bill Moyers on Faith and Reason." *Moyers and Company.* Posted online: July 29, 2006. Accessed November 23, 2015. http://www.pbs.org/moyers/faithandreason/portraits_atwood.html.

Banerjee, Neela, Lisa Song, and David Hasemyer. "Exxon: The Road Not Taken—Exxon's Own Research Confirmed Fossil Fuels' Role in Global Warming Decades Ago—Top Executives Were Warned of Possible Catastrophe from Greenhouse Effect, Then Led Efforts to Block Solutions." *Inside Climate News.* Published online September 16, 2015.

Accessed November 6, 2015. http://insideclimatenews.org/news/15092015/Exxons-own-research-confirmed-fossil-fuels-role-in-global-warming.

Baratta, Chris. *Environmentalism in the Realm of Science Fiction and Fantasy Literature*. Cambridge: Cambridge Scholars Publishing, 2012.

Baring-Gould, William S. *Sherlock Holmes of Baker Street: A Life of the World's First Consulting Detective*. New York: Random House, 1995.

Barthes, Roland. "The Death of the Author." In *Image-Music-Text*. New York: Hill and Wang, 1978.

Bennet, James. "We Need An Energy Miracle." *The Atlantic*, November 2015. Accessed online November 6, 2015. http://www.theatlantic.com/magazine/archive/2015/11/we-need-an-energy-miracle/407881/.

Bennett, Regina. "What Would Tolkien Drive? Ecopolitics in The Lord of the Rings." *5th Annual C. S. Lewis and the Inklings Conference: The New MythMakers*. Oklahoma City University, April 5, 2003. Unpublished essay.

Bernstein, Ellen. "Creation Theology: A Jewish Perspective." In *The Green Bible: New Revised Standard Version*, 55–57. San Francisco: HarperOne, 2008.

Berry, Wendell. *Bringing It to the Table: On Farming and Food*. Berkeley: Counterpoint, 2009.

———. *A Continuous Harmony: Essays Cultural and Agricultural*. Washington, DC: Shoemaker and Hoard, 1970.

———. "Stuck in the Middle." In *Our Only World: Ten Essays*, 73–74. Berkeley: Counterpoint, 2015.

Berwick, Isabel. "Lunch with the FT: George RR Martin." *Financial Times*. Posted online June 2, 2012. Accessed April 26, 2016. http://www.ft.com/cms/s/2/bd1e2638-a8b7-11e1-a747-00144feabdc0.html#axzz1wYzURCl0.

Beversluis, John. *C. S. Lewis and the Search for Rational Religion*. Grand Rapids, MI: Eerdmans, 1985.

Bramlett, Perry C. *I Am in Fact a Hobbit: An Introduction to the Life and Work of J. R. R. Tolkien*. Georgia: Mercer University Press, 2003.

Britt, Ryan. "Margaret Atwood's *MaddAddam* is *The Hunger Games* for Grown-Ups." *Tor.com*. Posted online September 18, 2013. Accessed September 2, 2016. http://www.tor.com/2013/09/18/margaret-atwoods-maddaddam-is-the-hunger-games-for-grown-ups/.

Britton, Piers D., and Simon J. Barker. *Reading between Designs: Visual Imagery and the Generation of Meaning in* The Avengers, The Prisoner, *and* Doctor Who. Austin: University of Texas Press, 2003.

Burke, Brianna. " 'Reaping' Environmental Justice through Compassion in the Hunger Games." *Interdisciplinary Studies in Literature and Environment* 22, no. 3 (Summer 2015): 547–48.

Burke, Daniel. "Pope Suggests It's Better to Be an Atheist than a Bad Christian." *CNN*. Posted nline February 24, 2017. Accessed February 28, 2017. http://www.cnn.com/2017/02/23/world/pope-atheists-again/index.html?sr=fbCNN022317pope-atheists-again0400PMStoryLink&linkId=34805927.

Burkholder, Kristen M. "Dreaming of Eggs and Bacon, Seedcakes and Scones." In *The Hobbit and History*, edited by Janice Liedl and Nancy R. Reagin, 86–87. New York: Wiley, 2014.

Burns, Marjorie. *Perilous Realms: Celtic and Norse in Tolkien's Middle-earth*. Toronto: University of Toronto Press, 2005.

Butler, Octavia E. *Parable of the Sower*. New York, Boston: Grand Central Publishing, 1993.

———. *Parable of the Talents*. New York, Boston: Grand Central Publishing, 1998.

Cahill, Tom. "Bill Gates: Only Socialism Can Save the Climate, 'The Private Sector is Inept.'" *U.S. Uncut*. Published online October 26, 2015. Accessed November 6, 2015. http://usuncut.com/climate/bill-gates-only-socialism-can-save-us-from-climate-change/.

Calvino, Italo. "Why Read the Classics?" Translated by Patrick Creagh. In *The Uses of Literature*. 128. New York: Harcourt Brace, 1986.

Campbell, Joseph. *The Hero with a Thousand Faces*. Princeton: Princeton University Press, 1972.

———, and Bill Moyers. *The Power of Myth*. New York: Doubleday, 1988.

Canavan, Gerry, and Kim Stanley Robinson, eds. *Green Planets: Ecology and Science Fiction*. Middletown, CT: Wesleyan University Press, 2014.

Carpenter, Charli. "Game of Thrones as Theory." *Foreign Affairs*. Posted online March 29, 2012. Accessed July 9, 2015. https://www.foreignaffairs.com/articles/2012-03-29/game-thrones-theory.

Carpenter, Humphrey. *J. R. R. Tolkien: A Biography*. Boston and New York: Houghton Mifflin, 1977.

Charlton, Bruce G. "A Companion to J. R. R. Tolkien's Notion Club Papers." *Tolkien's* The Notion Club Papers. Published online July 27, 2012. Accessed April 23, 2017. http://notionclubpapers.blogspot.com/2012/07/a-companion-to-jrr-tolkiens-notion-club.html.

Chism, Christine. "Middle-earth, the Middle Ages, and the Aryan Nation: Myth and History in World War II." In *Tolkien the Medievalist*, edited by Jane Chance, 63. London: Routledge, 2003.

Chumley, Cheryl. "Pope Francis Attacks 'Savage Capitalism' in Call for Charity." *Washington Times*, May 22, 2013. Washington, DC: News World Communications. http://www.washingtontimes.com/news/2013/may/22/pope-francis-attacks-savage-capitalism-call-charit/.

Cipriani, Casey. "Easy, Breezy, Brutal: CoverGirl Gets *The Hunger Games* Wrong." *Critic behind the Curtain*. Posted November 22, 2013. Accessed June 15, 2015. https://criticbehindthecurtain.wordpress.com/2013/11/22/easy-breezy-brutal-covergirl-gets-the-hunger-games-wrong/.

Colbert, Stephen. "Jesus Is a Liberal Democrat." *The Colbert Report*, December 16, 2010. New York: Comedy Central. http://www.colbertnation.com/thecolbert-report-videos/368914/december-16-2010/jesus-is-a-liberal-democrat.

Cole, Juan. "Leonard Nimoy to Palestinians and Israelis: Live Long and Prosper in Two States." *Informed Comment*. Posted online June 8, 2011. Accessed April 26, 2016. http://www.juancole.com/2011/06/leonard-nimoy-to-palestinians-and-israelis-live-long-and-prosper-in-two-states.html.

Collin, Robbie. "Elysium, Review." *The Telegraph*. Published online August 21, 2013. Accessed February 10, 2016. http://www.telegraph.co.uk/culture/film/filmreviews/10258064/Elysium-review.html.

Collins, Suzanne. *The Hunger Games Trilogy—Book I: The Hunger Games*. New York: Scholastic, 2010.

———. *The Hunger Games Trilogy—Book II: Catching Fire*. New York: Scholastic, 2013.

———. *The Hunger Games Trilogy—Book III: Mockingjay*. New York: Scholastic, 2014.

Cook, William R. *Francis of Assisi: The Way of Poverty and Humility*. Eugene, OR: Wipf and Stock, 1989.

Coontz, Stephanie, and Peta Henderson. "Introduction." In *Women's Work, Men's Property: The Origins of Gender and Class*, edited by Stephanie Coontz and Peta Henderson, 37. New York: Verso, 1986.

Crockett, Daniel. "Nature Connection Will be the Next Big Human Trend." *Huffington Post.* Posted online August 22, 2014. Accessed March 24, 2016. http://www.huffingtonpost. co.uk/daniel-crockett/nature-connection-will-be-the-next-big-human-trend_b_5698267.html.

Cronon, William. *Changes in the Land: Indians, Colonists, and the Ecology of New England.* New York: Hill and Wang, 1983.

Day, Dorothy. "Catholic Worker Positions." *The Catholic Worker,* May 1972. Accessed February 6, 2017. http://www.catholicworker.org/dorothyday/daytext.cfm?TextID=519/.

———. "Letter to Our Readers at the Beginning of Our Fifteenth Year." *The Catholic Worker,* May 1947. Retrieved from http://www.catholicworker.org/dorothyday/.

Dean, John W. *Conservatives without Conscience.* New York: Penguin Books, 1994.

Denby, David. "Endgames." *The New Yorker.* Posted online July 7, 2014. Accessed online April 26, 2016. http://www.newyorker.com/magazine/2014/07/07/endgames.

De Villiers, Marq. *The End: Natural Disasters, Manmade Catastrophes, and the Future of Human Survival.* New York: Saint Martin's, 2008.

De Waal, Frans. *The Age of Empathy: Nature's Lessons for a Kinder Society.* New York: Three Rivers Press, 2009.

Dewey, Arthur J. "Jesus as a Peasant Artisan." In *Profiles of Jesus,* edited by Roy W. Hoover, 77–79. Santa Rosa, CA: Polebridge Press, 2002.

Diamond, Sara. *Spiritual Warfare: The Politics of the Christian Right.* Boston: South End Press, 1989.

DiCaprio, Leonardo, and Kadeen Griffiths. "Transcript of Leonardo DiCaprio's Oscars Acceptance Speech Gets Political about Climate Change—VIDEO." *Bustle.* Posted online February 28, 2016. Accessed April 26, 2016. http://www.bustle.com/articles/144803-transcript-of-leonardo-dicaprios-oscars-acceptance-speech-gets-political-about-climate-change-video.

Dickerson, Matthew, and Jonathan Evans. *Ents, Elves, and Eriador: The Environmental Vision of J. R. R. Tolkien.* Lexington: The University Press of Kentucky, 2006.

Dickerson, Matthew, and David O'Hara. *Narnia and the Fields of Arbol: The Environmental Vision of C. S. Lewis.* Lexington: University Press of Kentucky, 2008.

DiPaolo, Marc. "Meeting Madonna and C. S. Lewis Again, For the First Time." In *Unruly Catholics from Dante to Madonna.* Lanham, MD: Scarecrow, 2013.

———. *War, Politics and Superheroes.* Jefferson, NC: McFarland, 2011.

Downing, David C. *Planets in Peril: A Critical Study of C. S. Lewis' Ransom Trilogy.* Amherst: University of Massachusetts Press, 1992.

Duriez, Colin. *The Oxford Inklings: Lewis, Tolkien, and Their Circle.* Oxford: Lion Hudson, 2015.

———. *Tolkien and C. S. Lewis: The Gift of Friendship.* Santa Monica: HiddenSpring, 2003.

Eckert, Win Scott. "An Expansion of Philip José Farmer's Wold Newton Universe." *PJFarmer. com.* Published online January 24, 2010. Accessed October 4, 2015. http://www.pjfarmer. com/woldnewton/Pulp.htm.

Eco, Umberto "Eternal Fascism: Fourteen Ways of Looking at a Blackshirt." Reprinted in Chris Hedges, *American Fascists: The Christian Right and the War on America,* xi. New York: Free Press, 2008.

Einenkel, Walter. "Conservative Talk Show Host Pens Attack on Neil deGrasse Tyson—Tyson Goes Supernova on Him." *Daily Kos.* Posted online August 23, 2016. Accessed September 2, 2016. http://www.dailykos.com/story/2016/8/23/1563180/-Conservative-talk-show-host-pens-attack-on-Neil-deGrasse-Tyson-Tyson-goes-supernova-on-him.

Elder, John. "Foreword." In Matthew Dickerson and Jonathan Evans, *Ents, Elves, and Eriador: The Environmental Vision of J. R. R.* Tolkien, x–xi. Lexington: The University Press of Kentucky, 2006.

Fernandes, Rio. "The Subfield That Is Changing the Landscape of Literary Studies." *The Chronicle of Higher Education.* Published online March 21, 2016. Accessed April 6, 2016. http://chronicle.com/article/The-Subfield-That-Is-Changing/235776?cid=rc_right.

Finn, Ed. "An Interview with Margaret Atwood." *Slate.* Posted online February 6, 2015. Accessed December 2, 2015. http://www.slate.com/articles/technology/future_tense/2015/02/margaret_atwood_interview_the_author_speaks_on_hope_science_and_the_future.html.

Finnigan, Ellen. "What We Missed in *The Hunger Games*." *LewRockwell.com.* Posted online December 11, 2013. Accessed September 2, 2016. https://www.lewrockwell.com/2013/12/ellen-finnigan/what-catholics-got-wrong-about-the-hunger-games/.

Flaherty, Colleen. "Prioritization Anxiety." *The Chronicle of Higher Education,* August 16, 2016. member.naicu.edu/news_room/detail/prioritization-anxiety; accessed September 5, 2016.

Forrest, Bethan. "Cli-Fi; Climate Change Fiction as Literature's New Frontier?" *Huffington Post.* Posted online July 23, 2015. Accessed October 11, 2015. http://www.huffingtonpost.co.uk/bethan-forrest/climate-change-fiction_b_7847182.html.

Foster, Michael. "An Unexpected Party." *Christianity Today* 78: J. R. R. Tolkien & Lord of the Rings, 2003. Accessed online April 8, 2017. http://www.christianitytoday.com/7812?type=issueNext&number=15&id=7824.

Fox, Margalit. "Octavia E. Butler, Science Fiction Writer, Dies at 58." *New York Times.* Posted online March 1, 2006. Accessed April 26, 2016. http://www.nytimes.com/2006/03/01/books/01butler.html?_r=0.

Fragoso, Alejandro Dávila. "The Planet Is Going Through a 'Catastrophic' Wilderness Loss, Study Says." *Think Progress.* Published online September 8, 2016. Accessed September 9, 2016. https://thinkprogress.org/most-wilderness-is-gone-thanks-to-humans-ad828409f4b6#.n1vlxbh7m.

Frainch, Darren. "*Star Trek VI: The Undiscovered Country* Is a Masterpiece until It's a Franchise Movie." *Entertainment Weekly.* Posted online June 7, 2016. Accessed November 24, 2016. http://www.ew.com/article/2016/06/07/star-trek-vi-undiscovered-country-geekly.

Frankel, Valerie Estelle. "Reflections in a Plastic Mirror." In *Of Bread, Blood, and* The Hunger Games*: Critical Essays on the Suzanne Collins Trilogy,* edited by Mary F. Pharr and Leisa A. Clark, 56. Jefferson, NC: McFarland, 2012.

Gagnier, Regenia. *Idylls of the Marketplace: Oscar Wilde and the Victorian Public.* Stanford: Stanford University Press, 1986.

Garrett, George, O. B. Hardison, and Jane R. Gelfman, ed. *Film Scripts, Volume 4: A Hard Day's Night, The Best Man, Darling—Classic Screenplays.* New York: Applause Theatre and Cinema Books, 2013.

Gilsdorf, Ethan. "J. R. R. Tolkien and C. S. Lewis: A Literary Friendship and Rivalry." *The Literary Traveler.* Published online October 1, 2006. Accessed August 1, 2015. http://www.literarytraveler.com/articles/tolkien_lewis_england/.

Giroux, Henry A. *University in Chains: Confronting the Military-Industrial-Academic Complex.* London: Routledge, 2007.

Glotfelty, Cheryll. "Literary Studies in an Age of Environmental Crisis." In *The Ecocriticism Reader: Landmarks in Literary Ecology,* edited by Cheryll Glotfelty and Harold Fromm. Athens and London: University of Georgia Press, 1996.

Glyer, Diana Pavlac. *The Company They Keep: C. S. Lewis and J. R. R. Tolkien as Writers in Community.* Kent, OH: Kent State University Press, 2007.

*The Golden Compass.* Written and Directed by Chris Weitz. DVD. New Line Home Video, 2008.

Goodman, Amy. "Fascism in the Church: Ex-Priest on 'The Pope's War,' Clergy Abuse and Quelling Liberation Theology." *Democracy NOW!* Posted online February 28, 2013. Accessed March 1, 2017.

Gore, Al. *An Inconvenient Truth.* Directed by Davis Guggenheim. 2006. Quoted in V. Arrow, *The Panem Companion: From Mellark Bakery to Mockingjays—An Unofficial Guide to Suzanne Collins' Hunger Games.* Dallas: SmartPOP, 2012.

Grady, Constance. "It's Margaret Atwood's Dystopian Future, and We're Just Living in It." *Vox.com.* Posted online June 8, 2016. Accessed September 2, 2016. http://www.vox.com/2016/6/8/11885596/margaret-atwood-dystopian-future-handmaids-tale-maddaddam-pigoons.

Grim, Ryan. "Senator Who Cited Snowball in Climate Change Debate Cites Scripture To Back Himself Up." *The Huffington Post.* Posted nline March 6, 2015. Accessed July 11, 2015. http://www.huffingtonpost.com/2015/03/06/jim-inhofe-genesis_n_6815270.html.

Gross, Doug. "Why We Love Those Rotting, Hungry, Putrid Zombies." *CNN.* Posted online October 2, 2009. Accessed August 27, 2010. http://www.cnn.com/2009/SHOWBIZ/10/02/zombie.love/index.html.

Gross, Terry. *Fresh Air: Stars: Terry Gross Interviews 11 Stars of Stage and Screen.* Audiobook. HighBridge, February 1, 2007.

Grove, Lloyd. "Barry Goldwater's Left Turn." *The Washington Post.* Posted online July 28, 1994. Accessed February 22, 2016. http://www.washingtonpost.com/wp-srv/politics/daily/may98/goldwater072894.htm.

Guite, Malcolm. "Poet." In *The Cambridge Companion to C. S. Lewis,* 294. New York: Cambridge University Press, 2010.

Harjo, Joy. "The Original Peoples of the Americas." *Facebook.* Posted online September 10, 2016. Accessed September 10, 2016. https://www.facebook.com/joyharjopoetsax/posts/10153757986091837?pnref=story.

———. "Yesterday Was Rough." *Facebook.* Posted online September 4, 2016. Accessed September 5, 2016. https://www.facebook.com/joyharjopoetsax/posts/10153743781611837?pnref=story.

Harmes, Marcus K. *Doctor Who and the Art of Adaptation: Fifty Years of Storytelling.* Lanham, MD: Rowman and Littlefield, 2014.

Harrelson, Walter J., editor. "Psalm 73: A Plea for Relief from Oppressors." In *The New Interpreter's Study Bible,* 815–16. Nashville: Abingdon Press, 2003.

Hedges, Chris. *American Fascists: The Christian Right and the War on America.* New York: Free Press, 2006.

———. "The Radical Christian Right and the War on Government." *TruthDig.* Posted online October 6, 2013. Accessed February 22, 2016. http://www.truthdig.com/report/item/the_radical_christian_right_and_the_war_on_government_20131006#14506663780421&action=collapse_widget&id=0&data=.

Helen, Daniel. "Tolkien's Favourite Tree to Be Cut Down." *The Tolkien Society.* Posted online July 30, 2014. Accessed September 29, 2015. http://www.tolkiensociety.org/2014/07/tolkiens-favourite-tree-to-be-cut-down/.

Hengen, Shannon. "Margaret Atwood and Environmentalism." In *The Cambridge Companion to Margaret Atwood*, edited by Coral Ann Howells, 84. Cambridge: Cambridge University Press, 2006.

Hiebert, Paul. "Are All Movie Heroes the Same Person?" *P-S. Pacific Standard*, June 20, 2014. Accessed June 14, 2015. http://www.psmag.com/books-and-culture/movie-heroes-person-joseph-campbell-monomyth-83796.

Hilder, Monika. "Jack, the 'Old Woman of Oxford'; Sexist or Seer?" In *Women and C. S. Lewis*, edited by Carolyn Curtis and Mary Pomroy Key. Oxford: Lion Books, 2015.

Hiscock, John. "Neill Blomkamp Interview: 'Elysium Isn't Science Fiction. It's Now.' " *The Telegraph*. Published online August 19, 2013. Accessed February 10, 2016. http://www.telegraph.co.uk/culture/film/10244979/Neill-Blomkamp-interview-Elysium-isnt-science-fiction.-Its-now.html.

"Hobbit Dinner in Rotterdam." *Tolkien Gateway*. Web resource. Accessed online April 8, 2017. http://tolkiengateway.net/wiki/%22Hobbit_Dinner%22_in_Rotterdam.

Hogan, Chuck, and Guillermo del Toro. *The Strain Book II: The Fall*. New York: HarperCollins, 2012.

"Honest Trailers—Game of Thrones." *Screen Junkies*. Published Apr 1, 2014. Accessed June 27, 2015. https://www.youtube.com/watch?v=SVaD8rouJn0.

Horkheimer, Max, and Theodor W. Adorno. "The Culture Industry: Enlightenment as Mass Deception." In *Dialectic of Enlightenment: Philosophical Fragments*, edited by Gunzelin Schmid Noerr; translated by Edmund Jephcott. Stanford: Stanford University Press, 2002.

Howells, Coral Ann. "Margaret Atwood's dystopian visions." In *The Cambridge Companion to Margaret Atwood*, edited by Coral Ann Howells, 161, 163. Cambridge: Cambridge University Press, 2006.

Hudson, Laura. "Rape Scenes Aren't Just Awful. They're Lazy Writing." *WIRED*. Posted online June 30, 2015. Accessed July 9, 2015. http://www.wired.com/2015/06/rape-scenes/.

Hughes, C. S. "George R. R. Martin: On the End of Thrones." *Nerdalicious*. Published online December 13, 2013. Accessed October 16, 2015. http://nerdalicious.com.au/books/george-r-r-martin-on-the-end-of-thrones/.

Hunter, I. Q. *British Trash Cinema*. London: BFI and Palgrave Macmillan, 2013.

"It's Cold and My Car Is Buried in Snow. Is Global Warming Really Happening?" *Union of Concerned Scientists*. Posted online December 17, 2015. Accessed February 25, 2016. http://www.ucsusa.org/global_warming/science_and_impacts/science/cold-snow-climate-change.html#.Vs9J0za9jzI.

Jackson, Holbrook. *The Eighteen Nineties*. New York: Capricorn Books, 1966.

Jennings, Kate, Dino Grandoni, and Susanne Rust. "How Exxon Went from Leader to Skeptic on Climate Change Research." *Los Angeles Times*. Published online October 23, 2015. Accessed November 6, 2015. http://graphics.latimes.com/exxon-research/.

"John Lennon's Last Interview, December 8, 1980." *Beatles Archive*. Posted online December 21, 2013. Accessed April 26, 2016. http://www.beatlesarchive.net/john-lennons-last-interview-december-8-1980.html.

Jones, Andrew Zimmerman. "Of Direwolves and Gods." In *Beyond the Wall: Exploring George R.R. Martin's* A Song of Ice and Fire, 115. Dallas: SmartPOP, 2012.

"J. R. R. Tolkien: The Mind of a Genius: Special *Newsweek* Edition." *Newsweek*, April 22, 2017.

Keenan, Hugh T. "The Appeal of *The Lord of the Rings*: The Struggle for Life." In *Tolkien and the Critics: Essays on J. R. R. Tolkien's The Lord of the Rings*. Notre Dame: University of Notre Dame Press, 1968.

Key, Keegan-Michael, and Jordan Peele. "Episode 5: Dueling Magical Negroes." *Key & Peele: Season One*. DVD. New York: Comedy Central, 2012.

Khoddam, Salwa. "The Book of Revelation, Ragnarök, and the Narnian Apocalypse in C. S. Lewis' *The Last Battle*." In *C. S. Lewis and the Inklings: Discovering Hidden Truth*, edited by Salwa Khoddam, Mark R. Hall, Jason Fisher. Newcastle: Cambridge Scholars Press, 2012.

Kaku, Michio. *Physics of the Future: How Science Will Shape Human Destiny and Our Daily Lives by the Year 2100*. New York: Anchor, 2012.

Kermode, Mark. "Pain Should not Be Sought—But It Should Never Be Avoided." *The Guardian*. Posted online November 5, 2006. Accessed September 12, 2016. https://www.theguardian.com/film/2006/nov/05/features.review1.

Kistler, Alan. *Doctor Who: A History—Celebrating Fifty Years*. Guilford, CT: Globe Pequot Press, 2013.

Klein, Naomi. *The Shock Doctrine: The Rise of Disaster Capitalism*. New York: Alfred A. Knopf, 2007.

———. *This Changes Everything: Capitalism vs. the Climate*. New York: Simon and Schuster, 2014.

Kurland, Philip B., and Ralph Lerner, eds. "Document 10: John Adams to Abigail Adams, 14 Apr. 1776." *The Founder's Constitution*. Chicago: University of Chicago Press. Online edition. Accessed April 26, 2016. http://press-pubs.uchicago.edu/founders/print_documents/v1ch15s10.html.

LaDuke, Winona. "Canadian Oil Companies Trample on Our Rights." *The Progressive*. Posted online June 18, 2013. Accessed September 8, 2016. http://www.progressive.org/taxonomy/term/850.

Le Guin, Ursula K. "The Carrier Bag Theory of Fiction." In *The Ecocriticism Reader*, edited by Cheryll Glotfelty and Harold Fromm, 151–53. Athens and London: University of Georgia Press, 1996.

———. "Introduction." In *The Left Hand of Darkness*. New York: Ace Books, 2003.

———. "Reviews: *The Dark Tower* by C. S. Lewis." In *Dancing at the Edge of the World: Thoughts on Words, Women, Places*, 243–44. New York: Grove, 1989.

Lewis, C. S. "A Case for Abolition." In *Animals and Christianity: A Book of Readings*, edited by Andrew Linzey and Tom Regan, 160–65. Eugene, OR: Wipf and Stock, 2007.

———. *The Chronicles of Narnia (with illustrations by Pauline Baynes)*. New York: HarperOne, 2005.

———. *The Collected Letters of C. S. Lewis, Volume 1. Family Letters: 1905–1931*. Edited by Walter Hooper. New York: Harper, 2004.

———. "The Dethronement of Power." In *Understanding* The Lord of the Rings: *The Best of Tolkien Criticism*, edited by Rose A. Zimbardo and Neil D. Isaacs. Boston and New York: Houghton Mifflin, 2004.

———. *The Space Trilogy: Out of the Silent Planet, Perelandra,* and *That Hideous Strength*. New York: HarperOne, 2013.

———. *Surprised by Joy: The Shape of My Early Life*. New York: Harcourt, Brace, Jovanovich, 1966.

Limbaugh, Rush. *The Way Things Ought to Be*. New York: Pocket Books, 1992.

Little, Lester K. *Religious Poverty and the Profit Economy in Medieval Europe.* Ithaca: Cornell University Press, 1983.

Loades, Ann. "On Women." In *The Cambridge Companion to C. S. Lewis*, 171. New York: Cambridge University Press, 2010.

Lob, Jaques, and Jean-Marc Rochette. *Snow Piercer, Vol. 1: The Escape.* London: Titan Books, 2014.

Loconte, Joseph. *A Hobbit, a Wardrobe, and a Great War: How J. R. R. Tolkien and C. S. Lewis Rediscovered Faith, Friendship, and Heroism in the Cataclysm of 1914–1918.* Nashville: Thomas Nelson, 2015.

Lovett, Jamie. "Stephen Colbert Schools Stephen Bannon on *Lord Of The Rings*." *Comic Book. com.* Posted online January 31, 2017. Accessed February 10, 2017. http://comicbook.com/popculturenow/2017/01/31/stephen-colbert-schools-stephen-bannon-on-lord-of-the-rings/.

"Mad Max: The Film Phenomenon." *Mad Max.* Blu-ray Disc Special Feature. Scream Factory, 2015.

Martin, George R. R. *A Song of Ice and Fire Book I: A Game of Thrones.* New York: Bantam, 2013.

———. *A Song of Ice and Fire Book II: A Clash of Kings.* New York: Bantam, 2013.

———. *A Song of Ice and Fire Book III: A Storm of Swords.* New York: Bantam, 2013.

———. *A Song of Ice and Fire Book IV: A Feast of Crows.* New York: Bantam, 2013.

———. *A Song of Ice and Fire Book V: A Dance with Dragons.* New York: Bantam, 2013.

———, Elio M. Garcia Jr. and Linda Antonsson. *The World of Ice and Fire: The Untold History of Westeros and the Game of Thrones.* New York: Bantam, 2014.

May, Charlie. "'We Beg for Your Forgiveness': Veterans Join Native Elders in Celebration Ceremony." *Salon.* Posted online December 5, 2016. Accessed February 4, 2017. http://www.salon.com/2016/12/05/we-beg-for-your-forgiveness-veterans-join-native-elders-in-celebration-ceremony/.

McDuffie, Dwayne. "Six Degrees of *St. Elsewhere* (aka The Grand Unification Theory)." *Dwayne McDuffie (1962–2011).* Posted online October 17, 2011. Accessed October 4, 2015. http://dwaynemcduffie.com/?p=47.

McFague, Sallie. "Theology of Nature: Remythologizing Christian Doctrine." In *Collected Readings*, edited by David B. Lott, 96–97. Minneapolis: Fortress Press, 2013.

McGrath, Alister. *C. S. Lewis—A Life: Eccentric Genius, Reluctant Prophet.* Colorado Springs: Tyndale House, 2013.

McGuire, Sean. "An Interview with Paul E. Kerry, Editor of *The Ring and the Cross: Christianity and The Lord of the Rings*." *Ignatius Insight.* Posted online May 23, 2011. Accessed February 6, 2017. http://www.ignatiusinsight.com/features2011/pkelly_tolkienintvw_may2011.asp.

McKibben, Bill. "Exxon's Climate Lie: 'No Corporation Has Ever Done Anything This Big or Bad.'" *The Guardian.* Posted online October 14, 2015. Accessed February 11, 2016. http://www.theguardian.com/environment/2015/oct/14/exxons-climate-lie-change-global-warming.

McLuhan, Marshall. *Counterblast* 1969: 132.

Mendlesohn, Farah. "Thematic Criticism." In *The Cambridge Companion to Fantasy Literature*, 125–26. Cambridge: Cambridge University Press, 2012.

Miller, Laura. *The Magician's Book: A Skeptic's Adventures in Narnia.* New York: Little, Brown, 2008.

Mooney, Chris. "People Really Do Pay Attention to Climate Change—When Leonardo DiCaprio Talks about It." *The Washington Post.* Posted online August 5, 2016. Accessed September 9, 2016. https://www.washingtonpost.com/news/energy-environment/wp/2016/08/05/the-leo-effect-when-dicaprio-talked-climate-change-at-the-oscars-people-suddenly-cared/?utm_term=.bbdc9f211159.

Moore, Alan, and Kevin O'Neill. *League of Extraordinary Gentlemen Omnibus*. New York: DC Comics, 2011.

Morton, Timothy. *Ecology without Nature: Rethinking Environmental Aesthetics*. Cambridge: Harvard University Press, 2007.

Munzenrieder, Kyle. "Jeb Bush Thinks Climate Change Will Be Fixed By 'A Person in a Garage Somewhere.'" *Miami New Times*. Posted online July 9, 2015. Accessed" November 6, 2015. http://www.miaminewtimes.com/news/jeb-bush-thinks-climate-change-will-be-fixed-by-a-person-in-a-garage-somewhere-7739675.

"NASA, NOAA Analyses Reveal Record-Shattering Global Warm Temperatures in 2015." *NASA*. Published online January 20, 2016. Accessed February 25, 2016. http://www.nasa.gov/press-release/nasa-noaa-analyses-reveal-record-shattering-global-warm-temperatures-in-2015.

Nasr, Seyyd Hossein. "Religion and the Resacralization of Nature." In *Many Heavens, One Earth: Readings on Religion and the Environment*, edited by Clifford Chalmers Cain, 86–87. New York: Lexington Books, 2012.

Newman, Kim. *Anno Dracula*. London: Titan Books, 2011.

———. *Doctor Who: BFI TV Classics Series*. London: BFI, 2005.

Niose, David. "Anti-intellectualism Is Killing America." *Psychology Today*. Posted online June 23, 2015. Accessed July 13, 2015. https://www.psychologytoday.com/blog/our-humanity-naturally/201506/anti-intellectualism-is-killing-america.

Nixon, Rob. *Slow Violence and the Environmentalism of the Poor*. Cambridge/London: Harvard University Press, 2011.

Norris, Kathleen. "Preface." In *Mere Christianity*, xvii–xix. New York: HarperOne, 2000.

O'Hanlon, Ryan. "Formula for a Hollywood blockbuster." *Salon*. May 7, 2013. Accessed June 14, 2015. http://www.salon.com/2013/05/07/formula_for_a_hollywood_blockbuster_partner/.

Okorafor, Nnedi. "*Parable of the Sower*—Not *1984*—Is the Dystopia for Our Age." *Modern Ghana*. Posted online February 17, 2017. Accessed February 21, 2017. https://www.modernghana.com/news/756213/parable-of-the-sower-not-1984-is-the-dystopia-for-our-ag.html.

Pavlik, Anthony. "Absolute Power Games." In *Of Bread, Blood, and* The Hunger Games: *Critical Essays on the Suzanne Collins Trilogy*, edited by Mary F. Pharr and Leisa A. Clark, 33–34. Jefferson, NC: McFarland, 2012.

Pearce, Joseph. "J. R. R. Tolkien: Truth and Myth." *Catholic Authors*. Posted online 2005. Accessed online February 6, 2017. http://www.catholicauthors.com/tolkien.html.

Petty, Anne C. *Tolkien in the Land of Heroes*. New York: Cold Spring Press, 2003.

Pope Francis. "Encyclical Letter, Laudato Si, of the Holy Father Francis, On Care for Our Common Home"" *The Holy See*. Published online May 24, 2015. Accessed September 21, 2015. http://w2.vatican.va/content/francesco/en/encyclicals/documents/papa-francesco_20150524_enciclica-laudato-si.html.

Potts, Robert. "Light in the Wilderness." *The Guardian*. Posted online. Accessed April 26, 2016. http://www.theguardian.com/books/2003/apr/26/fiction.margaretatwood.

Preddle, Jon. *Timelink: The Unofficial and Unauthorised Guide to the Continuity of Doctor Who*. Prestatyn, Denbighshire: Telos, 2006.

Rearick, Anderson III. "Why Is the Only Good Orc a Dead Orc? The Dark Face of Racism Examined in Tolkien." *Modern Fiction Studies* (Winter 2004): 50, 4.

Rieger, Joerg. *Religion, Theology, and Class: Fresh Engagements after a Long Silence*. New York: Palgrave Macmillan, 2013.

Rigby, Sam. "Peter Capaldi, David Tennant and Maisie Williams Want to Save the Arctic with Greenpeace." *Digital Spy*. Posted online July 14, 2015. Accessed October 16, 2015. http://www.digitalspy.com/celebrity/news/a658261/peter-capaldi-david-tennant-and-maisie-williams-want-to-save-the-arctic-with-greenpeace.html#ixzz3orQViFDG.

Robey, Tim. "Viggo Mortensen Interview: Peter Jackson Sacrificed Subtlety for CGI." *The Telegraph*. Posted online May 14, 2014. Accessed December 14, 2015. http://www.telegraph.co.uk/culture/film/10826867/Viggo-Mortensen-interview-Peter-Jackson-sacrificed-subtlety-for-CGI.html.

Rosebury, Brian. *Tolkien: A Critical Assessment*. London: Palgrave, 1992.

———. *Tolkien: A Cultural Phenomenon*. New York: Palgrave Macmillan, 2003.

Rosen, Elizabeth K. *Apocalyptic Transformation: Apocalypse and the Postmodern Imagination*. New York: Lexington Books, 2008.

Rovira, James. "*Ex Machina*: Girlbots vs. Geekboys and Creation Anxiety in the New *Frankenstein*." *Sequart*. Posted online January 10, 2016. Accessed September 5, 2016. http://sequart.org/magazine/62406/ex-machina-girlbots-vs-geekboys-and-creation-anxiety-in-the-new-frankenstein/.

Ruckelshaus, William D., Lee M. Thomas, William K. Reilly, and Christine Todd Whitman. "A Republican Case for Climate Action." *The New York Times*. Posted online August 1, 2013. Accessed April 26, 2016. http://www.nytimes.com/2013/08/02/opinion/a-republican-case-for-climate-action.html?_r=0.

Ruether, Rosemary Radford. *Integrating Ecofeminism Globalization and World Religions*. New York: Rowman and Littlefield, 2005.

Ruffalo, Mark. "'You Are Hurting Future Generations': Mark Ruffalo's Message to People Profiting from Fossil Fuels." *DemocracyNOW!* Posted online December 13, 2016. Accessed February 3, 2017. https://www.democracynow.org/2016/12/13/you_are_hurting_future_generations_mark.

Salamone, Gina. "James Cameron on 'Avatar': Fox Wanted Me to Take Out 'Tree-hugging, "FernGully" crap.'" *New York Daily News*. Published online February 18, 2010. Accessed September 19, 2015. http://www.nydailynews.com/entertainment/tv-movies/james-cameron-avatar-fox-wanted-tree-hugging-ferngully-crap-article-1.171225.

Sandifer, Philip. *TARDIS Eruditorum: An Official History of Doctor Who—Volume One: William Hartnell*. Second Edition. San Antonio: Eruditorum Press, 2013.

Santamaria, Abigail. *Joy: Poet, Seeker, and the Woman Who Captivated C. S. Lewis*. New York: Houghton Mifflin Harcourt, 2015.

Sargisson, Lucy. "What's Wrong with Ecofeminism?" *Environmental Politics* 10, no. 1 (2001).

Sarkeesian, Anita. "The Hunger Games Movie vs. the Book." *Feminist Frequency*. Published April 12, 2012. Accessed June 14, 2015. https://www.youtube.com/watch?v=3AilblBXlWU.

Schmitz, Matthew. "Ayn Rand Really, Really Hated C. S. Lewis." *First Things*. Published online March 27, 2013. Accessed October 6, 2015. http://www.firstthings.com/blogs/firstthoughts/2013/03/ayn-rand-really-really-hated-c-s-lewis.

Shippey, Tom. "Another Road to Middle-earth: Jackson's Movie Trilogy." In *Understanding* The Lord of the Rings: *The Best of Tolkien Criticism*, edited by Rose A. Zimbardo and Neil D. Isaacs, 236–37. Boston and New York: Houghton Mifflin, 2004.

Short, Sue. *Cult Telefantasy Series: A Critical Analysis of* The Prisoner, Twin Peaks, The X-Files, Buffy the Vampire Slayer, Lost, Heroes, Doctor Who, *and* Star Trek. Jefferson, NC: McFarland, 2011.

Shuster, David. "George R.R. Martin talks to David Shuster." *Al-Jazeera America*. Posted online November 13, 2014. Accessed November 17, 2015. http://america.aljazeera.com/watch/shows/talk-to-al-jazeera/articles/2014/11/13/george-rr-martintalkstodavidshuster.html.

Simms, Andrew. "Philip Pullman: New Brand of Environmentalism." *The Telegraph*. Posted online January 19, 2008. Accessed July 9, 2015. http://www.telegraph.co.uk/news/earth/3322329/Philip-Pullman-new-brand-of-environmentalism.html.

Snyder, Blake. *Save the Cat!: The Last Book on Screenwriting You'll Ever Need*. Studio City, CA: Michael Wiese Productions, 2005.

Suderman, Peter. "Save the Movie!" *Slate*. July 19, 2013. Accessed June 14, 2015. http://www.slate.com/articles/arts/culturebox/2013/07/hollywood_and_blake_snyder_s_screenwriting_book_save_the_cat.single.html.

Svoboda, Michael. "Climate Change at the Movies: A Summer 2015 Update." *Yale: Climate Connections*. Posted online August 12, 2015. Accessed November 8, 2015. http://www.yaleclimateconnections.org/2015/08/climate-change-at-the-movies-a-summer-2015-update/.

Symons, Emma-Kate. "How Pope Francis Can Cleanse the Far-Right Rot From the Church." *The Washington Post*. Posted online February 9, 2017. Accessed March 1, 2017. https://www.washingtonpost.com/news/global-opinions/wp/2017/02/09/how-pope-francis-can-cleanse-the-far-right-rot-from-the-catholic-church/?utm_term=.7869155b98ef.

Szabo, Ellen Briana. *Saving the World One Word at a Time: Writing Cli-Fi*. Charleston: CreateSpace, 2015.

Taylor, Jesse Oak. *The Sky of Our Manufacture: The London Fog in British Fiction from Dickens to Woolf*. Charlottesville and London: University of Virginia Press, 2016.

Tolkien, J. R. R. "Foreword to the Second Edition." In *The Lord of the Rings: 50th Anniversary One-Volume Edition*, xxiv. Boston and New York: Houghton Mifflin, 2004.

———. *The Hobbit, or There and Back Again*. Boston and New York: Houghton Mifflin, 1997.

———. *The Letters of J. R. R. Tolkien*. Boston and New York: Houghton Mifflin, 1981.

———. *The Lord of the Rings: 50th Anniversary One-Volume Edition*. Boston and New York: Houghton Mifflin, 2004.

———. "The Notion Club Papers." In *Sauron Defeated. The End of the Third Age: The History of the Lord of the Rings—Part IV*, 249. New York: Houghton Mifflin Harcourt, 1992.

———. "On Fairy Stories." *The Rivendell Community*. Posted online December 13, 2015. Accessed February 3, 2017. http://www.rivendellcommunity.org/Formation/Tolkien_On_Fairy_Stories.pdf.

———. "The Second Version of the Epilogue." In *Sauron Defeated. The End of the Third Age: The History of the Lord of the Rings—Part IV*, 121–28. New York: Houghton Mifflin Harcourt, 1992.

Trexler, Adam, *Anthropocene Fictions: The Novel in a Time of Climate Change*. Charlottesville: University of Virginia Press, 2015.

Tulloch, John, and Manuel Alvarado. *Doctor Who: The Unfolding Text*. New York: St. Martin's, 1983.

Turner, Laura. "C. S. Lewis Predicted Donald Trump." *The Washington Post*. Published online March 31, 2016. Accessed April 7, 2016. https://www.washingtonpost.com/news/acts-of-faith/wp/2016/03/31/c-s-lewis-predicted-donald-trump/.

Ullrich, J. K. "Climate Fiction: Can Books Save the Planet?" *The Atlantic*. Published online August 14, 2015. Accessed August 14, 2015. http://www.theatlantic.com/entertainment/archive/2015/08/climate-fiction-margaret-atwood-literature/400112/.

Vineyard, Jennifer. "Margaret Atwood on *Payback, The Handmaid's Tale* as Current Events, and *The Hunger Games*." *Vulture*. Posted online May 1, 2012. Accessed September 2, 2016. http://www.vulture.com/2012/05/margaret-atwood-payback-interview.html.

Wakim, Salena. "What Leonard Nimoy's Death Means to the Environment." *Examiner*. Posted online February 28, 2015. Accessed April 26, 2016. http://www.examiner.com/article/what-leonard-nimoy-s-death-means-to-the-environment.

Warner, Marina. "Boys Will be Boys: The Making of the Male." *The Independent*. Posted online February 2, 1994. Accessed April 20, 2016. http://www.independent.co.uk/life-style/the-reith-lectures-1994-boys-will-be-boys-the-making-of-the-male-marina-warner-in-the-second-lecture-1391550.html.

Warren, Karen. *Ecofeminist Philosophy: A Western Perspective on What It Is and Why It Matters*. Lanham, MD: Rowman and Littlefield, 2000.

Weiss, D. B., and David Benioff. "Hardhome." *Game of Thrones* (Season Five, Episode Eight). Transcribed online May 31, 2015. Accessed April 26, 2016. http://genius.com/Game-of-thrones-hardhome-script-annotated.

Whissel, Kristen. *Spectacular Digital Effects: CGI and Contemporary Cinema*. Durham: Duke University Press, 2014.

Whitbrook, James. "This Quote from Peter Capaldi Totally Nails the Appeal of *Doctor Who*." *I09*. Posted online November 22, 2016. Accessed February 3, 2017. http://io9.gizmodo.com/this-quote-from-peter-capaldi-totally-nails-the-appeal-1789281392.

Wilde, Oscar. "The Soul of Man under Socialism." In *The Collected Works of Oscar Wilde*, 1042. London: Wordsworth Editions, 1997.

Wilkinson, Loren. "Tolkien and the Surrendering of Power." In *Tree of Tales: Tolkien, Literature, and Theology*. Texas: Baylor University Press, 2007.

Williams, Doug. "Not So Long Ago and Far Away: *Star Wars*, Republics, and Empires of Tomorrow." In *The Science Fiction Film* Reader, edited by Gregg Rickman, 229–54. Milwaukee: Limelight, 2004.

Willoughby, Vanessa. "U.S. Army Veterans Apologized to Native Americans at Standing Rock." *Teen Vogue*. Posted online December 5, 2016. Accessed February 4, 2017. http://www.teenvogue.com/story/us-army-veterans-apologized-to-native-americans-at-standing-rock.

Wilson, Dan. "Doctor Who and Sherlock Holmes: Are They Really 'Opposites'?" Metro.co.uk. Posted online August 22, 2013. Accessed October 20, 2015. http://metro.co.uk/2013/08/22/doctor-who-and-sherlock-holmes-are-they-really-opposites-3934458/#ixzz3oyRKlFpl.

Wise Jr., James Waterman. "Fascism in America." *The Christian Century* 53 (February 5, 1936): 245.

*a*

# Index